First World War
and Army of Occupation
War Diary
France, Belgium and Germany

62 DIVISION
Headquarters, Branches and Services
Adjutant and Quarter-Master General
22 December 1916 - 31 March 1919

WO95/3072

The Naval & Military Press Ltd
www.nmarchive.com
Published in association with The National Archives

Published by

The Naval & Military Press Ltd

Unit 10 Ridgewood Industrial Park,

Uckfield, East Sussex,

TN22 5QE England

Tel: +44 (0) 1825 749494

www.naval-military-press.com

www.nmarchive.com

This diary has been reprinted in facsimile from the original. Any imperfections are inevitably reproduced and the quality may fall short of modern type and cartographic standards.

© **Crown Copyright**
Images reproduced by permission of The National Archives, London, England, 2015.

Contents

Document type	Place/Title	Date From	Date To
Heading	62 Nd Division 'A' & 'Q' Branch 1917 Jan-1919 Mar		
Heading	62 Div HQ 'A' Branch 1919 Jan-1919 March Box 2949		
War Diary	Beaford	22/12/1916	28/12/1916
War Diary	Southampton	09/01/1917	09/01/1917
War Diary	Frohen-Le-Grand	19/01/1917	22/01/1917
War Diary	Beaural	23/01/1917	23/01/1917
War Diary	Busles Artois	24/01/1917	31/01/1917
Miscellaneous	App I		
Miscellaneous	62nd Division	23/12/1916	23/12/1916
Miscellaneous	Order Of Embarkation 62nd Division	27/12/1916	27/12/1916
Miscellaneous	62nd Division		
Miscellaneous	App IV		
Miscellaneous	62nd Division	18/01/1917	18/01/1917
Miscellaneous	62nd Division	29/01/1917	29/01/1917
Miscellaneous	List Of Working Parties And By Whom Found App VII		
Miscellaneous	Distribution of units	27/01/1917	27/01/1917
Miscellaneous	62nd Division		
War Diary	Bus-Les Artois	01/02/1917	28/02/1917
Miscellaneous	Pack Trains		
Miscellaneous	62nd Division, Casualties During February 1917.		
Heading	62nd Division Standing Battle Orders		
War Diary	Bus-Les-Artois	01/03/1917	01/03/1917
War Diary	Englebelmer	04/03/1917	08/03/1917
Miscellaneous	Reinforcements Received By Division During North		
Miscellaneous	Appendix II List of Honours & Rewards Conferred on Officers and men of the 62nd Division During Month of March 1917.		
Miscellaneous	Casualties In 62nd Division During		
Miscellaneous	To Branch 62nd Division		
Miscellaneous	Suggested Formation Of Dumps		
Heading	War Diary Of HQ 62nd Division "A" Form 1st April To 30th April 1917 Vol IV		
War Diary	Engelbelmer	01/04/1917	01/04/1917
War Diary	Achiet-Le-Grand	02/04/1917	02/04/1917
War Diary	Engelbelmer	02/04/1917	02/04/1917
War Diary	Achiet-Le-Grand	04/04/1917	24/04/1917
Miscellaneous	Reinforcements Received By 62nd Division During April 19174. App I		
Heading	War Diary of 62nd Division "A" From: 1.5.17 To 31.5.17 Volume V		
War Diary	Achiet-Le-Grand	01/05/1917	31/05/1917
Miscellaneous	62nd Division Honours and Awards During May 1917		
Miscellaneous	62nd Division		
Heading	War Diary Of Assistant Adjutant And Quartermaster General's Branch 62nd Division. from 1st June 1917. to 30th June 1917 (Volume VI)		
War Diary	Achiet-Le-Grand	01/06/1917	16/06/1917
War Diary	Achiet-Le-Petit	29/06/1917	29/06/1917
War Diary	Bapaume Road H 15.c.4.5	29/06/1917	29/06/1917
Miscellaneous	Suggested Baths Establishment. App I		

Miscellaneous	62nd Division	02/08/1917	02/08/1917
Miscellaneous	Divisional Order No 189		
Miscellaneous	62nd Division. Casualties During June 1915. App III	03/07/1917	03/07/1917
Miscellaneous	62nd Division Honours and Awards Received during June 1914	03/07/1917	03/07/1917
Miscellaneous	App V 62nd Division.		
Miscellaneous	App VI 62nd Division.	28/06/1917	28/06/1917
Heading	War Diary of Administrative and Quartermaster General's Branch Headquarters, 62nd Division. From July 1st.1917. to July 31st. Vol.7		
War Diary	Bapaume Rd H15 C.4.5 Sheet 57c N.W.	03/07/1917	31/07/1917
Miscellaneous	Divisional Routine Orders by Major-General W.P. Braithwaite, C.B. Commanding 62nd Division. App I		
Miscellaneous	62nd Division Reinforcements Received	02/08/1917	02/08/1917
Miscellaneous	62nd Division	02/08/1917	02/08/1917
Heading	War Diary of Assistant Adjutant and Quartermaster General's Branch of 62nd Division From 1st August 1917 To 31st August 1917. Volume VIII		
War Diary	Bapaume Rd H.15.c.4.5 Sheet 57c N.W.	25/08/1917	28/08/1917
Diagram etc	Cross Section.		
Diagram etc	Infantry Brigade Transport Lines		
Miscellaneous	62nd Division	01/09/1917	01/09/1917
Miscellaneous	Appendix "D" Water Points.		
Heading	War Diary of 'A & Q' Branch, Headquarters,62nd Division From 010917 To 300917		
War Diary	Bapaume Rd H15c.4.5 Sheet 57c N.W.	02/08/1917	27/08/1917
Miscellaneous	62nd Division Special Order of The Day	14/09/1917	14/09/1917
Miscellaneous	62nd Division	02/10/1917	02/10/1917
Miscellaneous	62nd Division Reinforcements Received	02/10/1917	02/10/1917
Heading	War Diary Of Administrative Branch 62nd Division.from 1st October 1917 To 31st October 1917. Vol. X.		
War Diary	Bapaume Rd H 15 C 4.5 Sheet 57c NW	03/10/1917	04/10/1917
War Diary	Haplincourt	07/10/1917	13/10/1917
War Diary	I 34 A.3.7 57 C-40000	13/10/1917	30/10/1917
War Diary	Disposition And Movement Report No. 106. 62nd Division	24/10/1917	24/10/1917
Miscellaneous	62nd. Division. Disposition And Movement Report. App II		
Miscellaneous	62nd Division. Honours And Awards Conferred During October 1917. App III		
Miscellaneous	62nd Division. Casualties During October 1917. App IV		
Miscellaneous	App V 62nd Division.		
Heading	62nd Division War Diary of Assistant Adjutant And Quartermaster General's Branch From 1st November 1917 To 30th November 1917		
War Diary	Fosseux	01/11/1917	14/11/1917
War Diary	Neuville	14/11/1917	25/11/1917
War Diary	Havrincourt Chateau	25/11/1917	28/11/1917
War Diary	Haplincourt	29/11/1917	29/11/1917
Miscellaneous	Instructions For Operations	14/11/1917	14/11/1917
Miscellaneous	Appendix "B" Prisoners of War		
Miscellaneous	Appendix "C" Dumps.		
Miscellaneous	62nd Division	16/11/1917	16/11/1917
Miscellaneous	Amendment To Instructions For Operations	18/11/1917	18/11/1917

Miscellaneous	Additions To Instructions For Operations	20/11/1917	20/11/1917
Miscellaneous	Appendix II Administrative Notice on Operations 20th 30th November 1917.	03/12/1917	03/12/1917
Miscellaneous	Appendix III Brigade Notes.	03/12/1917	03/12/1917
Miscellaneous	Appendix IV 62nd Division.	05/12/1917	05/12/1917
Miscellaneous	62nd Division Casualties During Nov 1917	05/12/1917	05/12/1917
Miscellaneous	62nd Division Reinforcements Received During Nov 1917		
Heading	War Diary of Administrative and Quartermaster General's Branch, 62nd Division. From 1st December 1917 To 31st December 1917. Vol.2		
War Diary	Haplincourt	01/12/1917	01/12/1917
War Diary	Basseux	04/12/1917	04/12/1917
War Diary	Villers Chatel	06/12/1917	06/12/1917
War Diary	Labeuvriere	12/12/1917	12/12/1917
War Diary	Villers Chatel	19/12/1917	30/12/1917
Miscellaneous	62nd Division. Reinforcing Received During Dec 1917	03/01/1918	03/01/1918
Miscellaneous	62nd Division		
Heading	War Diary of Administrative and Quartermaster General's Branches, 62nd Division From 1st January 1918 To 31st January 1918 Vol XIII		
War Diary	Victory Camp	10/01/1918	17/01/1918
Miscellaneous	XII Corps "Q"	22/01/1918	22/01/1918
Miscellaneous	Reorganisation Of Infantry Battalions	01/02/1918	01/02/1918
Miscellaneous	62nd Div. No.	21/01/1918	21/01/1918
Miscellaneous	62nd (West Riding) Division	01/02/1918	01/02/1918
Miscellaneous	62nd (West Riding) Division.	01/02/1918	01/02/1918
Miscellaneous	62nd (West Riding) Division.		
Heading	War Diary of Administrative and Quartermaster General's Branch, 62nd (West Riding) Division From 1st February 1918 To 28th February 1918 (Volume 14)		
War Diary	In The Field	08/02/1918	28/02/1918
Miscellaneous	62nd (West Riding) Division		
Miscellaneous	Reinforcements Received During Feb		
Operation(al) Order(s)	Administrative Orders For 32nd Division Order No. 90	04/02/1918	04/02/1918
Miscellaneous	Table A		
Miscellaneous	Table B		
Miscellaneous	Table C		
Miscellaneous	Administrative Instructions With Reference To 62nd Divisional Order No 100	24/02/1918	24/02/1918
Heading	War Diary of Administrative and Quartermaster General's Branch, 62nd (W.R.) Division. From 1st March 1918 To 31st March 1918. (Volume15)		
Heading	War Diary 62nd (West Riding) Division March 1918 Appendices Attached Casualties Reinforcements Rewards		
War Diary	Villers Chatel	01/03/1918	03/03/1918
War Diary	Roclincourt	04/03/1918	23/03/1918
War Diary	Warlus	24/03/1918	26/03/1918
War Diary	Fonquevillers	26/03/1918	27/03/1918
War Diary	Souastre	28/03/1918	31/03/1918
Miscellaneous	Casualties During March 1918		
Miscellaneous	Reinforcements		
Miscellaneous	War Diary		

Heading	War Diary of Administrative and Quartermaster General's Branch, 62nd (West Riding) Division. From 1st April 1918. To 30th April 1918. (Volume 16).		
War Diary	Pas	01/04/1918	03/04/1918
War Diary	In The Field Pas	04/04/1918	06/04/1918
War Diary	Henu	07/04/1918	07/04/1918
War Diary	In The Field Henu	07/04/1918	21/04/1918
War Diary	Henu	22/04/1918	23/04/1918
War Diary	Authie	24/04/1918	30/04/1918
Miscellaneous	Reserve Area	01/04/1918	01/04/1918
Miscellaneous	Casualties-25.3.18-1/2.4.18		
Operation(al) Order(s)	Administrative Instructions in Connection With 62nd Division Order No. 108	06/04/1918	06/04/1918
Miscellaneous	62nd (West Riding) Division	16/04/1918	16/04/1918
Miscellaneous	Administrative Instructions In Connection With 62nd Division Order No 112	21/04/1918	21/04/1918
Operation(al) Order(s)	62 Div.No	13/04/1918	13/04/1918
Miscellaneous	62nd (West Riding) Division.		
Miscellaneous	Rewards Granted During April 1918.		
Miscellaneous	Casualties During April 1918		
Heading	War Diary Of Headquarters,62nd (West Riding) Division "A" 1st,May,1918 To 31st May, 1918. Volume 17.		
War Diary	Authie	01/05/1918	16/05/1918
War Diary	Henu	17/05/1918	31/05/1918
Miscellaneous	62nd Div. No.A		
Miscellaneous	Divisional Dump		
Miscellaneous	62nd Div. A/7555/8	05/05/1918	05/05/1918
Miscellaneous	Administrative Instructions In Connection With 32nd Division Order No 114	15/05/1918	15/05/1918
Miscellaneous	The following Allotment of Watering Places will come into force from 17th May, 1918, inclusive. App. E	16/05/1918	16/05/1918
Miscellaneous	Administrative Instructions In connection With 62nd Division Order No 114	16/05/1918	16/05/1918
Miscellaneous	62nd Div A/8393/8	28/05/1918	28/05/1918
Miscellaneous	Casualties During May 1918		
Miscellaneous	Reinforcements Received During May 1918	01/06/1918	01/06/1918
Miscellaneous	Rewards Granted During May 1918		
Heading	War Diary Of Headquarters 62nd (West Riding) Division 'A' 1st June 1918 To 30th June 1918 Volume XVIII		
War Diary	Henu	01/06/1918	24/06/1918
War Diary	Pas	25/06/1918	30/06/1918
Miscellaneous	Administrative Instructions Regarding This Office	06/06/1918	06/06/1918
Miscellaneous	Administrative Instructions In continuation of Those Issued	14/06/1918	14/06/1918
Miscellaneous	Administrations Instructions In connection With 62nd Division Order No 123	23/06/1918	23/06/1918
Miscellaneous	62nd Div		
Miscellaneous	Casualties During June 1918		
Miscellaneous	Rewards Granted during June 1918		
Miscellaneous	Reinforcements Received During June 1918		
Miscellaneous	Special Order		
Miscellaneous	62nd Division		

Heading	War Diary Of Headquarters, 62nd (West Riding) Division 'A' 1st July 1918 To 31st July 1918 Volume XIX.		
War Diary	Pas	01/07/1918	14/07/1918
War Diary	In The Train	15/07/1918	15/07/1918
War Diary	Arcis	16/07/1918	16/07/1918
War Diary	Tours Sur Marne	17/07/1918	17/07/1918
War Diary	Tours	17/07/1918	19/07/1918
War Diary	St. Imoges	20/07/1918	23/07/1918
War Diary	Hautvillers	24/07/1918	31/07/1918
Miscellaneous	Administrations Instructions In The Event Of Orders Being Received To Take up	08/07/1918	08/07/1918
Miscellaneous	IV Corps 'Q'		
Miscellaneous	Administrations Instructions With Regard To Division Order G.428	13/07/1918	13/07/1918
Miscellaneous	Special Order Of The Day By Lieutenant-General Sir A.J. Godley K.C.B. K.C.M.G. Commanding XXII Corps	31/07/1918	31/07/1918
Miscellaneous	Order General No. 63	30/07/1918	30/07/1918
Operation(al) Order(s)	Order Of This Day No.63	30/07/1918	30/07/1918
Miscellaneous	62nd (West Riding) Division		
Miscellaneous	Reinforcements Received During July 1918		
Miscellaneous	Administrative Notes On Operations In July 1918	27/07/1918	27/07/1918
Heading	War Diary Of Headquarters, 62nd (West Riding) Division 'A' 1st August 1918. to 31st August 1918. Volume XX.		
War Diary	Bisseuil	01/08/1918	04/08/1918
War Diary	Pas	05/08/1918	15/08/1918
War Diary	Authie	16/08/1918	18/08/1918
War Diary	Grenas	19/08/1918	19/08/1918
War Diary	Bavincourt	20/08/1918	21/08/1918
War Diary	Doullens	21/08/1918	22/08/1918
War Diary	Pas	22/08/1918	23/08/1918
War Diary	La Rezique	24/08/1918	24/08/1918
War Diary	Bienvillers And Quesnoy Pm	25/08/1918	30/08/1918
War Diary	Ervillers And Courcenes	31/08/1918	31/08/1918
Miscellaneous	Special Order By Lieutenant-General Sir A.J. Godley K.C.B. K.C.M.G. Commanding XXII Corps	01/08/1918	01/08/1918
Miscellaneous	Copy of G.H.O. letter O.B./2218 of 5/8/18 is forwarded for information. App B		
Miscellaneous	Divisional Routine Orders by Major-Gen Sir R.D. Whigham, K.C.B., D.S.O., Comdg 62nd (West Riding) Division		
Miscellaneous	Casualties During August 1918		
Miscellaneous	Rewards Granted During August 1918		
Miscellaneous	Reinforcements Received During August 1918		
War Diary	Courcelles And Triangle Wood	06/09/1918	09/09/1918
War Diary	Courcelles And Triangle Copse	09/09/1918	10/09/1918
War Diary	Courcelles And Sunken And Between Beugny Horchies	11/08/1918	14/08/1918
War Diary	Courcelles And Sunken Rd	15/09/1918	15/09/1918
War Diary	Triangle Copse	16/09/1918	26/09/1918
War Diary	Hermies Beaumetz	26/09/1918	28/09/1918
War Diary	Havrincourt Hermies	29/09/1918	30/09/1918
Miscellaneous	Administrative Instructions Reference 62nd Division Order No 141	08/09/1918	08/09/1918

Miscellaneous	Special Order Of The Day By Major General Sir R.D. Whigham K.C.B. D.S.O. Commanding 62nd (West Riding) Division	14/09/1918	14/09/1918
Miscellaneous	Correction To Para 2 Of Administrative Instructions	10/09/1918	10/09/1918
Miscellaneous	Casualties From 12.9.18 to 18.9.18. App C		
Miscellaneous	Administrative Instructions With Reference To 62nd Division Order No 143	15/09/1918	15/09/1918
Miscellaneous	Administrative Instructions With Reference To 62nd Division	22/09/1918	22/09/1918
Miscellaneous	Addition And Amendments To Administrative Instructions- 62nd Div A/2137/49. App F		
Miscellaneous	Amendment To Administrative Instructions 62nd Div	24/09/1918	24/09/1918
Miscellaneous	62nd (West Riding) Division Special Order Of The Day By Major-General Sir R.D. Wrigham K.C.B. D.S.O.	29/09/1918	29/09/1918
Miscellaneous	Casualties From 27-9-16-1-10-16. App I		
Miscellaneous	Appendix J. Casualties During September 1918.		
Miscellaneous	Rewards Granted During September 1918		
Miscellaneous	Reinforcements Received During September 1918		
Miscellaneous	Divisional Routine Orders by Major-General Sir R.D. Whigham K.C.B. D.S.O. Comdg 62nd (West Riding) Division	21/09/1918	21/09/1918
Miscellaneous	Divisional Routine Orders. by Major-General Sir R.D. Whigham K.C.B. D.S.O. Comdg 62nd (West Riding) Division		
Heading	Location Reports For Month of September 1918		
Miscellaneous	62nd (West Riding) Division.	01/09/1918	01/09/1918
Miscellaneous	62nd (West Riding) Division.	04/09/1918	04/09/1918
Miscellaneous	62nd (West Riding) Division.	07/09/1918	07/09/1918
Miscellaneous	62nd (West Riding) Division.	10/09/1918	10/09/1918
War Diary	62nd. (West Riding) Division.	17/09/1918	17/09/1918
Miscellaneous	62nd (West Riding) Division.	24/09/1918	24/09/1918
Miscellaneous	62nd (W.R.) Division.	25/09/1918	25/09/1918
Heading	War Diary Of Headquarters 62nd (West Riding) Division "A" 1st October 1918 To 31st October 1918. Volume XXII.		
War Diary	Hermies And Havrincourt	01/10/1918	08/10/1918
War Diary	Flesquieres	09/10/1918	09/10/1918
War Diary	Masnieres	10/10/1918	10/10/1918
War Diary	Petit Chautand Estourmel	11/10/1918	17/10/1918
War Diary	Bevillers	18/10/1918	30/10/1918
War Diary	Solesmes	31/10/1918	31/10/1918
Miscellaneous	Burial of Dead During an Advance	06/10/1918	06/10/1918
Miscellaneous	G.O.C. 185 th Infantry Brigade. App B	14/10/1918	14/10/1918
Miscellaneous	Administrative Instructions To accompany 62nd Division Order No. 154	18/10/1918	18/10/1918
Miscellaneous	Administrative Instructions To Accompany 62nd Division Order No. 154.	19/10/1918	19/10/1918
Miscellaneous	Casualties From 20/10/18 to 24/10/18. App.D		
Miscellaneous	62nd (West Riding) Division. Reinforcements Received During October. App H		
Miscellaneous	Statement Of Casualties Incurred Since August 25th to Date. App.E		
Miscellaneous	Appendix F Casualties During October 1918.		
Miscellaneous	Honours and Rewards		

Heading	War Diary of 62nd (West Riding) Division, 'A' Branch From 1st November 1918 To 30th November 1918 Volume XXII		
War Diary	Solesmes	01/11/1918	03/11/1918
War Diary	Escarmain	04/11/1918	04/11/1918
War Diary	Ruesnes	05/11/1918	06/11/1918
War Diary	Frasnoy	07/11/1918	08/11/1918
War Diary	Bavisiaux	09/11/1918	09/11/1918
War Diary	Le Trechon	10/11/1918	10/11/1918
War Diary	Neuf Mesnil	11/11/1918	11/11/1918
War Diary	Sous Le Bois	11/11/1918	17/11/1918
War Diary	Ham Sur Heure	18/11/1918	20/11/1918
War Diary	Loverval	21/11/1918	25/11/1918
War Diary	Bioul	25/11/1918	27/11/1918
War Diary	Leignon	27/11/1918	30/11/1918
Miscellaneous	Reinforcements Received During Month of November 1918		
Miscellaneous	Honours and Rewards Received During November 1918		
Miscellaneous	Casualties During November 1918		
Heading	War Diary of 62nd (West Riding) Division, "A" Branch From 1st December 1918 To 31st December 1918 Volume XXIII.		
War Diary	Leignon	01/12/1918	11/12/1918
War Diary	Hamoir	12/12/1918	13/12/1918
War Diary	Vielsalm	14/12/1918	17/12/1918
War Diary	Malmedy	18/12/1918	21/12/1918
War Diary	Schleiden	22/12/1918	31/12/1918
Miscellaneous	Honours and Rewards Granted During December 1918		
Miscellaneous	Subject:- Relese of Coalminers.		
Miscellaneous	Administrations Instructions on area Alloted To 62nd Division		
Map	App D		
Miscellaneous	62nd Div		
Heading	War Diary. Of 62nd (West Riding) Division Administrative Branch. From 1st January 1919 To 31st January 1919 Vol 25		
War Diary	Schleiden	01/01/1919	31/01/1919
Miscellaneous	Reinforcements Received During January 1919		
Heading	War Diary. Of 62nd (West Riding) Division Administrative Branch From 1st February 1919 To 28th February 1919 Vol 26		
War Diary	Schleiden	01/02/1919	28/02/1919
Miscellaneous	Honours And Rewards,		
Heading	War Diary Of Highland 62nd (West-Riding) Division Administrative Branch 1st March 1919 To 31st March 1919 Volume XXVII		
War Diary	Schleiden	01/03/1919	13/03/1919
War Diary	Duren	14/03/1919	31/03/1919

62ND DIVISION

'A' & 'Q' BRANCH.

~~JAN 1917 - DEC 1918~~

1917 JAN – 1919 MAR

62 DIV

HQ 'A' BRANCH

1919 JAN - 1919 MARCH

Box 2949

ORIGINAL.

Instructions regarding War Diaries and Intelligence Summaries are contained in F. S. Regs., Part II. and the Staff Manual respectively. Title pages will be prepared in manuscript.

HO Ap 062A SECRET.
62nd Division. A.   Army Form C. 2118.

WAR DIARY
or
INTELLIGENCE SUMMARY.
(Erase heading not required.)

Vol I

Place	Date	Hour	Summary of Events and Information	Remarks and references to Appendices
Beeford	27/12/16		G.O. Letter 12/85w3 (M) of 21.12.16 received ordering division to proceed to Southern on 5th January 1917. Intent of units see (Div Squadron not to go)	App I
do	28/12/16		Order of embarkation (G.O.QuG.2)	App II
do			Orders with detailed times for leaving Bedford	App III
				App IV
Southampton	19/1/17		HQ 1S division embarked. Embarkation of division proceed. Final location	
Frohen-le-Grand	19/1/17		Div. Cyclist left division on proceeding to Cyclist Battalion XVIII Corps. 3rd Army O.O. No. 167	App V
"	22/1/17		Division (less Div Arty) moved to BEAUVAL area. Location see	App VI & App VII
Beauval	23/1/17		do do BUS-les-ARTOIS area, and joined Vth Corps. Vth Army location	
BUS-les-ARTOIS	24/1/17		187th Inf Bde detailed for railway work – 185th, 186th Inf Bdes formed working parties	
BUS-les-ARTOIS	25/1/17		Div Arts reporting division with HQrs at BUS-les-ARTOIS.	
"	27/1/17		Took location for whole division	App VIII
"	28/1/17		Infantry Battalions completed to 2 Lewis Guns per battalion.	
"	29/1/17		202nd, 203rd, 204th & 208th Machine Gun Coys posted to division. V Army letter S.G. 254.	
"	24/1/17		Reorganization of Div Artillery under O.B. 1866 completed.	
"	31/1/17		Casualties sent evacuated during January	App IX

31.1.17.

W Macwinits? bvgv General
Comg. 62 v Division

T2/1331. Wt. W708-776. 500000. 4/15. Sir T. C. & S.

App I

Q/13358/454. App I

62ND DIVISION.

UNIT	PRESENT STATION.	ENTRAINING STATION.	REMARKS.
Headquarters 62nd Division	BEDFORD.	BEDFORD.	
62nd Divisional Cavalry Squadron.	TURVEY.	"	
62nd " Cyclist Company.	OLNEY.	"	
Headquarters 62nd Divl.R.Arty.	NORTHAMPTON.	NORTHAMPTON.	
310th Brigade, R.F.A.	"	"	
310th " Medium Trench Mr.Bty.	"	"	Personnel only.
311th " R.F.A.	"	"	" "
311th " Medium Trench Mr.Bty.	"	"	" "
312th " R.F.A.	"	"	
312th " Medium Trench Mr.Bty.	"	"	" "
312th " Heavy " " "	"	"	" "
62nd Divisional Ammunition Column.	"	"	
Headquarters, Royal Engineers.	BEDFORD.	BEDFORD.	
3/1st Field Coy. R.E.	"	"	
1/3rd " "	"	"	
2/3rd " "	"	"	
62nd Divl.Signal Coy.R.E.	"	"	
185th Infantry Brigade Headquarters.	"	"	
2/5th Bn. West Yorks Regt.	"	"	
2/6th -do-	"	"	
2/7th -do-	"	"	
2/8th -do-	"	"	
185th Infy.Bde.Light Tr.Mort.Bty.	"	"	Personnel & 8 Stokes Guns.
186th Infantry Brigade Headquarters.	"	"	
2/4th Duke of Welington's Regt.	"	"	
2/5th -do-	"	"	
2/6th -do-	"	"	
2/7th -do-	"	"	
186th Inf.Bde.Light Tr.Mort.Bty.	"	"	Personnel & 8 Stokes Guns.
187th Infantry Brigade Headquarters.	WELLINGBORO'.	WELLINGBORO'.	
2/4th Bn. K.O.Yorks.Light Infantry.	"	"	
2/5th -do-	"	"	
2/4th Bn. York & Lancs Regt.	RUSHDEN.	IRCHESTER.	
2/5th -do-	WELLINGBORO'.	WELLINGBORO'.	
187th Inf.Bde.Light Tr.Mort.Bty.	"	"	Personnel & 8 Stokes Guns.
Headquarters, 62nd Divl.Train.	BEDFORD.	BEDFORD.	
525th Company, A.S.C.	NORTHAMPTON	NORTHAMPTON.	
526th " "	BEDFORD.	BEDFORD.	
527th " "	"	"	
528th " "	"	"	
2/1st W.R.Field Ambulance.	WELLINGBORO'.	WELLINGBORO'.	
2/2nd -do-	BEDFORD.	BEDFORD.	
2/3rd -do-	"	"	
2/3rd -do- (Detachment).	WELLINGBORO'.	WELLINGBORO'.	"B" Section, 2/3rd W.R.Field Ambulance.
62nd Mobile Veterinary Section.	NORTHAMPTON.	NORTHAMPTON.	
62nd Divisional Sanitary Section.	BEDFORD.	BEDFORD.	
2/1st Northumbrian Cas.Clg.Station.	"	"	35 tons of baggage and no transport.

All Units will proceed up to War Establishments. Each Infantry Battalion will be accompanied by two (2) Limbered G.S.Wagons and four (4) draught horses in excess of W.E. Part VII General 1916, No.351/70 for the carriage of Lewis Gun Ammunition vide W.O.letter (secret) No.121/8543 (M) 21.12.16. Also that each Battalion will take with it, eight (8) Carts hand, Lewis Gun. 14 Supernumerary Officers and 14 batmen accompany each Battalion.

The Artillery is on War Establishments Part VII, 1916, 310th & 312th Brigades R.F.A. each consisting of 3 - 18 pr. 6 gun batteries & 1 - 4.5" 4 gun battery & the 311th Brigade R.F.A. of 2 - 18 pr. 6 gun batteries, and 2 - 4.5" gun batteries.

The Divisional Ammuntion Column at War Establishments for a Division having 16 Howitzers.

The following units have not been included, as their entraining stations are not known.-
    62nd (West Riding) Ammunition Sub Park (No.720 M.T.Coy. A.S.C.)
    62nd (West Riding Divisional Supply Column (No.719 M.T.Coy. A.S.C.)

Ed W.P. Braithwaite
MAJOR GENERAL.
COMMANDING 62ND DIVISION.

BEDFORD.
23.12.16.

SECRET.

App II

PROGRAMME NO. 35.

Order of Embarkation 62nd Division.

Index No.	Unit.	From	To
	December 30th		
I	Divisional Supply Column 2.and.Motor Ambulances	Avonmouth	Rouen
	January 5th		
II	Divisional Ammunition Sub Park	"	"
	1st Day, Jan., 5th		
III	2/5th West Yorks	Southampton	Havre
IV	312th Brigade, R.F.A.	"	"
V	312th Heavy Trench Mortar Battery	"	"
VI	312th Medium " " "	"	"
	2nd Day, Jan., 6th		
VII	2/6th West Yorks	"	"
VIII	311th Brigade, R.F.A.	"	"
IX	311th Med. Trench Mortar Battery	"	"
X	Cable Section	"	"
XI	H.Q., Div. R.A.	"	"
	3rd Day. Jan., 7th		
XII	2/7th West Yorks	"	"
XIII	310th Brigade, R.F.A.	"	"
XIV	310th Md. Trench Mortar Battery	"	"
	4th Day, Jan., 8th		
XV	H.Q. 185th Infy. Bde.	"	"
XVI	Div. Signal Coy. Section	"	"
XVII	Co. Divnl. Train	"	"
XVIII	Light Trench Mortar Battery	"	"
XIX	2/8th West Yorks	"	"
XX	H.Q., Div. Engrs.	"	"
XXI	3/1st W.Riding Field Co.R.E.	"	"
XXII	2/1st W.Riding Field Ambulance	"	"
XXIII	H.Q.& H.Q.Co. Divnl.Train	"	"
	5th Day, Jan., 9th		
XXIV	2/4th West Riding Regt.	"	"
XXV	Divn. Squadron	"	"
XXVI	H.Q. & No.1 Sec.Div.Sig.Co.	"	"
XXVII	2/2nd W.Riding Field Ambulance	"	"
XXVIII	2/1st Northumbrian Cas.Clg.Station	"	"
XXIX	Divisional H.Q.	"	"
	6th Day. Jan., 10th		
XXX	H.Q. 186th Inf. Bde.	"	"
XXXI	Section Div. Sig. Coy.	"	"
XXXII	Coy. Divnl. Train	"	"

Ligh

Index No.	Unit.	From	To
XXXIII	Light Trench Mortar Battery	Southampton	Havre
XXXIV	2/3rd W.Riding Regt.	"	"
XXXV	1/3rd W.Riding Field Co.	"	"
XXXVI	2/3rd W.Riding Field Co.	"	"
XXXVII	2/3rd W.Riding Field Ambulance	"	"
XXXVIII	Sanitary Section	"	"
XXXIX	Mobile Vet. Section	"	"
	7th Day, Jan., 11th		
XL	2/6th W.Riding Regt.	"	"
XLI	2/7th W.Riding Regt. (Portion)	"	"
XLII	H.Q. & No. 1 Sec. D.A.C.	"	"
	8th Day, Jan., 12th		
XLIII	2/7th W.Riding Regt. (Remainder)	"	"
XLIV	2/4th K.O.Y.L.I.	"	"
XLV	No.2 Sec. D.A.C.	"	"
XLVI	H.Q. 187th Infy. Bde.	"	"
XLVII	Sec. Divnl.Sig.Coy.	"	"
XLVIII	Company Divnl. Train	"	"
XLIX	Light Trench Mortar Battery	"	"
	9th Day, Jan., 13th		
L	2/5th K.O.Y.L.I.	"	"
LI	2/4th York & Lancs. (Portion)	"	"
LII	No.3 Sec. D.A.C.	"	"
	10th Day, Jan., 14th		
LIII	2/4th York & Lancs. (Remainder)	"	"
LIV	2/5th York & Lancs.	"	"
LV	No.4 Section D.A.C.	"	"
LVI	Divnl.Cyclist Coy.	"	"

War Office,(Q.M.G.2.
27th December, 1916.

SECRET

App III

62nd DIVISION.

1st DAY.

Train No.	Unit	Offrs:	Other Ranks	Horses	Guns	4-wh:V:	2-wh:V:	From	To	Starting Times Day	Starting Times Time	Arrival Times Day	Arrival Times Time
X.400 ½	"A" By: 312th Bde: R.F.A.	3	98	88	3	7	1	Northampton Cas:	Southampton dks:	Jan: 5th	3.55 am	Jan: 5th	9.0 am
X.401 ½	"A" -ditto-	2	68	89	3	7	1	-do-	-do-	,,	5.20 am	,,	10.30 am
X.402 ½	"B" -ditto-	3	98	88	3	7	1	-do-	-do-	,,	6.20 am	,,	11.30 am
X.403 ½	2/5 W.Yorks Regt:	22	495	32	-	9	6	Bedford, Bal:pit	-do-	,,	6.20 am	,,	11.50 am
X.404 ½	"B" By: 312th Bde: R.F.A.	2	98	89	3	7	1	Northampton Cas:	-do-	,,	7.25 am	,,	12.30 pm
X.405 ½	2/5 W.Yorks Regt:	22	494	32	-	8	6	Bedford, Bal:Pit	-do-	,,	7.30 am	,,	1.0 pm
X.406 ½	"C" By: 312th Bde: R.F.A.	3	98	88	3	7	1	Northampton Cas:	-do-	,,	8.25 am	,,	1.35 pm
X.407 ½	"C" -ditto-	2	83	89	3	7	1	-do-	-do-	,,	9.40 am	,,	2.45 pm
X.408 (½ "D" How:By:312th Bde:RFA (312th Hy:T.Mortar Bty:		3	69	66	-	5	1	-do-	-do-	,,	10.40 am	,,	3.45 pm
		3	66	-	-	-	-						
X.409 (½ (H.Q.312th Bde: R.F.A. (½ "D" How: Bty:312th Bde:RFA (312th Medium T.Mor:Bty:		5	49	45	-	5	2)	-do-	-do-	,,	11.50 am	,,	4.50 pm
		2	69	65	2	-	1)						
		2	23	-	-	-	1)						

2nd DAY.

Train No.	Unit	Offrs:	Other Ranks	Horses	Guns	4-wh:V:	2-wh:V:	From	To	Starting Times Day	Starting Times Time	Arrival Times Day	Arrival Times Time
X.410 ½	"A" By: 311th Bde: R.F.A.	3	98	88	3	7	1	Northampton Cas:	Southampton Dks:	6th	3.55 am	6th	9.0 am
X.411 ½	"A" -ditto-	2	68	89	3	7	1	-do-	-do-	,,	5.20 am	,,	10.30 am
X.412 ½	"B" -ditto-	3	98	88	3	7	1	-do-	-do-	,,	6.20 am	,,	11.30 am
X.413 ½	2/6 W.Yorks Regt:	22	495	32	-	9	6	Bedford, Bal:Pit	-do-	,,	6.20 am	,,	11.50 am
X.414 ½	"B" By:311th Bde: R.F.A.	2	98	89	3	7	1	Northampton Cas:	-do-	,,	7.25 am	,,	12.30 pm
X.415 ½	2/6 W.Yorks Regt:	22	494	32	-	8	6	Bedford, Bal:Pit	-do-	,,	7.30 am	,,	1.0 pm
X.416 (½ "D" How: Bty: (311th Medium Trench Mortar Battery		3	69	66	2	5	1	Northampton Cas:	-do-	,,	8.25 am	,,	1.35 pm
		2	23	-	-	-	1)						
X.417 (½ H.Q. Divl: Art: (½ "D" How:By:		5	23	20	-	2	2)	-do-	-do-	,,	9.40 am	,,	2.45 pm
		2	69	65	2	5	1)						
X.418	Cable Section	1	35	30	-	4	1	Hitchin	-do-	,,	10.0 am	,,	3.15 pm
X.419 ½	"C" How: Bty:	3	69	66	2	5	1	Northampton Cas:	-do-	,,	10.40 am	,,	3.45 pm
X.420 (½ H.Q. 311th Bde: R.F.A. (½ "C" How: Battery		5	49	45	-	5	2)	-do-	-do-	,,	11.50 am	,,	4.50 pm
		2	69	65	2	5	1)						

NOTE - It is most important that train loads, and that the Units, Batteries, Squadrons, etc., specified as allotted to each train, upon which the Embarkation Staff base their arrangements in allotting troops to ships, are very strictly adhered to. Any discrepancy between the authorised train load and the numbers arriving in the train leads to complication, inconvenience and discomfort to the troops, and delay in embarkation.

SECRET.

62nd DIVISION.

3rd DAY.

Train No.	UNIT	Offrs:	Other Ranks	Horses	Guns	4-w.Vh:	2-w.Vh:	From	To	Starting Times Day	Starting Times Time	Arrival Times Day	Arrival Times Time
X.421	"A" By: 310th Bde: R.F.A.	3	98	88	3	7	1	Northampton Cas:	Southampton Dks:	Jan: 7th	3.55 am	Jan: 7th	9.0 am
X.422	"A" -ditto-	2	98	89	3	7	1	-ditto-	-do-	,,	5.20 am	,,	10.30 am
X.423	"B" -ditto-	3	98	88	3	7	1	-ditto-	-do-	,,	6.35 am	,,	11.40 am
X.424	2/7 W.Yorks: Regt:	22	495	32	-	5	6	Bedford Bal:Pit	-do-	,,	6.35 am	,,	12.5 pm
X.425	"B" By: 310th Bde: R.I.A.	2	98	89	3	7	1	Northampton Cas:	-do-	,,	7.35 am	,,	12.45 pm
X.426	2/7 W.Yorks: Regt:	22	494	32	-	8	6	Bedford Bal:Pit	-do-	,,	7.50 am	,,	1.20 pm
X.427	"C" By: 310th Bde: R.I.A.	3	98	88	3	7	1	Northampton Cas:	-do-	,,	8.40 am	,,	1.45 pm
X.428	"C" By: -ditto-	2	98	89	3	5	1	-ditto-	-do-	,,	9.40 am	,,	2.45 pm
X.429	1/2 "D" How: Battery 1/2 (310th Med: Trench Mortar By:	3	69	66	2	5	2	-ditto-	-do-	,,	10.50 am	,,	3.55 pm
X.430	(H.Q.310th Bde: R.F.A. 1/2 ("D" How: Battery	5 2	43 69	45 65	- 2	5 5	2 1	-ditto-	-do-	,,	11.50 am	,,	4.55 pm

4th DAY.

Train No.	UNIT	Offrs:	Other Ranks	Horses	Guns	4-w.Vh:	2-w.Vh:	From	To	Starting Times Day	Starting Times Time	Arrival Times Day	Arrival Times Time
X.431	2/1 W.Riding Fd:Ambulance	10	232	53	-	14	4	Bedford Bal:Pit	-do-	8th	3.25 am	8th	9.0 am
X.432	2/8 W.Yorks: Regt:	22	495	32	-	6	6	-ditto-	-do-	,,	5.0 am	,,	10.30 am
X.433	2/8 -ditto-	22	494	32	-	8	6	-ditto-	-do-	,,	6.0 am	,,	11.30 am
X.434	3/1 W.Riding Fd:Coy: R.E.	3	106	39	-	5	4	-ditto-	-do-	,,	7.0 am	,,	12.30 pm
X.435	(H.Q.Div: R.E. (3/1 W.Riding Fd: Co: R.E.	3 3	12 106	11 39	- -	2 5	1 5	-ditto-	-do-	,,	8.0 am	,,	1.35 pm
X.436	(H.Q.185th Infy: Bde: (Sec:Div:Sig:Co: (526th Coy: Div: Train (185th Lt:Trench Mortar By: (F.G.Coy: (Train)	6 1 5 4 -	27 25 60 46 1	23 8 28 - 2	- - - - -	6 1 5 1 1	- - 1 - -	-ditto-	-do-	,,	9.15 am	,,	2.45 pm
X.437	(H.Q. & 525th Coy: Div: Train (Pioneer Bn: (Train)	10 -	110 4	57 8	- -	13 4	2 -	Northampton Cas:	-do-	,,	10.40 am	,,	3.45 pm

NOTE — It is most important that train loads, and that the Units, Batteries, Squadrons, etc., specified as allotted to each train, upon which the Embarkation Staff base their arrangements in allotting troops to ships, are very strictly adhered to. Any discrepancy between the authorised train load and the numbers arriving in the train leads to complication, inconvenience and discomfort to the troops, and delay in embarkation.

SECRET.

62nd DIVISION.

5th DAY.

Train No.	UNIT	Offrs:	Other Ranks	Horses	4-Wh:V:	2-Wh:V:	Stores	From	To	Starting Times Day	Time	Arrival Times Day	Time
X.438	2/- Northumbrian Cas:Clg:Stn:	11	88	-	-	-	*35	Bedford,Bal:Pit	Southampton Dks:	Jan: 9th	3.25 am	Jan: 9th	9.0 am
X.439	2/2 W.Riding Fd:Amb:	10	232	53	14	4	-	-do-	-do-	"	5.0 am	"	10.30 am
X.440	2/4 W.Riding Regt:	22	494	32	9	5	-	-do-	-do-	"	6.0 am	"	11.30 am
X.441	2/4 -ditto-	22	493	32	8	6	-	-do-	-do-	"	7.0 am	"	12.30 pm
X.442	H.Q. & No.1 Sec:Div:Sig:Coy:	3	137	83	12	8	-	-do-	-do-	"	8.0 am	"	1.35 pm
X.443	H.Q. 62nd Division	21	103	77	5	1	-	-do-	-do-	"	9.15 am	"	2.45 pm

*Vehicles will be in position for loading stores at 1.25 am.

6th DAY.

Train No.	UNIT	Offrs:	Other Ranks	Horses	4-Wh:V:	2-Wh:V:	Stores	From	To	Starting Times Day	Time	Arrival Times Day	Time
X.444	2/3 W.Riding Fd:Amb:	10	232	53	14	4	-	Wellingboro' Mid:Rly:	Southampton Dks:	10th	3.0 am	10th	9.0 am
X.445	½ 1/3 W.Riding Fd:Co: R.E. (Mobile Vet:Section)	3 1	106 29	39 26	5 3	5 -	- -	Bedford,Bal:Pit Northampton Cas:	-do- -do-	" "	4.55 am 5.0 am+)	"	10.30 am
X.446	½ 1/3 W.Riding Fd:Co: R.E. (Sanitary Section)	3 1	106 27	39 1	5 -	4 -	- -	)Bedford,Bal:Pit	-do-	"	6.0 am	"	11.30 am
X.447	½ 2/3 W.Riding Fd:Co: R.E.	3	106	39	5	5	-	-do-	-do-	"	7.0 am	"	12.30 pm
X.448	½ -ditto-	3	106	39	5	4	-	-do-	-do-	"	8.0 am	"	1.35 pm
X.449	2/5 W.Riding Regt:	22	495	32	9	6	-	-do-	-do-	"	9.15 am	"	2.45 pm
X.450	½ -ditto-	22	494	32	8	6	-	-do-	-do-	"	10.15 am	"	3.45 pm
X.451	(H.Q. 185th Inf:Bde: (Sec: Div: Sig: Co (527th Co: Divl: Train (186th Light Trench Mortar By: (F.G.Co: (Train)	6 1 5 4 -	27 26 60 46 1	23 8 28 - 2	6 1 5 1 1	- 1 1 - -	- - - - -	-do-	-do-	"	11.25 am	"	4.50 pm

+Connect with special at Bletchley.

NOTE. - It is most important that train loads, and that the Units, Batteries, Squadrons, etc., specified as allotted to each train, upon which the Embarkation Staff base their arrangements in allotting troops to ships, are very strictly adhered to. Any discrepancy between the authorised train load and the numbers arriving in the train leads to complication, inconvenience and discomfort to the troops, and delay in embarkation.

SECRET.

62nd DIVISION.

7th DAY.

Train No.	Unit	Offrs	Other Ranks	Horses	4-wh:V:	2-wh:V:	From	To	Starting Times Day	Time	Arrival Times Day	Time
K.452	1/2-2/6 W.Riding Regiment	22	434	32	8	6	Bedford Bal:Pit	Southampton Dks:	Jan: 11th	3.25 am	Jan: 11th	9.0 am
K.453	2/6 -ditto-	22	493	32	8	6	-do-	-do-	"	5.0 am	"	10.30 am
K.454	2/7 -ditto-	14	280	32	6	6	-do-	-do-	"	6.0 am	"	11.30 am
K.455	2/7 -ditto-	14	280	32	8	6	-do-	-do-	"	7.0 am	"	12.30 pm
K.456	No.1 Sec: D.A.C.	2	73	92	14	2	-do-	-do-	"	8.25 am	"	1.35 pm
K.457	-ditto-	2	72	91	14	1	Northampton Cas:	-do-	"	9.40 am	"	2.45 pm
K.458	H.Q. &1/3 No.1 Sec:D.A.C.	2	73	92	15	1	-do-	-do-	"	10.40 am	"	3.45 pm

8th DAY.

Train No.	Unit	Offrs	Other Ranks	Horses	4-wh:V:	2-wh:V:	From	To	Starting Times Day	Time	Arrival Times Day	Time
K.459	1/3 No.2 Sec: D.A.C.	1	59	75	12	1	Northampton Cas:	Southampton Dks:	12th	3.55 am	12th	9.0 am
K.460	1/3 -ditto-	1	50	74	12	1	-do-	-do-	"	5.20 am	"	10.30 am
K.461	1/3 -ditto-	1	59	74	12	1	-do-	-do-	"	6.20 am	"	11.30 am
K.462	2/7 W.Rdg:Reg:(remainder)	16	451	-	-	-	Bedford Bal:Pit	-do-	"	7.0 am	"	12.30 pm
K.463	2/4 K.O.Y.L.I.	22	495	32	9	6	Wellingboro' Mid: Rly:	-do-	"	7.30 am	"	1.35 pm
K.464	½ -ditto-	22	494	32	8	6	-do-	-do-	"	8.45 am	"	2.45 pm
K.465	½ (H.Q.187th Inf:Bde: (Sec: Divl: Sig:Co: (528th Co: Div: Train (187th Lt:Trench Mortar (Battery (M.G.Co: (Train)	6 1 5 4 -	27 26 50 46 1	23 8 28 - 2	6 1 5 - 1	- - 1 - -	-do-	-do-	"	9.45 am	"	3.45 pm

NOTE - It is most important that train loads, and that the Units, Batteries, Squadrons, etc., specified as allotted to each train, upon which the Embarkation Staff base their arrangements in allotting troops to ships, are very strictly adhered to. Any discrepancy between the authorised train load and the numbers arriving in the train leads to complication, inconvenience and discomfort to the troops, and delay in embarkation.

SECRET. 62nd DIVISION.

9th DAY.

Train No.	Unit	Offrs:	Other Ranks	Horses	4-wh:V:	2-wh:V:	From	To	Starting Times Day	Starting Times Time	Arrival Times Day	Arrival Times Time
X.466	1/3 No.3 Sec: D.A.C.	1	59	75	12	-	Northampton Cas:	Southampton Dks:	Jan: 13th	3.55 am	Jan: 13th	9.0 am
X.467	1/3 -ditto-	1	60	74	12	-	-do-	-do-	"	5.20 am	"	10.30 am
X.468	1/3 -ditto-	1	59	74	12	-	-do-	-do-	"	6.20 am	"	11.30 am
X.469	2/4 Yorks & Lancs:Reg:	14	328	32	9	6	Irchester,M.R.	-do-	"	6.35 am	"	12.30 pm
X.470	2/5 K.O.Y.L.I.	22	494	32	9	6	Wellingboro' Mid: Rly:	-do-	"	7.30 am	"	1.35 pm
X.471	2/4 Yorks:& Lancs:Reg:	13	328	32	8	6	Irchester,M.R.	-do-	"	8.50 am	"	2.45 pm
X.472	2/5 K.O.Y.L.I.	22	493	32	8	6	Wellingboro' Mid: Rly:	-do-	"	9.45 am	"	3.45 pm

10th DAY.

Train No.	Unit	Offrs:	Other Ranks	Horses	4-wh:V:	2-wh:V:	From	To	Starting Times Day	Starting Times Time	Arrival Times Day	Arrival Times Time
X.473	1/4 No.4 Section D.A.C.	1	68	91	14	-	Northampton Cas:	Southampton Dks:	14th	3.55 am	14th	5.0 am
X.474	1/4 No.4 -ditto-	1	68	91	14	-	-do-	-do-	"	5.20 am	"	10.30 am
X.475	1/4 No.4 -ditto-	1	68	91	14	-	-do-	-do-	"	6.30 am	"	11.40 am
X.476	1/4 No.4 -ditto-	1	68	90	13	1	-do-	-do-	"	7.30 am	"	12.45 pm
X.477	2/5 Yorks & Lancs Reg:	22	495	32	9	6	Wellingboro' Mid:Rly:	-do-	"	7.45 am	"	1.45 pm
X.478	1/2 2/5 -ditto-	22	494	32	8	6	-do-	-do-	"	8.45 am	"	2.45 pm
X.479	Cyclist Co:*	8	200	13	3	1	Bedford Bal:Pit	-do-	"	10.25 am	"	3.55 pm
X.480	2/4 York & Lancs Reg: (Remainder)	17	330	-	-	-	Irchester, M.R.	-do-	"	11.0 am	"	4.55 pm

*201 bicycles.

NOTE:- It is most important that train loads, and that the Units, Batteries, Squadrons, etc., specified as allotted to each train, upon which the Embarkation Staff base their arrangements in allotting troops to ships, are very strictly adhered to. Any discrepancy between the authorised train load and the numbers arriving in the train leads to complication, inconvenience and discomfort to the troops, and delay in embarkation.

App IV
A1.

DISTRIBUTION OF UNITS.

Divisional Headquarters	at Frohen le Grand
Divisional Supply Column	at Neuvillette
Ammunition Sub Park	at Villiers L'Hopital
H.Q.185th Infantry Brigade	at Bonnieres
2/5th Bn. West Yorks.Regt	at Fortel
2/6th Bn. " " "	at Bonnieres
2/7th Bn. " " "	at "
2/8th Bn. " " "	at "
Light T.M.Battery	at Beauvoir
2/1st R.F.Ambulance	at Bofflos
2/3rd R.E.Field Coy.	at "
526th Coy. M.G.C.	at Bonnieres
H.Q.186th Infantry Brigade	at Bachimont
2/4th Bn. West Riding Regt.	at Villers
2/5th Bn. " " "	at Noeux
2/6th Bn. " " "	at Buire au Bois
2/7th Bn. " " "	at Rougefay
Light T.M.Battery	at Bachimont
2/2nd R.F.Ambulance	at Villers
1/3rd R.E.Field Coy.	at Mamur Farm
527th Coy. M.G.C.	at Noeux
H.Q.187th Infantry Brigade	at Remaisnil
2/4th Bn. K.O.Y.L.I.	at Neuvillette
2/5th Bn. " "	at Barly and Remaisnil
2/4th Bn.York Lancs.Regt	at Barly
2/5th Bn. " " "	at Neuvillette
Light T.M.Battery	at Remaisnil
2/3rd R.F.Ambulance	at Ransart
3/1st R.E.Field Coy.	at Neuvillette
528th Coy. M.G.C.	at "
Headquarters, R.Arty.	at Chateau de Beauvoin
310th F.A.Brigade	at Drucas Wavans
310th F.A. " M.T.M.Battery	at Beauvoin
310th F.A. " H.T.M.Battery	at Drucas Wavans
311th F.A.Brigade	at Outrebois
311th F.A. " M.T.M.Battery	at "
312th F.A.Brigade	at Occoches
312th F.A. " M.T.M.Battery	at "
H.Q. Div.Amm.Column	at Mozerolles
No.1 Section D.A.C.	at Frohen le Grand
No.2 Section D.A.C.	at Mozerolles
No.3.Section D.A.C.	at "
No.4.Section D.A.C	at Drucas Wavans
Cable Section	at Frohen le Grand
H.Q. Divisional R.E.	at " " "
H.Q. Divisional Train	at " " "
525th Coy. A.S.C.	at " " "
H.Q.Div.Sig.Co.& No.1.Section	at " " "
Sanitary Section	at Various Brigade Headquarters
Mobile Veterinary Section	at Frohen le Grand

13.1.17.

SECRET.
62nd DIVISION.

App V Copy No. 21

Q/154/3

1. A table shewing location of Units of the Division, (less Divisional Artillery and 525th Company, A.S.C.) for the night of January 22nd - 23rd is attached.

2. The baggage section of 526th Company, A.S.C. will march immediately behind the 185th Infantry Brigade and the baggage section of 527th Company A.S.C. immediately behind the 186th Infantry Brigade.

The baggage section of 528th Company, A.S.C. will march immediately behind Divisional Headquarters, the tail being East of the road junction on the OCCOCHES - DOULLENS Road North of HEM Bridge by 1 p.m. January 22nd.

3. The Supply Sections of the Train will march under orders to be issued by O.C.Train.

4. 62nd Divisional Supply Column will billet at BEAUVAL on the night of Jan. 22nd - 23rd.

The Divisional Supply Column will proceed to BEAUVAL and dump the rations held in charge at BEAUVAL by 9 a.m. January 22nd - The requisite number of lorries required to load supplies for the whole Division will return to BOUQUEMAISON to arrive there and load at 11 a.m.

5. The refilling points on 22nd January will be as follows:-

Divisional Troops Supply Group (Artillery Units and No.525 Coy. A.S.C. only) on FROHEN-LE-GRAND - MEZEROLLES road (as at present) at 3 p.m.

185th, 186th and 187th Infantry Brigade Supply Groups (with balance of Divisional Troops) on the BOUQUEMAISON - DOULLENS Road immediately south of HAUTEVISEE at 2-30 p.m.

6. Billeting parties will precede their Units on January 21st.

18.1.17.

Lieut.Colonel.
A.A. & Q.M.G. 62nd Division.

Copies to:-

```
1 - 5   "Q"
6       C.R.A.
7       C.R.E.
8       A.D.M.S.
9       A.D.V.S.
10      185th Bde.
11      186th Bde.
12      187th Bde.
13      Camp Commandant.
14      "G"
15      Train
16      Supply Column
17      Signal Co.
18      V. Corps
19      XIII Corps
20      31st Division.
```

SECRET.   Night of 22/23rd January, 1917.

LOCATION OF UNITS - 62nd DIVISION.

Divisional Headquarters	BEAUVAL
Headquarters R.E.	BEAUVAL
3/1st W.R.Field Co.R.E.)	
2/3rd W.R.Field Co.R.E.) 3 Companies	BEAUQUESNE
1/3rd W.R.Field Co.R.E.)	
185th Infantry Brigade Headquarters)	
2 Battalions)	AMPLIER
1 Battalion	TERRAMESNIL
1 Battalion	SARTON
Trench Mortar Battery	AMPLIER

(leaving room for 61st Div.Art.H.Qrs.)

186th Infantry Brigade Headquarters	AUTHIEULE
1 Battalion	AUTHIEULE
2 Battalions	AMPLIER
Trench Mortar Battery	AUTHIEULE
187th Infantry Brigade Headquarters	BEAUVAL
4 Battalions	BEAUVAL
	1 Battalion in Camp.
Trench Mortar Battery	BEAUVAL
Divisional Train Headquarters	AUTHIEULE
526th Co.Divl.Train)	
527th Co.Divl.Train)	AUTHIEULE
528th Co.Divl.Train)	
Divisional Supply Column	BEAUVAL
2/1st W.R.Field Ambulance	BRETEL
2/2nd W.R.Field Ambulance	BRETEL
2/3rd W.R.Field Ambulance	BEAUVAL
Divl.Mobile Veterinary Section	BEAUVAL
Divisional Sanitary Section	BEAUVAL

18.1.17.

Lieut-Col.
A.A. & Q.M.G. 62nd Division.

SECRET.   Copy No. 22
                                                          G/525/3
                                                          App VI
                        62nd DIVISION.

1. A table showing proposed location of Units of this Division
(less Divisional Artillery and 525th Company, A.S.C.) for January
23rd 1917, and for Divisional Artillery and 525th Company, A.S.C.
for January 24th 1917, is attached.

   Billeting parties will be sent forward on 22nd and 23rd January
respectively. It is important that these parties should visit
Town Majors immediately on arrival in their billeting areas.

2. The baggage section of the Train Companies will march on the 23rd
and 24th January, as follows:-

     (a) 185 Bde. with waggons following units
     (b) 186 "   "   "   "   "   the Brigade Group
     (c) 187 "   "   "   "   "   units
     (d) Divisional Artillery on 23rd with waggons following
the whole formation, and on 24th inst. with waggons following units.

   The Supply Sections will march under orders to be issued by O.C.
Train, but to be clear of ORVILLE by 7 a.m. on January 24th.

3. The 62nd Divisional Supply Column will billet at LOUVENCOURT
on the nights 23rd-24th and 24th-25th January, after which it will
come under the orders of the 5th Corps.

   29 Lorries of Divisional Supply Column will proceed to LOUVEN-
COURT and dump rations held on charge. Of those lorries, 20 will
proceed in time to arrive at BELLE EGLISE to load supplies for the
Division (less Divisional Artillery & 525th Company A.S.C.) at 8.30
a.m. January 23rd. 9 lorries will return to BEAUVAL to pick up the
balance of rations held on charge and dump them at LOUVENCOURT.

4. Refilling points will be as follows:-

        January 23rd.- For the Division (less Divisional Artill-
                        ery and 525th Company A.S.C.), on the
                        AUTHIE - BUS Road in I.17 at 2 p.m.

                        For the Divisional Artillery & 525th Com-
                        pany A.S.C. on DOULLENS - BOUQUEMAISON
                        Road immediately south of HAUTE VISEE, at
                        2.30 p.m.

        January 24th.- For the whole Division, on AUTHIE - BUS
                        Road in I.17, at 12 noon.

                                            [signature]
                                            Lieut.-Colonel,
21. 1. 17.   A.A. & Q.M.G., 62nd Division.

Copies to:-
----

1. 185th Infantry Brigade.
2. 186th Infantry Brigade.
3. 187th Infantry Brigade.
4. 62nd Divisional Artillery.
5. C.R.E.
6. 62nd Divisional Signal Company.
7. 62nd Divisional Train.
8. 62nd Divisional Supply Column.
9. A.D.M.S.
10. A.P.M.
11. A.D.V.S.
12. Divisional Liaison Officer.
13. Divisional Post Office.
14. V. Corps.
15. V. Corps Artillery.
16. XIII Corps.
17. 19th Division.
18. 32nd Division.
19. "G".
20. "Q". — Major Lea
21. Camp Commandant. (H.Q. 62nd Division).
22. 23. War Diary.
24-28. Spare.

28 Col foot
27 " for APM.

SECRET.
Copy No. 22
C.253.

LOCATION OF UNITS - 62ND DIVISION.
(less Divisional Artillery & 525th Company A.S.C.)
JANUARY 23RD, 1917.

Divisional Headquarters	BUS
Headqrs.Divisional R.E.	BUS
" " Signal Coy. & No.1 Section.	BUS
Headqrs.185th Infantry Bde.	COIGNEUX
2/5th Bn.West Yorks.Regt.	COUIN
2/6th " " " "	ROSSIGNOL FARM
2/7th " " " "	ST.LEGER LES AUTHIE
2/8th " " " "	COIGNEUX
2/1st W.R.Field Ambulance	COIGNEUX
2/3rd W.R.Field Co.R.E.	COIGNEUX
526th Coy. A.S.C.	ST.LEGER LES AUTHIE (in tents)
Headqrs.186th Infantry Bde.	BUS
2/4th Bn.West Riding Regt.)	
2/5th " " " ")	
2/6th " " " ")	BUS
2/7th " " " ")	
2/2nd W.R.Field Ambulance	BUS
1/3rd W.R.Field Coy.R.E.	BUS
527th Coy. A.S.C.	WARNIMONT WOOD
Headqrs.187th Infantry Bde.	AUTHIE
2/4th Bn. K.O.Y.L.I.)	
2/5th Bn. " ")	LOUVENCOURT.
2/4th Bn.York & Lancs.Regt.	THIEVRES
2/5th " " " "	FAMECHON
2/3rd W.R.Field Ambulance	LOUVENCOURT
3/1st W.R.Field Co.R.E.	AUTHIE
528th Coy. A.S.C.	WARNIMONT WOOD
Sanitary Section	BUS
Mobile Veterinary Section	BUS
Headqrs. Divisional Train	BUS
Divl.Supply Column	LOUVENCOURT

DIVISIONAL ARTILLERY & 525TH COMPANY A.S.C.
January 24th 1917.

Headqrs.Royal Artillery	AUTHIEULE or AMPLIER	) This is upon
310th F.A.Brigade	LOUVENCOURT	) information
311th " "	ACHEUX WOOD	) received from
312th " "	LOUVENCOURT	) V.Corps Artillery.
H.Q.Divl.Ammn.Column	THIEVRES	) The accommodation
No.1.Section L.A.C. (		) for 62nd Divl.Arty.
No.2. " " (400	600	) will be very
No.3. " " (COUIN	THIEVRES	) much cramped for a
No.4. " " (		) few days.
525th Coy. A.S.C.	WARNIMONT WOOD	

Headquarters, Divisional Artillery will move to BUS on
January 25th.

21.1.17.

Lieut-Colonel,
A.A. & Q.M.G. 62nd Division.

Copies to:-
----

1. 185th Infantry Brigade.
2. 186th Infantry Brigade.
3. 187th Infantry Brigade.
4. 62nd Divisional Artillery.
5. C.R.E.
6. 62nd Divisional Signal Company.
7. 62nd Divisional Train.
8. 62nd Divisional Supply Column.
9. A.D.M.S.
10. A.P.M.
11. A.D.V.S.
12. Divisional Liaison Officer.
13. Divisional Post Office.
14. V. Corps.
15. V. Corps Artillery.
16. XIII Corps.
17. 19th Division.
18. 32nd Division.
19. "G".
20. "A".
21. Camp Commandant. (H.Q. 62nd Division).
22. 23. War Diary.
24-26. Spare.

Copy No. 5
Q/164/3
App. VI a.

SECRET.

Headquarters,
    62nd Divisional Artillery.

1.   The area allotted for the billeting of the Divisional Artillery on the night of January 23rd-24th, is - All accommodation on both roads between DOULLENS and ORVILLE (DOULLENS exclusive).

2.   Headquarters of 525th Company, A.S.C. and Baggage Section will move under orders to be issued by G.O.C. Divisional Artillery.

    The Supply Section of 525th Company A.S.C. will move under orders to be issued by O.C. 62nd Divisional Train.

3.   Billeting Parties will precede their Units on January 22nd.

19. 1. 17.
    Lieut.-Colonel,
    A.A. & Q.M.G. 62nd Division.

Copies to :-
----

    1.   "G"
  2 to 6.   "Q"
    7.   A.D.M.S.
    8.   A.D.V.S.
    9.   Div. Train
    10.   Div. Supply Column.
    11.   Signal Coy.
    12.   D.A.D.O.S.
    13.   A.P.M.
    14.   V Corps
    15.   XIII Corps
    16.   31st Div.

App VII

LIST OF WORKING PARTIES AND BY WHOM FOUND.

	ROADS.		FOUND BY.
1	D Coy. No.9 Labour Bn. LOUVENCOURT.	2 Coys.	186th Infantry Brigade
2	A Coy. No.6 Labour Bn. BUS	2 Coys. 2 Platoons	186th Infantry Brigade
3	D Coy. No. 6 Labour Bn. BEAUSSART.	2 Coys.	186th Infantry Brigade
4	B Coy. No.6 Labour Bn. COIGNEUX.	2 Coys.	185th Infantry Brigade
5	C Coy. No.6 Labour Bn. AUTHIE.	1 Coy.	185th Infantry Brigade
6	Town Major, VAUCHELLES.	1 Platoon	186th Infantry Brigade
7	Town Major, LOUVENCOURT.	2 Platoons	186th Infantry Brigade
8	Town Major, ACHEUX.	2 Platoons	186th Infantry Brigade
9	Town Major, BUS.	2 Platoons	186th Infantry Brigade
10	Town Major, BERTRANCOURT.	2 Platoons	186th Infantry Brigade

WORK UNDER C.E.

13	135 A.T. Coy. R.E. BERTRANCOURT.	1 Platoon	186th Infantry Brigade.
15	145th A.T. Coy. A.S.C. Dump, BELLE EGLISE.	2 Platoons	186th Infantry Brigade

UNDER G.O.C. R.A.

18	Constructing Dump, P.23.d.9.9.	1 Coy.	185th Infantry Brigade.
19	Constructing Dump, P.7.d.8.8. ACHEUX.	3 Coys.	186th Infantry Brigade

ORDNANCE, RAILWAYS, & A.S.C.

20	R.T.O., ACHEUX. Unloading Ammunition.	2 Platoons.	186th Infantry Brigade

TOTALS. 62nd Div. 17 Coys. - Platoons.

MISCELLANEOUS PARTIES.

e	P of W. Coy. ACHEUX	2 Platoons	186th Infantry Brigade.

SECRET

DISTRIBUTION OF UNITS.

Headquarters, 62nd Division.	BUS-les-Artois
Headquarters, 185th Infantry Brigade	COIGNEUX
2/5th Bn. West Yorks. Regt.	COUIN
2/6th Bn. " " "	ROSSIGNOL FARM
2/7th Bn. " " "	MAILLY WOOD WEST
2/8th Bn. " " "	FAMECHON
Headquarters, 186th Infantry Brigade	BUS-les-Artois
2/4th Bn. West Riding Regt.	"
2/5th Bn. " " "	"
2/6th Bn. " " "	" not yet arrived.
2/7th Bn. " " "	
Headquarters, 187th Infantry Brigade.	AUTHIE
2/4th Bn. K.O.Y.L.I. (2 Coys)	"
2/4th Bn. " " " (2 Coys)	ST. LEGER-les-Authie
2/5th Bn. K. " "	BUS-les-Artois
2/4th Bn. York & Lancs. Regt. (1 Coy)	AUTHIE
2/4th Bn. " " " (1 ")	SARTON
2/4th Bn. " " " (1 ")	HURTEBISE FARM
2/4th Bn. " " " (1 ")	ST. LEGER-les-Authie
2/5th Bn. " " " (3 Coys)	COIGNEUX
2/5th Bn. " " " (1 Coy)	BUS-les-Artois
Headquarters, 62nd Divisional Artillery	BUS-les-Artois
310th F.A. Brigade	VAUCHELLES-les-Authie
311th " "	ACHEUX WOOD
312th " "	LOUVENCOURT
D.A.C. Headquarters & Part	THIEVRES
" Part	COUIN
Headquarters, 62nd Divisional Engineers	BUS-les-Artois
3/1st W.R. Field Co.	MAILLY WOOD EAST
1/3rd " " "	MAILLY WOOD WEST
2/3rd " " "	COIGNEUX
Headquarters, and No.1. Section 62nd Divisional Signal Coy.	BUS-les-Artois
Headquarters, 62nd Divisional Train.	BUS-les-Artois
525th Coy. Divisional Train	BOIS du WARNIMONT
526th " " "	BUS-les-Artois
527th " " "	BOIS du WARNIMONT
528th " " "	" " "
2/1st W.R. Field Ambulance	BOIS LALEAU
2/2nd " " "	BUS-les-Artois
2/3rd " " "	LOUVENCOURT
62nd Divisional Sanitary Section	BUS-les-Artois
62nd Divisional Mobile Veterinary Section.	BUS-les-Artois.

26.1.17.

App IX

62ND DIVISION.

CASUALTIES during January 1917.

	Officers.	O.R.
Killed.	-	2.
Wounded.	-	11.

Sick evacuated from Divisional area.

Officers.	O.R.
10.	189.

VOLUME II

February 1917.

Army Form C. 2118.
SECRET.

WAR DIARY
of
62nd Division "A"

INTELLIGENCE SUMMARY.
(Erase heading not required.)

Vol 2

Instructions regarding War Diaries and Intelligence Summaries are contained in F.S. Regs., Part II. and the Staff Manual respectively. Title pages will be prepared in manuscript.

Place	Date	Hour	Summary of Events and Information	Remarks and references to Appendices
BUS-les-ARTOIS	1.2.17		62nd Div'l Arty. commenced relieving 7th Div'l Arty.	
do do	6.2.17		Two new Lewis guns issued per each battalion bringing numbers to 14 per battalion.	
do do	13.2.17		62nd Div'l Artillery completed relief of 7th Division in line.	
do do	14.2.17		185th & 186th Infantry Brig's completed relief of Inf. Bdes. 32nd Division in line.	
do do	2.2.17		[struck through]	
do do	20.2.17		Pack transport organised, as approach to front line had become impossible for wheeled vehicles.	App I
			This pack transport is used for rations, water, fuel and has worked well.	
do do	18.2.17		Thaw precautions came inforce. The entailed practically all lorries stopping. Precaution Continued to end of month. All administrative services became much hampered. Roads broke up very rapidly in spite of reduced traffic. A 3rd to 5 trans'l inspan on draught horses, horses being on a reduced scale of rations — full ration later resumed from 26th February. The advantage of gum boots, thigh for a/b trenches have not so marked in portions of the line, where trenches been disposed by gun fire and frost. The heavy mud in shell holes pulled the boots right off, and men got trench foot in consequence. Baths, laundries, canteens have all well started in February. A note to move that these institutions are vitally necessary, but showed to moved by men other than Category A.	

page 2

Army Form C. 2118.

SECRET.

62nd Division A

WAR DIARY
or
INTELLIGENCE SUMMARY.
(Erase heading not required.)

February 1917.

Instructions regarding War Diaries and Intelligence Summaries are contained in F. S. Regs., Part II. and the Staff Manual respectively. Title pages will be prepared in manuscript.

Place	Date	Hour	Summary of Events and Information	Remarks and references to Appendices
BOS-ec-ARTOIS			Casualties of February were officers 22 OR 333 details as attached in	App II
			28th February 1917	
			G.M. Larkins	
			Assistant Major General,	
			Commanding 62nd Division	

APPENDIX 1.

PACK TRAINS.

185th Infantry Brigade	162
186th Infantry Brigade	162
187th Infantry Brigade	162
3 Field Companies R.E.	42
3 Field Ambulances	18
Divisional Reserve (under C.R.A)	102

The animals were found, 120 from each Infantry Brigade, balance from Divisional Ammunition Column.

62nd DIVISION.

CASUALTIES DURING FEBRUARY 1917.

OFFICERS.

KILLED.

2nd Lieut. E.J.Trubshawe, 460th West Riding Field Co.R.E.	2.2.17
Lieut. H.Sinclair, 2/4th West Riding Regiment	16.2.17
Captain C.R.Bramley, 2/5th K.O.Y.L.I.	20.2.17

DIED OF WOUNDS.

2nd Lieut. S.D.Lang, 2/5th K.O.Y.L.I. Wounded 20.2.17, died of wounds. 24.2.17

WOUNDED.

Captain H.C.Lasbrey, 310th Brigade R.F.A.	11.2.17
Captain G.R.Nevitt, 2/8th West Yorkshire Regiment	15.2.17
Lieut. D.L.E.Davies, 2/6th West Yorkshire Regiment	18.2.17
2nd Lieut. S.A.Smith, 457th West Riding Field Co. R.E. (wounded slightly at duty)	19.2.17
Lieut. H.G.Hodgkinson, 2/5th West Riding Regiment	21.2.17
Chaplain F.L.Sugget, C.E. attd. 2/6th West Riding Regt.	20.2.17
Captain R.J.Preston, 2/5th K.O.Y.L.I. attached from 6th Norfolk Regt.	21.2.17
Captain W.N.Gale, 2/4th York.& Lancs.Regiment (wounded slightly at duty)	22.2.17
Lieut. A.E.Furniss, 2/5th York.& Lancs.Regiment	23.2.17
Lieut. G.K.Brown, 2/6th West Yorkshire Regiment (wounded slightly at duty)	20.2.17
2nd Lieut. T.B.Lyth, 2/5th York.& Lancs. Regiment	25.2.17
2nd Lieut. J.S.Mc.Ewen, 461st West Riding Field Co. R.E.	26.2.17
Major R.E.Negus, 2/8th West Yorks. attd. from 2/5th W.R.R.	26.2.17
2nd Lieut. H.A.Girling, 2/5th West Yorks. attd. from 1/10th Royal Scots	17.2.17

MISSING

Major F.A.Lupton, 2/8th West Yorkshire Regiment	19.2.17
Captain A.S.Furniss, 2/5th York.& Lancs. Regiment	22.2.17
Lieut. A.H.Hicks, 2/5th York.& Lancs. attd. from 2/7th Welsh Regiment	22.2.17
2nd Lieut. N.E.Bentley, 2/5th West Riding Regiment	6.2.17

OTHER RANKS.

Killed 88   Wounded 232   Missing 13.

SECRET.

62ⁿᵈ DIVISION
STANDING
BATTLE ORDERS

HQ AFQ SECRET
62nd Division. A

ORIGINAL
Army Form C. 2118.

WAR DIARY
or
INTELLIGENCE SUMMARY.
(Erase heading not required.)

March 1917.

Instructions regarding War Diaries and Intelligence
Summaries are contained in F. S. Regs., Part II.
and the Staff Manual respectively. Title pages
will be prepared in manuscript.

Place	Date	Hour	Summary of Events and Information	Remarks and references to Appendices
BUS-les-ARTOIS	1st March		Div H.Qrs still at B.O.S.	
ENGLEBELMER	4th		Div HQ A.Q. moved. General Staff at ENGLESART.	
"	1st		Town traps appointed for forward area BEAUMONT HAMEL to BEAUCOURT station.	
"	7th		Railhead moved to AVELUY	
"	19th		Town traps appointed for BEAUCOURT area and MIRAUMONT and ACHIET-le-PETIT. In these new areas vacated by the Germans nearly all houses & accommodation found to be destroyed, roads blocked by craters, wells fouled & blown in, all churches destroyed. During March the following units have been attached to the Division for working parties or reverts: 6th East Yorkshire Regt. 8th Northumberland Fusiliers. 3rd Cheshire Regt.	
"	19th		Railhead changed from AVELUY to BEAUCOURT-sur-ANCRE	
"	29th		Railhead moved from BEAUCOURT-sur-ANCRE to MIRAUMONT 2 Lewis guns per battalion raised bringing up total per battalion to 16.	
"	9th		Reinforcements received during month contained in The men born of good stamp and many had previous war experience, and had been wounded previously. Field General Courts martial held during month were 13.	App I

CONFIDENTIAL. Page 2

Army Form C. 2118.

62nd Division A

WAR DIARY
INTELLIGENCE SUMMARY
(Erase heading not required.)

Instructions regarding War Diaries and Intelligence Summaries are contained in F.S. Regs., Part II. and the Staff Manual respectively. Title pages will be prepared in manuscript.

March 1917

Place	Date	Hour	Summary of Events and Information	Remarks and references to Appendices
ENGLEBELMER	March 1917 1st	8½	208th Machine Gun Coy arrived from England & joined division	
			2/2nd & 213th Machine Gun Coys arrived from England & joined division	
			Honours & Rewards awarded for action round BEAUMONT HAMEL, SERRE, PUISIEUX, MIRAUMONT	App II
			ACHIET-LE-PETIT and ACHIET-LE-GRAND area	
			Casualties in action are as shewn in	App III
			Health of troops good throughout month, but a considerable number of diarrhea.	
			Equipment from Base arrived satisfactorily in spite of advance and difficulties by road and rail.	
			The supply of light lorries (15 cwt) in considerable numbers and to take the place of 30 cwt & 3 ton lorries might be the means of saving roads in bad weather.	
			Owing to the very bad state of the roads, the far back positions of railheads, the impossibility of using motor transport, the previous reduction of rations (since made up again) and the necessity of much of the transport having to be carried out with pack animals, the debility and subsequent losses of animals has become a serious difficulty affecting mobility	
			P.R.M. Taylor Lieut Col RHA, Major General Commanding 62nd Division	
	4 April 1917.			

Appendix I.

REINFORCEMENTS RECEIVED BY DIVISION
DURING MONTH OF MARCH.1917.

	Officers.	Other Ranks.
2/5th Bn. West Yorkshire Regt.	1	22
2/6th Bn. West Yorkshire Regt.	1	7
2/7th Bn. West Yorkshire Regt.	-	72
2/8th Bn. West Yorkshire Regt.	-	36
2/4th Bn. West Riding Regt.	2	29
2/5th Bn. West Riding Regt.	5	28
2/6th Bn. West Riding Regt.	3	19
2/7th Bn. West Riding Regt.	-	60
2/4th Bn. K. O. Y. L. I.	1	51
2/5th Bn. K. O. Y. L. I.	2	170
2/4th Bn. York & Lancaster Regt.	7	8
2/5th Bn. York & Lancaster Regt.	3	8
208 Machine Gun Company.	-	11
2/2nd W.R. Field Ambulance.	-	6
310th F.A. Brigade	11	10
312th F.A. Brigade	11	-
Divisional Ammunition Column	4	7
457th W.R. Field Coy. R.E.	-	5
460th W.R. Field Coy. R.E.	1	9
461st W.R. Field Coy. R.E.	-	2

Appendix II.

LIST OF HONOURS & REWARDS

CONFERRED ON OFFICERS AND MEN OF THE 62ND DIVISION DURING

MONTH OF MARCH 1917.

Military Crosses	2
Distinguished Conduct Medals	1
Military Medals	17

Appendix III

CASUALTIES IN 62ND DIVISION DURING MONTH OF MARCH 1917.

OFFICERS.

Date	Name	Unit	Status
March 1st.	Major A.P. Dale,	2/5th Bn. West Yorks. Regt.	Killed.
" "	2/Lt. W.O. de W. Silmon,	2/8th Bn. " " "	"
" "	Lieut. K.S. Sexton,	2/6th Bn. West Riding Regt.	Wounded.
" "	Major R.C. Williams,	310th F.A. Brigade	"
" 2nd.	2/Lt. R.G. Pickard,	2/4th Bn. K.O.Y.L.I. attd. from 2/7th Welsh Regt.	Died of Wounds.
" 3rd.	2/Lt. G. Ambler,	2/6th Bn. West Yorks. Regt.	Wounded.
" "	2/Lt. E.S. Smith,	2/6th Bn. " " "	Missing.
" "	Lieut. C.G. Bowler,	2/8th Bn. " " "	Wounded Acc.
" "	2/Lt. H.A. Sabelli,	310th F.A. Brigade	Wounded
" 5th	Lieut. E.N.J. Wethey,	2/6th Bn. West Yorks. Regt.	Wounded
" "	Lieut. E.W.F. Jephson,	310th F.A. Brigade	Wded. slightly at duty.
" 6th.	2/Lt. R. Holborn,	310th F.A. Brigade,	Wounded
" "	2/Lt. J.C. McIlroy,	310th F.A. Brigade	"
" 7th	Lieut. J.D. Conyers,	2/8th Bn. West Yorks. Regt.	"
" "	2/Lt. F. Warner,	2/5th Bn. York & Lanc. Regt.	Killed
" "	2/Lt. J.W. McHattie,	2/5th Bn. " " "	Wounded
" "	Capt. F. Wilson, RAMC.	attd. 2/5th York & Lanc. Rgt.	"
" 9th	Capt. W.H. Smith,	2/4th Bn. K.O.Y.L.I.	"
" "	2/Lt. A. Morris,	2/4th Bn. " "	Wded. slightly at duty.
" 11th	Lieut. R.E. Mainprice	2/4th Bn. York & Lanc. Regt.	Wounded
" "	Lt. Col. P. Prince,	2/5th Bn. York & Lanc. Regt.	"
" "	Lieut. S.S. Wainwright,	2/4th Bn. K.O.Y.L.I.	Killed
" 12th	Capt. C.E. Stuart	2/4th Bn. York & Lanc. Rgt. attd. from 2/6th Suffolk Rgt.	Wded. Died of wds. 15th
" 14th	Capt. H.E. Jenkinson,	2/4th Bn. York & Lanc. Regt.	Wounded.
" "	Lieut. E.B. Bilton,	Highland Cyc. Bn. attd. 2/5th Bn. K.O.Y.L.I.	Killed
" "	2/Lt. G.C. High,	6th Norfolk Regt. attd. 2/5th Bn. K.O.Y.L.I.	"
" "	Lieut. J. Mailer,	Highland Cyc. Bn. attd. 2/5th Bn. K.O.Y.L.I.	Wounded
" "	Lieut. C. Boden	Hunts. Cyc. Bn. attd. 2/5th Bn. K.O.Y.L.I.	"
" "	2/Lt. J.H. Lister	2/4th Bn. West Riding Regt.	"
" 15th	Capt. W. Bell,	2/4th Bn. K.O.Y.L.I.	Killed
" 13th	Capt. F.H. Seaman,	310th F.A. Brigade	Wded. (Gas)
" "	2/Lt. T.E.F. Russell,	2/5th Bn. York & Lanc. Regt.	Wounded.
" 20th	Capt. W. Graham,	2/4th Bn. West Riding Regt.	Wded. slightly at duty.
" 22nd	2/Lt. C.M. Pullan,	312th F.A. Brigade	Killed
" 21st	Major F.A. Lupton,	2/8th Bn. West Yorks. Regt.	Missing 21.2.17 Found dead.

OTHER RANKS.

Killed. 98   Wounded 386   Missing 17

URGENT.

SECRET.

62nd Divn.
G. 10

'Q' Branch,

    62nd Division.

    Herewith one copy of 62nd. Division "Battle Standing Orders" together with Addenda.

    These are to be taken into use forthwith.

    Acknowledge.

                                          Captain.
                              General Staff 62nd Division

10.3.1917.

FB.

The following Table cancels paras. 1 and 3 of 62nd. Division
"BATTLE STANDING ORDERS" :-

1. DRESS & EQUIPMENT.

   TABLE A. - To be carried by Battalions in the attack.

   (i) Each N.C.O. and man, except Lewis Gunners, Bombers, Rifle Grenadiers and such carriers and specialists (Signallers, Orderlies etc) as Commanding Officers consider should be exempt, will carry the following :-

   (a) Rifle and equipment, less pack.

   (b) 170 Rounds of S.A.A. except Platoon Sergeants who carry 120 Rounds only.

   (c) Haversack on the Back containing Emergency Ration, one full day's iron ration, mess tin packed with grocery ration, and solidified alcohol, spare oil tin and spare pair of socks.

   (d) One full water bottle.

   (e) Waterproof sheet fixed on the back of the waistbelt by the supporting straps of the pack, with cardigan jacket in sheet. In cold weather "Cap Comforter" in addition.

   (f) Three sandbags.

   (g) One Small Box Respirator and P.H. Helmet.

   (h) One tin of ground flares.

   (ii)
   (a) Each Platoon and Section Commander will carry one "P" bomb.

   (b) When specially ordered by the Division or Brigade, each man of the Rifle Sections will carry 2 No.25 Grenades with rods complete.

   (iii) Each Lewis Gun Team will carry 20 filled drums.

   Each Battalion will carry such additional filled drums to form a reserve as Battalion C.Os consider necessary.

   Each Lewis Gunner will carry 50 Rounds of S.A.A.

   (iv) 40 S.O.S. rifle grenades will be carried by each Battalion (8 per Company and 8 with Bn. H.Q.)

   (v) Whenever obtainable, either chocolate ration or a cocoa and milk ration, in small hermetically sealed tins, will be carried by all ranks in the haversack.

   NOTE: The number of tools, shovels and picks to be carried in the assault and their distribution will be ordered by the Brigade.

TABLE B. -- To be carried by Grenadiers and Bombers.

(a) RIFLE GRENADIERS.

    6 No.24 Grenades and cartridges for same.

    2 No.27 Grenades (smoke) and cartridges for same.

    50 Rounds of S.A.A.

(b) BOMBERS.

    7 No.25 Grenades and cartridges for same.

    1 "P" Bomb.

    50 Rounds of S.A.A.

    Rifle Grenadiers and Bombers will also carry all Table A. less 120 Rounds of S.A.A., picks and shovels, and ground flares.

STANDING BATTLE ORDERS.

THE FOLLOWING ORDERS WILL BE OBSERVED IN
ANY OPERATIONS IN WHICH THE DIVISION MAY TAKE PART:-
They are to be read in conjunction with the Pamphlet S.S.135
"Instructions for the Training of Divisions for Offensive Action"

1. **DRESS, EQUIPMENT etc.** (a) Every infantry soldier in the ranks, in addition to his ordinary equipment will carry :-

    120 rounds S.A.A. for each Rifleman.
    2 hand grenades, to form a reserve for recognised bombers.
    2 sandbags.
    A pick or shovel, in equal proportions.
    Iron ration and unexpired portion of the day's ration.

    (b) Haversacks will be worn, and all other kit including greatcoats if not worn, will be packed in men's packs. Packs will be labelled and stored under battalion arrangements, they should not contain articles of personal value.

    A Battalion dump will be established for all spare equipment and baggage under the Quartermaster.

    (c) Carrying parties, Bombers, Lewis and Machine Gunners, Scouts, runners, Signallers and personnel of Light Trench Mortar Batteries, will carry 50 rounds only.

    (d) All available wire cutters and wire breakers will be carried by selected men to deal with any wire remaining uncut by the artillery preparations.

Before going into action, as long beforehand as possible, the object of the operation and the method of carrying it out is to be most carefully explained to the men.

Para 1 (a) The 2 hand grenades carried by each soldier in the ranks are on no account to be thrown by the soldier. They are only carried as a reserve for recognised bombers. The soldier fights with rifle and bayonet and no more effective weapons exist if he is properly trained in the use of them and uses them with determination.

Para 1 (b) An alternative is to wear the pack and put the contents of the haversack, waterproof sheet and a full water bottle inside. This gives the soldier freedom in movement. Great coats can be worn while waiting prior to the assault. Prior to zero hour they will be collected under Regimental arrangements and stacked by platoons in the forming up place.

2. **SIGNALS.** (a) To mark the position which the attack has reached.

    <u>Hand flags</u>, 2'6" square, of Brigade colours, at the rate of two per platoon, will be carried and waved. These will only be waved as a signal to the artillery and to aeroplanes, <u>and will never be stuck in the ground</u>.

    (b) 400 flares per battalion will be carried to signal to contact patrol aeroplanes.

    (c) Ground sheets to signal to aeroplanes will be issued to battalions before going into action.

    (d) A special party will be told off to light flares or flash mirrors (Vigilant periscopes) to signal to aeroplanes from the front trenches.

    (e) Visual Stations must be carefully selected and protected from view, and should afford adequate protection.

    (f) Venetian blind shutters, pigeons, flares and trench wireless sets, must be made full use of. Pigeons should be kept with forward troops.

    (g) Messages sent from units in front line were often unnecessarily long. Long messages are rarely necessary during actual operations, and if sent, cause blocks in the signal service.

    (h) A Brigade advanced orderly report centre under a senior N.C.O. will be established. Company orderlies will run straight to Battalion Headquarters. Battalion Orderlies will return to the Brigade Advanced Orderly Report Centres.

    (i) Brigades and Battalions must keep their Signal Officers fully informed of what is going on or contemplated.

    (j) 12 S.O.S. rockets per company with port fires will be carried forward.

    Ground Signal Panels for communicating with contact aeroplanes will accompany Brigade and Battalion Headquarters and full use will be made of them when necessary.

    A code for signalling to aeroplanes is on page 71 of Pamphlet S.S. 135

    Runners should not be sent singly.

(3)

3. **GRENADES.** (a) All bombers will carry 12 bombs each.
   The bombs to include 3 Rifle Grenades. (Mill's Grenade fitted with a 9" rod).
   (b) Each platoon is to have one section of bombers.
   (c) Each bombing section will include 2 carriers to carry up extra supplies in 2 buckets, each bucket not holding more than 18 grenades; these carriers should only be armed with a rifle and 50 rounds S.A.A.
   Rifle grenades are most useful for assisting in the clearing of trenches.
   Grenade carriers should carry cartridges for these rifle grenades.

   (d) Grenades and bombs will be fuzed at the Divisional Dumps before passing up. An officer will be in charge of the fusing party.
   Grenade buckets must be collected and returned to these dumps as soon as possible.

4. **OFFICERS.** (a) 20 officers only will go into action with each Battalion. See Sec. XXX S.S.135.

   (b) The above is the absolute maximum number of officers who should go into an attack; this might with advantage be reduced to 15 if the operation is on a small scale.

   (c) In event of an attack being ordered, each Brigade will detail one thoroughly intelligent officer to report to D.H.Q. for Liaison work.

   (d) Officers in the attack should be dressed similarly to the men and should advance on the same alignment as the men, and not draw attention to themselves by being isolated from them.

5. **RUNNERS.** (a) The following runners will be detailed :-

   For Divnl. Hd. Qrs.   As required.

   For Brigade Hd. Qrs.   As detailed by Brigadiers.

   For Battalions.   16 per Battalion.

   (b) Runners sent back with demands for stores, S.A.A. etc., will remain at the store to guide back the carrying party to the desired point.

(4)

6. **TROPHIES.** Should there be likelihood of captured enemy's guns falling into our hands and it becomes necessary to destroy them, the following action will be taken:-

(a) <u>Field Guns.</u> Attack breech mechanism (open) with pick or axe, also the sights and their attachments to the gun or carriage. If time admits, fill the muzzle for a couple of feet or so with earth or any other material, load and fire the gun. As this will burst the gun, it is necessary to fire the gun by a string from a safe place.

(b) <u>Machine Guns.</u> Remove lock, feed block and fuze spring, and bend barrel in front of water jacket with pick axe.

(c) <u>Minnenwerfer.</u> If gun cannot be removed, it should be damaged by denting barrel or blowing up gun if time admits of this.

(d) <u>Prisoners.</u> No documents are to be taken from prisoners.

7. **DUMPS.** Dumps must be arranged beforehand behind each battalion, and as far to the front as is safe, in which will be stored (vide Appendix 1) :-

- Wire and standards.
- Ammun.
- Bombs.
- Trench Mortar ammun.
- Rations, one day's supply.
- Water.
- Sandbags.
- Tools.
- A second pair parts wallet for each Lewis Gun.

An officer must be placed in charge of each dump.

Rum to be stored under special arrangements for safety.

Small box Respirators, Boars Very Lights, Very Pistols, Rockets for S.O.S, Flares for aeroplane communications.

Sufficient must be stored to last for 3 days use.

8. **BADGES.** (a) The Divisional badge, cut out in red cloth, will be worn on the left shoulder by all individual men who are authorised to be outside the limits of the fighting. Any men found without this badge will be arrested by the police, or if wounded, passed on to the clearing stations.

(b) Other badges will be worn as laid down in S.S. 135.

9. **WORKING PARTIES.** In addition to the usual carrying parties, the following additional parties will as a rule be required :-

(a) By C.R.E. equivalent of 1 N.C.O. and 25 men per Bn.

(b) By each L.T.M.B ttery equivalent of 1 Officer and 40 men per Brigade.

(c) By each M.G.Coy. " " 1 N.C.O. and 25 men per Bde.

These men will be fully armed and will carry either a pick or a shovel.

10. **DISCIPLINE.**

(a) When reliefs are taking place, especially during the course of operations, a rear guard will be detailed by infantry units to collect stragglers. To allow stragglers to return indiscriminately to camp, instead of being collected and marched by parties, is harmful to discipline.

(b) The A.P.P.M. will arrange for extra patrols to be on duty two days after the operations have ceased.

(c) The word "Retire" does not exist. There can be no going back and if the word is heard, no attention is to be paid to it.

(d) No notice is to be taken of a white flag unless the enemy comes out of his trenches etc., unarmed and with hands up.

(e) No unwounded man is to fall out to help a wounded man back.

(f) No slightly wounded men are to go back.

(g) There is to be no collecting of trophies and souvenirs. Men found hunting for them are to be dealt with for breach of discipline.

(h) Wounded men must be taught that it is a point of honour to carry their arms as long as they possibly can. Medical Officers and Regimental police will send back men who have disobeyed this order, to fetch their arms and equipment.

11. **WATER.** The provision and care of water is most important.

 (a) There should be one day's supply in the men's water bottles, and Company Officers must see that water bottles are filled and the water used most sparingly.

 (b) There must be one day's water stored in petrol tins at the Divisional Advanced Dump and another day's supply in rear ready to be sent up as occasion may offer.

 (c) No food or water found in German trenches is to be eaten or drunk until it has been examined and passed fit by a Medical Officer.

12. **"MOPPING UP".**
 Mopping up Parties must be most carefully selected, be complete units and properly told off to their tasks beforehand.

 The first duty of all mopping up parties is to rapidly search for dugout entrances and to place a sentry at each entrance.

 In cases where the attacking troops stop in the captured trenches, Mopping up Parties are not required.

 Moppers up should take no prisoners. The reason for this is that should the enemy's barrage prevent our supporting lines following up the leading lines captured Germans might overpower their guards and then shoot on leading lines in the back.

13. CLEARING BATTLEFIELD AND SALVAGE COMPANY

(a) The clearing of the battle field will be carried out under the directions of the Divisional Staff.

(b) The Salvage Company will be responsible for all Salvage Work, but Commanding Officers should assist when possible, by collecting any equipment etc., into well defined places and informing the O.C. Salvage Company of their whereabouts.

Carrying and working parties should not be allowed to come back empty-handed from the front.

Every man should be put on his honour to bring back something.

Brigades and Battalions will be most careful to select sites for dumps which do not cause the men to go a long way out of their way when returning to billets. In Battalions - a site near its cookers is usually the most favourable.

Empty returning ration limbers or mules should be used to carry back the salvage to Brigade and Divisional dumps.

(c) Definite areas should be allotted to each salvage party and as those areas are cleared they should be hachured over on a map which will form a record of progress.

(d) Special parties should be detailed for the _immediate_ collection of rifles.

14. ACTION DURING ATTACK.

(a) There is to be no serious advance beyond the objective laid down.
This does not mean that local successes should not be exploited. Touch must be kept with the enemy by pushing forward patrols and Lewis Guns.

(b) Care must be taken in the advance that rear waves do not close on those in front. They must keep their distance, and when the objective is reached, it will be held only by the wave or waves which took it. Those in rear will stop where they are or look for cover.

(c) Directly a position is taken, consolidation will be carried out without delay. This is one of the chief duties of Commanding Officers, and specific instructions on this point should be included in all Operation Orders.

(d) Bridges for artillery and cavalry advance are to be placed in position prior to an attack. Men must keep clear of these, as if seen by the enemy they will be shelled.

(e) Gas should be released between 15 and 5 minutes before ZERO.

(f) Registration excepted, Stokes' mortars must not be kept in the front line trenches during our preliminary bombardment. During that period they will be kept under cover. On the Infantry advancing they will come into action between the front and support line trenches, and from there support the infantry advance.
The Stokes' Battery should, during an attack, remain in close touch with Brigade H.Q. Two guns are quite enough to send forward at a time, the remaining guns should be kept in reserve in some suitable place from which they can be sent forward, if required, to replace casualties. The Battery should move forward on the same principle that Artillery would move forward with a Division.

/The whole

The whole personnel of a battery, or a large portion of it, should be employed for carrying the bombs for the two guns sent forward.

The Brigadier should decide the special tasks of the battery.

Stokes guns can assist in the blocking of trenches along which hostile bombers can attack our flanks.

(g) Dividing lines between Brigades and between Battalions will be very carefully detailed in all operation orders.

(h) Tapes will be provided for the following purposes :-

  i To give a line for assaulting troops to form on.

  ii To be laid towards the enemy's positions to give the advancing troops proper direction.

  iii To guide troops up to the newly captured positions at night.

(i) The possible sites for Strong Points should be selected before the attack. Parties of R.E. and Pioneers should be told off to make these "Strong Points" and they should not go forward to commence work until it is certain that the place where the Strong Point is to be made is clear of the enemy. These parties should be detailed by the C.R.E. who will receive instructions from the General Staff.

Strong Points should not be placed in conspicuous positions, as, for instance, the corner of a wood.

It will usually be advisable to place machine guns <u>outside</u> a Strong Point, if hidden flanking positions can be found, as once a Strong Point is located, the enemy concentrates his artillery on to it.

(j) A Brigadier and his Brigade Major should never be absent at the same time from Brigade H.Q. unless a responsible Officer, in close touch with the situation is available to answer for them.

(k) <u>The Assault.</u>
<u>The all-important point is that the assault must follow absolutely on the heels of the lift of the barrage</u>
This is a matter of seconds.

Troops can advance safely to within 50 yards of a hostile trench while the barrage is on it. They should be at that point at least 1 minute before the barrage is timed to lift and then rush on.

(l) <u>Relief.</u>
No relief must be done on the first night after an attack. The men must hang on and consolidate. They may be <u>reinforced but</u> not relieved.

(m) The Regimental Police must see that nobody uses "up" trenches for down traffic and vice versa as long as operations are going on in that area.

(n) The opportunity of the Infantry is the moment at which the artillery lifts. Their success depends chiefly on keeping very close to the barrage, and jumping in the moment that it lifts.

(o)   Infantry must assault the whole front which is to be captured and held. It is not safe to leave gaps trusting to capture them by surrounding, bombing or other indirect methods.

(p)   Good communications and a good basis of attack are essential in those operations; if there are insufficient communications, the command cannot make its action felt and that troops cannot be properly supplied and are therefore not fresh. The best use to which flag and lamp signalling can be put requires careful thinking out before the assault.

(q)   As soon as a position is conquered, communications and trenches must be dug simultaneously with the utmost speed and the number of men required to carry out the work must be told off wherever they have to be taken from. It is less costly in the long-run suffering loss in the digging parties during the first two nights than suffering the constant wastage due to reliefs being carried out across the open etc.

15. **MISCELLANEOUS.**

(a)   **Reports.** Reports must be correctly written. They are useless unless the following are inserted :-

   1. Locality.
   2. Date.
   3. Time of Dispatch.

N.C.Os. must be taught to send in reports.
Nil reports must be sent in.

(b)   **Telescopic Sights.** Telescopic sights and periscopes will be stored in battalion dumps and only sent up to the firing line if required.

(c)   **Identifications.** It is essential that no orders, maps, or correspondence, which if captured by the enemy would disclose the identity of the Division should be carried into action.

(d)   German dug-outs, especially those under the front line parapet, are usually a complete system joined by passages. This enables the enemy :--

  (i)   to escape to a flank by underground passage.

  (ii)   to counter-attack from a flank by the same route unless all exits are guarded.

(e)   It is, therefore, necessary to close all dug-outs in the occupied area; to block all underground passages leading into dug-outs under the occupied area; to make a very thorough search for entrances to dugouts and place guards over them.

16. **MEDICAL.** (a) The Regimental Aid Post is to be as near as possible to Battalion Headquarters. As far as possible it is to be protected from shrapnel and rifle fire, and it must be able to protect from 12 to 20 wounded.

(b) The Battalion Stretcher Bearers are under the immediate Command of the Regimental Medical Officer and at the beginning of an attack they are to be formed up at the Battalion Aid Post, otherwise they get scattered and lost sight of, and a systematic evacuation of wounded is not obtained.

(c) At least four additional stretchers are to be drawn by each Battalion Medical Officer to bring the number up to twelve and Stretcher Bearers for these are to be supplied by the Commanding Officer, to enable the wounded to be cleared more quickly. If Stretcher Bearers of a Field Ambulance remove a wounded man on a Regimental stretcher they will leave a stretcher in the Battalion Aid Post in place of the one removed.

(d) Battalion Stretcher Bearers are not to work further back than the Battalion Aid Post. Their duties are to collect the wounded into the Battalion Aid Post.

(e) In order to locate their position to Stretcher Bearers wounded men are to endeavour to fix their bayonets and then fix the rifle in the ground, butt uppermost.

(f) Routes for Stretcher Bearers must be carefully selected and provided with guide posts.

(g) Stretcher Bearers are to learn their way about trenches and at the same time get more used to being under fire.

APPENDIX I.

SUGGESTED FORMATION OF DUMPS.

Dumps should be formed in the following order of importance :—

1. Wire.   )   Possessed of these four essentials,
2. Tools.   )   it has been found that our
3. S.A.A.   )   troops can resist the heaviest
4. Water   )   German counter-attacks.
5. Stokes' bombs.
6. Rations.
7. Grenades.
8. Sandbags.
9. Other R.E. material.

To take various items in detail :—

1. **WIRE**, more than anything else checks a German attack; it has been found that wiring by day is not always feasible, but the wire must be close at hand so that the wiring can go on vigorously by night.

½ picks 2. **TOOLS** To enable consolidation to be rapidly taken in hand,
½ shov- men must either carry entrenching tools, or tool dumps must
  ols   be established close at hand (also see note on consolidation)).

3. **S.A.A.** is stored in ½ Battalion and Brigade Dumps. (The Brigade should have at least 2 dumps, the idea being not to put all eggs in one basket).

4. **WATER.** The water question is a vital one. Every effort should be made to collect petrol tins; each Battalion should have 250 tins of its own, and there should be 3,000 tins at the Advanced Divisional Dump. Water is issued to nobody who cannot produce an empty tin, and requisitions for water on the Divisional Dump should be signed by an Officer. Supply Officers must have it impressed on them that they must supply their units with water as well as with rations etc., and must consider the water question when making their supply arrangements.

Normally, 1 quart of water per man is kept stored at the Divisional Dump.

5. **STOKES BOMBS** can be used with effect on previously reconnoitred targets (selected with a view to assisting our advancing infantry) if they come into action between the front and support line trenches when the bombardment is over. Dumps of ammunition therefore, for them should be accumulated there beforehand.

200 bombs per mortar has been found an adequate supply for a severe engagement.

SUGGESTED FORMATION OF DUMPS.
(continued.)

6. RATIONS. Except during exceptionally heavy bombardments rations have reached the troops in the trenches regularly.

To guard against any eventuality however, 8,000 additional iron rations should be spread about between the Brigade and advanced Divisional Dumps.

7 GRENADES. The question of grenades supply is an important one, and the Staff must establish grenade dumps intelligently after appreciation of the probable nature of the forthcoming battle. Should it be anticipated that the battle will be fought in trenches, hand grenades should preponderate in grenade dumps; if, however, open or village fighting is to be expected, rifle grenades should be in excess of hand grenades.

8. SANDBAGS. The chalky soil common to the neighbourhood in which the SOMME battles are being fought, does not require immediate revetment. Sandbags, therefore, though useful are not indispensable, and hence are placed No. 8 in order of importance. 32,000 sandbags should be stored in the Divisional Advanced Dump.

9. OTHER R.E. STORES. Dug-outs, machine gun and trench mortar emplacements etc., should be made on a sealed pattern, this enables the C.R.E. to prepare timber beforehand and greatly accelerates the construction of dugouts when they are required.

The tendency to push heavy R.E. stores up into the captured positions is to be resisted however, until consolidation has taken place, as if they are hastened forward they bet block approaches and frequently have to be abandoned on the enemy either counter-attacking or opening a heavy barrage.

The attached diagram shows the system of dumps found to be effective.

Below is a very approximate Table giving some indication of the amounts of some stores to be collected in dumps. It is liable to correction and is inserted as a guide only.

	Battalion Dump.	Brigade Dump.
S.A.A.	100 boxes	200 boxes.
Bombs (proportion of P bombs and rifle grenades)	2000	2000
Water	250 tins (maximum)	300 tins,
Very's lights	3 boxes	9 boxes
S.O.S. rockets	12	40
Stokes Ammunition	200 at each gun	200 per gun.
Picks) In addition	200	400
Shovels) to those	200	400
Sandbags) on the man.	8000	1600

Diagram Shewing Suggested System of Dumps.

o o   o o

½ Btn Dumps.

o o   o o

[ ]   2 Bde Dumps   [ ]

Advanced   [   ]   Water Fusers
Divl Dump.   Salvage Coy
                                          S.A.A.

D.H.Q.   [   ]   2 Lorries.
Dump.   8 G.S. Wagons.

Confidential
War Diary
H.Q. 63rd Division "A"
from 1st April 1917
to 30th April 1917
Vol IV.

SECRET.

Army Form C. 2118.

62nd DIVISION. A 90

Vol 4

ORIGINAL.

WAR DIARY
OF
INTELLIGENCE SUMMARY.
(Erase heading not required.)

APRIL 1917

Instructions regarding War Diaries and Intelligence Summaries are contained in F. S. Regs., Part II. and the Staff Manual respectively. Title pages will be prepared in manuscript.

Place	Date	Hour	Summary of Events and Information	Remarks and references to Appendices
ENGELBELMER	1st		Divisional Hqs. G at ENGLESART – A. @ ENGELBELMER	
ACHIET-G-GRAND	2nd		Divisional HQrs moved to ACHIET-le-GRAND into camp.	
ENGELBELMER	2nd		201st Machine Gun Coy joined division from England.	
ACHIET-G-GRAND	4th		Railead move from MIRAUMONT to ACHIET-le-GRAND.	
do do			Reorganisation of D.A.C. 5th Army S.G. 445/1 of 8-4-17.	
do do	13th		All horses transferred from B echelon to batteries, wagons to be packed and B echelon loads to be carried out by M.T. Owing to shortage of horses, owing to shortage from batteries & brigades was keen to reserve M.T.	
do do	18th		Owing to destruction of wells and watering places, arrangements made for sending vehicle to carry two gallons of water per horse in petrol tins: these tins to be filled in the vehicles and always kept full.	
do do	24th		1500 oblique reticules issued authorised for horses of a division. Honours & Rewards awarded during April. 7 Military Crosses. 1 Distinguished Conduct Medal. 25 Military hussars and 1 Meritorious Service medal. Casualties are as usual	

T2134. Wt. W708—776. 500000. 4/15. Sir J. C. & S.

SECRET. page 2.
Army Form C. 2118.

April 1917   62nd Division. A.

WAR DIARY
or
INTELLIGENCE SUMMARY.
(Erase heading not required.)

Instructions regarding War Diaries and Intelligence Summaries are contained in F.S. Regs., Part II. and the Staff Manual respectively. Title pages will be prepared in manuscript.

Place	Date	Hour	Summary of Events and Information	Remarks and references to Appendices
ACHIET-LE-GRAND			Killed Wounded Missing Officers 10 - O.R. 156. Officers 29 - O.R. 540 Officers Nil. O.R. 19. Evacuated Sick Officers 24. O.R. 826. Reinforcements shown in 11 Field General Courts Martial have been held Health of troops good. Prevalent sickness diarrhea.	App. I

10 May 1917.

Fairlie, Maj.
Brig. for G.O.C.
62nd Division

REINFORCEMENTS RECEIVED BY 62nd DIVISION DURING
APRIL 1917.

	Off.	O.R.
2/5th West Yorks. Regiment	9	21
2/6th -ditto-	-	10
2/7th -ditto-	11	19
2/8th -ditto-	4	19
2/4th West Riding Regiment	4	17
2/5th -ditto-	1	-
2/6th -ditto-	2	22
2/7th -ditto-	5	-
2/4th King's Own Yorkshire Light Infantry	3	11
2/5th -ditto-	2	53
2/4th York. & Lancs. Regiment	7	11
2/5th -ditto-	6	13
Royal Artillery	-	140
Royal Engineers	-	14
A.S.C.	-	1
Medical Units	-	15
201st Machine Gun Company	-	8
208th -ditto-	-	5
212th -ditto-	-	26
213th -ditto-	-	2
A.V.C.	-	1

7.5.17.

CONFIDENTIAL

Vol 5

WAR DIARY OF
63rd Division "A"

FROM: 1.5.17 TO: 31.5.17

VOLUME V

ORIGINAL

ORIGINAL

May 1917.

SECRET
Army Form C. 2118.

WAR DIARY
or
INTELLIGENCE SUMMARY.
(Erase heading not required.)

Instructions regarding War Diaries and Intelligence Summaries are contained in F. S. Regs., Part II. and the Staff Manual respectively. Title pages will be prepared in manuscript.

62nd Division A. E53

Place	Date	Hour	Summary of Events and Information	Remarks and references to Appendices
ACHIET-le-GRAND	1st		Route clothing withdrawn.	
"	7th		Experiments with gas masks for horses carried out.	
"	10th		Administration steps taken to conserve land which required hay & other crops such as lucerne, sainfoin, clover.	
A "	18th		Lean allotment raised from 4 to 6 per diem.	
"	19th		To preserve roads and to prevent congestion of traffic particular tracks have instituted across country; their success is evident and as the ground hardens they can be taken in any direction almost routes are thus obtained and time saved.	
"	13th		V Corps laundry was closed and V Army Laundry opened at ABBEVILLE.	
"	27th		Blankets returned. Bought 25%, which were cleaned & re-issued in case of an advance.	
"	28		Remounts became more easy to obtain & were of a good stamp.	
"	31st		V Corps, in which the division is, was transferred from VIth Army to 3rd Army.	

SECRET. Army Form C. 2118.

May 1917 page 2.

62nd Division A

WAR DIARY
or
INTELLIGENCE SUMMARY.
(Erase heading not required.)

Instructions regarding War Diaries and Intelligence Summaries are contained in F. S. Regs., Part II. and the Staff Manual respectively. Title pages will be prepared in manuscript.

Place	Date	Hour	Summary of Events and Information	Remarks and references to Appendices
ACHIET-le-GRAND		19"	At a Corps Conference the following points have been discussed, disposal of manure and cooperation with French authorities in concerning manure to a central and sanitary manure dealing with the plague of flies. Two papers to be administered by division and not by corps. Statistics: Courts martial. 23 F.G.C.M.s held. Honours & awards. Reinforcement. Casualties — Killed — Officers. 24 O.R. 254 Wounded Officers. 87 O.R. 1710 missing Officers. 32 O.R. 1320. Sick evacuated b.c.c.s. 14 Officers. 491 O.R.	see App I see App II

Haddl P. Maj
for GOC 62nd Division

T2134. Wt. W708—776. 500000. 4/15. Sir J. C. & S.

App I

62nd DIVISION.
HONOURS AND AWARDS DURING MAY 1917.

    D.S.Os.   3

    Military Crosses   21

    D.C.Ms.   8

    Military Medals   59

    M.S.Ms.   1

HONOURS AWARDED BY FRENCH GOVERNMENT.

    Croix de Chavilier   1

    Croix de Guerre   3

    Medal Militaire   1

62nd DIVISION.
REINFORCEMENTS RECEIVED DURING MAY 1917.

App II

	Offs.	O.R.
2/5th West Yorkshire Regiment	6	185
2/6th " " "	11	200
2/7th " " "	8	112
2/8th " " "	6	84
2/4th West Riding Regiment	3	45
2/5th " " "	3	120
2/6th " " "	12	78
2/7th " " "	8	56
2/4th K.O.Y.L.I.	4	91
2/5th "	11	146
2/4th York. & Lancs. Regiment	5	165
2/5th " " "	7	12
201st Machine Gun Company	1	18
208th " " "	2	36
212th " " "	4	15
213th " " "	-	32
Divisional Artillery	8	196
Divisional R.E.	-	10
Divisional Train	-	5
Medical Units	-	22
TOTAL	99	1628

DUPLICATE.   ORIGINAL

CONFIDENTIAL.

WAR DIARY

OF

ASSISTANT ADJUTANT AND QUARTERMASTER GENERAL'S BRANCH
62nd DIVISION.

FROM 1st JUNE 1917.   TO 30th JUNE 1917.

(VOLUME VI)

SECRET.

Army Form C. 2118.

62nd Division "A"

WAR DIARY
or
INTELLIGENCE SUMMARY.
(Erase heading not required.)

June 1917

Place	Date	Hour	Summary of Events and Information	Remarks and references to Appendices
ACHIET-LE-GRAND			The division having now been in France nearly six months the advantages of various organisations for the comfort, health and recreation of the men are recorded. 1. Baths. At least one bath house for infantry brigade is needed. French steam baths are found to be suitable. They can be erected in marquees or buildings, are easily put together and baths a dozen men at once. The Baths should be in the place where men get a clean change of underclothing. This is well worked by each man handing in his dirty underclothing and drawing a fresh set. The Baths staff are responsible for sorting dirty washclothing to the Laundry (Corps or Army). An ironing room is also required for ironing seams of clothing to kill eggs of lice. A Foden Thresh disinfector, though these all duty underclothing must pass before going to Laundry, is essential. The prevention of lice is important. It is not possible for men in trenches or in line generally to avoid having them, and official means to assist them are absolutely necessary. Lice plague has a comparing effect on men, and many be held the responsible for many cases of slight fever. Where lice is not merely breeding - Mufflers to supplement body vests are essential, and the staff of B supplied in the formation of a Div	

Page 2

Army Form C. 2118.

SECRET.

52nd Division. A

WAR DIARY
or
INTELLIGENCE SUMMARY.
(Erase heading not required.)

June 1917

Place	Date	Hour	Summary of Events and Information	Remarks and references to Appendices
ACHIET LE GRAND			Employment Company is entirely inadequate. A suggested establishment is in. This Establishment may be considered high, but the benefit to the health of the men and their efficiency will be found likely to warrant it.	App I
			2. SOCK LAUNDRY. Socks are not accepted at Corps or Army Laundries in sufficient advanced arrangements to meet demand. A copy of divisional order regarding socks is attached. The washing, temporary & sorting of socks takes a considerable amount of labour. This could be reduced if a washing machine was provided. A rotating machine with a wringer attached is recommended, but special sanction for this output cannot be acceded to. The staff necessary to handle the socks is asked to.	App II
			3. BAND & ENTERTAINMENTS. These have been found most valuable additions to all who have seen soldiers coming out from a turn in the trenches it must be patent that in addition to a profound physical fatigue, distraction from a certain mental apathy is needed. The Band and a Strength of 30 which provides for it informs that felt a concert party and a travelling cinematograph are valuable.	App I

June 1917   page 3

SECRET.

Army Form C. 2118.

62nd Division "A"

WAR DIARY
or
INTELLIGENCE SUMMARY.
(Erase heading not required.)

Place	Date	Hour	Summary of Events and Information	Remarks and references to Appendices
ACHIET-le-GRAND			The allowance in a division of Employment Company 1/12 men is to be two to substantive men than tan shown. To bring the First Class Substantive Employed to a total of Class A, is for higher all two men fit than in the fighting line. GAMES, a liberal supply of footballs, boxing gloves swimming shorts is always needed.	App I
Achiet-le-Grand	16-6-17		Divisional Hqrs moved to Achiet-le-Petit	
Achiet-le-Petit	29-6-17		Divisional Hqrs moved to Huts movement Corner of BAPAUME ROAD Sheet 57C N.W. B:15.c.4.5	
BAPAUME ROAD H.15.c.4.5	29-6-17		Railway changes from ACHIET-le-GRAND to BAPAUME	
			Casualties for June	App II
			Honors + awards awarded in June	App IV
			Reinforcements received during June	App V
			Courts martial held during June were four 15.	App VI

App 4

Army Form C. 2118.

SECRET

62nd Division A

WAR DIARY
or
INTELLIGENCE SUMMARY.
(Erase heading not required.)

June 1917

Place	Date	Hour	Summary of Events and Information	Remarks and references to Appendices
BARAUMESNIL H16.c.4.5.	29.6.17 29.6.17		Divisional Employment Company joined. Strength 1 officer 105 O.R. Division took over the line from 20th Division. LAGNICOURT & NOREUIL sectors with transport lines in and around FAVREUIL. A Divisional Machine Gun Corps officer ordered to be appointed with rank of Major and an extra captain holds his place in 3rd Company. Authority O.B/1704/1767 The Division has felt the want of a Pioneer battalion very much; this entails very heavy work of the Field Companies R.E. and divisions in the fighting strength of Infantry Brigades, who have to supply labour. The weather in June has been very hot, but there have been many heavy thunderstorms with torrential rain.	App VI

2nd July 1917

Sd J. Ingeby Maj-General
Comdg 62nd Division

App I

SUGGESTED BATHS ESTABLISHMENT.

1 Divisional Bath (to also serve one Infantry Brigade).

	Off.	N.C.Os.	Men.
To superintend all baths.	1.		
In charge of Divisional baths.		1.	
To attend to baths, issue of clean and reception of dirty clothing.			5.
Inspection and ironing clothes to render free from lice.			10.
To assist in working Foden disinfector.			2.
2 Brigade baths.		2.	10.
Sock laundry.		1.	10.
	1.	4.	37.

App. IV

62nd DIVISION.

HONOURS AWARDED DURING JULY 1917.

D.S.O.   1
M.C.   9
M.M.   6 (includes 2 to interpreters attached).
M.S.M.   1

2.8.17.

App II

Divisional Order No 189 of 10th February 1917.

SOCKS.

In order that every man in the trenches shall have his three pairs of socks for actual use, one pair will be withdrawn daily and replaced by a clean pair daily.

Commanding Officers will arrange for one pair of wet or dirty socks per man to be sent out of the trenches daily. Quartermasters will deliver them to the sock laundry at Divisional Headquarters each morning, and receive in exchange dry socks. These dry socks will be taken up with the day's rations, and issued to the men.

All socks whether serviceable/or unserviceable, will be returned by Quartermasters to the Sock Laundry. All socks issued which are not accounted for are to be made the subject of charges against individuals, as in the case of all other articles of underclothing.

[insertion above line: repairable]

62nd DIVISION.

CASUALTIES DURING JUNE 1915.

App III

12.6.17	2nd Lieut. F.AKROYD, 2/4th West Riding Regiment	Wounded accidentally.
19.6.17	2nd Lieut. F.G.HAY 312th F.A.Brigade	Wounded accidentally.
17.6.17	2nd Lieut. J.BROUGHTON, 2/6th West Riding Regiment	Injured accidentally.
18.6.17	2nd Lieut. G.E.GEE 2/4th York.& Lancs.Regiment	Wounded.
15.5.17	Lieut.T.P.CROSLAND, 2/5th West Riding Regiment	Wounded (Gas).
25.6.17	2nd Lieut. J.H.IRONS, 2/4th West Riding Regiment	Wounded accidentally at duty.
25.6.17	2nd Lieut. E.G.HARRIS, 2/7th West Riding Regiment	Accidentally wounded 25.6.17 Died of wounds 26.6.17.

OTHER RANKS.

Killed 7   Wounded 63.

3.7.17.

App IV

62nd DIVISION.

HONOURS AND AWARDS RECEIVED DURING JUNE 1917.

Military Crosses   2

Distinguished Conduct Medal   1

Military Medals   3

3.7.17.

62nd DIVISION.

REINFORCEMENTS RECEIVED DURING JUNE 1917.

	Off.	O.R.
2/5th West Yorkshire Regiment	9	24
2/6th -ditto-	3	64
2/7th -ditto-	2	83
2/8th -ditto-	-	91
2/4th West Riding Regiment	1	58
2/5th -ditto-	4	100
2/6th -ditto-	2	96
2/7th -ditto-	4	72
2/4th King's Own Yorkshire Light Infantry	6	27
2/5th -ditto-	3	35
2/4th York. & Lancaster Regiment	-	32
2/5th -ditto-	-	80
212th Machine Gun Company	-	8
213th -ditto-	-	3
201st -ditto-	-	1
208th -ditto-	-	7
62nd Divisional Artillery	6	155
62nd Divisional R.E.	3	-
62nd Divisional Train	1	8
62nd Divisional Medical Units	1	51.

3.7.17.

SECRET.   62nd DIVISION.   A/7152/49.

ADMINISTRATIVE INSTRUCTIONS ON TAKING OVER LINE FROM
20th DIVISION, VIDE D.O.NO.52 OF 22.6.17.

Map Reference
Sheet 57c. N.W.

1. AREA.

The Boundaries of the Area run in straight lines through the following points:-

C.5.a.5.10. - C.8.d.5.2. - C.8.c.7.2. - E.9.c.0.0. -
H.29.b.1.7. - I.5.d.0.0. - C.30.b.10.8.

2. LOCATION OF UNITS.

Location of Units will be as follows in accommodation to be taken over from 20th Division:-

Unit.	Location.	Date of arrival.
Divisional Headquarters	The Monument. H.15.c.4.5.	29.6.17
201st Machine Gun Coy.	L.10.c.central	24.6.17
Divisional Artillery.		
310th F.A.Brigade	H.Q. C.9.d.8.5. Wagon Lines H.17.a.	Moved on 22.6.17
312th F.A.Brigade	H.Q. C.26.d.1.6. Wagon Lines H.17.d. - H.18.d. H.24.b.	Moved on 22.6.17.
62nd Div.Ammn.Column	H.Q. L.22.b.0.5. No.1.Sec.H.22.a.& b. No.2.Sec.H.17.c. B.Echelon H.15.b.	Moved on 22.6.17.
62nd T.M.Batteries	H.17.d.	Moved on 22.6.17.
Divisional R.E.		
460th W.R.Field Co.R.E.	C.29.d.1.4. Transport I.8.a.2.2.	25.6.17.
457th W.R.Field Co.R.E.	C.10.c.0.2. Transport H.12.a.7.6.	27.6.17.
461st W.R.Field Co.R.E.	H.16.a.8.1. Transport H.16.a.8.1.	28.6.17.
62nd Div.Signal Co.	H.15.c.	29.6.17.
185th Infantry Brigade.		
Brigade Headquarters	C.29.c.3.3.	25.6.17
4 Battalions.	Right Sector	"
212th Machine Gun Company	" "	"
185th Trench Mortar Bty.	" "	"
Transport	FAVREUIL.	"

Unit.	Location	Date of arrival.
186th Infantry Brigade.		
Brigade Headquarters.	NOREUIL	27.6.17.
4 Battalions	Left Sector	"
213th Machine Gun Coy.	" "	"
186th Trench Mortar Bty.	" "	"
Transport	FAVREUIL	"
187th Infantry Brigade.		
Brigade Headquarters	FAVREUIL	28.6.17
1 Battalion	H.4.c. Camp B.	"
1 Battalion	H.5.d. Camp C.	"
1 Battalion	H.9.d. Camp D.	"
1 Battalion	I.8.c. Camp A.	"
208th Machine Gun Coy.	H.12.c.	"
187th Trench Mortar Bty.	H.12.c.	"
Transport	I.7.a. - I.13.a,b. & d.	"

In the event of Infantry Transport Lines not being cleared by Units of 20th Division in time, Infantry Transports of 62nd Division will park adjacent to the Lines of the Units they are relieving until the latter are cleared.

R.A.M.C.		
2/1st W.R.Field Ambce.	FAVREUIL)	25.6.17
2/2nd W.R.Field Ambce.	FAVREUIL) H.16.d.	27.6.17
2/3rd W.R.Field Ambce.	FAVREUIL)	27.6.17.
62nd Divisional Train.		
Headquarters	H.21.c.4.4.	29.6.17
525th Coy. A.S.C.	H.22.c.7.7.	25.6.17
526th Coy. A.S.C.)		25.6.17
527th Coy. A.S.C.) H.21.c.		26.6.17
528th Coy. A.S.C.)		28.6.17
Mobile Vet.Section.	FAVREUIL	29.6.17.
D.A.D.O.S.	H.15.c.1.8.	29.6.17
Divisional Gas Officer	FAVREUIL H.15.a.3.0.	29.6.17
Divl.Claims & Disbursement Officer.	H.15.c.4.4.	29.6.17

3. **MOVES.**

(1) The Divisional Train will move to its new locations under orders to be issued by Officer Commanding Divisional Train:-

    Headquarters   on 29.6.17.
    525th Coy. A.S.C.   on 25.6.17.
    526th Coy. A.S.C.   on 25.6.17.
    527th Coy. A.S.C.   on 26.6.17.
    528th Coy. A.S.C.   on 28.6.17.

(2) Field Ambulances will move under orders of A.D.M.S.

    2/1st W.R. Field Ambulance on 25.6.17
    2/2nd W.R. Field Ambulance on 27.6.17
    2/3rd W.R. Field Ambulance on 27.6.17

(3) Divisional Headquarters will move under orders of Camp Commandant on June 29th.

4. **ARTILLERY AMMUNITION.**

Dumps for gun ammunition are located at I.1.d.7.5., H.17.b.5.5. and I.19.d.2.6.

5. **S.A.A., GRENADES, ETC.**

The Divisional Grenade Store will be at BEUGNATRE (H.11.c.9.7), and will be taken over by the D.A.C. on June 26th.

6. **R.E. MATERIAL.**

The Divisional R.E. Dump is at VAULX at C.26.a.8.3.

7. **SUPPLIES.**

Railhead will be at BAPAUME from June 29th inclusive. Refilling will take place from June 30th inclusive as follows:-

Divisional Troops Group on BAPAUME - BEUGNATRE road in H.22.c. and 105th, 106th and 107th Infantry Brigade Groups on BAPAUME - FAVREUIL road in H.22.a. and H.16.c.

Supplies will be sent forward to the line by Regimental Transport, but it is hoped that the light railway may shortly be extended, so that it may be advantageously used for supply purposes.

8. **ORDNANCE REFILLING POINT AND DIVISIONAL SALVAGE DUMP.**

Ordnance Refilling Point and Divisional Salvage Dump will be at H.15.c.1.8.

9. **WATER.**

   Water Points are situated at :-

   FAVREUIL at H.16.a.1.1.   Water carts and horses

   BEUGNATRE at H.11.d.5.4. Horses and Petrol tins.
   H.17.b.6.0. Water carts
   H.17.b.5.7. Horses
   H.11.c.4.0. Horses and Petrol tins

   VAULX   at I.1.b.6.6. Horses and water carts.
   C.26.a.5.6. Horses and water carts.

   VRAUCOURT B.24.d.7.4. Horses and water carts.
   SUGAR FACTORY.

10. **MANURE DUMPS.**

    No sites having hitherto been fixed, these will be selected and notified as soon as possible.

11. **DIVISIONAL CANTEEN.**

    The Divisional Canteen is at H.17.a.5.7. between FAVREUIL and BEUGNATRE.

12. **BATHS.**

    Baths are being established at FAVREUIL, BEUGNATRE and VAULX. Allotments will be made on application to the Divisional Baths Officer.

13. **CEMETERIES.**

    The following are the authorised Cemeteries :-
    C.23.d.3.7. - C.16.a.5.5. - I.1.d.2.5. - H.16.d.5.5.

14. **PRISONERS OF WAR COLLECTING STATION.**

    The Prisoners of War Collecting Station is at VAULX at C.26.c.0.0.

15. **TRAFFIC CONTROL POSTS AND STRAGGLERS' POSTS.**

    Traffic Control Posts and Stragglers' Posts will be established by the A.P.M. as follows :-

    Traffic Control Posts at H.16.c.4.9. - H.16.c.5.9. - H.17.a.7.0. H.11.d.6.3. - I.1.b.10.5.

    Stragglers' Posts, which will also control road traffic, at
    C.26.c.7.9. and B.24.d.0.8.

16. MEDICAL ARRANGEMENTS.

Right Sector. Reg. Aid Posts.   C.23.b.6.9.
C.24.d.8.5.
C.30.a.8.5. (Support)

A.D.S.   C.29.a.5.0.

Loading Post.   C.26.d.central.

Line of Evacuation.   Hand carriage from Reg. Aid Posts by tracks direct to A.D.S.
From A.D.S. to Loading Post by wheeled stretchers via C.20 and C.27.
If track permits from A.D.S. to Loading Post at night by horsed ambulance or Ford Car.
All clearing by night except in urgent cases - From Loading Post to 2/1 W.R. Field Ambulance at H.16.d.7.5.

Left Sector. Reg. Aid Posts.   C.5.a.3.3.   C.5.a.2.3.
C.10.c.8.7.

Relay Post.   C.11.a.2.9.

Collecting Post.   C.10.c.7.7.

Loading Post   (night)   C.15.a.9.8.
Relay Post   (day)

A.D.S.   C.20.d.2.0.

Line of evacuation.   From Reg. Aid Posts by Relays of Field Ambulance Stretcher Bearers to Relay Post, thence by Ford Ambulance Cars by night via MORCHUIL to Advanced Dressing Station.
When weather bad or for any other reason cars cannot be used so far forward, by hand carriage or in wheeled stretchers to Collecting Post and Relay Post at C.15.a.9.8. thence by Ford Cars to Advanced Dressing Station.
All clearing by night except in urgent cases - from Advanced Dressing Station to 2/3rd W.R. Field Ambulance at H.16.d.9.8.

17. TRANSPORT RESTRICTION.

No Transport is allowed to enter VAULX during daylight.

24.6.17.

Lieut. Col.
A.A. & Q.M.G. 62nd Division.

DISTRIBUTION.

Copy No. 1.   A.D.C. for G.O.C.
"   "   2.   "G"
"   "   3.   Divisional Artillery.
"   "   4.   C.R.E.
"   "   5.   105th Infantry Brigade.
"   "   6.   106th Infantry Brigade.
"   "   7.   107th Infantry Brigade.
"   "   8.   Signal Coy.
"   "   9.   A.P.M.
"   "   10.   Divisional Train.
"   "   11.   A.D.M.S.
"   "   12.   201st Machine Gun Coy.
"   "   13.   D.M.G.O.
"   "   14.   A.D.V.S.
"   "   15.   Camp Commandant, Divl. Headquarters.
"   "   16.   V. Corps "Q".
"   "   17.   7th Division "Q".
"   "   18.   20th Division "Q".
"   "   19 - 24.   "A" & "Q".

SECRET.   Copy No. 21.

62nd DIVISION.   A/7346/49.

ADMINISTRATIVE INSTRUCTIONS NO.2. ON TAKING OVER LINE FROM
20th DIVISION, VIDE D.O.No.52 OF 22.6.17.

Map Reference
Sheet 57c. N.W.

1. **MANURE DUMPS.**

    Manure Dumps are to be established at the following points:-

    (a) H.17.c.3.3. under supervision of 62nd Divl.Artillery for H.Q. 'B' & 'C' Batteries 310th F.A.Brigade, H.Q. and 'C' & 'D' Batteries 312th F.A.Brigade, 2/1st, 2/2nd, 2/3rd W.R.Field Ambulances and 62nd Mobile Veterinary Section.

    (b) H.16.b.9.9. under supervision of 62nd Divl.Artillery for 'A' & 'D' Batteries 310th F.A.Brigade.

    (c) H.22.c.8.8. under supervision of 62nd Divl.Artillery, for H.Q. and Nos.1 & 2 Sections 62nd D.A.C. and 525th Coy. A.S.C.

    (d) H.24.b.7.7. under supervision of 62nd Divl.Artillery for 'A' Battery 312th F.A.Brigade.

    (e) H.19.a.4.9. under supervision of 62nd Divl.Artillery, for 'B' Battery 312th F.A.Brigade.

    (f) H.15.d.1.9. under supervision of 62nd Divl.Artillery, for No.3 Section D.A.C. Divl.H.Q. and Signal Coy.

    (g) H.12.b.7.8. under supervision of C.R.E. for 457th Field Coy.R.E. 460th Field Coy.R.E. 208th, 212th, and 213th Machine Gun Coys.

    (h) H.10.c.7.4. under supervision of 185th Infantry Brigade, for 185th Infantry Brigade Transport and 201st M.G.Coy.

    (i) H.16.b.1.2. under supervision of 186th Infantry Brigade, for 461st Field Coy. R.E. and 186th Infantry Brigade Transport.

    (j) I.13.b.1.1. under supervision of 187th Infantry Brigade, for 187th Infantry Brigade Transport.

    (k) H.21.c.4.4. under supervision of O.C. 62nd Divl.Train, for H.Q. 62nd Divl.Train and 526th, 527th and 528th Cos. A.S.C.

    These dumps are to be dealt with in accordance with instructions contained in Fifth Corps Special Routine Order dated 4th May 1917.

    When manure has been left uncovered by troops occupying the area in previous times, and is near camps or horse-lines, &c., in such condition as to still cause plagues of flies it must be dealt with by the nearest troops.

2. **WATER.- HORSES.**

Horses and mules will be watered by units as follows:-

Divisional H.Q.

H.Q. R.A.

H.Q. R.E.

461st Field Co. R.E.) at FAVREUIL at H.16.a.4.4.

Signal Co.

No.3 Section D.A.C.
201st Machine Gun Co.
186th Infantry Brigade
(less 213th M.G.Co.)

H.Q. and 'C' & 'D' Batteries 312th F.A.Bde.)
H.Q. and Nos. 1 & 2 Sections D.A.C.)
457th & 460th Field Cos. R.E.) at BEUGNATRE South
187th Infantry Brigade) at H.17.b.5.7.
525th Coy. A.S.C.)
2/1st, 2/2nd, 2/3rd W.R.Field Ambulances)

310th F.A.Brigade)
185th Infantry Brigade)
213th Machine Gun Co.) at BEUGNATRE West at H.11.d.5.4.
Mobile Veterinary Section)

'A' & 'B' Batteries 312th F.A.Brigade at FREMICOURT.

H.Q. Divl.Train and 526th,) at Sugar Factory at BAPAUME at
527th and 528th Cos. A.S.C.) H.27.a.7.4.

Programmes allotting times for watering will be issued to those concerned.

28.6.17.

Lieut.Col.
A.A. & Q.M.G. 62nd Division.

DISTRIBUTION.

Copy No. 1	A.D.C. for G.O.C.	Copy No.10.	Divl.Train.
" " 2	"G".	" " 11.	A.D.M.S.
" " 3	Divl.Arty.	" " 12.	201st M.G.Co.
" " 4	C.R.E.	" " 13.	D.M.G.O.
" " 5	185th Inf.Bde.	" " 14.	A.D.V.S.
" " 6	186th Inf.Bde.	" " 15.	Camp Comdt. Divl.H.Q.
" " 7	187th Inf.Bde.	" " 16.	V.Corps "Q".
" " 8	Signal Co.		
" " 9	A.P.M.	" " 17)	"A" &
		22)	"Q".

CONFIDENTIAL.

WAR DIARY

OF

ADMINISTRATIVE AND QUARTERMASTER GENERAL'S BRANCH

HEADQUARTERS, 62ND DIVISION.

FROM JULY 1ST. TO JULY 31ST.

1917.

---------o0o0o0o0---------

SECRET

Army Form C. 2118.

WAR DIARY
or
INTELLIGENCE SUMMARY.
(Erase heading not required.)

July 1917

62nd Division A

Instructions regarding War Diaries and Intelligence Summaries are contained in F. S. Regs., Part II. and the Staff Manual respectively. Title pages will be prepared in manuscript.

Place	Date	Hour	Summary of Events and Information	Remarks and references to Appendices
BAPAUME H15.c.4.6 Sheet 57c NW				
	3rd		Leave to England. Instructions received that leave will be allotted to officers & men in hand and g mn the references in army Expeditionary Force instructions to Staff Officers serving out of England.	fol
"	6		Musketry. Allotment of Lewis gun ranges for tyros & foot shooting on ranges.	
"	6		Anti-gas goggles abolished. Reason being that they are used by troops in advancing where they may possibly obscure the vision. GHQ letter OB/215 of 26-5-17.	fol
"	7		Postal orders. British postal orders returned not to pound as currency in France and British shopkeepers advised that they are not to be accepted as such.	fol
"	11		Telephones. New code named G.R.O. 2279.	fol
"	17		Despatching. The system for collection & payment for despatches carrying French guide questionnaires instituted. D.R.O. 710 of 17.7.17	App I
"	18		Trinity. All sports and betting clubs closed on issue life without Testimony to the Clergy of London ordered.	
"	25		The Grace the Archbishop of York to transmit his desire there a sermon to be delivered on Sunday 29th July.	fol
"	28		Establishment of horses in H.Qrs. divisional R.A.R.E. H.Qrs. etc. revised. O.B./2039 of 19.7.17	

Appx. 2.

SECRET Army Form C. 2118.

62nd Division A

WAR DIARY
or
INTELLIGENCE SUMMARY.
(Erase heading not required.)

July 1917.

Instructions regarding War Diaries and Intelligence Summaries are contained in F.S. Regs., Part II. and the Staff Manual respectively. Title pages will be prepared in manuscript.

Place	Date	Hour	Summary of Events and Information	Remarks and references to Appendices
BAPAUME Rd H16.c.4.5.	28th		**Gas precaution.** gas rattles issued at rate of 200 per mile of front & supplement shoulder horns. to 6 trench stores.	
Sheet 57c NW	31st		**Rations** issue of fresh meat stopped. unless preserved meat, fresh rabbits and tinned fish. Issue of stopping between	
"			Caen & England. Lots of Calais, Boulogne & Havre all to be used. allotment to be raised from 2000 per day to 4000 per day. Troops to leave from Havre in returning ammunition ships; from England in returning hospital ships.	
			Reinforcements during month of July	App II
			Casualties	App III
			Horses & mules	App IV
			Health of troops has not been so good. prevailing disease a kind of trench fever of obscure origin is obscure. Courts martial 18.	

2nd August 1917.

Maurice Jea Mor
Brig. G.G.S.
62nd Division

Copy No. 68

Abb I

DIVISIONAL ROUTINE ORDERS

by Major-General W.P. Braithwaite, C.B.,

Commanding 62nd Division.

17th July 1917.

ADMINISTRATIVE STAFF.

No 708. **HOT FOOD CONTAINERS - NUMBER OF.**

General Officers Commanding Brigades will report by the mid-day D.R. on the 22nd instant, the number of Hot Food Containers which they consider should be issued to Units for use during the Winter. These Containers will be trench stores.

No 709. **OPERATIONS - MERITORIOUS SERVICE DURING.**

The General Officer Commanding wishes to place on record his high appreciation of the gallant conduct of the following N.C.O's and men, which has been brought to his notice by the Brigadier-General Commanding the Divisional Artillery :-

No 685980 Bombr Hughes, T.,	C/293 Battery R.F.A.
No 685742 A/Bdr Loughlin, H.	" " "
No 686026 Gunner Wolding, J.	" " "
No 686689 " Binns, J.T.	" " "
No 686518 " Evans, A.E.	" " "
No 185632 " Vickers, W.	" " "

"On 7th July near LAGNICOURT, a detached gun of another Battery was shelled by enemy 8" Howitzer for 3 hours, and a direct hit obtained on a shelter in which the detachment had taken cover.
These men on being called on by their No 1 (Sergt Mackrill) left their dug-out, and followed him under heavy fire, helped him to rescue the wounded, and get them away from the position, carrying one man a distance of several hundred yards on a bed, and throughout this time the enemy continued to shell the position with 8" howitzers."

No 710. **DRIPPING.**

(a) The total amount of dripping returned to S.S.O. by units of the Division during April and May amounted to 10.446 lbs. The total cash received yesterday for this amount was only 495 francs (equal 1/5th of a penny per lb), the reduction below the price fixed being due to circumstances over which the Division had no control.

The distribution of the money has been sent to those concerned, and will be paid on application to "Q" Branch Divisional Headquarters, any afternoon between 2 and 5.

No 710 (contd)

(b) With reference to D.R.O.642, the following system will be adopted regarding payment, from July 20th :-

1. The S.S.O. will continue to hand in dripping in bulk to the R.S.O. and obtain him from him a receipt. This receipt in future will be in the form of a cheque which can be cashed at any branch of the E.F.C.

2. On the 1st and 15th of each month the S.S.O. will pay out to the units the amounts to which they are entitled.

3. The acknowledgments given by Brigade and Formation Supply Officers to Units are for approximate weights only, and are subject to verification at Railhead. Any alteration in the weight will be notified to the unit, and the acknowledgment altered and initialled accordingly.

No 711. RETURN - GRENADES &c.

With reference to D.R.O. 686, the weekly return of grenades, T.M.Ammunition, flares etc, will in future be made up to mid-night Saturday, and rendered to D.H.Q., by first D.R. on Sunday.

No 712. COURSES - MUSKETRY SCHOOL.

Parties proceeding to 5th Army Musketry Camp on 22nd July 1917, will report to R.T.O.ACHIET le GRAND at 3 p.m. on that day, detraining at VARENNES at 5-45 p.m.

No 713. WASTE.

VI Corps Routine Order No 2400 is to be republished in the orders of all units.

R.M.FOOT, Lieut-Colonel,
A.A. & Q.M.G.

NOTICE.

LOST on the night 11/12th July about C.16.a.0.0. (sheet 57C) rear carriage of a G.S.wagon.
Information to O.C., 62nd Divisional Train.

App. II

62nd DIVISION.
REINFORCEMENTS RECEIVED DURING JULY 1917.

	Off.	O.R.
2/5th West Yorkshire Regiment.	4	52
2/6th -ditto-	3	8
2/7th -ditto-	3	17
2/8th -ditto-	3	32
2/4th West Riding Regiment	1	13
2/5th -ditto-	2	6
2/6th -ditto-	3	14
2/7th -ditto-	4	15
2/4th K.O.Y.L.I.	7	8
2/5th -do-	1	13
2/4th York. & Lancaster Regiment	4	25
2/5th -ditto-	1	11
Royal Artillery	2	65
Royal Engineers	3	7
Medical Units	-	6
201st Machine Gun Company	1	3
208th -ditto-	1	5
212th -ditto-	-	1
213th -ditto-	-	8

2.8.17.

App III

62nd DIVISION.

CASUALTIES DURING JULY 1917.

OFFICERS.

Captain C.S.Wilson, 2/7th West Yorks.Regt. Wounded 2.7.17.
Captain H.N.Waller, 2/4th West Riding Regt. Died of wounds 4.7.17
2nd Lieut.T.F.Galpine, 2/7th West Yorks. Wounded 4.7.17.
Lt.F.L.Davies, 1/6th Norfolk attd.2/8 W.Yorks. Killed 8.7.17.
2nd Lieut.J.L.Rodger, 2/4th K.O.Y.L.I. Wounded 9.7.17.
2nd Lieut.R.L.Pickard, 310th F.A.Brigade Wounded 11.7.17.
Captain H.J.Behrens, 2/6th West Yorks. Wounded 13.7.17.
2nd Lieut.G.Ambler, 2/6th West Yorks. Wounded 13.7.17.
2nd Lieut.A.H.Metcalfe, 2/4th K.O.Y.L.I. Wounded 13.7.17.
2nd Lieut.A.Butler, 2/5th K.O.Y.L.I. Wounded 13.7.17.
2nd Lieut.T.B.Wills, 310th F.A.Brigade Wounded at duty 14th
2nd Lieut.W.H.Dawson, 2/7th West Yorks. Wounded 17.7.17.
Lt.Col.P.Prince, 2/5th York.& Lancs. Wounded 17.7.17.
2nd Lt.E.H.Vanderpump, 310th F.A.Brigade Wounded at duty 17th
2nd Lieut.H.C.O.Lawrie, 312th F.A.Brigade Wounded 17.7.17.
Captain C.D.Bennett, 2/6th West Riding Died of wounds 18.7.17
Lieut.C.G.Edwards, 2/7th West Yorks. Wounded 27.7.17.
2nd Lieut. F.Muff, 2/7th West Riding Wounded 28.7.17.
2nd Lieut.F.Abrahams, 310th F.A.Brigade Wounded at duty 30th

OTHER RANKS.

Killed	45
Wounded	189
Missing	4

2.8.17.

Original

War Diary

9/6778

CONFIDENTIAL.

WAR DIARY

OF

ASSISTAND ADJUTANT AND QUARTERMASTER GENERAL'S BRANCH OF 62nd DIVISION.

FROM 1st AUGUST 1917 TO 31st AUGUST 1917.

Volume VIII

SECRET

page 1.

Army Form C. 2118.

62nd Division "A"

WAR DIARY
or
INTELLIGENCE SUMMARY.
(Erase heading not required.)

August 1917.

Place	Date	Hour	Summary of Events and Information	Remarks and references to Appendices
BAPAUME R.4 H.15.C.4.5 Sheet 57c. N.W.			Promotion. Two additional captains sanctioned for infantry battalions. Authority G.R.O. 2494 dated 5th August 1917. Only 4 battalions in the Brigade. Adjutants, when holding the rank of 2nd Lieut. of unit to be acting captain. A.G. 1220 of 3.8.17.	
"			Winter hutting continued. The general scheme is to concentrate hutted camps on roads in the vicinity of FAVREUIL & BEUGNATRE. Accommodation to consist of NISSEN huts, ADRIAN huts and temporary structures. The camps proposed and in course of construction are attached in	App I
"			Horse standings in course of construction in all units. Brick floors made from bricks taken from ruined villages in vicinity. Timber frames corrugated iron roofs. Plans App II sanctioned Third Army Q.C/6232.	
"	25		Stores. Issues of 6 chaplains 2pr division sanctioned Third Army Q.C/6232. and Q.M.G. 2483 (Q.A.I.) of 24.8.17	
"	29		A fresh issue of 4 horses pack/riding was made under Third Army O.C/6232/2065 of 8.8.17 authorised to effect a saving in horses for A.Q's.	
"			D.A.C. reorganisation. G.H.Q. letter O.B. of 8.8.17 authorised to effect a saving in horses for A.Q's.	
"			2 sections each equivalent to an A.F.A. B.A.C. carrying gun ammunition.	
"			1 S.A.A. section for S.A.A. & grenades only	

Army Form C. 2118.

page 2

SECRET.

WAR DIARY
or
INTELLIGENCE SUMMARY.
(Erase heading not required.)

62nd Division A

August 1917.

Instructions regarding War Diaries and Intelligence
Summaries are contained in F. S. Regs., Part II.
and the Staff Manual respectively. Title pages
will be prepared in manuscript.

Place	Date	Hour	Summary of Events and Information	Remarks and references to Appendices
BAPAUME Rd H15 c.4.5. sheet 57c N.W.			D.A.C. Reorganization cont. The result of the reorganization is that a reduction of 155 horses is effected, and that the amount of ammunition carried approaches the same as before. Teams are reduced for waggons containing fieldwork stores etc.	
"	10.		Divisional tramways started. Line open from ECOUST ST MEIN to TOWER & RAILWAY trenches.	
"	27.		Bomb mors. Selection of mans suitable to breed from tomorrow. These mares to be transferred to England.	
"	28.		Care of arms. Orders to construct covered rifle racks issued.	App III
			Casualties.	App VI
			Reinforcements.	
			Courts martial. 13.	
			Health of division. Fair. There are still many cases of P.U.O.	
			Weather. Much rain and wind.	App V
			Horses & roads.	

1st September 1917.

[signed] Lewis Jew. Major
b.a.g. G.O.C.
62nd Division.

App II

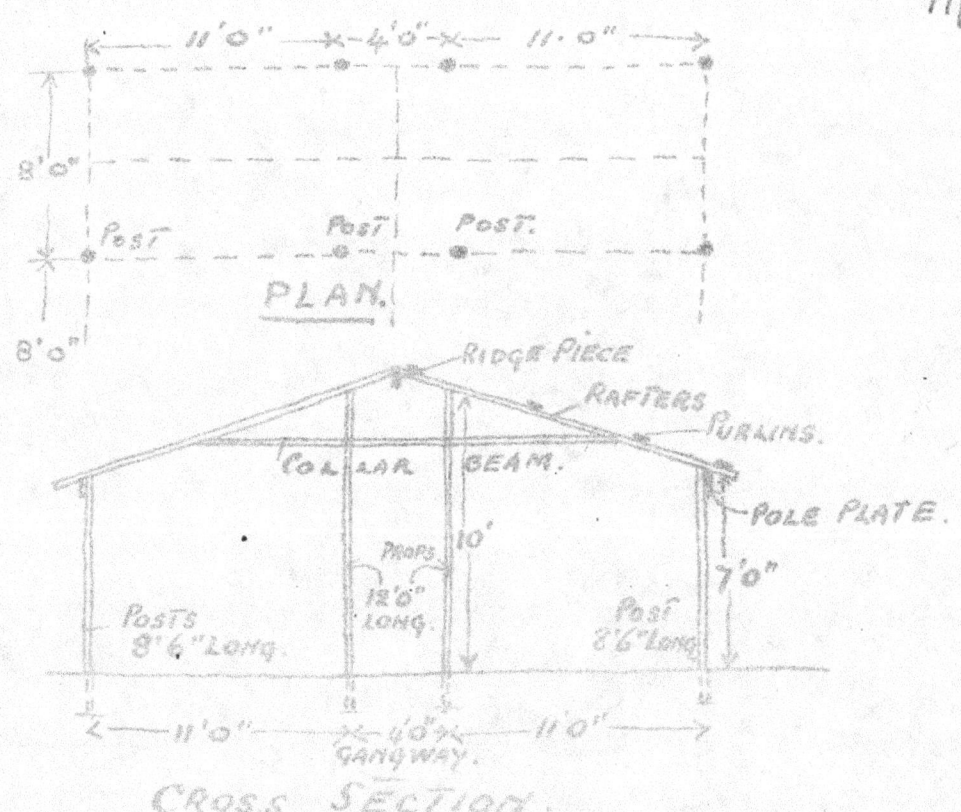

Timber for roof principals may be available from salvage timber.

App II

[Diagram: Camp layout plan showing parallel rows of buildings separated by a road, with dimensions]

Top section (left to right along vertical axis, with measurements 10', 60', 10', 10', 30', 20', 60', 20'):
- Latrines as required (10')
- (60')
- Ablution benches distribution as required
- Officers Quarters / Q.M. Stores
- Mens Quarters
- Harness Rooms & Forage Stores
- Park Battn. (210') | Park Battn. (210') | Park M.G. (162')
- Stable M.G. | Stable M.G. | Stable Bath | Stable Bath | Stable Bath | Stable Bath (26', 10, 26, 10, 26, 10, 26, 30')

ROAD

Middle section:
- Stable Bath | Stable Bath | Stable Bath | Stable Bath | Stable Bde H.Q. (20', 26, 10, 26, 10, 26, 10, 26, 30')
- Park Battn. (210') | Park Battn. (210') | Park Bde H.Q. (66')
- (30') (30')

ROAD

- Harness Rooms & Forage Stores
- Q.M. Stores / Mens Quarters / Officers Quarters
- Ablution Benches. Distribution as Required.
- Latrines as required

Infantry Brigade Transport Lines.

62nd DIVISION

CASUALTIES, AUGUST 1917.

App III

OFFICERS.

2nd Lieut. A.G.Bennett, V/62 Trench Mortar By. Wounded at duty 7.8.17.

2nd Lieut. G.H.Haigh, 2/6th West Yorks.Regiment Wounded 11.8.17.

Lt.Col.F.G.Chamberlin, 2/7th West Riding Regt. Wounded at duty 10.8.17.

2nd Lieut. G.Spedding, 2/4th K.O.Y.L.I. Killed 20.8.17.

2nd Lieut. J.A.Brown, 312th F.A.Brigade Wounded, shell shock 7.7.17.

OTHER RANKS.

Killed	27
Wounded	150
Missing	-

1.9.17.

App IX

62nd DIVISION.

REINFORCEMENTS - AUGUST 1917.

	Offs.	O.R.
2/5th West Yorkshire Regiment	1	126
2/6th -ditto-	6	110
2/7th -ditto-	3	195
2/8th -ditto-	5	103
2/4th West Riding Regiment	7	112
2/5th -ditto-	5	69
2/6th -ditto-	4	100
2/7th -ditto-	-	101
2/4th K.O.Y.L.Infantry	3	99
2/5th -ditto-	3	36
2/4th York.& Lancaster Regiment.	4	143
2/5th -ditto-	1	99
201st Machine Gun Company	1	3
208th -ditto-	-	4
212th -ditto-	-	9
213th -ditto-	2	15
Royal Artillery	2	22
Royal Engineers	-	4
Divisional Train	3	9
Medical Units	-	6
Mobile Veterinary Section	-	1

1.9.17.

App V

62nd DIVISION.

HONOURS AWARDED DURING AUGUST 1917.

Distinguished Service Order	2
Military Crosses	2
Chevalier de l'ordre de Leopold	1
Decoration Militaire	1
Military Medals	12
Meritorious Service Medal	1

1.9.17.

62nd DIVISION.

WINTER CAMPS.

App I

Map ref. sheet 57.c. N.W.

Headquarters, 62nd Division	H.15.c.
Signal School	H.15.c.
Ordnance and Salvage	H.15.c.
Employment Coy. & Divl. Canteen	H.15.c.
Battalion Camp	H.10.c.
" "	H.16.b.
" "	H.11.b.
" "	B.22.c.
185th Brigade Transport Camp	H.17.a.
186th " " "	H.15.b.
187th " " "	H.12.c.
460th W.R. Field Company R.E.	H.16.d.
461st " " " "	H.16.b.
457th " " " "	H.12.b.
2/3rd W.R. Field Ambulance	H.17.c.
2/1st " " "	H.16.d.
312th F.A. Brigade Wagon Lines	H.17.c.
310th " " " A,B,& C.Bys.	H.17.a.
310th " " " H.Q. & D.By.	H.22.b.
Divl. Ammunition Col. H.Q.& Sectioms	H.22.b.
R.F.C. Station	H.22.b.
525 Company A.S.C.	H.22.c.
526 " "	H.28.a.
527 " "	H.22.c.
528 " "	H.22.d.
Divisional Gas School	H.15.b.
Reserve Brigade Headquarters	H.16.central
201st Machine Gun Company	~~H.16.a. &~~ H.10.c.
Mobile Veterinary Section	H.16.a.
S.A.A. Dump	H.11.d.
Divl. Baths	H.16.a.
Divl. Classes and Reinforcement Camp	B.28.a.

1.9.17.

APPENDIX "D".

WATER POINTS.

Map reference.	Capacity.

UNDER CONSTRUCTION.

C.24.d.   )   (1 Water cart filler, 1 water bottle filler
D.25.a.   )   (1 Water Bottle filler.

J.10.a.   )   (2000 Horses per hour.
J.10.b.   )   (3 Water cart fillers.
                (1 Water bottle filler.

J.30.a.   800 Horses per hour.

P.17.d.   1000 Horses per hour.
           2 Water Cart fillers.
           1 Water bottle filler.

Q.10.a.   400 Horses per hour.
           1 Water cart filler.
           1 Water bottle filler.

Q.7.d.   1 Railway supply for filling tank wagons.
           1 Water bottle filler.

Q.8.a.   2 Water cart fillers.
           1 Water bottle filler.

Q.2.c.   400 Horses per hour.

Q.14.d.   2000 Horses per hour.
           3 Water cart fillers.
           1 Water bottle filler.

Q.25.b.   2000 Horses per hour.
           3 Water cart fillers.
           1 Water bottle filler

Q.21.c.   400 horses per hour, extendable to 800.

IN PREPARATION AS FAR AS POSSIBLE.

D.19.c.   400 Horses per hour.

K.32.b.   Up to 2000 Horses per hour.

Q.10.a.   800 Horses per hour extendable to 2000.
           800   "   "   "   "   "   2000.
           3 Water cart fillers.
           1 Water bottle filler.

PROPOSED.

Map reference	Capacity
D.16.a.	2000 G.P.H.
D.6.d.	6000 "
D.15.c.	2000 "
E.13.b.	2000 "
E.27.d.	6000 "
D.20.b.	1000 "
K.13.d.	2000 "
K.28.b.	4000 "

ORIGINAL

Vol 9

CONFIDENTIAL.

WAR DIARY

OF

'A & Q' BRANCH, HEADQUARTERS, 62nd DIVISION.

FROM 1.9.1917. TO 30.9.1917.

WAR DIARY / INTELLIGENCE SUMMARY

Army Form C. 2118.
Page 1.
62nd Division A

September 1917.

Place	Date	Hour	Summary of Events and Information	Remarks and references to Appendices
BAPAUME Rd.	2nd		Promotion. Authority given for promotion of all 2nd Lieutenants to Lieutenant (if recommended) after 18 months service. G.R.O. 2572 of 2.9.17.	
H.15.c.4.5	8th		Equipment. Special electric torch for intercommunication to front line issued.	
Sheet 57c NW	11th		Rattles for gas alarm issued only to be heard for that purpose.	
	15th		Return of French inhabitants. The district notified growing in said district is prohibited in view of truck experienced for cattle.	
	15th		Letter of commendation and congratulation from C-in-C, Commander VI Corps sent 62nd Division and a similar letter from the C-in-C to III Army congratulated in a Special Order of the Day	App. I
	21st		Divisional Routine Order published that no unnecessary work will be done in the Rison Area after 12 noon on Saundays.	
	25		Special Order & Leakage of Information. Sufficient copies reprinted to ensure up there were congregate	
	21st		Salvage. Special order that all empty ammunition tin chests, collated and track of the brass.	
			Bulletin issued of the rate of one per hour for winter	

Army Form C. 2118.

SECRET.
52nd Division

WAR DIARY
or
INTELLIGENCE SUMMARY.
(Erase heading not required.)

September 1917

Instructions regarding War Diaries and Intelligence Summaries are contained in F.S. Regs., Part II. and the Staff Manual respectively. Title pages will be prepared in manuscript.

Place	Date	Hour	Summary of Events and Information	Remarks and references to Appendices
BAPAUME Rd 27a H.15.c.4.5 Sheet 57a NW			Corps Reinforcement Camp established to further Reinforce its Army with Base. Each division to have (a) Depot Battalion HQrs. (b) 3 Depot Companies HQrs. Each Infantry Brigade will have its own Depot Training Company and furnish its necessary personnel. V Corps Reinforcement Camp to be located at ACHIET-LE-PETIT. Honours and Rewards during month Casualties during month Reinforcements received during the month Courts martial 20 F.G.C.Ms The health of the troops was good except for a continuance of trench fever, being caused by bad sanitary arrangements (about 30 men). The weather has been very fine & fine & fresh with barn owing days & cold sharp nights.	App II App III App IV

2nd October 1917

Hastings Hay?
Major GSO?
52nd Division

App I

Copy No..........

62nd DIVISION.

SPECIAL ORDER OF THE DAY.

The Divisional Commander has the honour to publish - with much gratification - the following two letters received from Army and Corps Headquarters respectively this morning :-

Third Army G.12/114.

VI Corps.

The Army Commander has the greatest pleasure in communicating the following message received from the Commander-in-Chief, and wishes to add his sincere congratulations to those who have prepared and carried out these successful enterprises :-

"The Commander-in-Chief congratulates you and your troops on the repeated successes gained in your local operations which show excellent spirit and skill. These successes help appreciably in the general plan."

(sd) Louis Vaughan,
Major-General,
General Staff, Third Army.

13th September 1917.

G.X.313/43.

62nd Division.

The Corps Commander desires me to convey to you, and through you to Brigadier-General Viscount Hampden, and the troops of the 185th Infantry Brigade, who have recently carried out successful raids and patrol work, as also to all ranks who repulsed the enemy's raid on the morning of the 13th instant, his high appreciation of their staunch and gallant behaviour.

The several recent successes of the Division, and the repulse of the enemy's storm troops after a severe bombardment, is a clear proof, if any proof were wanting, of the superiority of our troops. It is above all things important at the present time to maintain our moral ascendency over the enemy, and the more we can harass him now and show him that we are his masters, the easier and more quickly carried out will be his eventual defeat.

(sd) F.H.Dorling, Major, G.S.
for B.G.G.S.

VI Corps.
14th September 1917.

Major-General,
Commanding 62nd Division.

15/9/17.

App II

62nd DIVISION.

HONOURS AND REWARDS AWARDED DURING SEPTEMBER 1917.

Military Crosses	2
D.C.M.	1
Bar to Military Medal	1
Military Medals	23

2.10.17.

App III

62nd DIVISION.

CASUALTIES DURING SEPTEMBER 1917.

OFFICERS.

Lieut. H. Hutchinson, 2/5th West Yorks.	Died of wounds 1.9.17.
2nd Lieut. T.B. Wakefield, 2/6th West Yorks.	Killed 8.9.17.
2nd Lieut. J.N. Parker, 2/6th West Yorks.	Killed 8.9.17.
Captain A.H. Willats, 2/5th York. & Lancs.	Killed 7.9.17.
Captain J. Ellse, 2/5th York. & Lancs.	Wounded at duty 10.9.17
2nd Lieut. B. Bentley, 2/5th York. & Lancs.	Killed 11.9.17.
Captain G.C. Turner, 2/6th West Yorks.	Killed 13.9.17.
2nd Lieut. J. Buckley, 2/7th West Riding	Wounded 14.9.17.
2nd Lieut. J.H. Grisdale, 213th Machine Gun Co.	Wounded 14.9.17.
Lieut. W.E. Harris, Y/62 Trench Mortar Batty.	Killed 15.9.17.
Lieut. G.A. Craven. Z/62 Trench Mortar Batty.	Died of wounds 15.9
Lieut. W. Woolliscroft, Z/62 Trench Mortar Bty.	Wounded 15.9.17.
Captain G.F. Fitzgerald, 1/7th Welsh Regt. attd. 2/4th York. & Lancs.	Wounded accidentally S.I.W. 15.9.17.
Lt.Col. J. Josselyn, 2/5th West Yorks.	Wounded Shell shock 29.8
2nd Lieut. F. Calvert, 2/4th K.O.Y.L.I.	Wounded 19.9.17.
Captain G.B. Faulder, 2/5th West Riding attd. 2/4th K.O.Y.L.I.	Wounded 20.9.17.
2nd Lieut. H. Broomfield, 2/6th West Yorks.	Wounded Shell Shock 13.8
2nd Lieut. E.N. Kitcat, 2/7th West Yorks.	Wounded at duty 21.9.17.
2nd Lieut. A.A. Gould, 2/7th West Riding	Wounded Shell Shock 26.8
2nd Lieut. G.C. Beetham, 2/5th York. & Lancs.	Wounded at duty 26.9.17.

OTHER RANKS.

Killed	75
Wounded	296
Missing	8

2.10.17.

App IV

62nd DIVISION.

REINFORCEMENTS RECEIVED DURING SEPTEMBER 1917.

UNIT	OFF.	O.R.
2/5th West Yorks. Regiment	8	82
2/6th -ditto-	7	87
2/7th -ditto-	6	63
2/8th -ditto-	3	69
2/4th West Riding Regiment	3	146
2/5th -ditto-	6	76
2/6th -ditto-	3	83
2/7th -ditto-	4	40
2/4th K.O.Y.L. Infantry	5	78
2/5th -ditto-	3	93
2/4th York. & Lancs. Regiment.	3	75
2/5th -ditto-	3	76
Royal Artillery	1	80
Royal Engineers	-	12
Divisional Train	1	8
Medical Units.	-	2
201st Machine Gun Company	-	5
208th -ditto-	-	16
212th -ditto-	-	10
213th -ditto-	2	8

2.10.17.

C O N F I D E N T I A L.

WAR DIARY

OF

ADMINISTRATIVE BRANCH   62ND DIVISION.

FROM 1st OCTOBER 1917   TO   31st OCTOBER 1917.

Vol. X.

Army Form C. 2118.

SECRET
62nd Division ?
page 1.

WAR DIARY
or
INTELLIGENCE SUMMARY.
(Erase heading not required.)

October 1917

Instructions regarding War Diaries and Intelligence Summaries are contained in F.S. Regs., Part II. and the Staff Manual respectively. Title pages will be prepared in manuscript.

Place	Date	Hour	Summary of Events and Information	Remarks and references to Appendices
BAPAUME R.4	4th		D.A.C. a proportion of drivers to be substitutes for Drivers D officers + N.C.Os to proceed to ROUEN for 3 weeks course in handling motor vehicles etc. Third Army A/A 8964 of 2.10.17	
H.15.c.4.5 Sheet 57c NW	3rd		The division will be relieved in the line by the 3rd Division, relief to be completed by 10 a.m. 12th October	
			62nd Division passes to IV Corps. Winter time comes into force.	
HARPINCOURT	13th			
	7th		Parasitedly by returned to advance.	
I.34.a.5.7 57C 40000	13th		Divisional H.Qrs. Location return of all units Further registration of skilled tradesmen called for. Horse-clipping of lower halves to be clipped trace high - wool clipping on legs.	App I
	17th			
	19th			
	23rd		Warning against Epizootic Lymphangitis issued - all wounds to be most carefully treated.	
	26.		SOLDER. Collection of round solder to be melted into war arrangements to be made by Area Commandants.	

SECRET. Army Form C. 2118.

WAR DIARY
or
INTELLIGENCE SUMMARY.
(Erase heading not required.)

October 1917   62nd Division A.   page 2

Place	Date	Hour	Summary of Events and Information	Remarks and references to Appendices
I34.a.37	29th		**Armament.** 12 6" Newton Mortars issued in place of 12 2" Mortars.	
57c / H0000	26th & 27th		Blankets warmth clothing. Second blanket & jerkins undercutting issued.	
	31st		Lean period of leave increased from 10 days to 14 days via Boulogne to 15 days via HAVRE. Third Army letter A/C/30/862 of 28-10-17.	(a)(b)
	30th		Division H.Qrs moved to FOSSEUX Chateau	(c) App II
			Location of units	App III
			Honours & rewards in October	App IV
			Casualties in October	
			Courts martial in October 12.	App V
			Reinforcements in October	(d)
			Weather – stormy, high winds & frequent rain.	

3rd November 1917.

Harrat Jackson
DAAG. Thorp Bruce
Commanding 62nd Division

SECRET.

DISPOSITION AND MOVEMENT REPORT NO.106.
62ND DIVISION.

Period 6 p.m. 24th Oct. to 6 p.m. 25th Oct.1917.

Unit No.	Unit	Position of H.Q. 6 p.m.		Transport Lines.
1	H.Q. 62nd Division	I.34.a.3.7.		
2	201 M.G.Coy.	H.18.b.0.5.		H.18.b.0.5.
3	185th I.Bde.	O.16.a.2.7.	BARASTRE.	
4	2/5th W.Yorks.	O.10.d.3.8.	"	O.9.d.
5	2/6th "	O.10.d.2.9.	"	O.9.b.
6	2/7th "	O.10.c.5.0.	"	O.16.c.
7	2/8th "	O.16.d.5.5.	"	O.9.d.
8	212th M.G.Coy.	O.16.c.95.95	"	O.16.d.
9	185th T.M.Bty.	O.10.c.0.5.	"	C.16.c.
10	186th I.Bde.	N.24.b.1.4.	BEAULENCOURT	
11	2/4th D. of W's Regt.	N.18.c.3.8.	'A' Camp.	
12	2/5th "	N.24.d.5.9.	'D' "	
13	2/6th "	N.18.c.7.1.	'B' "	
14	2/7th "	N.18.c.4.1.	'C' "	
15	213th M.G.Coy.	N.18.b.1.4.		
16	186th T.M.Bty.	N.18.a.9.2.		
17	187th I.Bde.	P.25.d.i.9.	LECHELLE	
18	2/4th K.O.Y.L.I.	P.26.d.9.4.	VALLULART WOOD CAMP	
19	2/5th "	P.26.b.5.3.	LITTLE WOOD CAMP.	
20	2/4th Y. & L. Regt.	P.25.b.1.1.	GRAZING CAMP.	
21	2/5th "	P.31.b.9.5.	RAILWAY WEST CAMP.	
22	208th M.G.Coy.	P.25.a.2.5.		
23	187th T.M.Bty	O.30.b.9.6.		
24	R.A.H.Q.	I.34.a.3.7.		
25	310th F.A.Bde.	C.26.d.2.6.		H.17.a.
26	312th F.A.Bde.	B.17.b.2.6.		H.17.c.
27	62 D.A.C.	H.22.b.0.5.		H.22.b.
28	1,2 & 3 Sec.	H.22.Central		H.22.cen.
29	D.T.M.O.	C.26.a.9.1.		
30	R.E.H.Q.	I.34.a.2.5.		I.34.a.2.5.
31	460th Fld.Co.R.E.	O.16.d.2.8.		O.16.d.2.8.
32	457th "	N.18.c.5.2.		N.18.c.5.2.
33	461st "	P.26.b.5.3.		P.26.b.5.3.
34	H.Q. Signal Co.	I.34.a.3.7.		
35	A.D.M.S.	I.34.a.3.7.		
36	2/1st W.R.F.Amb.	O.15.b.9.9.		O.15.b.9.9.
37	2/2nd "	N.24.d.6.3.		N.11.d.6.2.
38	2/3rd "	P.25.c.2.4.		P.25.c.2.4.
39	H.Q., Div.Train	O.28.a.6.5.		
40	525 Co. A.S.C.	H.22.c.7.7.		
41	526 "	O.28.c.		
42	527 "	N.4.d.8.8.		
43	528 "	O.34.a.		
44	D.A.D.O.S.	I.34.a.3.7.		
45	D.A.D.V.S.	"		
46	A.P.M.	"		
47	Claims Officer	"		
48	Sen.Chap.C.of E.	"		
49	Sen.Chap.Non C.of E.	"		
50	French Mission	"		
51	Mob.Vet.Sec.	U.4.b.7.4.		
52	Salvage Officer	O.15.a.4.6.		
53	Div.Musk.Off.	I.34.a.3.7.		
54	Div.Gas School	I.34.a.3.7.		
55	Div.Depot Bn.	ACHIET LE PETIT C.19.d.1.7.		

24.10.17.

(Sd) C.E.Chandler, Capt.,
for Lt.Col., Gen.Staff,
62nd Division.

SECRET.   62ND. DIVISION.   No. 113

DISPOSITION AND MOVEMENT REPORT.

Situation at 12 noon 1st Novr. 1917.

Sheet 51.c. 1/40,000

No.	Unit.	Present Position	Moves tomorrow	Remarks
1.	62nd. Divnl. Hd.Qrs.	FOSSEUX CHATEAU.		
2.	185th Inf:Bde.Hd.Qrs.	BARLY.		
3.	2/5th W.Yorks.Regt.	BARLY		
4.	2/6th do	FOSSEUX		
5.	2/7th do	BAVINCOURT		
6.	2/8th do	BAVINCOURT		
7.	212th M.G.Co.	LAHERLIERE		
8.	185th T.M.Bty.	BARLY.		
9.	186th Inf:Bde.Hd.Qrs.	COUY en ARTOIS		
10.	2/4th D. of W's Regt.	SIMENCOURT		
11.	2/5th do	COUY		
12.	2/6th do	SIMENCOURT		
13.	2/7th do	COUY		
14.	213th M.G.Co.	MONCHIET		
15.	186th T.M.Bty.	MONCHIET.		
16.	187th Inf:Bde.Hd.Qrs.	BERNEVILLE.		
17.	2/4th K.O.Y.L.I.	SIMENCOURT		
18.	2/5th do	BERNEVILLE		
19.	2/4th York & Lancs Regt.	BERNEVILLE		
20.	2/5th do	SIMENCOURT		
21.	208th M.G.Co.	BERNEVILLE		
22.	187th T.M.Bty.	BERNEVILLE.		
23.	201st M.G.Co.	LAHERLIERE.		
24.	457th W.R.Fld.Co.R.E.	COUY		Less 3 Sections.
25.	460th do	-		Att. IV Corps.
26.	461st do	-		do
27.	2/1st W.R.Fld.Amb.	BARLY		
28.	2/2nd do	COUY		
29.	2/3rd do	BERNEVILLE.		
30.	310th Bde. R.F.A.			Att. VI Corps.
31.	312th do			do
32.	62nd Divl.Amm.Col.			do
33.	62nd.Divl.Train.	MONCHIET.		
34.	Mobile Vet. Section.	MONCHIET.		

for Lieut-Colonel.
General Staff 62nd Division.

App III

62nd DIVISION.

HONOURS AND AWARDS CONFERRED DURING OCTOBER 1917.

- Military Crosses   6
- D.C.Ms.   1
- Military Medals   9

App IV

62nd DIVISION.
CASUALTIES DURING OCTOBER 1917.

OFFICERS.

2nd Lieut. T.B.Lyth, 2/5th York & Lancs.Regt.	Wounded 3.10.17.
Captain S.Coates, 2/8th West Yorks.Regt.	Wounded 4.10.17.
Lieut. G.Bevington, 2/5th West Riding Regt.	Wounded accidentally 4.10.17.
Captain C.F.C.Taylor, 2/5th York & Lancs.Regt.	Wounded, shell shock 9.9.17.
2nd Lieut. A.Bray, 2/6th West Riding Regt.	Wounded, shell shock 17.9.17.
Lieut. J.E.David, 2/4th K.O.Y.L.I.	Wounded, shell shock 26.8.17.
Lieut. H.Sutherland, 312th F.A.Brigade	Killed 29.10.17.

OTHER RANKS.

Killed	9
Wounded	74
Missing	3

62nd DIVISION.

REINFORCEMENTS RECEIVED DURING OCTOBER 1917.

	Off.	O.R.
2/5th West Yorkshire Regiment	8	126
2/6th -ditto-	7	129
2/7th -ditto-	2	134
2/8th -ditto-	3	126
2/4th West Riding Regiment	5	122
2/5th -ditto-	2	123
2/6th -ditto-	8	103
2/7th -ditto-	2	88
2/4th K.O.Y.L.I.	-	83
2/5th -do-	3	62
2/4th York & Lancaster Regiment	4	109
2/5th -ditto-	3	120
201st Machine Gun Company	3	-
208th -ditto-	-	-
212th -ditto-	-	2
Royal Artillery	4	104
Royal Engineers	-	2
62nd Divisional Train	-	13

3.11.17.

CONFIDENTIAL.

62ND DIVISION.

WAR DIARY

OF

ASSISTANT ADJUTANT AND QUARTERMASTER GENERAL'S BRANCH

From 1st NOVEMBER 1917.   To 30th NOVEMBER 1917.

SECRET.

Army Form C.2...

62nd Division A

page 1.

NOVEMBER 1917. WAR DIARY or INTELLIGENCE SUMMARY.

(Erase heading not required.)

Instructions regarding War Diaries and Intelligence Summaries are contained in F. S. Regs., Part II. and the Staff Manual respectively. Title pages will be prepared in manuscript.

Place	Date	Hour	Summary of Events and Information	Remarks and references to Appendices
FOSSEUX	1st		Division training with Tanks	
	14th		Division left for concentration area.	
NEUVILLE	14th		H.Qs for attack on HAVRINCOURT	
	20th		Division took HAVRINCOURT and advanced to GRAINCOURT & ANNEUX cutting HINDENBERG main and support lines	App I
"	21/22/23rd		operation continued and division came out to billets in HAVRINCOURT WOOD, RUYAULCOURT, BERTINCOURT, BUS on 24th	
"			Administration orders for above operation air attached	App
"	25th		Division ordered to attack BOURLON WOOD	
HAVRINCOURT CHATEAU	25		Advance Div H.Q. moved to bivbs	
"	27th		Attack on BOURLON WOOD continued	
"	28th			
HAPLINCOURT	29th		Advance Div H.Q. moved to HAPLINCOURT, 2nd echelon joined train from NEUVILLE - Division located LEBUCQUIERE, BEAMETZ lu CAMBRAI on HINDENBERG Line	App

Army Form C.

WAR DIARY
or
INTELLIGENCE SUMMARY.
(Erase heading not required.)

SECRET.
62nd Division A
Page 2

NOVEMBER 1917

Instructions regarding War Diaries and Intelligence Summaries are contained in F.S. Regs., Part II. and the Staff Manual respectively. Title pages will be prepared in manuscript.

Place	Date	Hour	Summary of Events and Information	Remarks and references to Appendices
HAPLINCOURT			Comments on operations as attached under two headings	
			A. as concerning Corps	(a) App. II (b) App. III
			B. as concerning Brigade	(c) App. IV
			Honours & Rewards	(d) App. V
			Casualties	
			Courts martial in November = 7 7.9.C.M	
			Reinforcements	(e) App. VI
			[signature]	
			Brig-Genl Comdg 186	
			Infantry Bde 62nd Division	
			4th December 1917	

SECRET.   62ND DIVISION.   Copy No. 24
                                                         62nd Div.A/779/49.
                INSTRUCTIONS FOR OPERATIONS, NOVEMBER 1917.
Route Map.
Sheet 57C.N.E. & S.E. 1/20,000   APPENDIX I

1. **SUPPLIES.**

    Ration supply will be normal, i.e. Train delivery to transport lines of units.

    Up to and including rations for consumption Z plus 1 day, the supplies will be drawn from Railhead by Light Railway, or Train wagon where necessary.

    On Z day, the supplies will be drawn from the Railhead by the Divisional Supply Column, and will be retained by the Column until Refilling Points for Z plus 1 day (rations for consumption Z plus 2 days) is known.

    General Officers Commanding Brigades will be responsible for notifying their affiliated Train Companies the positions of the wagon lines of their units, i.e. Brigade Headquarters, Infantry Battalions, Trench Mortar Batteries and Machine Gun Companies.

    On arrival in the Concentration Area, the Senior Supply Officer will arrange for all Divisional Troops to be fed from Divisional Troops Dump, and accordingly, Commanders of these Troops will notify the Officer Commanding Divisional Train of the situation of their wagon lines.

    Supply Railhead will be moved to ROCQUIGNY on the 15th Nov.

    Reserve Supplies.
        Two days X. Rations for a Division.   ROCQUIGNY.
        Six days X. Rations for a Division.   FREMICOURT.

    These supplies do not include Hay for horses, and are placed by the Army at the disposal of the Corps. There is, however, about 300 tons of Hay stacked in the Area.

    Divisional Supply Column.
        The location of the 62nd Divisional Supply Column on change of Railhead will be LE MESNIL.

2. **RATIONS ON Z DAY.**

    Every man, in addition to the iron ration, will carry one full day's ration.
    A breakfast meal will be provided on Z day, so that the man shall advance with a complete day's ration on him.

3. **RUM.**

    An issue of rum will be made on Y/Z night, and will be issued with the breakfast meal on Z day.

4. **WATER.**

    The 185th and 187th Infantry Brigades will form water dumps ready for packing forward; these dumps should be calculated at not less than a quarter of a gallon per man.
    A further issue of tins may be indented for, to enable Battalions to supplement those already in possession.
    After the advance, no water is to be drunk until it has been tested by a Medical Officer, who will place a signed notice at the source stating if the water is fit for use. A.D.M.S. will arrange.

5. **WATERING OF HORSES.**

    Owing to the large number of horses to be watered in the Area, it is necessary that time tables be made for watering horses at the various water points. On arrival in IV Corps Area, all units will apply to the Town Major or Area Commandant, who will give them particulars as to time and place for watering. The watering places are:-
        HAPLINCOURT.   LECHELLE.   BUS.   VILLERS AU FLOS.
                       BARASTRE.

6. **S.A.A., GRENADES, and EXPLOSIVES.**

   The Divisional Dump will be at RUYAULCOURT, P.9.d.9.1.

   Brigade Dumps will be formed at :-

   HAVRINCOURT WOOD   Q.1.c.central.
        "   "   Q.2.b.central.

   They will be traversed and dug in, or scattered in small dumps.

   Machine Gun Ammunition will be drawn from the Divisional Dump under allotment made by the Divisional Machine Gun Officer, which will not exceed 500000 rounds.

   S.A.A., Grenades, and explosives will be allotted as under :-

	185 Bde.	186 Bde.	187 Bde.	Reserve	Total.
S.A.A.	300000	100000	300000	800000	1500000.
P.Bombs.	400	200	400	-	1000.
No. 5.	8000	2000	8000	2000	20000.
No.23 Rifle.	4000	2000	4000	2000	12000.
No.20 or 24.	1600	800	1600	1000	5000.
No. 27.	400	200	400	-	1000.
Stokes.	1212	-	1212	1076	3500.
Rings.	1212	-	1212	1076	3500.
1" White	4200	600	4200	1000	10000.
1½" White	250	-	250	500	1000.
1½" Green.	-	-	-	300	300.
1½" Red.	-	-	-	300	300.
Flares.	5000	2000	5000	2000	14000.
Webley.	3000	3000	3000	1000	10000.
S.O.S.	180	180	180	60	600.

   Includes that for Machine Gun Companies.

   Until Z day, Grenades will not be issued detonated from the Divisional Dump.

   Brigades will make their own arrangements for detonating.

7. **STORES - WIRE CUTTERS AND GLOVES.**

   A table is appended below: These stores can be drawn from Advanced D.A.D.O.S. at BARASTRE, O.15.b.8.7.

		C.R.E.	185 Bde.	186 Bde.	187 Bde.
Wire cutters,	S.A.A.	-	500	200	200.
" "	Small.	-	300	140	140.
" "	long.	160	100	90	100.
Wire breakers		-	450	300	250.
Hedging gloves.		160	400	240	400.

8. **ACCOMMODATION IN FORWARD AREA.**

   The 185th, 186th and 187th Infantry Brigades will send forward advanced parties on the night previous to moving, to take over accommodation and make the necessary sanitary arrangements.

   Accommodations in the Forward Area are shown in .G.425/S of 14.11.17.

   Unit areas will be allotted by Brigade Commanders.

9. POLICE, TRAFFIC CONTROL, STRAGGLERS, PRISONERS OF WAR.

Traffic Control Posts will be established at :-

1. P.1.c.9.2.
2. P.7.b.9.5.
3. P.7.b.0.4.
4. P.2.d.0.4.
5. P.10.a.9.6.
6. P.10.c.5.8.
7. P.15.b.5.4.

Stragglers' Posts will be established at :-

1. J.34.d.9.5.
2. P.10.a.9.6.
3. P.17.d.6.6.

Stragglers' Collecting Station will be at :-

P.10.c.5.9.

Brigade Commanders will arrange for the Stragglers' Collecting Station to be visited every six hours by a conducting N.C.O. to take stragglers to their Battalion wagon lines, where they will be fed, re-armed if necessary, and marched to their units when rations are sent up.

Brigade Commanders will arrange for Regimental Police to be used at suitable places for blocking stragglers.

Prisoners of War. The Corps Pen will be established at RUYAULCOURT; when prisoners of war are handed over, Divisional responsibility will cease.

A Divisional Pen will be established at J.34.d.5.7. Brigades will send prisoners of war to the Divisional Pen, where they will be handed over to the M.M.P. except that where the Corps Pen is the nearer, prisoners may be marched there direct. All prisoners of war will be disarmed before sending them to the Corps or Divisional Pen. Officer prisoners of war will be searched by Brigades for papers, documents, etc., but other ranks will not be searched except for arms, bombs, etc.

The Reserve Brigade will detail 1 Officer, 1 Sergeant, 1 Corporal and 6 Privates, to take charge of the Divisional Pen under the A.P.M. This guard will report at Divisional Pen at 6 p.m. on Y/Z night, and they will bring two days rations with them.

10. CASUALTIES.

The reporting of "estimated casualties" by units to Brigades, and by Brigades to Divisional Headquarters, is of special importance, as on this depends the supply of reinforcements.

The estimates should be made at the earliest possible moment after heavy casualties occur, and reported as soon as possible to Divisional Headquarters (A).

Round numbers are to be given, officers and other ranks seperately, and no distinction is to be made between killed, wounded, and missing.

Full instructions for reporting "estimated casualties" are laid down in Third Army Circular No.42 of 1.8.17 circulated from this office.

The reports referred to in page 3, para.1, of the above circular, will be sent by telegram to this office daily not later than 7 p.m. and if heavy casualties occur during the night, as soon as possible the following morning.

10. CASUALTIES. (contd.)

In reporting to Divisional Headquarters, there is no need to use code letters.

It must be distinctly understood that "estimated casualty" telegrams in no way affect the daily casualty wires, which are to be rendered immediately actual casualties have been determined.

Further copies of Third Army Circular No.42 can be obtained at Divisional Headquarters (A).

11. STORAGE OF KITS, BLANKETS. ETC.

Officers' Kits, men's packs, blankets and great coats, and all equipment not actually carried forward, will be stored by units under Brigade arrangements.

12. PACK TRANSPORT - YUKON PACKS.

Pack saddles will be allotted as follows :-

25 additional pack saddles per Battalion can be drawn from Advanced D.A.D.O.S.

16 Yukon packs per Battalion can be drawn from Advanced D.A.D.O.S.

13. GUARDS ON CAMPS.

All Units will arrange for guards to be placed over their billets or camps.

14. CORPS REINFORCEMENT CAMP.

The Corps Reinforcement Camp will close on November 15th.

All personnel with the exception of the Commandant, his Staff, and such officers and men as are detailed for Corps duties, will join their units on this day. The camp will be available as a staging area or for the accommodation of troops by mid-day November 15th.

Divisional Wing Staffs are not included as a portion of the Staff that will remain.

The Camp will continue to accept reinforcements and details on and after November 15th, and will pass them on to their units with as little delay as possible, until instructed to retain them.

15. COLLECTING AND DISPOSAL OF DEAD.

The Divisional Burials Officer will be given a party of men, and will proceed to J.34.c.0.6, where accommodation will be found. He will reconnoitre the ground round the Cemetery at J.36.a.6.2., and select a spot for the burial of the dead. Stretchers will be drawn from A.D.M.S.

Should more men be required, application should be made to Divisional Headquarters (A).

Major HILL will act as Corps Burials Officer. His Headquarters will be at Corps Reinforcement Camp, ROCQUIGNY.

16. **COLLECTION OF STORES IN CASE OF ADVANCE.**

    Instructions have been issued under "Q" Circular No.7 of 11.11.17.

17. **APPENDICES.**

    The following Appendices are attached:-

    Appendix "B"   Instructions regarding prisoners of war.
    Appendix "C"   Dumps.
    Appendix "D"   Water points.

14.11.17.

[signature]
for Lieut. Colonel,
A.A.& Q.M.G., 62nd Division.

DISTRIBUTION.

    1.   A.D.C. for Divisional Commander.
    2-3   "G".
    4-5-6   "A" & "Q".
    7.   62nd Divisional Artillery.
    8.   62nd Divisional Engineers.
    9.   185th Infantry Brigade.
    10.   186th Infantry Brigade.
    11.   187th Infantry Brigade.
    12.   62nd Divisional Signal Company.
    13.   A.D.M.S., 62nd Division.
    14.   62nd Divisional Train.
    15.   S.S.O., 62nd Division.
    16.   A.P.M., 62nd Division.
    17.   D.A.D.V.S., 62nd Division.
    18.   D.A.D.O.S., 62nd Division.
    19.   201st Machine Gun Company.
    20.   IV Corps "Q".
    21.   51st Division "Q".
    22.   36th Division "Q".
    23.   56th Division "Q".
    24-25   War Diary.
    26-27. File.

APPENDIX "B"

PRISONERS OF WAR

An Advanced Corps Cage for prisoners of war has been established at RUYAULCOURT, and all prisoners captured by Divisions will be passed there as soon as possible under Divisional arrangements as to escort.

The escort will hand them over to the Officer in charge of the Cage, who will, together with the Guard, be found by the Corps.

The Corps A.P.M. will make the necessary arrangements for guarding prisoners at RUYAULCOURT, and for their transfer by escort to the Army Cage. Divisions will form such collecting stations for prisoners as they may consider necessary, the locations being reported to IV Corps "A".

RETURNS OF PRISONERS OF WAR.

The following returns are required :-

A.P.M. will render a return daily made up to 6 p.m. to Division "A" stating the number of prisoners of war remaining in the Divisional Collecting Stations at that hour.

Also a return showing the number evacuated during the previous 24 hours ending at 7 p.m. specifying whether evacuated to Corps Cage or evacuated sick or wounded.

A.D.M.S. will render a return to Division "A" daily made up to 7 p.m. of the numbers of sick or wounded prisoners of war admitted to Field Ambulances during the previous 24 hours.

In all the above cases "NIL" returns will be rendered and the returns will be sent by wire.

The above orders will come into force on Zero Day.

APPENDIX "C".

DUMPS.

The following dumps either now exist or will be made in IV Corps Area :-

ARTILLERY.

Corps Reserve Dumps.

Light Ammunition	YTRES.	P.20.c.3.8.
Heavy Ammunition	BUS.	Q.24.a.3.5.
Light Ammunition	VALLULART WOOD.	P.33.a.3.8.

Ammunition Refilling Points.

BEUGNY	I.21.central.
RUYAULCOURT	P.9.d.9.0.

The following Decauville Railheads and Sidings will be used for delivery of ammunition :-

B.W.20. METZ-en-COUTURE. (in case of emergency)

B.W.40.)
B.W.50.) HAVRINCOURT
) WOOD.
Siding asked for at Q.1.a.3.2. if approved)

HERMIES
BOURSIES
LAGNICOURT

When the Corps advances the following Ammunition Refilling Points will be formed, for delivery of ammunition by Decauville:-

(a) TRESCAULT   B.W.54.
(b) CLAYTON CROSS B.W.62.   (Of these (b)
(c) HERMIES   (and (d) are the
(d) BOURSIES   (principal.
(e) LAGNICOURT

DIVISIONAL GRENADE AND BOMB STORES.

BEUGNY	I.22.b.1.7.
RUYAULCOURT	P.9.d.9.1.

BRIGADE GRENADE AND BOMB STORES.

HAVRINCOURT WOOD	Q.1.c.central
" "	Q.8.b.central.

R.E. STORES.

Corps Dumps.   HUN DUMP.
YTRES DUMP.

56th Divl. Reserve Dump.	BEUGNY.
36th Divl. Reserve Dump.	VELU.
62nd Divl. Reserve Dump.	RUYAULCOURT.
51st Divl. Reserve Dump.	METZ.

56th Divl. Advanced Dumps.   1. LAGNICOURT.
2. On Light Railway between LOUVERVAL and BOURSIES.

36th Divl. Advanced Dumps.   1. DEMICOURT.
2. HERMIES.

62nd Divl. Advanced Dumps.   HAVRINCOURT WOOD.
                                    1. B.W.26   K.31.c.
                                    2. Between B.W.60 and
                                        B.W.62 at Q.7.b.

51st Divl. Advanced Dumps.   1. B.W.54   Q.10.a.
                                    2. TRESCAULT.

CORPS WATER SUPPLY. -   Left   BEUGNY.
                        Right   METZ.
                        Main   BERTINCOURT.

CORPS MAIN BRIDGING DUMPS.   1. YTRES,   P.32.d.
                                    2. HUN DUMP.

CORPS ADVANCED BRIDGING DUMP.   BEAUMETZ.

RESERVE SUPPLY DUMPS.

                                    FREMICOURT,   I.20.c.2.9.
                                    ROCQUIGNY RAILHEAD.

SECRET.   62nd DIVISION.   62 Div. ../817/49.
                                                       Copy No. ......

ADDITIONS AND AMENDMENTS TO INSTRUCTIONS FOR OPERATIONS,

NOVEMBER 1917.
----

1.   TOWN MAJORS.

             The following Officers have been detailed as
Town Majors to place in charge of such inhabited villages
and towns as may be recaptured from the enemy :-

        2nd Lieut. C.A.CORKE, 2/5th West Yorks.Regiment.
        Lieut. T.H.CHAMBERS, 2/7th West Riding Regiment.
        Captain B.E.POPPLETON, 2/4th K.O.Y.L.I.

             These Town Majors will be located at
Divisional Headquarters, and detailed at the very
earliest opportunity, i.e. as soon as the Divisional 'A'
Staff have been informed that a village containing
inhabitants has been recaptured. They will report at
Divisional Headquarters at 2 p.m. on 18th November.

             Each Town Major will be in possession of a
copy of Orders for Town Majors and also of all copies
of notices, etc., required to be posted, which will be
furnished to them by Divisional Headquarters.

             Should the number of villages captured be
larger than can be dealt with as laid down, Divisions
will group them into Areas and place the Town Major in
charge of each Area.

             Until the arrival of the Town Major, the
Officer Commanding a Unit who enters an inhabited village
(unless he is passing through fighting) is responsible
that such measures are taken as will ensure that no
civilian enters or leaves the village.

             Should the evacuation of inhabitants be
decided upon, the procedure is described in S.S.425, and
orders will be issued by Corps. No such evacuation is to
take place without Corps Orders.

2.   S.A.A., GRENADES AND EXPLOSIVES.

             Paragraph 6 is amended to read as follows :-

	185 Bde.	186 Bde.	187 Bde.	Reserve	Total.
Stokes.	1212	804	1212	272	3500
Rings	1212	804	1212	272	3500.

3. **POLICE, TRAFFIC CONTROL, STRAGGLERS, PRISONERS OF WAR.**

Paragraph 9, sub-para.4, is amended to read as follows :-

Prisoners of War. The Corps Pen will be established at RUYAULCOURT; when prisoners of war are handed over, Divisional responsibility will cease.

Divisional forward collecting stations will be established at J.36.b.8.3. and Q.15.a.8.6. Brigades will send prisoners of war to collecting stations, where they will be handed over and will be brought to the Corps Cage by a M.M.P. guard.

All prisoners of war will be disarmed before sending them to the collecting stations. Officer prisoners of war will be searched by Brigades for papers, documents, etc., but other ranks will not be searched except for arms, bombs, etc.

The Reserve Brigade will detail 1 Officer, 1 sergeant or 1 Corporal, and 6 Privates for each collecting station to take charge of prisoners under the A.P.M. The Officers will report to A.P.M. for instructions at Divisional Headquarters at 12 noon on Y day.

The guards will arrive at the collecting stations at 6 p.m. on Y/Z night, and will bring 2 days rations with them.

4. **POSITIONS OF TRANSPORT LINES ON COMPLETION OF CONCENTRATION.**

On completion of concentration positions of Transport Lines will be as follows :-

185th Infantry Brigade	HAVRINCOURT WOOD.
186th Infantry Brigade	BERTINCOURT.
187th Infantry Brigade	RUYAULCOURT.

16.11.17.

Lieut.Colonel,
A.A.& Q.M.G., 62nd Division.

Copies to all recipients of "Instructions for Operations, November 1917" dated 14.11.17.

SECRET.   62nd DIVISION.   62 Div. A/866/49.
                                                             Copy No...24...

AMENDMENT TO INSTRUCTIONS FOR OPERATIONS, NOVEMBER 1917.

POLICE, TRAFFIC CONTROL, STRAGGLERS, PRISONERS OF WAR.

Prisoners of War.

   The Divisional Collecting Station will now be at Q.8.a.1.9., 100 yards N of CLAYTON CROSS.
   All former instructions on this subject are cancelled.

18.11.17.   [signature]   Lieut.Colonel,
                                       A.A. & Q.M.G., 62nd Division.

Copies to all recipients of "Instructions for Operations, November 1917" dated 14.11.17.

SECRET.

62 Div. A/906/49.
Copy No........

ADDITIONS TO INSTRUCTIONS FOR OPERATIONS, NOVEMBER 1917.
----

1. TRAFFIC.

    Road from DOIGNIES to DEMICOURT will be a one way horse traffic route from West to East.

    Road from DEMICOURT to HERMIES will be a two way horse traffic route.

    Pontoon wagons carrying bridging material will be accorded every facility to proceed to the sites selected for Bridges; A.P.M's and traffic control posts will be warned accordingly. It is essential that Bridges be erected with the utmost despatch.

2. ADVANCED VETERINARY AID POSTS.

    Advanced Veterinary Aid Posts will be established at I.30.b.2.0., and F.4.a. Cross Roads, LEBUCQUIERE.

20.11.17.   [signature] Lieut.Colonel,
                                        A.A.& Q.M.G., 62nd Divn.

Copies to all recipients of "Instructions for Operations, November 1917" dated 14.11.17.

APPENDIX II

ADMINISTRATIVE NOTES ON OPERATIONS 20th to 30th NOVEMBER 1917.

TRANSPORT.

The usual course adopted in a limited advance has been for the Corps to order a number of wagons from each Division to assist the R.E. in maintenance and repair of roads. In the recent advance of this Division a distance of 8500 yards was covered by noon on Z plus 1 day, the artillery advancing to very forward positions adjacent to GRAINCOURT. 34 wagons were demanded for road work, and in view of the artillery advance, no risk could be incurred by taking away from the D.A.C. and there was only the Train to fall back on. The obvious counter to this is that the baggage wagons of the Train are free to do this ; but this will not stand in the case under consideration,

The furthest point supply lorries could at any time have run was TRESCAULT, and this (owing to congestion of traffic and difficulties of dumping places) was eventually put back to METZ.

The journey from METZ to HAVRINCOURT, where advanced first line transport lines were, was on a bad road, up a severe hill and round two difficult deviations - to save foundering horses, and to ensure food getting up, wagons had to be double-teamed, and the only horses available for this were the baggage wagon horses.

It is considered that when objections are known to be well ahead beforehand, arrangements should be made to bring up transport from Divisions in rest to meet the needs of road repair etc.

All Divisional Transport and horses should be at the disposal of Divisions - any taking away of Divisional transport will limit a Division's mobility, and consequently will cramp the Commander's power to take advantage of circumstances, which render possible a bold advance.

Much of this might be avoided in future by a more extended use of DECAUVILLE Railway ; the need in this instance was for more truckage, which, it is suggested, might have been collected beforehand from areas, where operations were not in progress.

PACK TRANSPORT.

Packing is often attempted for too long a distance ; it means small loads and many animals compared to limbers, which can go almost anywhere. Every effort should be made to carry forward as far as possible in limbers : packsaddles should be on limbers, and the loads transferred when necessary - this is not popular owing to the extra trouble of changing loads from limber to pack.

D.A.C.

The D.A.C. was up to the last under the orders of another Corps only arriving in the Area at 12 noon on Z day, zero hour having been 6-20 a.m.

This is not soon enough to enable proper Divisional control to be maintained, and actually in this instance it was found that the S.A.A. Section was not filled up on arrival. At least 24 hours before zero on Z day the S.A.A. Section of the D.A.C. should be placed under the orders of Division 'Q'.

PERSONNEL.

The standard method of taking away personnel from Divisions to man Corps Troops is strongly deprecated.

Instances occurred as follows :-

(a) R.A.M.C.

3 Medical Officers, 3 N.C.Os., and 24 men were detailed for work at C.C.S.

It is submitted that this is the wrong end of the chain from which the C.C.S. Staff ought to be supplemented. Field Ambulances have at no time during operations any personnel to spare, and when an advance of any considerable distance is made, they require every officer and man in their establishment.

Surely C.C.S. personnel could be augmented from further back.

(b) SUPPLY PERSONNEL.

1 Corporal and 3 men Supply details were ordered to assist Corps Troops Supply Column

The same remarks apply in this case. If accurate accounts are still to be demanded, all available supply details are needed in a Division, more especially in view of the recent "combing out" of Divisional Train personnel.

In spite of this additional personnel being sent to Corps Troops Supply Column, this Division was at one time asked to undertake the supply of the R.A., R.E., and Pioneer Battalion of another Division and a proportion of the Heavy Artillery.

AMMUNITION.

Ammunition was ordered to be handed over for issue as equipment ammunition from supplies held by the Division formerly occupying the front line. To a Division coming new into the Area and only taking over the front line just before Z day, this is a difficult and harassing method.

Moreover in this case the front line was taken over by two Divisions and some considerable difficulties were experienced, both "taking over" Divisions being new to the line.

3.12.17.

(Sgd). Harold.F.Lea. Major.
D.A.A.G. 62nd Division.

BRIGADE NOTES.

RE-EQUIPMENT AFTER BATTLE.

The importance of ascertaining losses of equipment immediately after coming out of action does not seem to be always realised. It is understood that both Brigade and Regimental Staffs are tired, but the omission to take stock at once invariably adds to the final labour, and exposes Commanders to periods of anxiety, which they should be spared.

The recent operations point the moral very clearly. The Division was "put in" again within 36 hours, and in any case, there must have been a rush.

Again after coming out from the second phase, all 3 Infantry Brigades were almost immediately placed at the disposal of other Divisions, or held in readiness.

The main items requiring immediate attention are Lewis Guns and magazines, rifles and all ammunition and boots. Staff Captains should commence to ascertain, by personally visiting units, losses, immediately on leaving the forward area (not waiting till their Brigade gets to a problematical rest area), and the information should be wired to Divisional Headquarters forthwith stating that it is an approximate estimate.

This enables Divisional "Q" Staff, in conjunction with D.A.D.O.S. to get up equipment and stores and to obtain the necessary Army authority.

Indents, when sent in, should be properly completed stating reason for replacement, and adding the necessary certificate.

LEWIS GUN MAGAZINES.

Very heavy demands are sent in for these, and it has been observed that at times when Brigades' demands are most urgent, no notice is taken of the scores of drums lying in trenches.

L.G. Magazines have to be obtained from the back, but no reserve on Divisional charge is allowed. As transport to the nearest Gun Park and back to units takes time, it is recommended that personnel from the wagon lines or carrying parties be detailed to look round for them. In two recent instances enough magazines were seen within $\frac{1}{4}$ mile of wagon lines to have met the emergency. Every effort should be made to reload empty magazines, which are equipment, and should not be treated like empty cartridge cases.

SUPPLIES.

The importance of Brigades keeping in touch with their Supply Officer is not always appreciated. The affiliated Company of the train should be kept aware of any movement of wagon lines. If communications are difficult such wires can be repeated to D.H.Q. who will always endeavour to ensure that the Train Company is informed, but the direct communication is the normal method.

Increases of the normal rations (Trench rations) should be demanded by units. It frequently occurs that the obtaining of these rations is left to the Supply Officer concerned; the correct method is for the unit to know what can be drawn and to demand it.

Attention is directed to S.S.571, which gives schedules of everything that can be drawn.

CASUALTIES.

Before going into action a careful check should be made of officers' names and initials. If a really correct nominal roll was available, it would do away with much needless telegraphing for corrections.

GUIDES.

To ensure special delivery of rations, ammunition or store guides of intelligence should be selected.

Several demands in recent operations, though arranged for with a good deal of trouble, were nullified through guides told off to meet the stores etc doing unexpectedly foolish things.

                                    (sd) H.F.LEA, Major,
3/12/17.   D.A.A.G., 62nd Division.

APPENDIX IV

62ND DIVISION.

HONOURS AND REWARDS AWARDED DURING NOVEMBER 1917.

Distinguished Conduct Medals   2.

5.12.17.

APPENDIX V

62ND DIVISION.
CASUALTIES DURING NOVEMBER 1917.

	Killed	Wounded	Missing
Officers	36	116	4
Other Ranks	435	2330	469

Names of officers as per attached list.

5.12.17.

NAMES OF OFFICER CASUALTIES.

2/Lieut.	W.B.Diver. 6th Norfolk Regt. attd. 2/4.th. K.O.Y.L.I.	Wounded.S.S.
Lieut.	J.E.David. 2/4th K.O.Y.L.I.	Wounded.S.S.
2/Lieut.	E.W.Davis. 310th F.A.Brigade.	Wd. at duty.
2/Lieut.	N.H.Smith. 2/5th West Yorks.Regt.	Killed.
2/Lieut.	N.G.Airey. 2/5th West Yorks.Regt.	Killed.
2/Lieut.	A.J.Watson. 2/5th West Yorks.Regt.	Wounded.
2/Lieut.	L.F.Walker. 2/5th West Yorks.Regt.	Wounded.
2/Lieut.	R.M.Davidson. 2/5th West Yorks.Regt.	Wounded.
Captain.	R.Bickerdike.M.C. 2/6th West Yorks.Regt.	Killed.
Captain.	G.Barker. 2/6th West Yorks.Regt.	Killed.
2/Lieut.	A.W.Bedford. 2/6th West Yorks.Regt.	Killed.
2/Lieut.	J.G.Booth. 2/6th West Yorks.Regt.	Killed.
2/Lieut.	P.Haywood. 2/6th West Yorks.Regt.	Killed.
2/Lieut.	W.Moorhouse. 2/6th West Yorks.Regt.	Killed.
Captain.	G.E.J.Brooksbank. M.C. 2/6th West Yorks.Regt.	Wounded.
Captain.	G.R.S.Walker. 2/6th West Yorks.Regt.	Wounded.
2/Lieut.	J.W.Worth. 2/6th West Yorks.Regt.	Wounded.
2/Lieut.	J.R.Allett,M.C. 2/6th West Yorks.Regt.	Wounded.
Lieut.	F.C.Lawrence. 2/6th West Yorks.Regt.	Wounded.
2/Lieut.	J.Moor. 2/6th West Yorks.Regt.	Wounded.
2/Lieut.	H.Potterton. 2/6th West Yorks.Regt.	Wounded.
2/Lieut.	G.L.Bonsor. 2/6th West Yorks.Regt.	Wounded.
2/Lieut.	D.N.Vize. 2/6th West Yorks.Regt.	Wounded.
Lt.Col.	C.H.Hoare,D.S.O. 2/6th West Yorks.Regt.	Wd. at duty.
2/Lieut.	W.Mellor. 2/6th West Yorks.Regt.	Wd. at duty.
2/Lieut.	B.J.A.Pratt. 2/6th West Yorks.Regt.	Missing.
Captain.	H.Smith,M.C. 2/6th West Yorks.Regt.	Missing.
2/Lieut.	W.R.Brown,M.C. 2/7th West Yorks.Regt.	Killed.
2/Lieut.	J.Swift. 2/7th West Yorks.Regt.	Killed.
2/Lieut.	W.R.Hutchinson. 2/8th West Yorks.Regt.	Killed.
Captain.	H.R.Burrows. 2/8th West Yorks.Regt.	Wounded.
Lieut.	T.A.H.Orr. 2/8th West Yorks.Regt.	Wounded.
Lieut.	P.Jowett. 2/8th West Yorks.Regt.	Wounded.
Lieut.	G.M.Hirst. 2/8th West Yorks.Regt.	Wounded.
2/Lieut.	O.R.Pogson. 2/8th West Yorks.Regt.	Wounded.
2/Lieut.	V.L.Patch. 2/4th West Riding Regt.	Killed.
Lieut.	L.Cordingley. 2/4th West Riding Regt.	Wounded.
Lieut.	W.L.Oldroyd. 2/4th West Riding Regt.	Wounded.
2/Lieut.	H.E.Hoyle. 2/4th West Riding Regt.	Wounded.
2/Lieut.	G.R.V.Peel. 2/4th West Riding Regt.	Wounded.
2/Lieut.	G.F.Hotson. 2/4th West Riding Regiment.	Wounded.
2/Lieut.	H.A.Esden. 2/4th West Riding Regiment.	Wounded.
2/Lieut.	W.Kennett. 2/4th West Riding Regt.	Wounded.
2/Lieut.	J.P.Castle. 2/4th West Riding Regt.	Wd. at duty.
Lt.Col.	T.A.D.Best,D.S.O. 2/5th West Riding Regt.	Killed.
Lieut.	J.E.Ridgway. 2/5th West Riding Regt.	Killed.
Lieut.	J.G.Bodker. 2/5th West Riding Regt.	Killed.
Captain.	C.S.Moxon. 2/5th West Riding Regt.	Wounded.
Lieut.	J.A.Haigh. 2/5th West Riding Regiment.	Wounded.
Lieut.	W.L.Thomas. 2/5th West Riding Regt.	Wounded.
2/Lieut.	C.Wright. 2/6th West Riding Regt.	Killed.
Lieut.	J.Stocks. 2/6th West Riding Regt.	Wd. at duty.
Lieut.	H.H.Peet. 2/6th West Riding Regt.	Wd. at duty.
Captain.	J.C.K.Alexander,M.C. 2/8th West Yorks.Regt. attd. 2/7th West Riding Regt.	Wounded.
Captain.	A.F.Gloag. M.C. Highland Cyclist Battn. attd. 2/7th West Riding Regt.	Wounded.
Lieut.	C.G.Stott. Highland Cyclist Battn. attd. 2/7th West Riding Regt.	Wounded.
Lieut.	J.Maden. 2/7th West Riding Regt.	Wounded.
2/Lieut.	A.E.Crookson. 2/7th West Riding Regt.	Wounded.
2/Lieut.	C.Hirst. 2/4th K.O.Y.L.I.	Wounded.
2/Lieut.	H.A.E.Barker. 2/4th K.O.Y.L.I.	Killed.
2/Lieut.	C.P.Maddox. 2/4th K.O.Y.L.I.	Killed.
2/Lieut.	A.G.Hill. 2/4th K.O.Y.L.I.	Wounded.S.
Captain.	G.H.Roberts. 2/4th K.O.Y.L.I.	Wounded.

Captain.	M.McNicoll. 2/4th K.O.Y.L.I.	Wounded.
Lieut.	A.R.Mosley. 2/4th K.O.Y.L.I.	Wounded.
Lieut.	R.Hale-White. 2/4th K.O.Y.L.I.	Wounded.
2/Lieut.	H.Anderson. 2/4th K.O.Y.L.I.	Wounded.
2/Lieut.	S.A.V.Butler. 2/4th K.O.Y.L.I.	Wounded.
2/Lieut.	A.Kilner. 2/4th K.O.Y.L.I.	Wounded.
2/Lieut.	E.Morris. 2/5th K.O.Y.L.I.	Wounded.
2/Lieut.	J.A.V.Jago. 2/5th K.O.Y.L.I.	Wounded.
Captain.	A.Robinson. 2/5th K.O.Y.L.I.	Wd. at duty.
2/Lieut.	E.McLaren. 2/4th York & Lancs.Regt.	Killed.
Captain.	C.G.Vickers. 2/4th York & Lancs.Regt.	Killed.
2/Lieut.	W.E.Laidlaw. 2/4th York & Lancs.Regt.	Wounded.
Captain.	R.C.Hall. 2/5th York & Lancs.Regt.	Killed.
2/Lieut.	C.A.G.Bertram. 2/5th York & Lancs.Regt.	Wounded.
Captain.	S.O'R.Surridge. 2/5th York & Lancs.Regt.	Wd. at duty.
T/Chaplain,3rd Class.	C.M.Chavasse.H.Q. 62nd Divn.	Wounded.
T/Chaplain,4th Class.	A.B.Wright. H.Q. 62nd Divn.	Wounded.
Brig-General.	R.B.Bradford,V.C.,M.C. H.Q.186th Inf.Bde.	Killed.
Lieut.	G.B.Foster. 2/5th West Yorks.Regt.	Wounded.
2/Lieut.	G.R.Hutchinson. 2/5th West Yorks.Regt.	Killed.
2/Lieut.	T.E.Gibson. 2/5th West Yorks.Regt.	Killed.
2/Lieut.	B.Hick. 2/6th West Yorks.Regt.	Wounded.
Captain.	C.L.Sagar-Musgrave, 2/7th West Yorks.Regt.	Wounded.
Lieut.	A.E.Leeson. 2/7th West Yorks.Regt.	Wounded.
2/Lieut.	G.W.Curry. 2/7th West Yorks.Regt.	Wounded.
2/Lieut.	J.W.Pugh. 2/7th West Yorks.Regt.	Wounded.
Lieut.	G.E.Raven. 2/7th West Yorks.Regt.	Wounded.
Captain.	G.R.Nevitt. 2/8th West Yorks.Regt.	Killed.
Lieut.	E.M.Boxall. 2/8th West Yorks.Regt.	Wounded.
Lieut.	H.Coles. 2/8th West Yorks.Regt.	Wounded.
2/Lieut.	A.W.Shann. 2/8th West Yorks.Regt.	Killed.
Lieut.	A.T.Hodgson. 2/8th West Yorks.Regt.	Wd. at duty.
Captain.	G.M.Fletcher. 2/4th West Riding Regt.	Wounded.
Lieut.	G.F.Robertshaw. 2/4th West Riding Regt.	Wounded.
2/Lieut.	B.Stott. 2/4th West Riding Regt.	Wounded.
2/Lieut.	A.Shaw. 2/4th West Riding Regt.	Wounded.
2/Lieut.	W.Saunders. 2/4th West Riding Regt.	Wounded.
2/Lieut.	H.Metcalfe. 2/4th West Riding Regt.	Wounded.
2/Lieut.	G.Liddle. 2/5th West Riding Regt.	Wounded.
Captain.	F.A.Sykes. 2/5th West Riding Regt.	Wounded.
Lieut.	E.W.Harris. 2/5th West Riding Regt.	Wounded.
Lieut.	D.Black. 2/5th West Riding Regt.	Wounded.
2/Lieut.	A.S.Jack. 2/5th West Riding Regt.	Wounded.
2/Lieut.	J.Bower. 2/5th West Riding Regt.	Wounded.
2/Lieut.	V.Greaves. 2/5th West Riding Regt.	Wounded.
2/Lieut.	W.O.Davies. 2/5th West Riding Regt.	Killed.
2/Lieut.	J.Melville. 2/5th West Riding Regt.	Missing.
Captain.	W.Robertson,R.A.M.C. attd. 2/5th W.Rid.Rgt.	Wounded.
Captain.	W.F.Luckman. 2/6th West Riding Regt.	Wd. at duty.
Captain.	B.S.Mann. 2/6th West Riding Regt.	Killed.
2/Lieut.	A.F.Melton. 2/6th West Riding Regt.	Killed.
2/Lieut.	A.J.Alexander. 2/6th West Riding Regt.	Killed.
Captain.	A.Somervell, 2/6th West Riding Regt.	Wounded.
Captain.	T.J.Howell. 2/6th West Riding Regt.	Wounded.
2/Lieut.	M.Elwin. 2/6th West Riding Regt.	Wounded.
2/Lieut.	T.C.Sharples. 2/6th West Riding Regt.	Wounded.
2/Lieut.	G.A.Cartwright. 2/7th West Riding Regt.	Wounded.
2/Lieut.	H.Hartley. 2/7th West Riding Regt.	Wounded.
2/Lieut.	C.Sexton. 2/7th West Riding Regt.	Wounded.
2/Lieut.	A.V.Spafford. 2/7th West Riding Regt.	Wounded.
Lieut.	N.T.Lawton. 2/7th West Riding Regt.	Wounded.
2/Lieut.	J.W.Berryman, 2/4th K.O.Y.L.I.	Died of Wds.
2/Lieut.	F.MacCunn. 2/4th K.O.Y.L.I.	Wounded.
Lieut.	H.L.Hollard. 2/4th K.O.Y.L.I.	Wounded.
Lieut.	A.E.Earle. 2/4th K.O.Y.L.I.	Wounded.
2/Lieut.	F.Cocker. 2/4th K.O.Y.L.I.	Wounded.
2/Lieut.	A.Brealey. 2/4th K.O.Y.L.I.	Wounded.
Captain.	O.S.Roper. 2/5th K.O.Y.L.I.	Killed.
2/Lieut.	G.A. Eardley. Royal Lancs. Regt. attd. 2/5th K.O.Y.L.I.	Killed.

NAMES OF OFFICER CASUALTIES.
(Contd).

2/Lieut.	L. Melhuish. Yorkshire Regt. attd. 2/5th K.O.Y.L.I.	Killed.
Captain.	H.O.Brown. 2/5th K.O.Y.L.I.	Wounded.
2/Lieut.	R.A.Waters. 2/5th K.O.Y.L.I.	Wounded.
2/Lieut.	P.Cartwright. 2/5th K.O.Y.L.I.	Wounded.
2/Lieut.	C.E.Townend. 2/5th K.O.Y.L.I.	Wounded.
2/Lieut.	W.McArthur. 2/5th K.O.Y.L.I.	Wounded.
2/Lieut.	G.W.V.Hughes. 2/5th K.O.Y.L.I.	Wounded.
Lieut.	C.H.Wilson. 2/5th K.O.Y.L.I.	Wd. at duty.
Lieut.	H.L.Field. 2/5th K.O.Y.L.I.	Wd. at duty.
Captain.	M.Barber. 2/4th York & Lancs.Regt.	Killed.
Captain.	C.Walker. 2/4th York & Lancs.Regt.	Wounded.
2/Lieut.	P.A.Wortley. 2/4th York & Lancs.Regt.	Wounded.
2/Lieut.	A.H.Halliday. 2/4th York & Lancs.Regt.	Wd. at duty.
Captain.	G.A.G.Hewitt. 2/5th York & Lancs.Regt.	Killed.
Captain.	J.Ellse. 2/5th York & Lancs.Regt.	Wounded.
Captain.	S.O'R.Surridge. 2/5th York & Lancs.Regt.	Wounded.
2/Lieut.	H.E.Newton. 2/5th York & Lancs.Regt.	Wounded.
Lieut.	E.L.H.Dunkerton. 2/5th York & Lancs.Regt.	Wd. at duty.
Lieut.	G.Thompson. 2/5th York & Lancs.Regt,	Wd. at duty.
2/Lieut.	H.Ashton. 2/5th York & Lancs.Regt.	Wd.& Missing.
2/Lieut.	W.Barber. 2/5th York & Lancs.Regt.	Wd.& Missing.
Lieut.	C.G.Harrison. 2/5th York & Lancs.Regt.	Missing.
Captain.	C.B.R.King. 208th Machine Gun Company.	Wounded.
2/Lieut.	A.P.McClare. 208th Machine Gun Company.	Wounded.

62ND DIVISION.

REINFORCEMENTS RECEIVED DURING NOVEMBER 1917.

	Off.	O.R.
2/5th West Yorkshire Regiment	1	131
2/6th " " "	-	134
2/7th " " "	-	171
2/8th " " "	1	133
2/4th West Riding Regiment.	11	22
2/5th " " "	3	51
2/6th " " "	8	85
2/7th " " "	6	177
2/4th K.O.Y.L.I.	5	144
2/5th "	3	137
2/4th York & Lancaster Regt.	2	192
2/5th " " "	6	120
201st Machine Gun Company.	2	-
208th " " "	-	29
212th " " "	-	20
213th " " "	-	18
R.A.	1	44
R.E.	-	7
A.S.C.	-	9
R.A.M.C.	-	46
Mob. Veterinary Section.	-	2

CONFIDENTIAL.

WAR DIARY

OF

ADMINISTRATIVE AND QUARTERMASTER GENERAL'S BRANCH, 62ND DIVISION.

From 1st December 1917 to 31st December 1917.

WAR DIARY or INTELLIGENCE SUMMARY

Army Form C. 2118. SECRET

DECEMBER 1917

62nd Division A

Place	Date	Hour	Summary of Events and Information	Remarks and references to Appendices
HAPLINCOURT	1st		HQ Division. Brigades in LEBUCQUIERE, BEAUMETZ les CAMBRAI & HINDENBERG Line	A1
BASSEUX	4th		Division staging through BLAIRVILLE, BAILLEULVAL & ARRAS.	A1
VILLERS CHATEL	6th		Division (less Artillery) moved to MONCHY BRETON Area. 13th Corps Reserve Area	A1
LABEUVRIERE	12th		Division (less Artillery) moved to 1st Corps Area. Brigades in LAPUGNOY, VENDIN, ANNEZIN, GONNEHEM, FOUQUIERES, HOUCHIN	A1
VILLERS CHATEL	19th		Division (less Artillery) returned to 13th Corps Reserve Area	A1
"	22nd		Hoedwin and Berry French Horton Batteries rejoined Division.	A1
"	29th		Divisional Artillery rejoined Division accommodated in BETHONSOURT, BERLES, GAUCHIN LEGAL, LA TARGETTE and CAUCOURT	A1
"	30th		3 officers 150 O.R. Infantry attached to 185 Tunnelling Coy.	A1
			1 officer 40 O.R. Infantry attached to 176 Tunnelling Company for work on forward area	A1
			Number of Field General Courts Martial during month 5	
			With the exception of the Artillery and Hoedwin and Berry French Motor Batteries the Division was in rest from December 4th	A1
			A heavy fall of snow occurred about the middle of the month, interfering to a certain extent with mechanical transport but	A1

Army Form C. 2118.

Page 2

WAR DIARY
or
INTELLIGENCE SUMMARY.
(Erase heading not required.)

Instructions regarding War Diaries and Intelligence Summaries are contained in F.S. Regs., Part II. and the Staff Manual respectively. Title pages will be prepared in manuscript.

Place	Date	Hour	Summary of Events and Information	Remarks and references to Appendices
VILLERS CHATEL	4-1-18		with the exception of 1 day these precautions had not to be resorted to	
			Reinforcements	
			Appendix A Honours and Rewards	
			Appendix B Casualties	
			Appendix C	
				Initialled for Colonel commanding the 8th Green Howards B. Division

62ND DIVISION.

REINFORCEMENTS RECEIVED DURING DECEMBER 1917.

	Off.	O.R.
2/5th West Yorkshire Regiment	3	202
2/6th West Yorkshire Regiment	12	258
2/7th West Yorkshire Regiment	4	128
2/8th West Yorkshire Regiment	7	188
2/4th West Riding Regiment	5	307
2/5th West Riding Regiment	8	175
2/6th West Riding Regiment	1	133
2/7th West Riding Regiment	2	132
2/4th King's Own Yorkshire Light Infantry	7	91
2/5th King's Own Yorkshire Light Infantry	3	123
2/4th York & Lancaster Regiment	15	43
2/5th York & Lancaster Regiment	6	216
201st Machine Gun Company	-	9
208th Machine Gun Company	2	26
212th Machine Gun Company	-	10
213th Machine Gun Company	1	42
62nd Divisional Artillery	8	76
62nd Divisional Royal Engineers	4	25
Army Service Corps	1	8
Medical Units	-	20
Veterinary Section	-	2
	89	2214

3.1.18.

62ND DIVISION.

Honours and Rewards conferred upon Officers, N.C.Os. and Men during December 1917.

Bars to Distinguished Service Orders	3
Distinguished Service Orders	13
Bars to Military Crosses.	2
Military Crosses	59
Bar to Distinguished Conduct Medal	1
Distinguished Conduct Medals	22
Bars to Military Medals	3
Military Medals	262

CONFIDENTIAL.

WAR DIARY

OF

ADMINISTRATIVE AND QUARTERMASTER GENERAL'S BRANCHES, 62nd DIVISION.

from 1st January 1918.   to 31st January 1918.

Vol. XIII

****

CONFIDENTIAL.

Original

WAR DIARY
or
INTELLIGENCE SUMMARY.

Army Form C. 2118.

"A" 62nd Div

Place	Date	Hour	Summary of Events and Information	Remarks and references to Appendices
VICTORY CAMP	Jan 10th 1918		Commencing Jan 7th the 62 Division relieved the 56th Division in the Riffle-Villa of the 13th Corps front. The relief was completed at our Div HQrs 10th own 11 a.m. Jan 10th. The Divisional sector was taken over after a heavy fall of snow. The weather having been snowy & frosty once report & the 1st Army, there were reserve Coy ty" but put in force again 6 am Jan 16th. They were finally taken off 6 am Jan 24th.	
	Jan 22		Commencing 27 Dec/17 the 13th Corps introduced a Cumulative Reduced scale of rations in view of the increasing holdings of food. Repts were called for by the G.O.C. the Division from all formations & separate Units, stating whether in all the reduced rations considered practicable to report being upon that half pounders other Corps Jan 22. A copy of the report attached. Table showing previous & reduced rates is attached.	W.D.

Army Form C. 2118.

Original

WAR DIARY
or
INTELLIGENCE SUMMARY.
(Erase heading not required.)

"A" 62nd Division

Instructions regarding War Diaries and Intelligence Summaries are contained in F. S. Regs., Part II. and the Staff Manual respectively. Title pages will be prepared in manuscript.

Place	Date	Hour	Summary of Events and Information	Remarks and references to Appendices
	Jan 25		In accordance with A.G. 2223(c) of 24.12.17 a draft of 12 other personnel numbering 10 f/m 125 OR arrived fr. the OTC	Nil
	Jan 30		In accordance with G.O.C. 08/1851/A.G. of 23.1.18 instructions were received to form Battalion x a Pioneer Battalion consisting of the division into three Battalions x a Pioneer Battalion. Instructions were received for 3 Battalions to be disbanded and for 3 Battalions the amalgamated. viz. Three comprising 1st line Battalions. The 49th division on/under the HQs & a nucleus of each Battalion for this purpose. The Battalion chosen for disbandment being the 2/6 West York 15; 2/6 Duke of Wellington's x 2/5 York x Lancs. Reg'. The 49th Division on/under for amalgamation is 1/5 West York by 1/5 Duke of Wellington's x 1/5 York x L.R. The surplus personnel of the disbanded Battalion after completing the vacancy of Battalion to establishment being sent to the Corps event at PERNES. Owing to the 167 Inf. Bde being in the line the organization of these Bde could not take place during January. Instructions were received	

Army Form C. 2118.

WAR DIARY
or
INTELLIGENCE SUMMARY.

(Erase heading not required.)

Original

"A" 62nd Div.

Instructions regarding War Diaries and Intelligence Summaries are contained in F.S. Regs., Part II. and the Staff Manual respectively. Title pages will be prepared in manuscript.

Place	Date	Hour	Summary of Events and Information	Remarks and references to Appendices
			that the 50th Division would supply the Pioneer Battalion. The name of the Battalion to relieve had not been received. Even 3rd/5th a table is attached showing the organisation of Bns.	Nil. Appendix B
Nœux	Jan 17.		In accordance with G.R.O. 2986 of 17.12.18. Inventions and separate kits were ordered to held. My convictions that reductions in personnel & equipment could be effected without efficiency being in any way impaired. A recommendation based upon their any replies was sent forward. Appendix C	Nil. Appendix C Nil. Appendix D Appendix E
			Honours and Rewards. a list is attached	
			Casualties	"
			Reinforcements list attached. Ma only draft being Indian personnel for the D.A.C. draft just to fight from the 49th Div. on reorganisation 1 section complete July 201 M.G.C to replace the section that was taken away in October 1917.	h.h. Appendix F
			Field Services Routh Marting. 11 were held during the month.	Nil.

b. Lloyd Captain
fr. major fr. Copt. 62 Division

XIII Corps "Q".   Q/10306/10.

In compliance with Corps Routine Order No. 1268 of 23rd December 1917, I forward a report on the experimental reduction in the soldier's rations as laid down in S.S.571.

BREAD.   The reduction in this has since been cancelled, and I cannot recommend that any reduction should again be contemplated.

PRESERVED MEAT.   When troops are not in the line I can recommend the reduction from 9 oz to 6 oz as long as the normal percentage of 60/40 fresh and preserved meat obtains, for troops in the line I am not so certain and, though willing to agree to try it for a longer period, I do not care to give a final opinion now.

Reports from units are shortly in this tone : while the ration of 6 oz is sufficient, it does not leave a margin for making up rissoles etc which are more called for now that the cheese ration is reduced.

JAM.   I agree that the reduced ration is, with care, just sufficient.

CHEESE.   Generally speaking, I find no complaints about this reduction.

SUGAR.   I find from reports and from personal interviews that this reduction is felt in all units. I am of opinion that some reduction is possible, but that $2\frac{1}{4}$ oz is not enough in winter months and recommend that $2\frac{3}{4}$ oz be the issue in winter.

TEA.   There seems to be no doubt in the mind of any Commander that the reduction in the tea ration is inadvisable, and after careful consideration I agree with them.

Life in the trenches at this time of the year is very materially affected by the ability to constantly supply hot drinks - tea is what the men like.

I do not think that experiments carried out at Army Cookery Schools, where ther are a fixed number of men having their meals at fixed hours, and where the arrangements for cooking are naturally of the best, can be held to govern the circumstances in which a Division in the Line lives.

Isolated posts, sentries, runners, transport drivers, dispatch riders and others require special meals at uncertain hours - it is tea always that is most looked for.

I am therefore, of the opinion that the tea ration should not be reduced by more than 1/8th oz of the ration laid down in S.S.571 issued with General Routine Order No. 2523.

GENERAL.   I have further to report that the importance of the scheme has been fully recognised by both officers and men, and that all ranks have loyally co-operated. I am of opinion that there is a great saving possible, but hope that reductions will not be pressed further than I have indicated in this letter. The time of year and the inevitable extra hardship in wet and cold trenches do not conduce to making reductions in food easy.

Further reductions in the summer can undoubtedly be made without hardship to the men.

(sgd) W.P. Braithwaite.
Major General.
22nd January 1918.   Commanding 62nd (West Riding) Division.

SCALE OF RATIONS.

	New scale.	Old scale.	
PRESERVED MEAT.	6 ozs	9 ozs	
BISCUIT.	8 ozs	10 ozs	
CHEESE.	1½ ozs	2 ozs	
JAM.	2 ozs	3 ozs	
TEA.	3/8 ozs	5/8 ozs	+ 1/8 oz in Trenches.
SUGAR.	2¼ ozs	3 ozs	+ 3/4 oz in Trenches.

REORGANISATION OF INFANTRY BATTALIONS.

Designation before reorganisation.	Disbanded	Amalgamated with H.Q. & nucleus of 1st line unit from 49th Divn.	Present order of battle.
185th Infantry Bde.			**185th Infantry Bde.**
2/5th West Yorks.			8th West Yorks.
2/6th West Yorks.	2/6th West Yorks.		2/5th West Yorks.
2/7th West Yorks.			2/7th West Yorks.
2/8th West Yorks.		2/8th West Yorks.	
186th Infantry Bde.			**186th Infantry Bde.**
2/4th West Riding			5th West Riding
2/5th West Riding		2/5th West Riding	2/4th West Riding
2/6th West Riding	2/6th West Riding		2/7th West Riding
2/7th West Riding			
187th Infantry Bde.			**187th Infantry Bde.**
2/4th K.O.Y.L.I.			5th K.O.Y.L.I.
2/5th K.O.Y.L.I.		2/5th K.O.Y.L.I.	2/4th K.O.Y.L.I.
2/4th York & Lancs.			2/4th York & Lancs.
2/5th York & Lancs.	2/5th York & Lancs.		

1.2.18.

XIII Corps "Q".

62nd Div. No.
Q/10246/5/1.

With reference to G.R.O. No.2985 of 17.12.17, I have to report with regard to possible economies in Q.M.G's Services.

1. I consider that the essence of all economy in the issue of equipment, clothing and stores is contained in the recent Order (G.R.O. 1317 of 7.1.18). If this can be rigorously enforced throughout all Armies, I believe a surprisingly large saving will be made.

The closer co-operation there is between Salvage work, and the Ordnance Department, the more will the economy be felt.

2. Among the many stores issued, I have noted the following as being ones that can be reduced :-

<u>Bicycles.</u> As per attached table.
<u>Barr & Stroud Range Finders</u>, from 3 to 1 in a Battalion.
<u>Bombing Shields.</u> a few to be kept in Divisional Store.

3. <u>Supplies.</u>

This is now being tested in this Corps, and I withold any remarks on this point.

4. <u>R.E. Material.</u>

I have no recommendations to make with regard to R.E. material in the line. But in the billeting and camp areas there appears to me to be waste, much of which is due to avoidable causes.

The care of many billets and camps is in the hands of Area Commandants with small staffs of wardens and is due to two causes.

(a) troops coming in cold and burning anything they can lay their hands on.
(b) billets and camps being left vacant and local inhabitants taking out fittings.

To stop this the Area Commandants require larger Staffs, which increases personnel, and the economic advantages require weighing one against the other.

(sd) W.P. Braithwaite,
Major-General,
Commanding 62nd (West Riding) Division.

21.1.18.

XIII Corps 'Q'.

PROPOSED REDUCTION OF BICYCLES.

Unit.	Establish-ment.	Proposed Establishment.	Saving per Division.
Battalion H.Q. & No.1.)	9	7	24
Sec.Sig.Co)	21	12	9
Div.Train.	43	30	13
Field Coy.	33	13	60
		Total	106

SECRET.
XIII Corps A.

62nd Div. No.
A/3044/62.

With reference to General Routine Order No.2986 of 17.12.17, I have but few suggestions to make with regard to any reduction of personnel.

The establishments have been calculated to meet certain needs, and there is no personnel that I know of that is superfluous.

Two items have occurred to me that might be considered -

(a) R.E. The carrying of pontoons has been frequently discussed; in my experience in France of over a year, pontoons have only once been used, and even in that instance another form of bridge could have been used.

If pontoons were removed from the establishment of Field Companies R.E. there would be, taking the Armies in France as a whole, an appreciable saving in both personnel and horses.

(b) R.A.M.C. The establishment of 3 Field Ambulances for a Division is, as a rule, excessive when a Division is not engaged in operations; on the other hand in operations the personnel can largely cope with the work. As soon as an advance, such as was achieved at CAMBRAI, takes place, the strain is immediately felt, and it is difficult to efficiently evacuate the wounded.

To meet this, and at the same time to effect an economy, and also bearing in mind the imminent reduction of Divisions to a strength of 9 Battalions, I suggest that the reduction of the numbers of Field Ambulances from 3 to 2 in a Division is possible; but to meet the needs of operations, there should be Field Ambulances on some similar footing as Army Field Artillery Brigades.

Thus, supposing there are 60 Divisions in the Field, an establishment of 120 Field Ambulances with 30 Army Field Ambulances, who would be moved to the scene of operations, might suffice, and 30 Field Ambulances would by this means be saved.

(sd) W.P?Braithwaite,
Major-General,
Commanding 62nd (West Riding) Division.

21.1.18.

62nd (WEST RIDING) DIVISION.

HONOURS AND REWARDS AWARDED DURING JANUARY 1918.

NEW YEAR'S HONOURS GAZETTE.

Brevet Colonelcy	1
Brevet Lieut.Colonelcy	2
Brevet Majorities	2
C.M.G.	1
Bars to D.S.O.	2
D.S.Os.	13
M.Cs.	21
D.C.Ms.	6
M.S.Ms.	6

FOR GALLANTRY DURING OPERATIONS.

D.S.O.	1
Bar to M.C.	1
M.Cs.	2
D.C.Ms.	2
M.Ms.	4

1.2.18.

62nd (WEST RIDING) DIVISION.
CASUALTIES DURING JANUARY 1918.

OFFICERS.

```
2nd Lieut. L.M.C.Collins, att.2/5th York & Lancs.  Missing 9.1.18.
2nd Lieut. E.G.Mackenzie, 2/5th West Riding  Missing believed
                                                     killed 20.1.18.
2nd Lieut. T.R.Sykes, 2/5th West Riding          Wounded 20.1.18.
2nd Lieut. E.Williams, 2/5th York & Lancs.  Accid.Killed 25.1.18.
Captain J.L.Thompson, 2/5th West Yorks.          Wounded 28.1.18.
2nd Lieut. E.Morton, 2/5th K.O.Y.L.I.            Wounded 29.1.18.
Lieut. S.A.Thorn, 2/7th West Yorks.              Wounded 31.1.18.
2nd Lieut. L.Keen, 2/5th K.O.Y.L.I.  Wounded, shell shock 27.11.17
2nd Lieut. L.A.Clack, 2/5th K.O.Y.L.I.   "      "      "      "
2nd Lieut. G.R.Maskell, 2/4th W.Riding   "      "      "   26.11.17
```

OTHER RANKS.

Killed	22
Wounded	70
Missing	1

1.2.18.

62nd (West Riding) Division.

Reinforcements received during January.

	Officers.	O.R.	
2/5th West Yorkshire Regiment	5	17	
2/6th " " "	17	23	
2/7th " " "	12	12	
2/8th " " "	22	26	
2/4th West Riding Regiment	8	34	
2/5th " " "	7	69	
2/6th " " "	3	38	
2/7th " " "	9	127	
2/4th K.O.Y.L.I.	25	361	Includes draft from 1st Line 9 Offs. 230 OR
2/5th " "	23	107	
2/4th York & Lancaster Regiment	-	12	
2/5th " " "	-	20	
62nd (West Riding) Divisional Artillery	4	297	Includes 1 Off. 125 OR Indian personnel.
62nd (West Riding) Divisional Engineers	-	18	
62nd (West Riding) Divisional A.S.C.	-	12	
201st Machine Gun Company	2	47	
208th Machine Gun Company	-	2	
212th Machine Gun Company	-	7	
	138	1219	

ORIGINAL.

CONFIDENTIAL

WAR DIARY

OF

ADMINISTRATIVE AND QUARTERMASTER GENERAL'S BRANCH,
62nd (WEST RIDING) DIVISION.

From 1st February 1918   to 28th February 1918.

(Volume 14)

Original

Army Form C. 2118.

Page 1.

SECRET

WAR DIARY
FEBRUARY for 1918
INTELLIGENCE SUMMARY. 62 DIVISION "A"
(Erase heading not required.)

Instructions regarding War Diaries and Intelligence Summaries are contained in F. S. Regs., Part II. and the Staff Manual respectively. Title pages will be prepared in manuscript.

Place	Date	Hour	Summary of Events and Information	Remarks and references to Appendices
In the field	Feb 8th–11th		The Division moved from the Right centre XIII Corps front into XIII Corps reserve about VILLERS CHATEL. The accommodation at no time too food, was further strained in both the villages of LACOMTE and BAJUS were out of bounds for troops owing to measles and also ACQ a large village with food store standing was earmarked for A.F.A. Bde. The great difficulty was to find horse-lines for the Divisional R.A. eventually the H.Qrs of 1 Bde and an Battery were located in XVII Corps area and 1 Battery had to be kept in half-finished horse-lines at FREVANT – CAPELLE	Rtn
" "	12th		9th Bn. D.L.I. (T.F.) from the 50th Division was transferred to the Division as a Pioneer Bn. They arrived in buses from the YPRES salient, organised in 4 companies. They had a fine fighting record, commencing with 2nd battle of YPRES, they were also at the time commanded by Brig-General BRADFORD V.C. who died for life in 2 CAMBRAI BATTLE commanding a Bde of the Division. 9 D.L.I were re-organised on a 3 Company basis, the re-organisation was completed on the 29/2/18	Rtn
" "			During the month No. 62 M. G. Battn. was directed to be formed from the 201, 208, 212	Rtn

SECRET

Army Form C. 2118.

WAR DIARY
FEBRUARY or 1916
INTELLIGENCE SUMMARY. 62nd (WR) DIVISION
Page 2

(Erase heading not required.)

Instructions regarding War Diaries and Intelligence Summaries are contained in F.S. Regs., Part II. and the Staff Manual respectively. Title pages will be prepared in manuscript.

Place	Date	Hour	Summary of Events and Information	Remarks and references to Appendices
In the Field	20		and 213th M.G. Coys. Deficiencies in Personnel & Transports were made up from Units disbanded under the reorganisation scheme of the Division	Rtn
" "	21		A parade was arranged so the Field at HERUN-LE-VERT when the G.O.C. was to have inspected the Division. This programme was cancelled and the C in C eventually visited the G.O.C. Division and the C.R.A., C.R.E., G.S.O.1. and A.A.& Q.M.G. at VILLERS CHATEL on 24-2-15	Rtn
" "			During the month a reorganisation of the Heavy and Medium Lewis Mortar Batteries took place. Details of the reorganisation were carried out & checked by the 1st Army Heavy Trench Mortar Batteries. Heavy Corps troops and also R.G.A personnel employed and the medium Trench Mortar Batteries were transferred to the Heavy Trench Mortar Batteries	Rtn
" "	28		The Division commenced the relief of the 31st Division in the left section of the XIII Corps	Rtn
			Health :- Sick rate high chiefly P.U.O.	Rtn
			Weather :- Weather has been very changeable ranging from bright spring day	Rtn

Army Form C. 2118.
page 3.

SECRET.

WAR DIARY
62nd Division A.
FEBRUARY 1918.
INTELLIGENCE SUMMARY.
(Erase heading not required.)

Instructions regarding War Diaries and Intelligence Summaries are contained in F.S. Regs., Part II. and the Staff Manual respectively. Title pages will be prepared in manuscript.

Place	Date	Hour	Summary of Events and Information	Remarks and references to Appendices
In the Field	Feb		Extreme cold with heavy winds, storms and rain, and occasionally a little snow.	A/1
			NOTES (1) Divisional Horse Show took place on 26-2-18 at HERLIN-LE-VERT and was a great success.	A/1
			(2) Finals of the football league were played off at TINCQUES on 27-2-18. Winners 2nd/3rd (W.R.) Field Ambulance	A/2
			APPENDICES.	
			Honours and Awards :- A list showing those who attacks) APPENDIX I	
			Casualties :- A table " " II	
			Reinforcements ; " " " " III	
			General Courts Martials during the month of Feby. 1.	A/1
			F.G.C.M. " 12.	
			2nd March 1918.	

Lancelot Kidson
Major General
Comdg. 62nd (W.R.) Division

Appendix 1.

62nd (WEST RIDING) DIVISION.

HONOURS AND REWARDS AWARDED DURING FEBRUARY 1918.

Military Medals   6

BELGIAN.

Croix de Guerre   34

Decoration Militaire   1

Appendix II.

62nd (WEST RIDING) DIVISION.
CASUALTIES DURING FEBRUARY 1918.

OFFICERS.

Captain C.S.Wilson, 2/7th West Yorkshire Regiment Wounded at duty 2/2/18.

2nd Lieut. C.R.Witcher, 310th Brigade R.F.A. Wounded at duty 6/2/18.

2nd Lieut. J.H.Hawkins, 8th West Yorkshire Regt. Wounded 7/2/18.

OTHER RANKS.

Killed	13
Wounded	46
Missing	1

APPENDIX 3.

Reinforcements received during February.

	Officers.	O.R.
8th West Yorkshire Regiment.	-	120
2/5th " " "	1	53
2/7th " " "	-	159
5th West Riding Regiment.	-	143
2/4th " " "	1	228
2/7th " " "	-	263
5th K.O.Y.L.I.	1	91
2/4th " "	-	78
2/4th York & Lancaster Regiment.	-	120
62nd (W.R) Divisional Artillery	2	49
62nd (W.R) Divisional Engineers	2	38
62nd (W.R) Divisional Train.	2	7
A.D.M.S. 62nd (W.R) Divl. R.A.M.C.	-	39
9th Durham Light Infantry (Pioneers)	2	4
208th Machine Gun Company.	-	37
212th " " "	1	29
213th " " "	2	18.
	14	1476

SECRET.

62 Div.A/3566/49
Copy No. 38

ADMINISTRATIVE ORDERS
for 62nd (West Riding) Division Order No.80.

1. A move table is attached, Appendix A.

2. A Location for the Reserve Area is attached, Appendix B.

3. Infantry Brigades (D.A.G.A. in case of 201st Machine Gun Company) will arrange accomodation for the Machine Gun Companies on relief.

4. Trains on broad gauge will be notified by 'Q'. Numbers will be notified as early as possible.
Trains on light railways will be arranged by Brigades, who will notify relieving Brigades direct.

5. Infantry Brigades will wire immediately on receipt of these instructions which are A, B and C Battalions.

6. All Area Employment will be relieved by 2 p.m. on 8th February by 56th Division. List attached, Appendix C. List of transport details to be relieved is also attached, Appendix D.

7. 1st Line Transports will move on the same day as their units. Transport lines in the Forward Area will be handed over to units of 56th Division on the days on which units of 62nd Division move either into MAIZEUL Staging Area or into a 'Working Battalion' Camp. Locations of transport lines for 'Working Battalions' are as follows :-

  AUBREY Camp at   ST CATHERINE.
  SCTTINE Camp   to be notified.
  WAKEFIELD Camp at   ST CATHERINE.

8. C.R.E., 62nd Division will arrange with C.R.E., 56th Division, all details of relief of Field Companies R.E.

9. AREA & TRENCH STORES. All trench stores, ammunition, supplies in Supporting Points, Etc., will be handed over. A.F. G.3405 receipted by both incoming and outgoing units will be forwarded to 62nd Division 'Q' within three days after relief.

Water and petrol tins, less those carried on water carts, and all soyer stoves, except those on the establishment of Field Ambulances, will be handed over.

The white overall suits for patrols (vide G.R.O.3030) will be handed into the D.A.D.O.S. 62nd Division at the first opportunity after relief.

Gum boots and inner soles will be handed in to the Store at ROCLINCOURT and receipts obtained.

All area and billet stores will be handed over to incoming units, receipts obtained and countersigned by Area Commandants and Town Majors.

Detailed separate receipts, showing accurate locations for all water and rations held in the defence system, will be obtained from relieving units and forwarded to Divisional Headquarters.

10. CAMPS AND BILLETS. All camps, billets and horse lines will be handed over in a clean and sanitary condition, and clearance certificates will be obtained from Area Commandants or relieving units.

11. CHAFF CUTTERS. All Infantry units will hand over chaff cutters to relieving units.

12. BATHS.   Baths will be at :-

   TINCQUES.
   MAGNICOURT.
   CAUCOURT.

   and will be ready for use on 8th February.
   Baths in Forward Area will be handed over to 56th Division on 8th February.

13. The Divisional Concert Party will perform at Theatre, VICTORY Camp, up to and including 11th February.

14. WORK IN PROGRESS.   C.R.E., 62nd Division will hand over all details of work in progress to C.R.E., 56th Division.

15. The Divisional Gardens Officer will hand over full details of land selected for gardens, and progress report, to Divisional Gardens Officer, 56th Division.

14. SANITATION IN FRONT LINE.   The schemes prepared by 185th and 186th Infantry Brigades, with maps, will be sent to Divisional Headquarters on relief, marked up to date.

4/2/18.

Lieut.Colonel,
A.A.& Q.M.G., 62nd (West Riding) Division.

DISTRIBUTION.

Copy No.	
1	A.D.C. for G.O.C.
2-3	"G"
4-5-6	"A" & "Q".
7	62nd Divisional Artillery
8	62nd Divisional Engineers.
9	185th Infantry Brigade.
10	186th Infantry Brigade.
11	187th Infantry Brigade.
12	62nd Divisional Signal Company.
13	A.D.M.S., 62nd Division.
14	62nd Divisional Train.
15	S.S.O., 62nd Division.
16	201 Machine Gun Company.
17	A.P.M., 62nd Division.
18	D.A.D.O.S., 62nd Division.
19	D.A.D.V.S., 62nd Division.
20	Camp Commandant, 62nd Division.
21	XIII Corps 'Q'.
22	56th Division.
23	62nd Divisional Tramway Officer.
24	62nd Divisional Water Officer.
25	62nd Divisional Graves Registration Officer.
26	62nd Divisional Baths Officer.
27	62nd Divisional Gardens Officer.
28-29	Area Commandants.
30-31	War Diary.
32-33	File.

SECRET.

TABLE "A".

"C" Battalions are Working Battalions, also B. 187

Locations shown are those after relief on any one day, on the assumption that the reliefs will finish before mid-night.

The Headquarters of the Battalion, 62nd Div. in the RED LINE are shown as at WAKEFIELD CAMP.

DATE	BREVILLERS AREA	CHILLERS AREA	ORLENCOURT AREA	MARONIL	MARONIL	ST. AUBIN	TRAFALGAR CAMP	AUDRUY CAMP	STEWART CAMP	ROCLINCOURT W. CAMP	WAKEFIELD CAMP	BOUVIRES	LEFT BDE. SUPPORT	LEFT BDE. LINE	RIGHT BDE. SUPPORT	RIGHT BDE. LINE	RIGHT BDE. LINE
Feb. 6th.	A.B./169	A.B./167	A.B./168	A./187	B./187	—	C./169	C./187	C./189	C./185	C./187	—	B./185	A./185	C./185	A./185	B./185
7th.	A./187	A.B./187	A.B./168	A./169	B./187	B./169	C./169	C./187	C./189	C./185	C./187	—	B./185	A./185	C./185	A./185	B./186
8th.	A./187	A.B./187	A.B./168	A./186	B./186	B./183	—	C./187	C./188	C./185	C./187	B./187	B./185	A./185	C./189	A./189	B./189
9th.	A./187	A.B./187	A.B./186	A./186	B./188	C./186	—	C./187	C./188	C./185	C./187	C./187	B./185	A./185	C./189	A./189	B./189
10th.	A.B./187	A.B./187	A.B./185	A./185	B./185	C./187	—	C./185	C./186	C./168	C./187	B./187	B./168	A./168	C./169	A./169	B./169
11th.	A./187	A.B./188	A.B./185	A./187	B./187	—	—	C./185	C./186	C./168	C./187	B./187	B./168	A./168	C./169	A./169	B./169
12th.	A.C./187	A.B./169	A.B./185	A./187	B./187	—	—	C./185	C./186	C./168	C./187	D./187	D./168	A./168	C./189	A./189	B./189

SECRET. TABLE "B".

62nd (W.R) Division Location Table on completion of relief.

UNIT.	LOCATION.
62nd (W.R) Divn. Headquarters, D.A.D.O.S.	VILLERS CHATEL, MINGOVAL, TINCQUES.
62nd (W.R) Divn. Train	SAVY.
62nd (W.R) Divn. Signal School	SAVY.
62nd (W.R) Divn. N.C.O.s School	BAILLEUX-AUX-CORNAILLE.
201st Machine Gun Company	BAILLEUX-AUX-CORNAILLE.
185th Inf.Bde Headquarters.	ORLENCOURT.
Machine Gun Company	MARQUAY.
Trench Mortar Battery	MARQUAY
1 Battalion	MONCHY BRETON.
1 Battalion	LA THIEULOYE.
1 Battalion	AUBREY CAMP.
Train Company	ROCOURT
Pioneer Company	HOUVELIN.
Field Ambulance	HOUVELIN.
186th Inf.Bde Headquarters	CHELERS
Trench Mortar Battery	CHELERS
Pioneer Company	CHELERS
1 Battalion	TINCQUES.
1 Battalion	VILLERS BRULIN, BETHONSART.
1 Battalion	STEWART CAMP.
Machine Gun Company	TINCQUETTE.
Train Company	TINCQUETTE
Field Ambulance	BAILLEUX-AUX-CORNAILLE.
187th Inf.Bde Headquarters	FREVILLERS.
Machine Gun Company	FREVILLERS.
Trench Mortar Battery	FREVILLERS.
Pioneer Company	FREVILLERS.
1 Battalion) H.Qrs,& 2 Coys.	CAUCOURT.
) 2 Companies	HERMIN.
1 Battalion	Forward Area.
Train Company	HERMIN.
Field Ambulance	HERMIN.
1 Battalion.	MAGNICOURT.
Pioneer Battalion	CAMBLIGNEUL.
Mobile Veterinary Section	VANDELICOURT.

TABLE "C".

LIST of AREA EMPLOY furnished by
62nd DIVISION to be relieved by 56th DIVISION at 2 p.m. 16.5.18.

Serial No.	Lost	Offs.	NCOs.	Men	Nature of work	Where reliefs to report	By whom rationed
1	A.C. MADAGASCAR	-	1	3	Clerk, Billet Wardens &c.	A.C. MADAGASCAR	A.C. MADAGASCAR
2	" PONT du JOUR	-	-	7	do.	G.6.d.8.7.	A.C. PONT du JOUR.
3	" ROCLINCOURT	-	-	6	do.	do.	A.C. ROCLINCOURT.
4	" ST AUBIN	-	-	4	do.	A.C. ST AUBIN	A.C. ST AUBIN.
5	" ST CATHERINE	-	1	10)	Work on roads	A.C. ST CATHERINE	Unit. Daily party.
		-	1	10)			" "
6	T.M. ANZIN	-	1	10	do	T.M. ANZIN	" "
7	Div.Water Service	1	6	29	Water Wardens	62nd Div. Water Service Officer c/o A.C. ECURIE.	Under arrangements made by D.W.S.O.
8	Div.Burials Officer	To be arranged between Burials Officers of 62nd & 56th Divisions.					
9	Tramway Officer ROCLINCOURT.	1	2	3	On Tramways	ROCLINCOURT Station No.7 A.T.Coy.	No.7 A.T.Coy.
10	No.7 A.T.Coy. R.E. ROCLINCOURT.	-	-	26	Tramway maintenance	do	do
11	Musketry Ranges :- MAROEUIL.	-	-	2	Wardens	T.M. MAROEUIL.	T.M. MAROEUIL.
	ROCLINCOURT	-	-	2	do.	A.C. ROCLINCOURT	A.C. ROCLINCOURT.
12	R.E. Dump, ROCLINCOURT	-	1	20	Loading & unloading party.	R.E. Dump, ROCLINCOURT	C.R.E.
13	Div. Amn. Dump.	-	1	3	Holding party	At Dump	O.C. Employment Co.
14	XIII Corps S.C.	-	-	1	Thatcher at Corps Straw Depot	XIII Corps S.C. MAROEUIL.	XIII Corps S.C.
15	R.E. Park, MAROEUIL	-	-	5	Tinsmiths making stoves.	R.E. Park, MAROEUIL.	O.C., R.E. Park.

Serial No.	Post	Offrs.	N.C.Os.	Men	Nature of work	Where relief to report.	By whom rationed.
16	148 A.T.Co. MARŒUIL.	-	-	3	Sappers supervising Chinese labour.	148 A.T.Co. MARŒUIL.	148 A.T.Co.
17	M.& R.Camp, FLORINGHEM	-	1	3	Sappers erecting buildings.	M.& R.Camp.	M.& R.Camp.
18	Div.S.A.A.& Grenade Dump, G.11.b.9.5.	1	1	9	Work and to include 1 batman & 1 clerk.	Off.i/c Dump, G.11.b.9.5.	O.i/c Dump.
19	Traffic Control.	To be arranged between A.P.Ms.of 62nd & 56th Divisions.					
20	Div.Baths	To be arranged between Baths Officers of 62nd & 56th Divisions.					
21	Corps Roads Officer B.15.c.7.0.	1	-	10	Sappers superintending repair of Forward Roads.	Corps Roads Off. B.15.c.7.0.	C.R.E.
22	Rest Camp, ST POL.	1 W.O.			Light Duty	Rest Camp, ST POL.	At Camp.
23	XIII Corps Troops Supply Column.	-	1	2	(Div.Train) Loaders	XIII Corps S.C. MARŒUIL.	XIII CORPS S.C.
24	Reinforcement Camp BOOIVRES.	1	1	9	Div.Disbursing Off. Staff 3 cooks, 3 clerks, 3 carpenters or handymen	At Camp.	C.O., Camp.
25	No.33 Ordnance Workshop.	-	1	5	Employed in workshop.	No.33 Ordnance Workshop. A.26.b.central	At workshop.
26	Gum Boot Store, ROCLINCOURT.	-	1	10	Cleaning gum boots	O.i/c Store.	Daily party. Haversack ration required.
27	62nd Sanitary Sec.	-	1	4	Making sanitary appliances.	62nd Sanitary Sec. ANZIN.	62nd San.Sec.
28	T.M. MARŒUIL	1	2	20	General Work.	T.M. MARŒUIL.	Daily party.
29	Y.M.C.A. MARŒUIL.	1	1	10	Erecting Y.M.C.A.hut.	Y.M.C.A.Official.	To report 1 p.m. daily.
30	Div.S.A.A.& Grenade Dump, G.11.b.9.3.	1	1	3	Guard	Off.i/c Dump.	Relieved 10 a.m. daily.
31	VICTORY CAMP	-	1	20	Winter proofing	Camp Comdt	Daily party.
32	C.R.E., VICTORY CAMP.	1	-	15	do	C.R.E.	Daily party.
33	Corps Salvage Officer	1	-	1		Corps Salvage Off. MARŒUIL.	

DETAILS OF TRANSPORT TO BE TAKEN OVER BY 56th DIVISION
FROM 10th JANUARY 1918 INCLUSIVE.

Serial No.	Detail	Found by	For	Rationed by
			PERMANENT DETAILS.	
1	1 G.S.wagon (G.P.O.)	R.A.M.C.	XIII Corps M.e R.Camp, FLORINGHEM.	M.e R.Camp.
2	2 mules and driver	187th Inf.Bde.	127 Labour Company, ST AUBIN	127 Labour Co.
3	2 mules and driver	185th Inf.Bde.	169 Labour Company, G.6.a.6.4.	169 Labour Co.
4	14 H.D.horses with drivers	R.A.M.C.	Assistance to Farmers, MAROEUIL.	'M' Corps Supply Colu Report T.M. MAROEUIL.
5	2 G.S.wagons	62 Div.Train	ditto	ditto
			DAILY DETAILS.	
6	1 G.S.Wagon	R.A.M.C.	Town Major ANZIN	
7	1 G.S.Wagon	R.A.M.C.	Town Major, ST CATHERINE.	
8	6 G.S.Wagons	62 Div.Train	341 Road Construction Co, MADAGASCAR. 8 a.m.	
			DAILY DETAILS TO BE TAKEN OVER BY 56th DIVISIONAL ARTILLERY ON RELIEF OF 62nd DIVISIONAL ARTILLERY.	
9	2 G.S.Wagons	62 Div.Arty.	135 Tunnelling Company, ..26.b.5.3. 3 p.m.	
10	10 G.S.Wagons	"	249 Labour Company, R.E. Dump, ROCLINCOURT. 8 a.m.	

SECRET.

62 Div.A/4830/49.
Copy No.24.

ADMINISTRATIVE INSTRUCTIONS WITH REFERENCE TO
62nd DIVISIONAL ORDER NO. 100 OF 24.2.18.

Reference maps
51B, 51C, 36C.

The following information with regard to the new area is circulated for information :-

1. **ADMINISTRATION.** The Divisional Area is shown on the attached map. The portion of the Area West of a line drawn from T.26.c.7.5. to B.15.c.5.3. is divided into 5 Sub-areas for administrative purposes.

    Areas and Area Commandants are as follows :-

		NAME.	OFFICE.
Town Major.	ECOIVRES	Major D.L.BAINE.	F.18.b.8.4.
Area Comdt.	BRAY.	Capt C.L.PROSSER	BRAY.
" "	BRUNEHAUT.	Lt-Col.T.W.JONES	F.22.d.6.2.
" "	ECURIE.	Major C.H.GRAY.	A.26.b.6.2.
" "	NINE ELMS.	Lt. J.C.HICKMAN.	A.28.b.7.2.
" "	BAILLEUL	Major W.JOYCE.	G.6.d.8.7.

    The above named officers are responsible for the administration of their Area as regards accommodation, tentage, huts, etc, and will see that nothing is removed in the way of huts, billet stores etc, without authority from D.H.Q.

    This does not relieve Units of their responsibility for the sanitation and cleanliness of their respective camps.

    The remainder of the Divisional Area is administered by the Brigades holding the line respectively.

2. **ACCOMMODATION.** The accommodation in the area is as follows :-

    ECOIVRES AREA.

    | VILLAGE CAMP. | 1 Bn. in French and Nissen Huts. |
    | YORK CAMP | 1 Bn. do. |
    | LANCASTER CAMP. | 1 Bn. in French Huts. |
    | DURHAM CAMP. | 1 M.G.Coy. & T.M.Bty in billet and French Huts. |

    Each Camp has its own transport lines and a Recreation Room.

    BRAY AREA.

    | BRAY CAMP | 1 Bn in Nissen Huts. |
    | | 1 Divnl Musketry Schl in Nissen Huts. |

    There is also good accommodation for 110 horses.

    BRUNEHAUT AREA.

    There are no Battalion Camps in this area, which consists chiefly of Training Ground.

    There is a labour company camp of 22 Nissen Huts at A.20.b.0.3. and a R.N.A.S Squadron Camp of 18 Nissen and 14 Miscellaneous Huts at F.15.b.1.9.

    Four Coys of Divisional Train are accommodated in Nissen Huts on ARRAS - SOUCHEZ ROAD.

    ECURIE AREA.

    Most of the Divisional accommodation is in this Area, and is as follows :-

    | ECURIE WOOD CAMP. | 40 Nissen Huts. |
    | SPRINGBALE CAMP. | 37 do |
    | ROBERTS CAMP. | 27 do |
    | FLANDERS CAMP. | 17 do |
    | TUNNELLING COY CAMP. | 17. do |
    | ESSEX CAMP. | 6 do |

Sheet 2.

3 Nissen Hut Camps, each of 11 Huts, for the 3 Field Coys R.E. with transport lines.
3 Inf.Bdes Transport Lines, each containing 34 Nissen Huts.
There is also a single camp of 4 Nissen Huts and Transport lines for Divnl M.G.Coy.

NINE ELMS AREA.

DIVISIONAL HEADQUARTERS at WEXFORD CAMP, consisting of 27 Nissen Huts and various small huts.
MARLBORO' CAMP. 6 Nissen Huts and small corrugated huts occupied by Heavy Artillery Group.
ROCLINCOURT WEST CAMP. 32 Nissen Huts (at present loaned to Right Division.
STEWARTS CAMP 40 Nissen Huts.
LABOUR CAMP. 3 Nissen and small corrugated iron Hu
There are also on Ridge Track 2 dugout Camps as follows :-
WORCESTER CAMP. A.24.c.4.4. to accommodate 4 officers and 100. O.R.
OLIVE CAMP. 6 Nissen Huts occupied by A.A.Bty
ARGYLE CAMP. 4 Nissen Huts & 3 Other Huts occupied by H.T.M.B.

BAILLEUL AREA.

The accommodation in this area consists almost entirely of shelters and dug-outs, and its total capacity is about 25 Officers and 550 O.R.
The following is the full list of named Camps in the Divisional Area.

BAILLEUL
CURRAGH CAMP. B.19.a.4.7. to accommodate 4 Officers and 100 O.R.

ECOIVRES.
LANCASTER.	F.8.c.7.6.	Battalion.
DURHAM.	F.8.c.8.2.	M.G.C.& T.M.B. (with billet)
YORK.	F.13.b.3.6.	Battalion.
VILLAGE	F.13.b.2.4.	"

ECURIE.
ECURIE WOOD.	A.27.b.0.7.	Battalion.
SPRINGVALE.	A.22.c.5.2.	"
ROBERTS	A.27.b.6.9.	M.G.Coys.
FLANDERS.	A.27.b.	Bn.H.Q. & 1 Coy.
ESSEX. (	A.14.d.1.5.	6 huts.
(	A.27.d.	3 Fld Coys R.E.

BRUNEHAUT	A.14.c. & A.20.a.	H.Q. & all Train Coys.
BRAY.	F.20.a.8.5.	Battalion.

NINE ELMS.
WORCESTER.	A.24.c.4.4.	1 Coy.
LABOUR.	A.29.a.	6 officers, 80 O.R.
STEWARTS	A.29.b.	Battalion.
WEXFORD.	A.28 & 29.	D.H.Q.
MARLBORO'	A.28.a.	T.M.Bty.
OLIVE.	A.23.d.2.3.	A.A. Bty.
ARGYLE.	A.28.b.5.3.	3 huts.
ROCLINCOURT WEST.	A.28.a & b.	Battalion.

Sheet 3.

3. **LIGHT RAILWAYS & TRAMWAYS.**

   ROCLINCOURT WILLERVAL LINE.. Runs from ROCLINCOURT through Ridge Station ("Daylight Railhead) B.19.d.5.9. to Tunnel Dump B.15.c.3.2 runs via LONG WOOD to WILLERVAL. At LONG WOOD B.15.a.3.4. a branch line runs to SUGAR FACTORY B.16.a.3.7. known as SUGAR SPUR, from thence it continues to join the ARLEUX Line at B.10.d.2.2.

   ROCLINCOURT ARLEUX LINE. Runs through ROCLINCOURT to ASHFORD JUNCTION along the TUNNEL DUMP Line, as far as B.19.d.2.7., then passes through B.20.d.5.3. - B.21.a.3.2. - B.21.central - B.16.c. B.16.a.1. - B.16.d.0.0. to ARLEUX.
   At B.11.a.2.1. there is a branch line called SEVERN SPUR which goes as far B.11.b.7.8. The HUDSON Line branches off the ARLEUX Main Line at B.5.c.8.0. and passes through B.5.c.7.6 - B.29.central to B.23.b.7.8. SEVERN SPUR is a push line only, also that part of the HUDSON Line north of ANTELOPE ALLEY. The line passing through B.15.d.1.0. connects TUNNEL DUMP B.15.c.3.2. to CRUCIFIX JUNCTION at B.16.c.0.1. on main ARLEUX Line.

   RAILWAY PASSENGER SERVICE.

   ECOIVRES. Dept. 8 a.m.   6.45 p.m.
   ROCLINCOURT. arr. 9.30 a.m. 7.10 p.m.

   ROCLINCOURT. Dep. 10. a.m.   8.30 p.m.
   ECOIVRES.   arr. 11.30 a.m. 10.0 p.m.

   ROCLINCOURT   dep. 9.30 a.m.
   DAYLIGHT RAILHEAD   arr. 9.50 a.m.

4. **WATER:** Divisional Water Service Officer :-
   2/Lieut. R.J. FOSTER, 2/5th West Yorks Rgt.
   A list of horse troughs, water cart and bottle filling points is given below

   PIPE LINES. A 4 pipe line runs from ANZIN to ECURIE and thence on through B.14.c. to CRUCIFIX CORNER. From here a 2" pipe runs to SUGAR FACTORY.
   Branch Pipes run from SUGAR FACTORY to S.P. at B.15.b.6.7.. and B.16.a.2.9., also to two-100 gallon Tanks at B.9.95.00

   WATER POINTS IN DIVISIONAL AREA.

   F.13.c.2.9.   Bottle Filler.   A.14.b.7.4.   2 Horse Troughs
   F.13.a.5.1.   3 Horse Troughs.   Bottle Filler.
   F.14.a.1.1.   4 Stand Pipes.   A.20.d.4.7.   2 Stand Pipes.
                  Bottle Filler.   Bottle Filler.
   F.14.central. Bottle Filler.   A.21.c.9.1.   Bottle Filler.
   F.14.a.1.2.   3 Horse Troughs.   A.22.c.7.4.   Bottle Filler.
   F.29.a.3.6.   1 Stand Pipe.   A.28.a.0.0.   1 Horse Trough
                  Bottle Filler.   Bottle Filler.
   A.13.b.5.   1 Horse Trough.   A.20.b.3.2.   Bottle Filler.
                  4 Stand Pipes.   A.29.b.0.6.   1 Horse Trough.
                  Bottle Filler.   2 Stand Pipes.
                                                    Bottle Filler.
                  B.14.d.1.0.   Bottle Filler.
                  B.15.c.5.2.   Bottle Filler.
                  B.19.a.2.5.   Bottle Filler.
                  B.19.b.7.5.   Bottle Filler.
                  B.19.b.7.8.   Bottle Filler.
                  B.10.c.0.0.   Bottle Filler.

Sheet 4.

5. **AMMUNITION.** Ammunition Railhead - MAROEUIL.

Main Ammunition Refilling Point (Gun & Howitzer) is at G.9.central.
Ammunition is delivered to the A.R.P. by Light Railway and sent up to Battery Positions either by Light Railway or in horse drawn vehicles, according to the location of the Batteries.

GRENADES & S.A.A.
The Main Divisional S.A.A. and Grenade Dump is at A.29.b.3.8.
O.i/c Lt. F.KENSETT Div'l Ammn. Column.
BRIGADE DUMPS have been established at
Left Brigade Dumps:- T.23.d.0.3. & T.28.c.4.9.
Right Brigade Dump:- B.10.d.9.7.

6. **R.E. MATERIAL.** The Main Divisional Dump is at CHELSEA DUMP, ROCLINCOURT A.29.c.0.2., and is supplied by Light Railway from XIII Corps Dump at MAROEUIL. Stores from this dump can only be drawn on production of authority signed by Adjutant R.E.

ADVANCED R.E. DUMPS.
Left Brigade Sector. T.23.d.8.1. & T.20.c.3.6.
Right Brigade Sector. B.11.a.3.3.
These Dumps are kept supplied by Light Railway.
From Advanced Dumps Stores can be drawn on authority signed by an R.E. Officer, or Brigade Staff Captain.

7. **SUPPLIES.** Supply Railhead - ECURIE STATION. A.20.central.
Refilling Points are on the SOUCHEZ-ARRAS Road.
Div.Troops. A.20.central.
92nd Bde. Group. A.26.d.5.5.
93rd Bde. Group. A.20.d.4.6.
94th Bde. Group. A.20.b.4.1.
FUEL Divisional Coal Dump is at ROCLINCOURT A.29.d.0.3..
Coal is delivered there from Artillery Corner by Light Railway.
Wood, coke and charcoal are drawn from the dump at A.20.central.
From each dump units draw with First Line Transport.

8. **BATHS.** Baths are established as follows :-
   (a) ECURIE. Capacity 72 men per hour. All men using these Baths have their service dress disinfected. Application for use of these Baths is made to 62nd Divl Baths Officer.
   (b) TUNNEL DUMP Capacity.25-30 per hour (B.15.c.4.0)
   (c) NEUVILLE ST VAAST Controlled by 11th Canadian Inf. Bde. Application to be made for use of Baths to 11th Canadian Inf. Bde. rear H.Q. FORT GEORGE

9. **GUM BOOT STORES.** The Gum Boot Store is established at ROCLINCOURT. A.29.c.9.2. Gum Boots will be dried and repaired there. Other Stores are established as follows :-

   Left Brigade. Junction of HUDSON & BRANDON Trenches.
   Right Brigade. LONG WOOD-B.9.c.0.0.
   Units draw from the Divisional Store, by Light Railway, if possible, and take to Bde or Battalion Stores, where issues are made.

10. **GASSED CLOTHING STORES.** A Gassed Clothing Store is established for the Right Brigade at TUNNEL DUMP B.15.c.5.2. at which 100 complete sets of Service Dress and underclothing are kept. N.C.O. i/c issues on demand signed by O.C. Units concerned to men whose clothing has become tainted from contact with Yellow cross gas.

Sheet 5.
No 10.
(contd)

A Gassed Clothing Store is under construction for the Left Brigade at T.23.a.4.1. where, on completion, clothing will be issued under the same conditions as above.

A further store of 1000 sets S.D.Clothing is kept at the Divisional Underclothing Store, ROCLINCOURT. A.29.c.6.4. to replace tainted clothing.

Tainted clothing is treated at the Corps Gassed Clothing disinfecting plant at ECURIE Distillery. A.28.a.4.4.

Each Battery R.F.A., in addition to the above keeps a store of 50 sets complete change at the Battery position, for the same purpose.

11. CLOTHING FOR PATROLS.

50 complete changes of clothing are kept at the store at TUNNEL DUMP, which can be drawn on production of C.Os certificate, by men of Right Brigade who have been out on patrol and got wet through. T.25.d.8.3.

50 complete changes of clothing are also kept at T.25.d.8.3. for use of patrols of Left Brigade under arrangements of Left Brigade.

12. SALVAGE.

The Main Divisional Salvage Dump is established at ECURIE, A.27.b.3.8. Headquarters of Divisional Salvage Coy. and 62nd Divisional Salvage Officer, Lieut. S.Smith, are accommodated here.

Stores are returned direct to the Dump, and Salvage Officer arranges disposal.

13. DRYING ROOM

A drying room is established at the Divisional Salvage Dump. Units will apply to the Divisional Salvage Officer for its use.

14. ORDNANCE.

D.A.D.O.S. office and stores are on the ARRAS-SOUCHEZ Road at A.26.b.6.7.

15. MEDICAL ARRANGE- MENTS.

The following are the Medical Arrangements which will be taken over from the 31st Division :-

Field Ambulance Headquarters. at ROCLINCOURT (Main Dress.St
                                                         at ANZIN.
                                                         at MONT ST.ELOI.

Medical Posts in Forward Area
  RIGHT SECTOR
    Regimental Aid Post. B.12.a.4.5. (TOMMY ALLEY)
    Relay Posts.   B.11.d.8.8.
                             B.16.b.4.4.

    Advanced Dressing St. B.15.c.5.1. (TUNNEL DUMP)
    Advanced Dressing St. B.10.b.6.0. (under construction)

Two methods of evacuation.
(i) From R.A.P. in TOMMY ALLEY by hand carriage via Relay Posts B.11.d.8.8. and B.16.b.4.4. in TOMMY ALLEY to A.D.S. at TUNNEL DUMP.

(ii) From R.A.P. in TOMMY ALLEY by hand carriage via MACHINE GUN TRENCH on to ARLEUX - EN - GOHELLE - SUGAR FACTORY Road and thence along road to A.D.S. at B.10.b.6.0.

  LEFT SECTOR.
    Regimental Aid Post. T.29.b.5.8.
    Relay Post.   T.23.b.6.0.
    Advanced Dressing Station A.6.b.9.7. (VANCOUVER ROAD)

Evacuation by hand carriage via HUDSON TRENCH to VANCOUVER Road at T.28.a.5.1. thence by wheeled stretcher along VANCOUVER Road to A.D.S. There is also a Bearer Post at T.29.d.1.8. for the collection of local casualties Evacuation from this point is cross the open to the A.D.S. in VANCOUVER ROAD.

Sheet 6.

Main Dressing Station - ROCLINCOURT.

Cases are cleared from these Advanced Dressing Stations to the M.D.S. as follows :-

(a) By Night   A.D.S. - VANCOUVER Road   By Motor Ambulance Cars and Light Railway.
               A.D.S. - B.10.b.6.0.
               A.D.S. - TUNNEL DUMP.   By Light Railway.

(b) By Day.   A.D.S. - VANCOUVER Road.   By hand stretcher to Commandant's House and thence by motor ambulance car.
               A.D.S. - B.10.b.6.0.
               A.D.S. - TUNNEL DUMP.   By hand carriage via OUSE ALLEY to DAYLIGHT RAILHEAD & thence by motor amb. car or Light Railway.

16. VETERINARY. The 52nd Mobile Veterinary Section is situated at A.30.b.3.2.

17. PROVOST ARRANGEMENTS.
Traffic Control Posts are established in the Divisional Area as follows :-
1. ECURIE X ROADS.   A.28.a.5.3.
2. ROCLINCOURT X ROADS.   A.29.c.5.5.
3. MADAGASCAR X ROADS.   A.26.d.8.2.
4. CONCRETE Rd (Duck Board Patrol) A.29.b.4.5.
5. ZEHNER WEG.   B.19.b.6.1.
6. OUSE ALLEY.   B.19.b.2.5.

Battle Straggler Posts.
1. CONCRETE ROAD.   B.19.d.5.8.
2. ZEHNER WEG.   B.19.b.6.1.
3. OUSE ALLEY.   B.19.b.2.5.
4. COMMANDANT'S HOUSE.   B.7.d.6.2.

A.P.M.   Adv. H.Q.   )
Stragglers Collecting   ) B.19.central.
Stn.
P. of W. Pound.   A.28.a.7.2.

18. CANTEENS. Divisional Canteens are established at ECURIE (A.27.b.cen.) ECURIE RAILHEAD, MONT ST.ELOI.(F.8.d.4.2) Div. Cinema (near MADAGASCAR X ROADS), ROCLINCOURT (A.28.d.7.8.) Bottom of RIDGE TRACK (A.29.a.3.2.), DAYLIGHT RAILHEAD (B.19.b.7.0.)

19. SOUP KITCHENS. A soup kitchen is established at TUNNEL DUMP, B.15.a.5.1.

20. SOLDER INCINERATORS. Solder incinerators are established at the undermentioned places. Bully beef tins, M. & V. tins are sent to these incinerators.

INCINERATOR.	IN CHARGE OF.
A.29.a.3.4.	Area Comdt. NINE ELMS.
A.14.c.9.2.	" " BRUINEHAUT.
A.27.b.7.6.	" " ECURIE.
B.19.a.0.6.	" " BAILLEUL.
F.20.a.8.7.	" " BRAY.
F.14.a.0.5.	Town Major ECOIVRES.

Sheet 7.

21.	RECREATION ROOMS ETC.	The Divisional Recreation Room is established close to the Baths at ECURIE, and the Divisional Theatre at the same place. The Divisional Cinema Hall is near MADAGASCAR Cross Roads. A.27.c.5.7.

Divisional Recreation & Reading Room ECURIE.A.27.b.co
Church Army Hut at ECURIE Cross Roads.A.28.a.5.3.
Y.M.C.A.Hut at ECURIE WOOD. A.27.c.6.8.
Officers' Club.- close to ECURIE CROSS ROADS. A.28.a.
Haircutting. Officers' Hair Cutting Saloon is established close to the Baths at ECURIE.

22. A Location Table of 31st Division is attached for information.

23. BILLETS & CAMPS. Clearance Certificates will be obtained from incoming units or from Area Commandants, in all cases.

[signature]

Lieut-Colonel,
24/2/18.   A.A. & Q.M.G., 62nd (West Riding) Division.

DISTRIBUTION

Copy No.

1. A.D.C. for G.O.C.
2. G.
3-5. Q.
6. 62nd Divl Artillery.
7. 62nd Divl Engineers.
8. 185th Infantry Bde.
9. 186th Infantry Bde.
10. 187th Infantry Bde.
11. 9th Durham L.I.
12. A.D.M.S.62nd (W.R)Divn.
13. Signal Coy.
14. 62nd Divisional Train.
15. 201st Machine Gun Coy.
16. XII Corps Q.
17. 31st Division Q.
18. Camp Commandant.
19. D.M.G.O.
20. A.P.M., 62nd (W.R) Divn.
21. D.A.D.O.S.62nd (W.R) Div.
22. D.A.D.V.S.62nd (W.R) Div.
23. Divl Baths Officer.

SECRET.   12.2.18.
           LOCATION OF UNITS 31st DIVISION.   Map refs.
           ---------------------------   51B, 51C, 36C.

Divisional Headquarters.   A.29.a.3.4.
S.S.O.   A.20.b.3.4.
D.A.D.O.S.   ECURIE.
A.P.M.   A.28.a.6.3.
D.A.D.V.S.   A.29.a.3.4.
Div. Burial Officer.   A.24.c.4.4.
Div. Water Service Officer.   A.26.b.6.4.
Div. Gas School.   A.20.d.4.0.

Div. Arty. Headquarters.   A.29.a.3.4.
165th Bde. R.F.A.   B.14.d.4.4.   Wagon Lines A.26.c.
170th   do   B.8.a.3.0.   "   "   A.26.d.
D.A.C. Headquarters.   G.1.d.6.5.
S.A.A. Section.   G.2.a.2.2.
H.Q. R.E.   A.29.a.1.2.
210th Field Coy. R.E.   A.27.a.8.9.
211th   do   A.27.a.7.5.
223rd   do   A.27.a.8.3.
Div. Signal Coy.   A.29.a.3.4.

4th Guards Bde. H.Q.   B.20.a.3.7.
4th Grenadier Guards   Transport   ECURIE WOOD.
3rd Coldstream Guards. Lines   B.10.a.6.4.   SUPPORT.
2nd Irish Guards   A.27.c.&.d.   B.11.b.9.9.   LINE.
94th M.G. Coy.   B.4.c.6.5.
4th Guards T.M.B.   F.8.c.8.2.

92nd Inf. Bde. H.Q.   B.14.a.65.30.
10th E. Yorks R.   Transport   T.28.a.5.2. SUPPORT.
11th   do   Lines   SPRINGVALE CAMP.   RESERVE.A.28.c.5.2.
11th E. Lancs. R.   A.27.c.   T.23.d.85.50 LINE.
92nd M.G. Coy.   T.28.c.3.4.
92nd T.M. Bty.   T.24.c.70.35.

93rd Inf. Bde. H.Q.   WHITE HOUSE, MONT ST. ELOY.
15th W. Yorks R.   Transport   LANCASTER CAMP. F.8.c.7.6.
13th York & Lancs. R.   Lines (VILLAGE CAMP,   F.13.b.2.4.
                        A.27.c. (YORK CAMP,   F.13.b.3.6.
                                  BRAY CAMP,   F.20.b.0.6.
18th Durham L.I.   ROBERTS CAMP. A.27.b.6.9.
93rd M.G. Coy.   DURHAM CAMP.   F.8.c.
93rd T.M. Bty.

243rd M.G. Coy.   ROBERTS CAMP.   A.27.b.6.9.
Pioneer Bn. (12th K.O.Y.L.I.) H.Q.   FLANDERS CAMP. A.27.b.1.7.

Div. Train H.Q.   A.20.b.3.4.
No.1 Coy.   do   A.20.b.3.4.
No.2 Coy.   do   A.14.c.9.9.
No.3 Coy.   do   A.20.a.7.9.
No.4 Coy.   do   A.14.c.7.8.
No.31 Supply Column.   ACQ.

A.D.M.S.   A.29.a.3.4.
93rd Field Ambulance.   DURHAM CAMP.   F.8.c.
94th   do   ROCLINCOURT.
95th   do   ANZIN.

31st Div. Salvage Coy.   A.27.b.7.7.
41st Mob. Vet. Section.   A.20.b.3.2.
228th Employment Coy.   Billet 56, MONT ST. ELOY.

CONFIDENTIAL.

WAR DIARY

OF

ADMINISTRATIVE AND QUARTERMASTER GENERAL'S BRANCH, 62nd (W.R) DIVISION.

FROM 1st MARCH 1918.   TO 31st MARCH 1918.

(VOLUME 15)

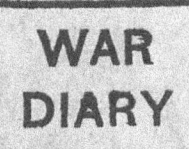

A. & Q.

62nd (West Riding) DIVISION

MARCH 1918

Appendices attached :-

    Casualties.
    Reinforcements.
    Rewards

SECRET

62nd Division "A"

WAR DIARY or INTELLIGENCE SUMMARY

Army Form C. 2118.

March 1918 P.1

Place	Date	Hour	Summary of Events and Information	Remarks and references to Appendices
VILLERS Chatel	March 1st		187th Inf. Bde relieved 4th Guards Bde 31st Div'n in Right Section Left Div'l Front XIII Corps	A/1
do	2nd		186th Inf Bde moved from CHELERS Area to Reserve Bde Area (ETOUARS) Left Division XIII Corps	B/1
do	3rd		186th Inf Bde relieved 92nd Inf Bde in Left Section, Left Divisional Front. XIII Corps	C/1
ROCLINCOURT	4th		185th Inf Bde moved from MONCHY BRETON Area to Reserve Bde Area ECOIVRES. Divl HQ's opened at ROCLINCOURT at 11 a.m. at which hour GOC 62nd Division assumed Command of Left Sector XIII Corps front	D/1
do	5th		Nothing to Record	E/1
do	6th		do. Weather Fine	F/1
do	7th		do Weather Dull. Some Rain.	G/1

Army Form C. 2118.

WAR DIARY
or
INTELLIGENCE SUMMARY.
(Erase heading not required.)

March 1918 p. 2.

Instructions regarding War Diaries and Intelligence Summaries are contained in F.S. Regs., Part II. and the Staff Manual respectively. Title pages will be prepared in manuscript.

Place	Date	Hour	Summary of Events and Information	Remarks and references to Appendices
ROEUX COURT	8th		Nothing to Record	A
do	9th		do	A
do	10th		do	A
do	11th		do	A
do	12th		XIII Corps warn us that attack by Enemy in ARRAS area might be expected at Early date. G's gave orders that from 6 p.m. Division to maintain a state of immediate Readiness and will stand to at 5 a.m. on 13th Inst. — Instructions re Traffic Control issued to MPM. in case attack materialises. — During Night ROEUX COURT and Divl HQs shelled. 185 Inf Bde relieved 187 Inf Bde in Right Bde Section —	A
	13th		Division stood down at 8 a.m. Reserve Bde placed under 1 hours notice —	A

T2134. Wt. W708—776. 500000. 4/15. Sir J. C. & S.

Army Form C. 2118.

WAR DIARY
or
INTELLIGENCE SUMMARY.   March 1918   p. 3
(Erase heading not required.)

Instructions regarding War Diaries and Intelligence Summaries are contained in F. S. Regs., Part II. and the Staff Manual respectively. Title pages will be prepared in manuscript.

Place	Date	Hour	Summary of Events and Information	Remarks and references to Appendices
ROCLINCOURT	14th		Nothing to Record	
do	15th		do	
do	16th		do	
do	17th		186th Inf.Bde carried out Raid on Enemy Trench N.of FRESNOY.	
do	18th		Nothing to Record.	
do	19th		Orders issued for 31st Bn to relieve 62nd Division in Left Sector and for latter to sideslip and take over Right Sector from 56th Division	
do	20th		Administrative Instructions issued re above. Capt J. SAUNDERS M.C. arrived from 43rd Division to take over duties DAAG vice Major A.F. NATION apptd DAAG	
			Till Corps	
do	21st		Relief Orders cancelled – Warning Rec'd that Division will be relieved by 3rd Canadian Division by night 22/24 March	
do	22nd		Orders rec'd and cancelled for Division to concentrate in MONCHY BRETON Area	
do	23rd		On Relief by 3rd Canadian Division, 62nd (W.R.) Division Brigades disposed as follows – 186 Inf.Bde at BOIS des MLEUX (Can.Corps Area), 187 Inf.Bde at ECOIVRES and 185 Inf.Bde at ROCLINCOURT.	

WAR DIARY or INTELLIGENCE SUMMARY

Army Form C. 2118.

March 1918 p. 4.

Place	Date	Hour	Summary of Events and Information	Remarks and references to Appendices
ROLLINCOURT	23rd		Orders rec'd for Division to be transferred to XVII Corps 3rd Army. Brigade to Brigade as it comes out of the line — 127th Inf Bde thereon moved to ARRAS 3rd Canadian Division completed Relief of 62nd Division by Midnight 23/24 pm	
WARLUS	24th		185th Inf Bde moved to DAINVILLE and BERNEVILLE. 186th Inf Bde moved to "Y" Huts near AGNEZ les DUISANS. 187th Inf Bde (at ARRAS) placed at disposal of 13th Division. 3 Field Coys R.E. and Pioneer Bn moved to General RONVILLE St SAUVEUR. Divl HQ's to WARLUS —	
	25th	12.15 AM	Orders Received that Division (less 187th Inf Bde) would move at once to ARCT TE where orders would be received — DHQ's accompanied by G.S.O.3 was sent on at once to IV Corps HQ's MAILLY MAILLET instructions — which were for Division to concentrate around BUCQUOY and receive further orders there from. HQ's 40th Division — Areas allotted at BUCQUOY for 3 Bdes, Divl Artillery and RE's — Division moved to MEZTE concerning 3 AM. Surplus Kit etc being dumped under guard in BILLETS	

Army Form C. 2118.

WAR DIARY
or
INTELLIGENCE SUMMARY.   March 1918. P.5.
(Erase heading not required.)

Place	Date	Hour	Summary of Events and Information	Remarks and references to Appendices
	25th	10.0am	Leading Troops of Division (185th Inf.Bde.) began to arrive in BUCQUOY — Followed by 186 Inf.Bde and R.E. Field Coys — All Roads blocked by all kinds of Transport — much delaying progress of Troops.	R
		3pm	185 and 186 Inf. Bdes moved to positions E. of ACHIET LE PETIT — dumping packs etc on Road E. of BUCQUOY — Echelon B "1st" Line Transport and Train Wagons moved to HANNESCAMPS — Lorries with Blankets were sent on some Cases to LANZERVILLERS. —	R R
		7pm	Div. HQ's took over 41st Div. HQ's at BUCQUOY	
		10pm	187th Inf. Bde. began to arrive and came into Div. Reserve at BUCQUOY — Packs were dumped to WEST of BUCQUOY. Transport etc. moved to HANNESCAMPS. Div. Headquarters moved to GOMIECOURT and thence to BONQUEVILLERS.	R R
	26th		Wagon Lines of Infantry Units moved as follows to HANNESCAMPS — POMMIERS Road 185 Inf.Bde. E.g. BIENVILLERS, 186 Inf.Bde W. of HANNESCAMPS, 187 Inf.Bde Ed. POMMIERS — M.G.B." W. of HANNESCAMPS Train Corp to POMMIERS — Field hsp remained at BONQUEVILLERS	R

Army Form C. 2118.

WAR DIARY
or
INTELLIGENCE SUMMARY.
(Erase heading not required.)

March 1918 p. 6.

Place	Date	Hour	Summary of Events and Information	Remarks and references to Appendices
FONQUEVILLERS	26th	7pm	4th Australian Brigade arrived and came under Orders of G.O.C. 62nd Division. Any moved to HEBUTERNE. Estimated Casualties since 23/24 March 8th W. Yorks. 5 Officers and 50 O.R. 2/5 W. Ridings 2 Officers and 50 O Ranks	
do	27th		Heavy fighting on Divisional front. New 2nd MND Division arrived and took over to Right of Divisional front. Large elements of Bards which were sent up infantry to BOMMECOURT. 10th and 13th M.G. coys arrived from GHQ School CAMIERS in lorries with approx. 500,000 Rds S.A.A. and came under orders of 62nd Division 62nd D.A.C. moved to camp on SOUASTRE Road. Estimated casualties since 23/24 March 8th W.Yks. 8 Officers and 100 O.R. 2/5 W.Yks. 2 Officers and 50 O.R. 2/7th 2/7 K W.Yks. 2 Officers and 50 O.R. M.G. 13th 10pn and 20 O.R.	
SOUASTRE	28th	7am	Divisional HQrs moved to SOUASTRE — Adv.HQ. Div. Caly. — A&Q Offices located in School. G Office in Small Chateau. Some difficulty experienced with Ammunition Supply. Heavy attacks made on Divisional front during day. —	

Army Form C. 2118.

WAR DIARY
or
INTELLIGENCE SUMMARY.
(Erase heading not required.)

March 1918 p. 7

Place	Date	Hour	Summary of Events and Information	Remarks and references to Appendices
SOUASTRE	28th		Estimated Casualties from 27/28 March	
			2/7th W.Yks. 6 Offrs and 180 o.ranks 5th KOYLI 20 Offrs and 90 o.ranks	
			5th D of W 3 — and 170 — 2/4th York' 6 Offrs and 300 o.ranks	
			2/4 do — — — 50 — 2/4 C.Yks 8 Offrs and 140 o.ranks	JM
			9th D.L.I. 50 o.ranks	
SOUASTRE	29th		Further attacks on Divisional Front — Counter attacks by 4th Aust. Rifles and 187 Brigade on ROSSIGNOL Wood — 155 Infantry Bde relieved by 42nd Division and wounded Support Trenches. Shipe received for Bands owing to Bombing attacks by both sides on Rossignol Wood. Demands met but with some difficulty — If Division had not moved from XIII Corps not full Echelon Ammunition situation would have been at times critical.	
			Estimated Casualties from 28/29 March	
			2/4 D of W 20 Offrs and 100 o.ranks 2/7 W.Riding 100 o.ranks	JM
			5th KOYLI 13 Offrs and 300 o.ranks	
SOUASTRE	30th		A Comparatively quiet day — Orders received for relief of 62nd Division by 37th Division.	JM
			Estimated Casualties M.G.Bn: 4 Officers and 60 o.ranks.	JM

Army Form C. 2118.

WAR DIARY
or
INTELLIGENCE SUMMARY.
(Erase heading not required.)

March 1918 p. 8.

Instructions regarding War Diaries and Intelligence Summaries are contained in F.S. Regs., Part II. and the Staff Manual respectively. Title pages will be prepared in manuscript.

Place	Date	Hour	Summary of Events and Information	Remarks and references to Appendices.
SOUASTRE	31st		A Quiet Day. 186 Infantry relieved by a Brigade of 37th Division and moved to PAS and HENU. Some confusion as to Areas occasioned by the fact that 31st Division also attempted to billet a Brigade in PAS, which up to the evening had been in Corps Area. This Brigade was eventually sent elsewhere — Estimated Casualties 2/4th Royl. 9 Officers and 350 O.Ranks.	
			F.G.C.M. during month 10	

Appendices:-
 'A' - Casualties during March 18.
 'B' - Reinforcements recd   "   "
 'C' - Rewards conferred   "   "

22/4/18

Arthur Solly-Flood
Major-General
Commanding 62nd (West Riding) Division

APPENDIX A

CASUALTIES DURING MARCH 1918.

OFFICERS.

Date.	Rank & Name.	Unit.	Nature of Casualty.
7.3.18.	2/Lt. C.H.CROFT.	5th K.O.Y.L.I. (attd from K.O.R.Lanc.Regt).	wounded.
9.3.18.	2/Lt. F.KIRK.	2/4th West Riding Regt.	wounded.
11.3.18.	A/Capt.J.H.IRONS.	2/4th West Riding Regt.	wounded.
11.3.18.	2/Lt. B.SHELDON.	2/4th West Riding Regt. (attd from W.Yks Rgt)	wounded.
17.3.18.	Capt. C.B.STEAD.	8th West Yorks Regt.	wounded.
17.3.18.	2/Lt. J.F.BLAKEY.	9th Bn D.L.I.	wounded.
17.3.18.	2/Lt. C.J.EASTON	62nd Bn M.G.C.	wounded.
18.3.18.	Lt. J.R.SYMONS.	8th West Yorks Regt.	wounded.
18.3.18.	2/Lt. A.NAYLOR.	8th West Yorks Regt.	wounded.
18.3.18.	2/Lt. C. .ALLEN	8th West Yorks Regt.	wounded.
18.3.18.	2/Lt. R.C. ICKE	8th West Yorks Regt.	wounded.
21.3.18.	2/Lt. H.G.GOLDSMITH.	310 Bde R.F.A.	wounded.
21.3.18.	2/Lt. L.W.NOTT.	461 Field Coy. R.E.	wounded.
20.3.18.	2/Lt. S.L.PERRY.	8th West Yorks Rgt.	wounded (gas)
29.3.18.	Bt.Major F.W.L.BISSETT,M.C., D.of Corn.L.I. G.S.O.2. 62nd Div.		wounded.
26.3.18.	A/Lt-Col.A.M.JAMES,D.S.O. N.Fus. 8th West Yks Rgt.		killed.
26.3.18.	Capt. E.MURGATROYD. D.C.M. 8th West Yorks Rgt.		killed.
26.3.18.	Lieut. H.EVANS.	8th West Yorks Regt.	killed.
26.3.18.	Lieut. J.H.NUSSEY.	8th West Yorks Regt.	wounded.
26.3.18.	2/Lt. W.H.HARTLEY.	8th West Yorks Regt.	wounded.
26.3.18.	2/Lt. C.J.PRIESTLEY.	8th West Yorks Regt.	wounded.
26.3.18.	2/Lt. C.WAITE,	8th West Yorks Regt.	wounded.
26.3.18.	2/Lt. W.D.CATTERMOLE.	8th West Yorks Regt.	wounded.
28.3.18.	Capt. J.D.BALLANTYNE.	8th West Yorks Regt.	wounded.
29.3.18.	Capt. B.HUTCHINSON.	8th West Yorks Regt.	wounded.
29.3.18.	2/Lt. H.SOWDEN.	8th West Yorks Regt.	wounded.
31.3.18.	Capt. W.G.KEMP, M.C.	8th West Yorks Regt.	wounded.
26.3.18.	2nd Lt. J.L.PERCIVAL	8th West Yorks Regt.	wounded at duty.
27.3.18.	2nd Lt. F.W.POTTER.	2/7th West Yorks Regt.	wounded.
28.3.18.	Lieut. W.H.C.JEFFCOCK.	2/7th West Yorks Regt.	wounded.
28.3.18.	2/Lt. J.G.HEWITT.	2/7th West Yorks Regt.	wounded.
28.3.18.	2/Lt. T.F.GALPINE.	2/7th West Yorks Regt.	wounded.
28.3.18.	2/Lt. A.E.TARGETT.	2/7th West Yorks Regt.	wounded.
28.3.18.	Capt. B.H.PICKERING.	2/7th West Yorks Regt.	W. at duty.
27.3.18.	2/Lt. J.A.WEBDALE.	8th West Yorks Rgt.	W. at duty.
		185th T.M.B.	
28.3.18.	2/Lt. P.MOSLEY.	5th West Riding Regt.	Killed.
29.3.18.	2/Lt. J.SUGDEN.	5th West Riding Regt.	Killed.
28.3.18.	2/Lt. N.H.WEIGHILL, 1st W.Yks. 5th West Rid.Rgt.		wounded.
28.3.18.	Lieut. B.MOLLETT.M.C.	5th West Riding Regt.	wounded.
27.3.18.	Capt. H.O.BROWNING.M.C.	5th West Riding Regt.	wounded.
29.3.18.	Capt. G.L.TINKER.	5th West Riding Regt.	wounded.
29.3.18.	Capt. T.GOODALL.D.S.O. M.C. 5th West Riding Regt.		wounded.
26.3.18.	A/Lt-Col. J.WALKER.	5th West Riding Regt.	W. at duty.
28.3.18.	A/Major F.BROOK. K.O.Y.L.I., 5th West Riding Regt.		W. at duty.
29.3.18.	2nd Lieut F.CHAPMAN.	5th West Riding Regt.	W. at duty.
28.3.18.	Lieut J.W.SHERRICK.	U.S.M.C.attd 5th W.Rid Rgt.	wounded.
29.3.18.	2nd Lieut A.CAWTHRA.	5th West Riding Rgt.	Missing.
30.3.18.	2/Lt. L.MARTINDALE.	2/4th West Riding Regt.	Killed.
26.3.18.	Capt J.GROVES.	2/4th West Riding Regt.	wounded.
27.3.18.	2/Lt T.LAWSON.	2/7th West Riding Regt.	wounded.
27.3.18.	Capt F.H.THREAPPLETON.	2/4th W.Rid. 186 T.M.B.	W. at duty.
28.3.18.	Lieut R.M.SKELSEY.	2/4th W.Rid. 186 T.M.B.	Missing.
26.3.18.	2/Lt. F.J.B.DIXON.	62nd Bn M.G.C.	Wounded.
27.3.18.	2/Lt. J.McFARLANE.	62nd Bn M.G.C.	wounded.
28.3.18.	2/Lt. W.H.BAILIE.	62nd Bn M.G.C.	wounded.
28.3.18.	2/Lt. H.A.WATERHOUSE.	62nd Bn M.G.C.	wounded.
28.3.18.	2/Lt. L.C.GANE.	310th Bde R.F.A.	wounded.
28.3.18.	Lieut C.V.MONTGOMERY.	312th Bde R.F.A.	wounded.
28.3.18.	A/Lt-Col. C.C.S.WATSON. D.S.O., Mid Yeom.5thKOYLI.		killed.
28.3.18.	T/2nd Lieut G.C.M.GREEN. Wst Yks R. 5th K.O.Y.L.I.		killed.
28.3.18.	2/Lt F.C.LAMBERT.	5th K.O.Y.L.I.	killed.
28.3.18.	Lieut. E.H.FRANK.	5th K.O.Y.L.I.	wounded.

Date	Name	Unit	Status
28.3.18.	Capt. B.A.BEACH.	5th K.O.Y.L.I.	missing.
28.3.18.	Capt. A.D.THOMSON.A.S.C.	5th K.O.Y.L.I.	missing.
28.3.18.	Capt. E.ROBERTS.	5th K.O.Y.L.I.	missing.
28.3.18.	Lieut. R.CRIGG.	5th K.O.Y.L.I.	missing.
28.3.18.	T/2nd.Lieut.R.APPLETON.	Wst Yks Rgt.	missing.
28.3.18.	T/2nd.Lieut.T.WELDON.	Wst Yks Rgt. 5th K.O.Y.L.I.	missing.
28.3.18.	T/2nd.Lieut.W.C.IBBOTT.M.C.	5th K.O.Y.L.I.	missing.
28.3.18.	T/2nd.Lieut.B.P.JENKINSON.	5th K.O.Y.L.I.	missing.
28.3.18.	T/2nd.Lieut.M.HAMER.	Wst Yks Rgt. 5th K.O.Y.L.I.	missing.
28.3.18.	T/2nd.Lieut.H.G.NORTHEY.	5th K.O.Y.L.I.	missing.
28.3.18.	T/Lt. H.A.SMITHEN.	5th K.O.Y.L.I.	killed.
27.3.18.	T/2nd.Lieut.F.DRAKE.	Wst Yks Rgt. 2/4th KOYLI	killed.
27.3.18.	T/2nd.Lieut.J.RAINFORD.Wst Yks Rgt.2/4 KOYLI.		wounded.
27.3.18.	T/2nd.Lieut.J.W.PARR.	2/4th K.O.Y.L.I.	wounded.
27.3.18.	Capt. A.E.PILLEY.	2/4th K.O.Y.L.I.	missing.
27.3.18.	Capt. G.L.HUDSON.	2/4th K.O.Y.L.I.	missing.
27.3.18.	2nd Lieut.D.O.C.MAGGS.	2/4th K.O.Y.L.I.	missing.
27.3.18.	2nd Lieut.H.W.SPINK.	2/4th K.O.Y.L.I.	missing.
28.3.18.	T/2nd.Lieut.W.W.POWNALL.	W.Yks Rgt. 2/4 KOYLI.	missing.
27.3.18.	T/2nd.Lieut.N.ROGERSON.	W.Yks Rgt. 2/4th York & Lanc.	wounded.
27.3.18.	Lt-Col.F.St.J.BLACKER.D.S.O.	2/4th York & Lanc.Rgt.	wounded.
26.3.18.	Capt H.K.WILSON.	2/4th York & Lanc.Rgt.	wounded.
26.3.18.	Capt R.C.BARNES.M.C.	2/4th York & Lanc.Rgt.	wounded.
27.3.18.	T.2nd.Lt. J.C.FERNELEY.	2/4th York & Lanc.Rgt.	wounded.
28.3.18.	T.2nd.Lt. J.R.DRAPER.	2/4th York & Lanc.Rgt.	wounded.
28.3.18.	2nd Lt. H.MITCHELL.	2/4th York & Lanc.Rgt.	wounded.
28.3.18.	2nd Lt. E.BUTTERFIELD.W.Rid.R.	2/4th Y & L.Rgt.	wounded.
28.3.18.	Lieut.P.REID.M.C.	2/4th York & Lanc.Rgt.	wounded.
28.3.18.	T.2nd Lt.J.W.THORNTON.	2/4th York & Lanc.Rgt.	killed.
28.3.18.	Lieut.W.G.WYLIE.M.C.	9th Bn D.L.I.	killed.
28.3.18.	2nd Lt.A.W.BELL.	9th Bn D.L.I.	killed.
30.3.18.	Capt.R.E.B.LISLE.	9th Bn D.L.I.	wounded.
26.3.18.	Lieut.G.F.BOLAM.	9th Bn D.L.I.	wounded.
27.3.18.	Lieut.J.FISHER.	9th Bn D.L.I.	wounded.
26 and 30.3.18.	Major.P.P.WILSON.	9th Bn D.L.I.	W.at duty.
30.3.18.	Lieut.J.G.WEIGHTMAN.	9th Bn D.L.I.	W.at duty.

OTHER RANKS.

Killed.   225.
Wounded.   1289.
Missing.   570.

APPENDIX "B"

REINFORCEMENTS - MARCH.

	Officers.	O.R.
8th West Yorkshire Regiment.	6	21
2/5th West Yorkshire Regiment.	3	66
2/7th West Yorkshire Regiment.	1	14
5th West Riding Regiment.	-	48
2/4th West Riding Regiment.	1	55
2/7th West Riding Regiment.	4	94
5th K.O.Y.L.I.	4	14
2/4th K.O.Y.L.I.	-	125
2/4th York & Lancaster Regiment.	2	73
Royal Engineers.	1	22
Royal Army Medical Corps.	-	3
Divisional Train.	2	6
Machine Gun Battalion.	2	54
9th Bn. Durham Light Infantry (Pioneers)	1	38
	27	633

APPENDIX "C"

REWARDS CONFERRED DURING MARCH 1918.

Bar to Military Medal.	1.
Military Medal.	7.

Administrative

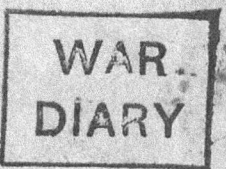

A. & Q.

62nd DIVISION

APRIL 1 9 1 8

Appendices .- Instructions.
Casualties.
Reinforcements
Rewardsz

Vol 16

CONFIDENTIAL.

WAR DIARY OF

ADMINISTRATIVE AND QUARTERMASTER GENERAL'S BRANCH, 62nd (WEST RIDING) DIVISION.

From 1st April 1918. To 30th April 1918.

(VOLUME 16).

SECRET

62nd (WEST RIDING) DIVISION

WAR DIARY or INTELLIGENCE SUMMARY.
(Erase heading not required.)

Army Form C. 2118.

APRIL 1918 page 1.

Instructions regarding War Diaries and Intelligence Summaries are contained in F.S. Regs., Part II. and the Staff Manual respectively. Title pages will be prepared in manuscript.

Place	Date	Hour	Summary of Events and Information	Remarks and references to Appendices
PAS	1st		Relief continued 162nd by 37th Division. 20ths 185 and 20ths 186 Inf. Bde. moved on Relief in line to COUIN-BIENVILLERS and SOUASTRE areas respectively in early morning. Troops in former moving by lorries — Pioneer Bn. to SOUASTRE in evening. Remaining Bns. of 185 and 186 Bde moved to BARBICOURT and HENU in evening — Divisional HQrs moved to PAS CHATEAU	Appendix A
	2nd		Divisional HQrs moved from PAS to AUTHIE in early morning by Rly — 187 Inf Bde moved from Rue to AUTHIE. Relief of 62nd by 37th Division complete about 6 a.m. In Afternoon Troops of Division concentrated in Reserve Area as under. 185 Inf Bde Troops. VINCENT and MARIEUX including Pioneer Bn. 186 do do do PAS and HENU do M.G.Bn 187 do do do AUTHIE and ST LEGER les AUTHIE. Divisional Artillery remained in Action under 37th Division — Billets generally very crowded and some Troops under Canvas.	GM
	3rd		Weather changed to wet — Divisional Army arrived from XIII Corps Renft Camp and accommodated in PAS.	GM

WAR DIARY
or
INTELLIGENCE SUMMARY.

(Erase heading not required.)

Army Form C. 2118.

April 1918. Page 2.

Place	Date	Hour	Summary of Events and Information	Remarks and references to Appendices
In the field PAS	4th		Weather showery. 2 rest men. Casualties since 24.3.18. forwarded to Corps. A. See Appendix.	Appendix B
"	5th		Weather dull. 2/4th Duke of Wellington Regt. moved to SAILLY AU BOIS in reserve owing to S.O.S. sent up on N.Z. front.	
"	6th		Weather dull, turning to rain in the evening. Division received orders to relieve 42nd Divn in the line & HENU Lineal Group 6th & 7th. Relief to be complete by 7th. See Administrative Instructions dated 6.4.18 attached. 185 Bde moved by bus from MARIEUX to SOUASTRE, commencing 7 p.m. Approx. 1 hour delay occasioned by Corps traffic preventing troops embussing at point fixed by Army. — 185 Bde moved to Purple Line relieving 4/8th of 22nd DIVISION there.	Appendix C
HENU	7th		Weather fine — moving turning to rain in afternoon. 62nd Division took over line from 42nd Divn and units were distributed as follows: HENU — 185th I.B. line right Sector — 185th I.B. line left Divisional Hd. Quarters at HENU	

WAR DIARY or INTELLIGENCE SUMMARY

April 1918. Army Form C. 2118.
Page 3.

Place	Date	Hour	Summary of Events and Information	Remarks and references to Appendices
In the field HENU	7th		Infte. Bde. – 187th Infantry Bde. La BRAYELLE FARM (reserve). – 9th D.L.I. (Pioneers) VAUCHELLES. – M.G. Bn. – H.Q. HENU. – Divl. Artillery attached 37th Division. – R.E. H.Q. HENU, Companies at SOUASTRE. All three Infantry Bdes. with our Hd. Quarters and details at SOUASTRE, the Hd. Quarters and details in billets, remainder personnel in VALLEY CAMP, SOUASTRE. Hotts VALLEY CAMP consist of 34 huts and 46 tents, the camp very cut-up and muddy. B.de. transport on standings in the open, very muddy and cut-up.	
"	8th		Steady rain all day. 1/9th D.L.I. (Pioneers) moved from VAUCHELLES to SOUASTRE.	
"	9th		Dull all day & some rain. Roads and ground very heavy	
"	10th		Dull & misty, little rain.	
"	11th		Weather dull morning turning to bright sunshine in afternoon. Conditn. of roads & ground greatly improved by weather	

Army Form C. 2118.

WAR DIARY
or
INTELLIGENCE SUMMARY.
(Erase heading not required.)

April 1918
Page 4.

Place	Date	Hour	Summary of Events and Information	Remarks and references to Appendices
In the field. HENU	12"		Very fine all day. Roads and ground considerably drier. 187 I.B. relieved 185 I.B. in the line during night of the 12/13.	
" " "	13"		Weather dull & misty, no rain. Reinforcements 62nd Div: Bing arrived also mid-day as under:-	
			Serjeant. Rank & file. Staff.	
			2/5th D. Yorks 5. — 1.	
			2/7" do 6. 12. 7.	
			8" " 3/6. 28. 9.	
			2/4 S. Ridings 6" — 3.	
			5" do 1 1 4.	
			2/7" do — 1 4.	
			2/4" N.O.Y.L.I. — 2. 1.	
			5" do 5. 43. 1	
			2/4" Y. & L. — 20. 10.	
			9" D.L.I. 1 2 1	

Continued.

Army Form C. 2118.

WAR DIARY
or
INTELLIGENCE SUMMARY.
(Erase heading not required.)

April 1918.
Page 5.

Place	Date	Hour	Summary of Events and Information	Remarks and references to Appendices
In the field	13th (Contd)		460. 2nd C. R.E. — Trained reinforcements. Untrained. Staff	Appendix D
HENU			TOTAL 338 — 109 — 1 — 40.	
			All except untrained joined their units. Untrained stood by. Appendix G	G
			R.E.	
"	14th		Weather dull, strong wind.	G
"	15th		Dull, no rain.	G
"	16th		Orders received to prepare to accommodate advanced HQ 57th Division in HENU at any time in case of necessity. Billets arranged for in the village. Weather dull + some rain.	
"	17th		Divisional rear echelon on under moved into billets in PAS. (a) Rear Divisional HQ. — D.A.D.V.S. — D.A.D.O.S and Staff — O.C. 252 Employment Coy Staff. Oil Salvage Officer & Section — D.C.O. — Entertainment Officer & Concert Party — Munition Officer + M.O.I. Vet's Section.	

WAR DIARY
or
INTELLIGENCE SUMMARY.
(Erase heading not required.)

Army Form C. 2118.

April 1918. Page 5.

Place	Date	Hour	Summary of Events and Information	Remarks and references to Appendices
In the field HENU	17th (Contd)		(b) Hd. Quarters & the Co. Divisional Train. (c) Divisional Wing. - Reinforcements not required in the line. Nucleus of Staff & Brigade Classes. (d) 2/1st (W.R.) Field Ambulance. Weather dull. Some rain.	Appendix E
"	18th		Weather dull & cold. Some rain. Roads & transport lines becoming heavy again. Details moved to PAS as ordered above	M
"	19th		Weather cold with intervals of Sun and Sleet. Personal arrangements made to establish Officers Rest House in PAS.	M
"	20th		Weather finer. - New phase Estimated Casualties commenced midnight 20th/21st April. Orders received for relief 162nd by 37th Division	M
"	21st		Weather Fine. - Preparations continued for Relief	M

WAR DIARY or INTELLIGENCE SUMMARY.

Army Form C. 2118.
April 1918 Page 6

Place	Date	Hour	Summary of Events and Information	Remarks and references to Appendices
HENU	22nd		Weather Dry Cold - Administration Instructions re Relief Issued. Attached	Appendices F
do	23rd		Weather fine - 63rd Inf Bde relieved 187 Inf Bde in Right Sector, later Relief moved by Bus from SOMBRIN to AUTHIE during night 23/24 April where they took over Camps in AUTHIE Wood.	A
AUTHIE	24th		Divisional HQ's moved to AUTHIE taking over from 37th Division at 4pm. On Night 24/25 186 and 185 Inf Bdes were relieved and moved to AUTHIE ST LEGER and LOUVENCOURT by Bus.	A
do	25th		On Relief by 37th Division - 63rd Division accommodated as follows. 185 Inf Bde Train Company and Field Coy in Gnr Billets at LOUVENCOURT 186 Inf Bde HQ's, 1 Battalion, Field Amb. in Crowded Billets at ST LEGER to AUTHIE 2 Battalion in Tents in BOIS de WARNIMONT 187 Inf Bde HQ's in AUTHIE. 3 Bn's field Coy in Tents AUTHIE Wood M.G. Bn in Tents BOIS de WARNIMONT. Pioneers Bn Tents BOIS LUCIEN	A

WAR DIARY or INTELLIGENCE SUMMARY

Army Form C. 2118.

April 1915 Page 7

Place	Date	Hour	Summary of Events and Information	Remarks and references to Appendices
AUTHIE	25th (Continued)		All Troops under Cover though crowded. Divisional HQs reconnoitred dispersed and scattered Kingshood billets. Copy attached on subject. Divisional WAY moved from PAS to AUTHIE and most of personnel despatched to Minie. Personal Instructions issued with regard to disposal of baggage & Town Wagons in event of having to clear out to make room for French Troops. Baths taken over at VAUCHELLES AUTHIE and proportion of DOUDENCOURT. Bathing commenced in all 3 Properties. Relief Completed of N.G.R.H. during night and Details moved by bus to Bois de WARNIMONT	
AUTHIE	26th		Weather Dull and colder.	
AUTHIE	27th		Weather Fine and Warm: D.A.D.O.S. moved to AUTHIE and Salvage Corps to BOIS MALEAU	

Army Form C. 2118.

WAR DIARY
or
INTELLIGENCE SUMMARY.
(Erase heading not required.)

April 1918 p. 8.

Instructions regarding War Diaries and Intelligence Summaries are contained in F. S. Regs., Part II. and the Staff Manual respectively. Title pages will be prepared in manuscript.

Place	Date	Hour	Summary of Events and Information	Remarks and references to Appendices
AUTHIE	28th		Weather dull – Combined Church Parade of 186, 187 Inf/Bdes – M.G. and Pioneer B'ns – Divl. Commander present. Troops marched past – Section 62nd M.T. Coy moved to AUTHIE, exchanging billets with 37th M.T. Coy.	
do	29th		Warmer. Rain in evening –	
do	30th		Warm. Dull. Some Rain.	
			Reinforcements received during April	Appendix H
			Rewards " " "	" J
			Casualties during April	" K
			F.G.C.M. during April 26	
			G.C.M. " " 1	

B. Saunders
Major
D.A.A.G. 62nd (West Riding) Divn.

SECRET.   Copy No......
                                 62 Div.A/6195/49.

RESERVE AREA.

1.   Owing to readjustment of Areas, those detailed
by this office No.A/6173/49 of 31.3.18 are altered.
       By 6 p.m. on 3rd April the troops of 62nd Division
will be located as under, and billetting arrangements
will be made forthwith:-

Formation.	Suggested distribution at discretion of Brigade Group Commanders.
(a) 185th Inf.Bde.Group. VAUCHELLES les AUTHIE MARIEUX. Note: Bulk of accommodation in MARIEUX is in hangars and huts.	Bde. H.Q. VAUCHELLES les AUTHIE. 1 Battn. -do- 2 Battns. MARIEUX. Fld Coy. VAUCHELLES les AUTHIE. Fld Ambce. MARIEUX. Train Co. -do- T.M.Bty. -do-
(b) 186th Inf.Bde.Group, plus MG Pioneer Bn. & Mob.Vet.Sec. PAS. HENU (less Chateau). Note: PAS has not hitherto been used as a billetting Area, and the Mayor will have to be approached with tact; stringent orders will also have to be issued to prevent damage to billets. There is, however, ample accommodation there.	Bde. H.Q. PAS. 1 Battn. PAS. MG Pioneer Bn. PAS. Fld Coy. PAS. Fld Ambce. PAS. Train Co. PAS. T.M.Bty. PAS. M.V.Sec. PAS. 2 Battns. HENU.
(c) 187th Inf.Bde.Group, plus Pioneer M.G. Battalion. AUTHIE. ST LEGER les AUTHIE. Note: Details of billets from Town Major, AUTHIE.	Bde. H.Q. AUTHIE. 2 Battns. AUTHIE. Pioneer M.G. Battn AUTHIE. Fld Coy. AUTHIE. Train Co. AUTHIE. T.M.Bty. AUTHIE. 1 Battn. ST LEGER les AUTHIE. Fld Ambce. -do-

-2-

2. Orders as to dates and times of moves will be issued later.

3. Divisional Headquarters, Headquarters R.E., and Headquarters Train will be at PAS.

Saunders
Major.
D.A.A.G. 62nd (West Riding) Division.

1.4.1918.

Distribution.

Copy No.		
1	-	A.D.C. for G.O.C.
2	-	'G'
3-5	-	'Q'.
6	-	G.O.C.R.A.
7	-	C.R.E.
8	-	185th Bde.
9	-	186th Bde.
10	-	187th Bde.
11	-	Camp Comdt.
12	-	Signals.
13	-	A.D.M.S.
14	-	O.C., Train.
15	-	A.P.M.
16	-	62nd Bn. M.G.C.
17	-	9th D.L.I.
18	-	D.A.D.V.S.
19	-	Mob. Vet. Sec.
20	-	D.A.D.O.S.
21	-	IV Corps 'Q'
22	-	IV Corps 'G'
23	-	42nd Division.
24	-	37th Division.
25	-	N.Z. Divn.

CASUALTIES 25.3.18 - 1/2.4.18.

	Killed		Wounded		Missing	
	Off.	O.R.	Off.	O.R.	Off.	O.R.
Divisional Headquarters	-	-	1	4	-	-
8th West Yorks.	3	18	10	103	-	16
2/5th West Yorks.	-	16	-	56	-	4
2/7th West Yorks.	-	28	6	70	-	6
185th T.M.B.	-	-	1	4	-	-
5th West Riding	2	31	9	119	1	50
2/4th West Riding	1	12	1	76	-	-
2/7th West Riding	-	17	1	51	-	7
186th T.M.B.	-	1	1	3	1	-
5th K.O.Y.L.I.	4	28	1	106	10	246
2/4th K.O.Y.L.I.	1	15	2	82	6	218
2/4th York & Lancs.	-	16	9	100	-	7
187th T.M.B.	-	-	-	2	-	-
9th D.L.I. (Pioneers)	3	21	4	85	-	1
62nd Bn. M.G.C.	-	7	4	50	-	1
310th Bde. R.F.A.	-	-	1	3	-	-
312th Bde. R.F.A.	-	-	1	6	-	-
460th Field Co. R.E.	-	-	-	2	-	-
461st Field Co. R.E.	-	1	-	3	-	-
62nd Divl. Signal Coy. R.E.	-	1	-	4	-	2
2/1st W.R. Field Ambce.	-	2	-	3	-	-
2/2nd W.R. Field Ambce.	-	-	-	2	-	-
2/3rd W.R. Field Ambce.	-	-	-	1	-	-
252 Employment Coy.	-	-	-	1	-	-
	14	214	52	936	18	558

SECRET.   Copy No. 32

                           62 Div. A/6351/49.

   ADMINISTRATIVE INSTRUCTIONS IN CONNECTION WITH 62nd
        Division Order No.108 dated 5.4.18 and Amendment No.1
                         dated 6.4.18.
   ----

1.   Wagon Lines will be taken over as follows under arrangements made by Brigades and Units concerned; all to be clear of present locations by 2 p.m. on 7th instant:-

        185th Inf.Bde. from 125th Inf.Bde. at D.22.b.
        186th   do   do   127th   do   at D.22.a.
        187th   do   do   126th   do   at D.21.d.
        9th Bn. D.L.I. do   1/7th Nath'd Fus. at D.27.b.
        62nd Bn M.G.C. do   42nd Bn M.G.C. at D.28.a.

2.   Rear Headquarters of Brigades etc., will be taken over from relieved Units, whose present locations are:-

        125th Inf.Bde. H.Q. (Rear) Billet 24 SOUASTRE.
        126th   -do-   do   69 SOUASTRE.
        127th   -do-   do   117 SOUASTRE.
        1/7th North'd Fus   do   74 SOUASTRE.

3. MEDICAL.
                                                        Wagon Lines.
2/3rd W.R.Fld.Amb Adv. Dressing Stn. at BIENVILLERS,   HENU D.19.b.
2/2nd   do   Main Dressing Stn. at SOUASTRE.   -do-
2/1st   do   in Reserve.   at SOUASTRE.   -do-

4. BURIALS.

        Divisional Burials Officer will be at SOUASTRE.
        All burials will take place at BIENVILLERS Military
Cemetery E.7.b.4.1, at 3 p.m. daily. Bodies will be brought down/on
returning ration wagons by units and placed in the mortuary there.
They will then be dealt with by Divisional Burials Officer.
Dressing Stations will be cleared in the same manner by Field Ambces.
        185th Infantry Brigade will detail 6 men for duty at the
Cemetery, who will report to Divisional Burial N.C.O. at Advanced
Dressing Station 2/3rd W.R.Field Ambulance, BIENVILLERS at 4 p.m.
on the 7th inst. They will be accommodated by Advanced Dressing
Station and rationed by them from 9th inst. inclusive

5. SALVAGE.

        62nd Divisional Salvage Company will be at HENU, and all
dumps etc., will be taken over from 42nd Division by 12 noon 7th inst

6. **TRAFFIC CONTROL, STRAGGLERS POSTS, PRISONERS OF WAR.**

    Stragglers Posts D.17.d.8.2. D.23.c.4.4.

    Stragglers Collecting Station SOUASTRE.

    Prisoners of War Collecting Post.
        SOUASTRE.

    A.P.M. will be located at SOUASTRE, same Headquarters as formerly.

7. **RAILHEAD.**

    For supplies AUTHIEULE.
    For personnel returning from leave. Normally BELLE EGLISE. Brigades etc., will still hold guides at WARLINCOURT & AUTHIEULE.

8. **NUCLEUS PERSONNEL.**

    Nucleus personnel will be accommodated under Brigade arrangements at SOUASTRE. VALLEY Camp is divided into Brigade Group Areas - These Areas will be taken over from relieved Brigades and used to accommodate nucleus personnel and reinforcements arriving.
    Brigade Rear Headquarters will forward to Divisional Headquarters by noon daily commencing 8th inst. a state showing numbers available for work exclusive of Brigade Classes. These will be held at disposal of Division, who will issue orders direct to Rear Brigade Headquarters repeating to Advanced Headquarters.

9. **D.A.D.O.S.**

    D.A.D.O.S. will take over from D.A.D.O.S. 42nd Division at HENU by 6 p.m. 7th inst.

10. **TENTS.**

    Tents are to be left standing and handed over to relieving units, receipts being obtained in each case and forwarded to Divisional Headquarters.
    Units of 42nd Division are being similarly instructed. Formations will report to Divisional Headquarters by noon 10th inst. numbers and positions of all tents taken over.
    Applications for extra tentage required will be made to Divisional Headquarters, stating numbers of Officers and men requiring accommodation.

-3-

11. Divisional Train will be located -
   Headquarters at HENU.
   Nos. 525, 526, 527 and 528 Companies at SOUASTRE.

12. Divisional Water Officer, Divisional Entertainment Officer, Divisional Claims Officer and Road Mending Parties will complete taking over from 42nd Division by noon 7th inst and will be located at SOUASTRE, billet 92 (formerly Divisional 'B' Mess).

13. Divisional Baths Officer will take over Baths at SOUASTRE from 42nd Divisional Baths Officer by 6 p.m. 7th inst. His Headquarters will be at SOUASTRE.

14. AMMUNITION.

   S.A.A. Section D.A.C. is at J.2.b.2.9.

SUPPLIES. Refilling Points are on HENU - SOUASTRE Road in D.20.

15. GASSED CLOTHING.

   For the present, demands for clothing to replace gassed clothing will be sent to D.A.D.O.S. Gassed clothing will be stored away from any personnel until arrangements can be made to deal with it.

C.P.Saunders Major
for Lieut.Colonel.
A.A.& Q.M.G. 62nd (West Riding) Division.

6.4.1918.

Copies to:-
1. A.D.C. for G.O.C.
2. 'G'.
3-5. 'Q'.
6. G.O.C.R.A.
7. C.R.E.
8. 185th Inf.Bde.
9. 186th Inf.Bde.
10. 187th Inf.Bde.
11. Camp Comdt.
12. Signals.
13. A.D.M.S.
14. O.C.Train.
15. A.P.M.
16. Div.M.G. Bn.
17. 9th D.L.I.
18. D.A.D.V.S.
19. Mob. Vet.Sec.
20. D.A.D.O.S.
21. Div.Burials Off.
22. Div.Baths Off.
23. Div. Water Off.
24. Div. Enter. Off.
25. Div.Salvage Off.
26. Div.Claims Off.
27. IV Corps 'Q'
28. 42nd Div. 'Q'.
29. 37th Div. 'Q'.
30. N.Z.Div.

SECRET.   62 Div. No.A/6751/49.
                  62nd (WEST RIDING) DIVISION.   Copy No......
                      ADMINISTRATIVE ORDERS.

1.   The following will be located at PAS, moving thereto
on Wednesday 17th April, by 12 noon :-

(a) Rear Divisional Headquarters.

    D.A.D.V.S.
    D.A.D.C.S. and staff.
    O.C. 252 Employment Company and staff.
    Divisional Salvage Officer and Salvage Section.
    Divisional Claims Officer.
    Divisional Entermainment Officer and Concert Party.
    Divisional Musketry Officer.
    Mobile Veterinary Section.

(b) Headquarters, Divisional Train.
    526 Company A.S.C.
    527 Company A.S.C.
    528 Company A.S.C.

(c) Divisional Wing.
    Reinforcements not required in line.
    Nuclei of Battalions.
    Brigade Classes.

(d) 2/1st W.R. Field Ambulance.

2.   Billets will be arranged by D.A.A.G. and advance parties
will meet him at Town Hall, PAS, at 10 a.m. 17th April.

3.   Store Rooms - Surplus Kit.

        Brigade Group store rooms will also be allotted by D.A.A.G.,
and all surplus kit will be removed from wagon lines and Q.M. Stores
in SOUASTRE.
        A guard will be found for each store room.

4.   Any extra transport required will be demanded by 8 p.m. tonight.

[Signature]
Lieut. Colonel,
A.A. & Q.M.G., 62nd (W.R.) Division.

16/4/18.

DISTRIBUTION.

A.D.C. for G.O.C.
185th Infantry Brigade
186th   "   "
187th   "   "
185th   "   "   Rear
186th   "   "   "
187th   "   "   "
C.R.E.
A.D.M.S.
Train
D.A.D.V.S.
Mob.Vet.Sec.
D.A.D.O.S.
A.P.M.
D.M.C.
Camp Commandant.
Salvage Officer.
Major Whiteaway, O.C. Divl.Wing.
252 Employment Company.
"G"

SECRET.

Copy No.
62 Div.A/6959/49.

ADMINISTRATIVE INSTRUCTIONS IN CONNECTION WITH
62nd (W.R.) DIVISION ORDER NO.112 DATED 21/4/18.

Reference 57.D. 1/40.000.

1. **ACCOMODATION IN NEW AREA.**

    185th Infantry Brigade Group   LOUVENCOURT.
        Brigade Headquarters, 3 Battalions, 461st W.R.Field Company R.E. and Train Company in Billets.
        1 Company Pioneer Battalion in Tents.
        2/1st W.R.Field Ambulance at MARIEUX.

    186th Infantry Brigade Group   BOIS de WARNIMONT & ST LEGER les AUTHIE.
        Brigade H.Q. and 1 Battalion, Billets and Tents, ST LEGER.
        2/2nd W.R.Field Ambulance   "   "   "   "   "   "
        1 Battalion   BOIS de WARNIMONT   Tents, I.24.a.
        1 Battalion   ditto   do   I.17.d.
        1 Battalion   ditto   do   I.24.a.
        457th W.R.Fld.Co. ditto
        Train Company will be accomodated under arrangements made by O.C. Divisional Train.

    187th Infantry Brigade Group   AUTHIE & BOIS de l'AUTHIE.
        Brigade H.Q.   AUTHIE   Cure's House.
        3 Battalions   BOIS d'AUTHIE, I.16.b. and d. Tents.
        460th W.R.Fld.Co. ditto   ditto   do
        2/3rd W.R.Fld.Ambce. AUTHIE Mill. Corps Rest Station.
        Train Company will be accomodated under arrangements made by O.C. Divisional Train.

    62nd Battalion M.G.C.   BOIS de WARNIMONT, I.17.b.   Tents.

    9th D.L.I. (less 1 Company at LOUVENCOURT.)
        BOIS LALEAU, I.10.b.9.2.   Tents.

    Headquarters 62nd Divisional Artillery and Royal Engineers will be at PAS, and will exchange Billets with 37th Division.

2. **BATHS.**
        Divisional Baths Officer will hand over Baths at SOUASTRE to 37th Division and take over Baths at AUTHIE and VAUCHELLES by noon 24th April.
        Arrangements with N.Z.Division re use of Baths at LOUVENCOURT will also be taken over.

31. **SALVAGE.**
        Salvage Company will remain at PAS.

ORDNANCE.

D.A.D.O.S. will remain at PAS.

TRAFFIC PERSONNEL AND STRAGGLERS' POSTS.

Traffic personnel and Stragglers Posts, etc., will be relieved by noon 24th April under arrangements to be made by A.P.M., and move to AUTHIE.

6. **WATER.**

Water trough and Well Wardens (6 N.C.Os. and 44 men) will be relieved by 37th Division by noon 24th April.

On relief Water Points will be policed under arrangements to be made by Divisional Water Officer, who will take over from 37th Division by 12 noon 24th April. Any water personnel surplus to requirements will be returned to duty with units; a nominal roll being sent in each case.

7. **BURIALS.**

The Burial Party at BIENVILLERS Cemetery will be relieved by 12 noon 24th April by 37th Division and return to their units.

8. **TOWN MAJOR, FONQUEVILLERS** and staff will be relieved by 12 noon 24th April and return to their units.

9. A.D.M.S., D.A.D.V.S., Divisional Gas Officer, Baths Officer, Claiming Officer and O.C. 252 Employment Company will be located at AUTHIE.

10. **GAS CLOTHING.**

Divisional Gas Officer will hand over gas clothing to D.G.O., 37th Division, and obtain receipts.

11. **AMMUNITION.**

S.A.A. Dump will be handed over to 37th Division by 12 noon 24th April.

Dumps of S.A.A., Grenades, etc., ordered to be established in PURPLE Line under G.411 of 10.4.18 will be handed over to relieving units of 37th Division and receipts obtained.

All units will move with full echelons.

Units will take over dumps of practice ammunition in Reserve Area.

12. **RESERVE RATIONS.**

Rations in FONQUEVILLERS (2000 tins P.M. 2000 lbs. Biscuit) will be handed over to incoming unit of 37th Division by 9th D.L.I. and a receipt obtained.

15. R.A.

Details of Infantry Brigades at present quartered at PAS will be disposed of as follows :-

(a) Nuclei of Battalions will rejoin their units on latter arriving in Reserve Area.
Brigade Schools and Classes remain at PAS.
Stores of surplus kit, etc., remain in PAS pending arrangements for their transfer elsewhere.

(b) **Divisional Wing** remains in present billets at PAS.

(c) **Infantry attached R.A.M.C.**
The 50 men attached to each Field Ambulance will join the Divisional Wing at PAS, on completion of relief of each Medical Unit, under arrangements to be made between A.D.M.S. and O.C. Divisional Wing.

14. TENTS.

All tents and trench shelters in occupation will be handed over to relieving units of 37th Division and receipts obtained.

[signature]

22.4.18.
Lieut.Colonel,
A.A.& Q.M.G., 62nd (West Riding) Division.

D I S T R I B U T I O N.

Copy No.				
1	A.D.C. for G.O.C.		17	D.A.D.V.S.
2	"C"		18	D.A.D.O.S.
3-5	"Q"		19	A.P.M.
6	G.O.C. R.A.		20	IV Corps 'Q'.
7	C.R.E.		21	37th Division 'Q'.
8	186th Inf.Bde.		22	Div.Baths Officer.
9	185th Inf.Bde.		23	Div.Water Officer.
10	187th Inf.Bde.		24	Div.Salvage Officer.
11	Signal Co.		25	Div.Burials Officer.
12	Train		26	Town Major, FONQUEVILLERS.
13	A.D.M.S.		27	Divisional Wing.
14	M.G.Bn.		28	Div.Gas Officer.
15	9th D.L.I.		29	O.C., 252 Employment Coy.
16	Camp Comdt.			

62 Div. No. A/6602/11.

185th Infantry Brigade & Rear.   9th Bn. Durham Light Infantry.
186th Infantry Brigade & Rear.   S.S.O., 62nd Division.
187th Infantry Brigade & Rear.   "G", 62nd Division.
C.R.E., 62nd Division.

Following are arriving about noon from 62nd Divisional Wing to-day, rationed for 13th only.

	(a) Trained Reinforcements.	(b) Untrained Reinforcements.	(c) Staff.
2/5th West Yorks.	5	-	1
2/7th do	6	12	7
8th do	316	28	9
2/4th West Riding.	5	-	3
5th do	-	1	4
2/7th do	-	1	4
2/4th K.O.Y.L.I.	-	2	1
5th do	5	43	-
2/4th York & Lanc.	-	20	10
9th Bn. D.L.I.	1	2	-
460 Field Coy R.E.	-	-	1
	338	109	40

1.   All except Untrained Reinforcements will rejoin Units, names of any officers arriving, and Units to which posted, being reported to this office.

2.   Untrained Reinforcements, (except 2 O.Rs. D.L.I., who will join Battalion), will be sent forthwith for attachment to affiliated R.E. Company - one officer per Brigade being also attached - These untrained reinforcements will remain on the strength of their Battalions.
        All arrangements to be made between C.R.E. and Brigades direct - C.R.E. will accommodate them from to-night inclusive.

3.   Rolls of Other Ranks, with postings, will be forwarded to D.A.G., 3rd Echelon.

(sd) Harold F. Lea, Lt-Colonel,
for Major,
D.A.A.G., 62nd (West Riding) Division.

13.4.1918.

as per following table :-

2/7th W.Yorks.	12)	to 460 Field Coy R.E.
8th W.Yorks.	28)	
5th K.O.Y.L.I.	43	to 461 do.
5th W.Riding.	1)	
2/7th do.	1)	to 457 do.
2/4th K.O.Y.L.I.	2)	
2/4th Y. & L.	20)	

62nd (West Riding) Division.

Reinforcements received during April.

	Officers.	Other Ranks.
8th West Yorkshire Regiment.	13	667
2/5th West Yorkshire Regiment.	1	133
2/7th West Yorkshire Regiment.	6	331
5th West Riding Regiment.	4	239
2/4th West Riding Regiment.	16	127
2/7th West Riding Regiment.	4	104
5th K.O.Y.L.I.	11	478
2/4th K.O.Y.L.I.	15	268
2/4th York & Lancaster Regiment.	9	143
Royal Artillery.	1	90
Royal Engineers.	4	55
Divisional Train. A.S.C.	-	3
Royal Army Medical Corps.	3	33
62nd Bn. Machine Gun Corps.	3	86
9th Durham Light Infantry. (Pioneers).	4	169
Divisional Signal Company.	-	18

REWARDS GRANTED DURING APRIL 1918.

Military Cross.	2.
Distinguished Conduct Medal.	2.
Bar to Military Medal.	3.
Military Medal.	45.

FRENCH.

Legion D'Honneur (Chevalier)	1.
Medaille Militaire.	1.
Croix de Guerre.	3.

ITALIAN.

Bronze Medal.	1.

CASUALTIES DURING APRIL 1918.
OFFICERS.

3.4.18	Major J.Willey,	312th Brigade R.F.A.	Killed
5.4.18	Lieut. J.C.F.Nowill, MC.	310th Brigade R.F.A.	Wounded
	2nd Lt.F.W.G.Sharpling	310th Brigade R.F.A.	Wounded.
6.4.18	Major M.R.H.Crofton DSO.	312th Brigade R.F.A.	Wounded - gas.
	Captain A.Senior	312th Brigade R.F.A.	Wounded - gas.
	Lieut. J.B.Boden, M.C.	312th Brigade R.F.A.	Wounded - gas.
	Lieut. S.A.Rissik	312th Brigade R.F.A.	Wounded - gas.
	2nd Lt.E.J.W.Puttock	312th Brigade R.F.A.	Wounded - gas.
	2nd Lt.A.E.Stuttle	312th Brigade R.F.A.	Wounded - gas.
7.4.18	Lt.E.H.Vanderpump	310th Brigade R.F.A.	Wounded - gas.
	Capt.T.Whitelaw, R.A.M.C.att.2/7th West Yorks.		Killed.
	2nd Lieut.E.N.Temple	2/7th West Yorks.	Wounded.
	2nd Lt.H.D.Forrest, W.Yorks.att.5th West Riding		Killed.
8.4.18	Lieut. A.A.Campbell	9th D.L.I.	Wounded.
9.4.18	2nd Lt.A.Walker	5th West Riding	Wounded.
10.4.18	Lieut.W.O.P.Gibb, R.Scots att.2/4th K.O.Y.L.I.		Wounded.
11.4.18	2nd Lt.E.C.J.Sheppard	310th Brigade R.F.A.	Wounded.
12.4.18	Lt.Sir R.C.Muir-Mackenzie,MC, 9th D.L.I.		Killed.
	2nd Lt.R.J.Dangerfield	62nd Bn. M.G.C.	Wounded.
13.4.18	Lieut.W.Douglass	9th D.L.I.	Wounded.
	2nd Lt. F.J.Doherty	R.Lancs.att.5th K.O.Y.L.I.	Wounded.
12.4.18	Capt. A.J.Neilan	312th Brigade R.F.A.	Wounded.
14.4.18	2nd Lieut. A.H.Fehr	5th K.O.Y.L.I.	Missing
15.4.18	Capt.G.A.McK.Morant	2/5th West Yorks.	Killed.
	2nd Lt.O.C.Gardiner	461st Field Co.R.E.	Wounded.
16.4.18	2nd Lt.J.M.Wilson	Yorks.Regt.att.2/4 KOYLI.	Wounded.
17.4.18	2nd Lieut. A.Hall	2/7th West Yorks.	Wounded.
18.4.18	2nd Lt.A.Marshall	2/7th West Yorks.	Wounded.
17.4.18	Lieut.J.C.McIlroy	310th Brigade R.F.A.	Wounded.
14.4.18	Lieut. T.F.B.Hall	5th KOYLI att.187 T.M.B.	Wounded - gas.
22.4.18	Major W.F.Tuthill	312th Brigade R.F.A.	Wounded - gas.
	2nd Lt.A.E.Cockerell	312th Brigade R.F.A.	Wounded - gas.
	Capt.W.Vero	2/5th West Yorks.	Wounded.
	Lt.J.G.Weightman	9th D.L.I.	Wounded.
	Lt.Col.N.A.England, W.Rid.Regt.Cmdg.8th W.Yorks.		Wounded at duty.
23.4.18	2nd Lt.R.J.Machin	5th West Riding	Wounded at duty.
30.3.18	2nd Lieut.S.H.Bell	2/4th West Riding	Wounded.

OTHER RANKS.

Killed	83
Wounded	456
Missing	10

CONFIDENTIAL.

WAR DIARY

OF

HEADQUARTERS, 62ND (WEST RIDING) DIVISION "A".

1ST. MAY, 1918   to   31ST. MAY, 1918.

VOLUME 1.

SECRET.

Army Form C. 2118.

62nd Division
A. D. WAR DIARY or INTELLIGENCE SUMMARY.
MAY 1918
P. 1.

(Erase heading not required.)

Instructions regarding War Diaries and Intelligence Summaries are contained in F. S. Regs., Part II. and the Staff Manual respectively. Title pages will be prepared in manuscript.

Place	Date	Hour	Summary of Events and Information	Remarks and references to Appendices
AUTHIE	1st		Much Colder — Instructions issued re Watering Arrangements in work area.	See Appendix A
do	2nd		Fine and Warm — Increase in P.V.O. noted in Units occupying Camps in Bois d'AUTHIE Area	
do	3rd		Weather — Arrangements made for Bn. of 187 Inf. Bde. and Qr. Det. 1 Border Regt. Camps in 4th Inst. to Ars at WARNIMONT in order to dig a Purple Line — Lt Col NASH Col 2/4/ W. Riding appointed to command 49th Inf. Bde. Capt HARPER Bde. Major 186 Inf. Bde. appointed GSO2 32nd Division	B.M.
do	4th		Weather Colder. Some Rain — Capt HAWTHEN M.C. Borden Regt. appt. Bde. Major 186th Inf. Bde. —	B.M.
do	5th		Weather Warm. Heavy Rain during Day. Divisional Dump for Surplus Kit arranged at WAVANS near Nr.E. CHATEAU. Instructions issued	See Appendix B
do	6th		Weather Fine and Warm during day — Some Rain in Evening — Leave for N.C.Os. Men entitled to Months Reengagement Leave issued	

Army Form C. 2118.

WAR DIARY
or
INTELLIGENCE SUMMARY.
MAY 1918 page 2.

(Erase heading not required.)

Place	Date	Hour	Summary of Events and Information	Remarks and references to Appendices
AUTHIE	7		Weather dull and damp	GW
do	8		Weather fine and much warmer — Owing to damp and unhealthy Conditions in Bois d'AUTHIE Camps 4/187 Infantile Mortem moved to Orchard just South of it. Letter from GHQ re Economy in Man Power sent out to Ades etc.	GW
do	9		Weather very fine — Special Reference of Divisional Commander presented Medal Ribbon to 186 INF. BDE.	GW
do	10		Weather Fine.	
do	11		Weather Fine.	
do	12		Weather dull — Sunday. Deputy Chaplain General — Bishop GWYNNE — Visited Division and attended Parade Services of 186 and 187 Inf Bdes.	GW
do	13		Weather dull and cold.	

Army Form C. 2118.

WAR DIARY
or
INTELLIGENCE SUMMARY.
(Erase heading not required.)

MAY 1918 Page 3

Place	Date	Hour	Summary of Events and Information	Remarks and references to Appendices
AVITNE	14th		Weather Fine. Administrative Instructions re relief of 37th by 62nd Division on 16th to 17th not issued	3rd Appendix D
AVITNE	15th		Weather Fine and Much Warmer - 187 Inf. Bde had very successful Sports Meeting during Afternoon at AVITNE	GW
AVITNE	16th		Weather Fine - 186 Brigade Relieved 63rd Inf. Bde during night in Left Brigade Left Division Front - 62nd Brigade moved to ST.LEGER et. Allotment of Watering Points issued	GW Appendix E
HENU	17th		Weather Fine and Hot - Divl HQ.s moved to HENU, taking over from 37th Divisn. Relief of 37th by 62nd Division Completed during Night - P.O.w.as at Chateau - Camp at ORVILLE taken over from 37th Divisn for 62nd Div. Wing and Reinft Camp	62nd Appendix F
HENU	18th		Weather Fine in Morning - Some Rain in Afternoon - Divl HQ.s shelled by Long Range Gun from 11 a.m to 12 Noon -	GW

Army Form C. 2118.

WAR DIARY
or
INTELLIGENCE SUMMARY.
(Erase heading not required.)

O.a.O   May 1918   p. 4.

Instructions regarding War Diaries and Intelligence Summaries are contained in F.S. Regs., Part II. and the Staff Manual respectively. Title pages will be prepared in manuscript.

Place	Date	Hour	Summary of Events and Information	Remarks and references to Appendices
HENU	19th		Weather Fine — G.O.C. presented Medal Ribbons to 2 O.R. Artillery after Church Parade — Reconnaissance made of Pits with a view to installing D.L.L. M.G's. Three if HENU became untenable	8/1
HENU	20th		Weather Fine	8/1
HENU	21st		Weather Fine	8/1
HENU	22nd		Weather Fine — Anti-aircraft received concepts L.M. Guns to scale E —	8/1
HENU	23rd		Weather Fine. Cooler —	8/1
HENU	24th		Weather Wet — Arrival of American Officers and N.C.O's for instructional attachment	8/1
HENU	25th		Weather Fine — Cooler — 187 hrs/Adc relieved 185 Bepple in Right Bde Section	8/1
HENU	26th		Weather Fine	8/1
HENU	27th		Weather Fine — Some shelling of SOASTRE during Evening	8/1
HENU	28th		Weather Fine — Leave allotment of 3 per day ordinary & 2 per day Recuperment received to commence June 1st — RE allotment issued	8/1 Appendix G
HENU	29th		Weather Fine	8/1
HENU	30th and 31st		Weather Fine — Some shelling of SOASTRE and Wagon Lines on BIENVILLERS Road	8/1

Army Form C. 2118.

WAR DIARY
or
INTELLIGENCE SUMMARY.
(Erase heading not required.)

A.A. & Q.M.G.   May 1918   Page 5.

Instructions regarding War Diaries and Intelligence Summaries are contained in F. S. Regs., Part II. and the Staff Manual respectively. Title pages will be prepared in manuscript.

Place	Date	Hour	Summary of Events and Information	Remarks and references to Appendices
			Casualties during May 1918 — Appendix H	
			Reinforcements received May 1918 — " I	
			Rewards granted during May 1918 — " J	
	31/5/18		[signature] Lieut Colonel a/Major General Commanding 62nd (W.R.) Division	

App. A.

62nd Div. No.A/7328/43

The following Horse Troughs, Water Cart and Water Bottle Filling Points are available in the Reserve Divisional Area :-

Village.	Location etc.	Capacity in 2 hours.
1. AUTHIE.	I.16.a.3.8. Horse Troughs.	300 Horses.
2. AUTHIE.	I.9.d.9.0. W.C.F.Point.	50 Carts.
3. AUTHIE.	I.16.a.8.6. Horse Troughs.	500 Horses.
4. AUTHIE - ST LEGER Rd.	I.11.c.3.0. Horse Troughs.	1200 Horses.
5. AUTHIE - ST.LEGER Rd.	I.11.d.0.0. Horse Troughs.	500 Horses.
6. ST LEGER.	I.12.c.1.7. W.C.F. Point.	100 Carts.
7. ST LEGER.	I.12.b.1.1. Horse Troughs.	1200 Horses.
8. LOUVENCOURT (Station)	C.4.b.2.8. Horse Troughs.	3168 Horses.
9. LOUVENCOURT.	I.34.b.3.0. W.C.F. Point.	80 to 100 Carts.
10. LOUVENCOURT Baths.	I.34.b.7.0	Water bottle filling point.
11. VAUCHELLES Baths.	I.32.b.2.1. Horse Trough & W.C.F. Point.	500 Horses.

1/5/1918.

Major,
D.A.A.G., 62nd (West Riding) Division.

Copies to :- all concerned.

App B

62 Div. No.A/7512/49.

DIVISIONAL DUMP.

1. Divisional Stores for surplus Kit are at Billets Nos. 21 and 51.A., WAVANS.

2. Brigades etc will transport all surplus Kit there on Tuesday 7th instant. Applications for lorries to move this will reach Division "Q" by 4 p.m. tomorrow 6th instant, stating time and place lorries are required to report, and number of loads required - They will then be allotted as available.

3. Units will be grouped as under :-

Group.	Unit.	Storemen allowed.
Groups 1 to 3.	Each Infantry Brigade, Field Ambulance, Field Coy. Train Coy.	1 N.C.O. 5 O.Rs.
Group 4.	62nd Divl. Artillery. No.1 Coy., Train.	1 N.C.O. 3 O.Rs.
Group 5.	62nd Divl. Headquarters. 9th Bn. Durham L.I. 62nd Battn. M.G.Corps. 62nd Divl. Signal Coy.	1 O.R. 1 N.C.O. 1 O.R. 1 O.R. 1 O.R.

4. In addition, 186th Infantry Brigade will detail a senior N.C.O. to be in charge of the whole Dump, and report name direct to Divisional Headquarters by 4 p.m. 6th instant.

5. Lieut. GORE, York & Lancs. Regiment, Divisional Burials Officer, will proceed to WAVANS on 7th instant to allot the accommodation, and make all necessary arrangements as to rationing etc. He will return when those are complete.
Lorries will report to him at Billet No.21, WAVANS, on arrival.

/3.

6. Personnel will proceed with one blanket per man and rationed up to 10th instant inclusive. Area Commandant will ration after that date.

7. Address of men at Dump for letters etc. :-
   Rank, Name & Unit,
   62nd Divisional Dump,
   c/o FROHEN Sub-Area Commandant, AUXI-LE-CHATEAU.

8. Each N.C.O. or Storeman in charge of Brigade or separate Units stores will be in possession of duplicate list showing clearly what is in Dump. He will retain one copy and hand one to N.C.O. in charge, Divisional Dump.

E. Saunders
Major,
5/5/1918. D.A.A.G., 62nd (West Riding) Division.

Distribution :- all concerned.

3 Bdes   HDqrs
RA   9th DLI
RE   MG Btn
Sig. Coy   CCdt
Train   R Gore
              Frohen Sub Area Cdt

185th Inf. Bde.   62nd Bn. M.G.C.   62nd Div. A/7555/8.
186th Inf. Bde.   9th Bn. D.L.I.
187th Inf. Bde.   Camp Cmdt.
62nd Div. Arty.   D.A.D.V.S.
62nd Div. R.E.   D.A.D.O.S.
A.D.M.S.   D.G.O.
O.C. Train.   Signal Coy.

Reference reverse.

Paras 1 and 2. Applications for special leave will continue to be forwarded to Divisional Headquarters as heretofore.

Para. 3. Vacancies for one month's leave on re-engagement are sub-allotted as under and commence forthwith. (G.R.O.3758 only applied to men eligible for ordinary leave at the same time as due for one month's re-engagement leave). Applications for this leave must be submitted as hitherto to Divisional Headquarters for approval where same has not already been given. If any unit or formation is unable to fill their allotment, Divisional Headquarters will be notified without delay.

	Sun.	Mon.	Tues.	Wed.	Thurs.	Fri.	Sat.	Day of embarkation.
185 Bde.	-	1	1	1	-	-	-	-
186 Bde.	-	-	1	-	1	-	-	-
187 Bde.	-	-	1	-	1	-	1	-
9th D.L.I.	-	-	-	-	-	1	-	-
M.G. Bn.	-	-	-	-	-	1	-	-
R.A.	1	-	-	-	3	-	-	-
R.E.	-	-	-	-	-	1	-	-
A.D.M.S.	1	-	-	-	-	-	-	-
Train.	1	-	-	-	-	-	-	-
D.H.Q. (spare)	-	3	-	-	-	-	-	-

NOTE: Units not included in above table will forward applications to Divisional Headquarters for allotment from spares by noon on Saturdays.

Officers proceeding on leave will report to R.T.O. DOULLENS at 3 p.m. and other ranks by 6 p.m. daily, and will cross by boat sailing following day.

C. Waunders Major.
D.A.A.G. 62nd (West Riding) Division.

7.5.1918.

IV Corps. A.G./441/P.S.

While ordinary leave is closed, G.O.C., Armies, Corps and L. of C. Area may grant Special Leave in the following cases :-

1. Leave not to exceed 14 days on the grounds of Urgent private affairs and this should be curtailed to a lesser period if it is considered sufficient for the purpose for which leave is requested.

The following are considered reasonable grounds for the granting of such special Leave :-

(a) Urgent private affairs which necessitate the individual's presence and which do not admit of delay.

(b) Dangerous illness of parent, wife or child.

(c) Death of parent, wife or child.

(d) Misconduct of wife: other circumstances which makes it desirable that the custody of children should be arranged for.

In all cases where any doubt exists the bona-fides of applications should be vouched for (police evidence etc.) Attention is directed to G.R.O. 2145 as amended by 2833.

2. Up to 30 days' leave under Army Council Instruction 2327 of 1916 (leave granted to officers and men owing to exigencies connected with their civil profession or business affairs) may be granted.

3. One month's leave may continue to be granted to those Warrant Officers, Non-commissioned Officers and men who are eligible and are recommended for the month's leave under the terms of G.R.O. 3474 (as amended by G.R.O. 3758) and G.R.O. 3867.

For this purpose, a special allotment has been given to G.O.C. Armies & G.O.C. L. of C. Area who will sub-allot to lower formations.

This allotment which will be revised from time to time by G.H.Q. is based on the number of Corps and Divisions in each Army on the 2nd. May, 1918.

Under no circumstances will this allotment be exceeded nor will any Warrant Officer, Non-commissioned Officer or man be allowed to proceed who has been on leave within the previous four months.

All Labour personnel will be included in this allotment.

The left-hand portion of the Warrant of any Warrant Officer, Non-commissioned Officer or man proceeding on this month's leave on re-engagement will be clearly marked with a large "R".

4. Leave on the grounds of sickness will not be granted to officers except under the conditions allowed by paragraphs 25 & 26 of Regulations regarding Leave - S.S. 525. A.

5. Leave under M.S. Circular letter 19898 will not be granted.

6. No Officer, Warrant Officer, Non-commissioned officer or man will be allowed to embark unless the authority of the Adjutant General, Army, Corps or L. of C. Area is quoted on the Warrant.

This will not apply to the month's leave granted under the terms of para. 3.

G.H.Q., 1st. Echelon,
5th. May, 1918.

(Sgd.) L.H.BODDAM-WHETHAM, Capt., S.C.
for Adjutant General.

SECRET.

App D

Copy No.
62 Div.A/7794/49.

ADMINISTRATIVE INSTRUCTIONS IN CONNECTION WITH 62nd (W.R.) DIVISION ORDER NO. 114 dated 13/5/18.

Reference 57.D. 1/40,000.

1. **REAR H.Q., WAGON LINES & QUARTERMASTER'S STORES.**

   Rear Headquarters, Wagon Lines, and Quartermaster's Stores will be taken over as follows, under arrangements made between Brigades and Units concerned:—

Formation or Unit.		Rear H.Q.	Wagon Lines.	Q.M. Stores.
185 Inf.Bde.	from 112 I.Bde.	D.13.c.5.2.	D.13.c.	SOUASTRE.
186 " "	" 63 "	Billet 69 SOUASTRE.	D.21.d.	ditto
187 " "	" 111 "	Billet 24 SOUASTRE.	D.25.a.	ditto
9th D.L.I.	" Pioneers (S.Staffs)	SOUASTRE.	D.20.b. 9.3.	ditto
62nd Bn.M.G.C.	" 37th Bn. M.G.C.	HENU.	D.19.c. 9.2.	ditto
3 Field Coy.	" 3 Field Coys.	—	D.22. a & c.	—

   R.A., R.E., and A.D.M.S. Headquarters will be at HENU.

2. **MEDICAL.**

   Advanced Dressing Station   BIENVILLERS   2/2nd W.R. Field Ambulance
   Main Dressing Station   SOUASTRE   2/1st   ditto
   Reserve Field Ambulance   PAS   2/3rd   ditto

   Wagon Lines will be taken over from relieved Units at HENU and PAS.

3. **SALVAGE.**

   62nd Divisional Salvage Company will take over from 37th Divisional Salvage Company by noon 16th instant.
   Salvage Company Headquarters will be at PAS, near D.A.D.O.S. Store.

4. **ORDNANCE.**

   D.A.D.O.S., 62nd Division, will take over from D.A.D.O.S., 37th Division, by noon 16th instant, and be located at PAS.

5. **BURIALS.**

   Divisional Burials Officer will be at SOUASTRE.
   All burials will take place at BIENVILLERS Military Cemetery, E.7.b.4.1., at 3 p.m. daily. Bodies will be brought down on returning Ration wagons and placed in Mortuary there. They will then be dealt with by the Divisional Burials Officer.

/Dressing

Dressing Stations will be cleared similarly by Field Ambulances

186th Infantry Brigade will detail 6 men for duty at Cemetery, who will report to Divisional Burial N.C.O. at Advanced Dressing Station, 2/2nd W.R. Field Ambulance, at 4 p.m. on 16th inst. They will be accommodated by Advanced Dressing Station and rationed by them from 18th instant inclusive.

6. A.P.M., TRAFFIC CONTROL, ETC.

A.P.M. and Traffic Personnel will be at SOUASTRE.

Stragglers Posts - D.22.d.8.4. - D.23.a.1.5.
Collecting Station - SOUASTRE.
P. of War do - SOUASTRE.
Left Stragglers Post of Centre Division - D.29.c.8.4.

A.P.M., 62nd Division, will take over from A.P.M., 37th Division, by noon 16th instant.

7. R.E. MATERIAL.

Divisional Dump at SOUASTRE, D.22.b.9.0.

8. VETERINARY.

D.A.D.V.S. will be at HENU.
Mobile Veterinary Section remains at PAS.

9. DIVISIONAL TRAIN.

Headquarters Train, 525, 527, and 528 Coys. remain in present lines at PAS. 526 Coy. will move to Lines previously occupied at PAS.

10. BATHS.

Divisional Baths Officer will take over Baths at SOUASTRE, and hand over Baths in present Area by noon 16th instant.
He will arrange for sock-drying room to be in operation and exchange to commence by 17th instant.

11. BRIGADE CLASSES AND DIVISIONAL WING.

Reference para (9) of Division Order 114, further instructions will be issued

12. ENTERTAINMENTS ETC.

Divisional Entertainment Officer and Troupe, Musketry and Educational Officers will be at ORVILLE.

13. TENTAGE.

Tents are to be left standing and handed over to relieving Units; receipts being obtained and forwarded to Divisional Headquarters Units of 37th Division are being similarly instructed.
Numbers and position of all tents and shelters taken over will be reported to "Q", 62nd Division, by last D.R., 19th instant.

14. **SOUASTRE.**

Duties of Town Major, SOUASTRE, will be taken over by Captain R. CANDLISH, O.C. 252nd Employment Company, from Officer of 37th Division now acting as such, by noon 16th instant.
Headquarters, 252nd Employment Company, will be at SOUASTRE.

15. **WATER WARDENS.**

Divisional Water Control Officer (2/Lieut.R.J.FOSTER), will take over Water Control Posts from 37th Division by noon 13th instant.
He will be located at SOUASTRE.
Posts in Reserve Area will be handed over to 37th Division by noon 16th instant.

16. **S.A.A. SECTION, D.A.C.**

S.A.A. Section will move to HENU, D.19.c. central, taking over from 37th Division.

17. **DIVISIONAL CANTEENS.**

Divisional Canteens will be established at SOUASTRE and ORVILLE.

[signature]
Lieut-Colonel,
A.A. & Q.M.G., 62nd (West Riding) Division.

13/5/1918.

DISTRIBUTION.

Copy No.			
1	A.D.C. for G.O.C.	17	D.A.D.V.S.
2	"G"	18	D.A.D.O.S.
3-5	"Q"	19	A.P.M.
6	G.O.C. R.A.	20	IV Corps "Q".
7	C.R.E.	21	37th Division "Q".
8	185 Inf.Bde.	22	Divnl. Baths Offr.
9	186 Inf.Bde.	23	Divnl. Water Offr.
10	187 Inf.Bde.	24	Divnl. Salvage Offr.
11	Signal Coy.	25	Divnl. Burials Offr.
12	Train.	26	Divnl. Gas Offr.
13	A.D.M.S.	27	Divnl. Wing.
14	M.G. Battn.	28	O.C., 252 Emp.Coy.
15	9th D.L.I.		
16	Camp Cdt.		

App. E

62 Div.No.A/7886/46.

The following Allotment of Watering Places will come into force from 17th May, 1918, inclusive :-

Water at

H E N U.

(i)	All horses North of HENU-PAS Road, and West of HENU-GAUDIEMPRE Road.	C.18.b.8.3.
(ii)	All horses North of HENU-SOUASTRE Road, and West of HENU-ST.AMAND Road.	D.13.b.5.3.
(iii)	All horses South of HENU-SOUASTRE Road, and West of SOUASTRE-COUIN Road.	C.24.a.6.4. (W.C.F.Pt.)

S O U A S T R E.

(i)	All horses South of HENU-BIENVILLERS Road.	D.27.d.9.2.
(ii)	All horses North of HENU-BIENVILLERS Road, and East of SOUASTRE-ST.AMAND Road.	D.22.a.4.7. (W.C.F.Pt.)
(iii)	All horses North of HENU-SOUASTRE Road, and West of SOUASTRE-ST.AMAND Road.	D.21.d.8.9. (W.C.F.Pt.)

C.Maunders
Major,
D.A.A.G., 62nd (West Riding) Division.

16/5/1918.

D I S T R I B U T I O N.

185th Inf. Bde.	4 copies.	A.D.M.S.	4 copies.
186th " "	4 "	Train.	5 "
187th " "	4 "	Sig.Coy.	1 "
Div. Arty.	5 "	M.G.Bn.	5 "
C.R.E.	4 "	9th D.L.I.	1 "

Town Major SOUASTRE & HENU. 10 copies.

SECRET. 62 Div.No.A/7907/49.Copy No.

ADMINISTRATIVE INSTRUCTIONS IN CONNECTION WITH
62nd DIVISION ORDER NO.114, para 9, of 13-5-18.

DIVISIONAL WING AND BRIGADE CLASSES AT ORVILLE.

1. C.R.E. will arrange to carry on all work at present in hand and started by 37th Division.

2. A.D.M.S. will detail one G.S. Wagon and one Water Cart (complete turn-out) for duty at Camp, to report to Commandant, Divisional Wing, tomorrow, 17th May.

3. A.D.M.S. will arrange for Medical supervision and evacuation of sick.

4. 62nd Divisional Signal Company will supply one telephone.

5. D.A.D.O.S. will supply one bicycle on loan.

6. Rations will be delivered by Mechanical Transport. Attention is drawn to Q/2580/33 of 14-5-18.

7. LEWIS GUNS.
185th and 187th Infantry Brigades will furnish one Lewis Gun each for A.A. defence, and arrange to man them.

8. BATHS.
Divisional Baths Officer will arrange for a supply of clean clothing, and for the clearing of dirty clothing.

9. A Divisional Canteen will be opened forthwith.

10. The Entertainment Officer, Educational Officer, and Divisional Musketry Officer will be at the disposal of Commandant, Divisional Wing, for such duties as he may allot to them.

11. Brigade Classes will come supplied with sufficient proportion of Cooks and Cookery utensils.

Harold Lea
Lieut-Colonel,
16/5/1918.   A.A. & Q.M.G., 62nd (West Riding) Division.

D I S T R I B U T I O N.

Copy No.				
1	A.D.C. for G.O.C.		13	Camp Commdt.
2	"G".		14	D.A.D.O.S.
3-5	"Q".		15	Div.Baths Offr.
6	C.R.E.		16	Div. Entrt Offr.
7	185 Inf.Bde.		17	Div.Canteen Offr.
8	186 Inf.Bde.		18	Divnl. Wing.
9	187 Inf.Bde.		19	Divnl.Ed. Offr.
10	Signal Coy.		20	Divnl. Mus. Offr
11	Train.			
12	A.D.M.S.			

App G

CONFIDENTIAL.   62nd Div.A/8393/8.

To......................

      With reference to G.R.O.4110 and Confidential Circular A.G/441/PS/1 of 25.5.18.

1.   This comes into force on June 1st 1918 and leave allotment will be as under from 1st to 14th June 1918 inclusive:-

Boat sailing.	Leave other than Re-engagement Leave.	Re-engagement leave.
June.		
June.		
June.		

    Note (a) Camp Commandant's allotment includes Divisional Employment Company and Mobile Veterinary Section.

    (b) Para. 4 of G.H.Q.Circular A.G/441/P.S/1 states that if vacancies for Re-engagement Leave cannot be filled they may be used for Ordinary Leave.

2.   All applications for Special Leave for Officers and Other Ranks who have been in the Country for less than 5 and 12 months respectively will be submitted for approval of G.O.C. Army through this office. If granted they will come out of above allotment.

3.   Leave under M.S.Circular 19898 (30 days for tired officers) may be submitted for consideration; such leave, if granted, will normally come out of allotment above.

4.   A copy of Leave Train Service is on reverse.

5.   Leave for Commanders of Formations, Commanding and Staff Officers, will be submitted to this office for approval before being granted.

6.   The above allotment cancels that for Re-engagement Leave issued under this office letter A/7555/8 of 7/5/18.

                                  (sd) C.J.SAUNDERS.
                                                       Major,
28th May 1918.   D.A.A.G.,62nd (West Riding) Division.

TRAIN CIRCULAR 17.

LEAVE TRAIN SERVICE TO BOULOGNE
FROM 1st JUNE UNTIL FURTHER NOTICE.
------

1. All leave men for BOULOGNE will proceed from Railhead by return empty supply trains via ABBEVILLE.

2. The approximate times of departure from Railheads are shown below.

3. R.T.O., DOULLENS, will arrange, as far as possible, to collect all leave men from the returning empty supply trains at DOULLENS EXCHANGE, and forward them to ABBEVILLE together on the best convenient train.

4. On the return journey leave men will be sent from BOULOGNE to ETAPLES to be forwarded by REINFORCEMENT trains.

APPENDIX H

CASUALTIES DURING MAY 1918.

OFFICERS.

10.5.18.	Lieut.	J. OWEN	310th Bde R.F.A.	Wounded.
16.5.18.	Lieut.	C.E. MORIER	5th West Rid. Regt.	do
"	2/Lt.	R.B. HILL	do	do
"	"	J. SCOTT	2/7th do	do
18.5.18.	Capt.	W.G. JAMES, D.S.O.	5th K.O.Y.L.I.	do
19.5.18.	Lt. Col	C.K. JAMES, D.S.O.	(Border Regt, Cmdg (2/7th West Yorks.	Killed.
"	2/Lt.	S. POWELL	2/7th West Yorks.	Wounded.
21.5.18.	2/Lt.	R. DONKERSLEY	2/5th do	do
22.5.18.	"	C.H. CROFTS	(K.O.R.L. attd (5th K.O.Y.L.I.	W at duty.
24.5.18.	2/Lt.	R. LANCE	8th West Yorks.	Wounded.
"	"	R.J. INGLEBY	do	do
"	Lieut.	E. PEPPER	do	Missing.
"	Capt.	G.F.M. LING	(2/7th West Yorks (attd 185th T.M.B.	Killed.
"	2/Lt.	A.C. POTTER	2/4th West Riding	W at duty.
26.5.18.	"	A. MCKINNON	62nd Bn. M.G.C.	Wounded.
29.5.18.	"	P. DE LACY	2/5th West Yorks	do
"	"	H. NEWTON	2/4th York & Lancs	do
"	1st Lt.	A.P.H. SAGE	(M.O.R.C., U.S.A. attd (2/1st W.R. Fld Ambce	Killed.
30.5.18.	Capt.	J.J.G. GREENWOOD	2/5th West Yorks.	Wounded.

OTHER RANKS.

Killed	...	62.
Wounded	...	392.
Missing	...	14.

App 1

REINFORCEMENTS RECEIVED DURING MAY 1918.

	Offrs.	O.R.	
8th West Yorkshire Regiment	2	94	
2/5th West Yorkshire Regiment	2	78	
2/7th West Yorkshire Regiment	5	78	
5th West Riding Regiment	-	80	
2/4th West Riding Regiment	1	72	
2/7th West Riding Regiment	-	37	
5th K.O.Y.L.I.	1	104	
2/4th K.O.Y.L.I.	1	167	
2/4th York & Lancaster Regiment	-	28	
Royal Artillery	10	181	Includes 5 Indians.
Royal Engineers	1	64	
62nd (W.R) Divisional Signal Co.	-	23	
62nd (W.R) Divisional Train	1	17	
62nd (W.R) Divisional R.A.M.C.	5	63	
62nd Bn. Machine Gun Corps	5	184	
9th Durham L.I. (Pioneers)	6	22	
	40	1292	

1.6.18.

APPENDIX J

REWARDS GRANTED DURING MAY, 1918.

Victoria Cross.	1
D.S.O.	4
Bar to M.C.	6
M.C.	39
Bar to D.C.M.	3
D.C.M.	21
Bar to M.M.	5
M.M.	143

Original. Vol 18

CONFIDENTIAL.

WAR DIARY

OF

HEADQUARTERS, 62ND (WEST RIDING) DIVISION 'A'.

1ST JUNE 1918 to 30TH JUNE 1918.

VOLUME XVIII.

Army Form C. 2118.

SECRET.

WAR DIARY
or
INTELLIGENCE SUMMARY.

62nd (West Riding) Division
A.J.Q.

JUNE 1918
p. 1.

(Erase heading not required.)

Place	Date	Hour	Summary of Events and Information	Remarks and references to Appendices
HENU	1st		Weather Fine — Intimation rec'd that 1/5 Devons and 2/4 Hants would arrive shortly and replace 2/7 W. Yorks and 2/7 W. Riding Regt., who would be formed into Training Bns. after reinforcing 1/5 and 1/6 Devons — Balance to go to Base	BJD
HENU	2nd		Weather Fine — V.C. awarded to 203590 Pte T. YOUNG 9th Bn D.L.I.	BJD
HENU	3rd		Weather Fine — Altogether 3 Offrs 70 O.Rs rec'd fr Third Army Rest Camp to depart on 9th Inst.	BJD
HENU	4th		Weather much Colder — Intimation received 1/5th Devons and 2/4th Hants arriving shortly and to go to FONCTION and AMPLIER Respectively	BJD
HENU	5th		Weather Fine and Warm — 1/5th Devons Rev'd Devons and Hants arriving — latter arrived DOULLENS 5pm and marched to Billets at AMPLIER. No news of former due at MONDICOURT 10 a.m.	BJD
HENU	6th		Weather Fine — Learnt that Devons sent in Error to MFQ OES . Second Army Area — and finally arrived at MONDICOURT at 7.10 pm	BJD
HENU	7th		Administrative Instructions re Breakup of 2/7 W. Yorks and 2/7 W. Ridings issued to all Officers	BJD
HENU	8th		Weather Still Fine and Very Dry	BJD
HENU	9th		SUNDAY — Weather Fine in Morning Some Rain in Evening — Colder	BJD

Army Form C. 2118.

WAR DIARY
or
INTELLIGENCE SUMMARY.
(Erase heading not required.)

JUNE 1918

Place	Date	Hour	Summary of Events and Information	Remarks and references to Appendices
HENU	10		Weather Cooler – Some Rain during Day. G.O.C. presented Medal Ribbons to R.A. in Afternoon – Certain Horses of HANTS and DEVONS used in EGYPT found to be mangy	BM
do	11th		Weather Fine and Warmer. Brigade of 59th Div Arty withdrawn to Rest near PITS and 312th Add. RFA (Tactically under 57th Div) withdrawn to town, not at 1 hours Notice	BM
do	12th		Weather Fine	
do	13th		Weather Fine. Instructions Received that Battalion Training Staff Cadres 1/7 W.Yorks and 2/7 W. Ridings were to leave Divl. Area on 16th inst and proceed to join 145 (Training Cadre) DIVISION. Hence they would go to ENGLAND. Arrangements made for the 2 O/Ns to be withdrawn from the Line on 15th inst, and proceed to Relief at FAMECHON and AMPLIER which would then be vacated by DEVONS and HANTS to relieve them in the Line – Administrative Instructions issued	BM Appendix B
do	14th		Weather Fine. 1/5 DEVONS and 2/4 HANTS moved to Line in Busses which returned to FAMECHON and AMPLIER with 1/7 W. Yks and 2/7 W. Ridings. AA & QMG proceeded on leave to U.K.	BM

Army Form C. 2118.

WAR DIARY
or
INTELLIGENCE SUMMARY.   JUNE 1918 p 3
(Erase heading not required.)

Instructions regarding War Diaries and Intelligence Summaries are contained in F. S. Regs., Part II. and the Staff Manual respectively. Title pages will be prepared in manuscript.

Place	Date	Hour	Summary of Events and Information	Remarks and references to Appendices
HENU	16th		Weather Fine. Training Staff Cadres of 2/7 W.Yorks and 2/7 W.Ridings proceeded by Rail from MONDICOURT to BOULOGNE via ABBEVILLE. Divl Commander presented Indian Distinguished Service Medals to 3 Indians of 62nd D.A.C. N.Z. Division Horse Show during afternoon. Neighbourhood of Divl Hrs Bombed between 12 Midnight and 1 a.m.	GW BW GW
HENU	17th		Weather Fine - Estb. of new Buses raised to 28 (rubbed) as per 2/7/9 8"	GW
HENU	18th		Weather Fine. Divl Cdr. presented Medals to 187 hep.tble of vants in morning	GW
HENU	19th		Weather Fine. Transport of 2/7 W.Yorks and 2/7 W.Ridings proceeded to Base by Road and Surplus Personnel (some 8 NCOs recently Trans to BASE - Break up of 2 Bns this completed, on 2 Remaining Bns. June 185 and 186 Inf Bdes had been made to Strength 1,40 Officers and 900 O Ranks + 5% in each Case	GW
			during early part of week.	
HENU	20th		Some much needed Rain during Day and Night	
HENU	21st		Weather Fine and Cooler - Divl Cdr. presented Medal Ribbons to 186 Inf Bde in morning	GW
do	22d		Some Rain. Intimation received that 37th Division would relieve 62nd Division at an early date - Leave in France in allotment of Twenty 60pt and 30 oRs per 10 days	GW
			for Division sanctioned	

Army Form C. 2118.

WAR DIARY
or
INTELLIGENCE SUMMARY.
(Erase heading not required.)

June 1918 p. 4

Instructions regarding War Diaries and Intelligence Summaries are contained in F. S. Regs., Part II. and the Staff Manual respectively. Title pages will be prepared in manuscript.

Place	Date	Hour	Summary of Events and Information	Remarks and references to Appendices
HENU	23rd		Weather cool – Estb phones from tanks to 32 Inf Bde B² Administrative Instructions re Relief of 62nd by 37th Division on 24/25th and 25/26 June issued	BM Appendix
HENU	24		Weather cool and some Rain – Relief of Division commenced. Troops of 37 Division coming up by Bus relieved Troops returning by them	BM Appendix "C"
PAS	25		Weather cool and finer – Relief complete and Division passed into G.H.Q. Reserve to be prepared for move at 9 hours notice to join XXII Corps – Dispositions after Relief as follows:– Divisional HQs at PAS 185 Inf Bde gp AUTHEULE AMPLIER, TERRAMESNIL 186 Inf Bde gp HENU THIEVRES 187 Inf Bde gp LOUVIN with Rly of AMPLIEUX R.A. at SARTON, ORVILLE with DHQ at AMPLIER Instructions re Statistical Return issued	BM
PAS	26		Weather Fine Cool – Number Influenza Cases noticeable in Division	BM
PAS	27		Weather Fine – Divis Cdr. proceeded on leave – Brig. Genl. ANDERSON GOC Assumed Command	BM
PAS	28		Weather Fine Summer – AA & QMG Returned from Leave	BM

Army Form C. 2118.

WAR DIARY
or
INTELLIGENCE SUMMARY.
(Erase heading not required.)

JUNE 1918
p. 5

Place	Date	Hour	Summary of Events and Information	Remarks and references to Appendices
PAS	28		(continued) IV Corps Boxing Championship at Corps HQ in afternoon. G-in-C represented in Finals. Light and Right Heavy Weights. But no wins were secured for the Division. Instructions re Tactical Trains issued	G.O.
PAS	29		Weather Fine. Instructions issued to deal with Influenza Epidemic.	G.O. Appendix D
PAS	30		Sunday. Weather Fine. Casualty Pierre closes and reopens midnight.	G.O.
			June 30/July 1 - Brigadier General T.W. Viscount HAMPDEN C.M.G. Coldstream Guards returned from Course at GRANTHAM and assumed Temporary Command of the Division.	G.O.

Appendix E - Casualties during June.
" F - Rewards granted during June.
" G - Reinforcements received during June.

[signature]
Lieutenant Brigadier General
Commanding 62nd (West Riding) Division.

30-6-18

SECRET.   62 Divn. No.A/8742/66.

ADMINISTRATIVE INSTRUCTIONS REGARDING THIS OFFICE A/8670/66 of 4-6-18.

1. An establishment for the Battalion Training Staff is attached herewith.
   Nominal rolls of Officers, N.C.Os and men selected for this will be rendered in triplicate. The Company Officers should, when possible, be of the rank of Captain.

2. Personnel of the 2/7th West Yorkshire Regiment and 2/7th Duke of Wellington's Regiment should be selected to make up the 8th and 2/5th West Yorkshire Regiments and the 5th and 2/4th Duke of Wellington's Regiments to a strength of 40 Officers and 900 other ranks. The basis of these Battalions' strengths may be taken to be column "A" in strength return on 15th June - 5% may be added for unascertainable sick wastages.
   Nominal rolls of above will be prepared in triplicate.

3. Nominal rolls of Officers, N.C.Os and men surplus after paras 1 and 2 have been complied with will be rendered in triplicate.

4. All rolls will be submitted to Divisional Headquarters.

5. Regimental funds will be dealt with in accordance with Third Army letter SQ/361 of 13-5-18, copies of which are attached for guidance.

6. Instructions with regard to ordnance stores, horses, etc., are being issued separately.

7. Detached and employed personnel of 2/7th West Yorkshire Regiment and 2/7th Duke of Wellington's Regiment will be dealt with as under :-

(a) DIVISIONAL EMPLOY.

   Such Officers and other ranks on Divisional Employ as are administered by the Camp Commandant and are NOT on the establishment of Divisional Headquarters will be included amongst those cross posted to Battalions within the Brigades. The Camp Commandant will forward a nominal roll to each of the 185th and 186th Infantry Brigades of the personnel concerned. This will be returned to him shewing Battalions to which posted.
   "A" men attached to 252 Employment Company and employed as above will be included in the roll which will be endorsed accordingly. When cross posted they will be in excess of the numbers required to bring the strength of the two other Battalions up to 900 other ranks, as they are already supernumerary to the strength of their present Battalions.

(b) DIVISIONAL AREA EMPLOY.

   Men employed as water police, burial duty, etc., etc., whom it is not desired to retain will be relieved as soon as possible under Brigade arrangements, the Officer under whom they are working being notified prior to arrival of relief.

(c) BRIGADE EMPLOY, CORPS & ARMY EMPLOY, HOSPITAL, LEAVE AND COURSES.

   Officers and men whom it is desired to retain will be cross posted within Brigades and the remainder included on the nominal rolls of men to be despatched to Base. Extra regimentally employed personnel will be relieved as soon as possible under Brigade arrangements, the Officer under whom they are working being notified in each case. Personnel for Base who return to Division after the main party has been despatched will be sent to Base under Brigade arrangements. Nominal rolls will be endorsed when for any reason it is not possible to despatch men with the main party to Base.

(d) <u>Divisional Wing.</u>

Instructional Staff will be cross posted within Brigades.
O.C. 62nd Divisional Wing will send nominal rolls to each of 185th and 186th Infantry Brigades of Staff concerned. This will be returned to him shewing Battalions to which posted.
Reinforcements not yet sent to join Battalions will be disposed of as desired by Brigades. O.C. Wing has been instructed to forward nominal rolls forthwith to Brigades, and to notify them immediately names of any further men arriving.

8. A.D.M.S. will issue instructions as to disposal of Medical Officers and Medical equipment and stores not already provided for.

9. The nominal rolls referred to in paras 1, 2 and 3 will be commenced forthwith, and finally rendered by last D.R. on 17th June.

Lieut-Colonel,
A.A. & Q.M.G., 62nd (West Riding) Division.

6/6/1918.

<u>D I S T R I B U T I O N.</u>

185th Inf. Bde.	4 copies.
186th Inf. Bde.	4 copies.
A.D.M.S.	1 copy.
Camp Commdt.	1 copy.
Divisional Wing	1 copy.
"G"	1 copy.

SECRET.   62 Div. No.A/9055/42.

ADMINISTRATIVE INSTRUCTIONS IN CONTINUATION OF THOSE ISSUED UNDER A/8742/66 dated 6-6-18, and reference G.834/S of 13-6-18.

1. Orders as to the move of CADRES from Divisional Area will be issued later.

2. On relief of 2/7th West Yorks and 2/7th West Riding Regiments on night 15/16th instant, the whole of each Battalion will proceed to billets at FAMECHON and AMPLIER respectively vacated by 1/5th Devons and 2/4th Hants Regiments. - The Battalions not being split up at SQUASTRE as directed in G.834/S.
   Wagon Lines and Q.M. Stores will move to FAMECHON and AMPLIER during 15th instant under Brigade arrangements.
   Application for lorries to move stores being made to Headquarters 62nd Division "Q" forthwith.
   Arrangements, which will be notified later, are being made to move the two Battalions, on relief, to their Billets.

3. The nominal rolls required by paras 1, 2 and 3 of A/8742/66 will reach this office by first D.R. on 15th instant.

4. Brigades will be responsible that a provisional Staff, consisting of a C.O., A/Adjutant, and A/Q.Mr. is formed forthwith within each of the Battalions to be broken up, which will be ready to carry on with the Administration of the remainder of the Battalion after departure of the Battalion Training Staff Cadre. This Staff will complete the settling of outstanding accounts, and preparing Balance Sheets in accordance with para 5 of A/8742/66, and the settlement of any other outstanding matters.

5. Until the parties for the Base have been despatched, the remaining personnel of the 2/7th West Yorks and 2/7th West Riding Regiments will be known within the Division for purposes of Administration, as the 2/7th West Yorks Regt. and 2/7th West Riding Regt. respectively. They will continue to be rationed as at present.

6. Personnel composing the Bands of the 2/7th West Yorks and 2/7th West Riding Regiments will be shown on a separate nominal roll to any of the three categories detailed in the instructions.
   Further orders will be issued as to their disposal.

7. Brigades will arrange to absorb personnel for cross-posting to the other two Battalions at the earliest possible date after the departure of the Cadre. Division "A" being notified on 18th instant as to proposed dates.

8. Brigades will arrange with O.C. Divisional Wing direct, as to withdrawal of any personnel.

C.F.Saunders
Major,
D.A.A.G., 62nd (West Riding) Division.

13/6/1918.

DISTRIBUTION.
185 Inf. Bde.   6 copies.(3 for Adv.Hqrs & 3 for Rear Hqrs).
186 Inf. Bde.   6 copies.(3 for Adv.Hqrs & 3 for Rear Hqrs).
62 Div. Wing.   1 copy.
"G".   1 copy.

SECRET.   62 Div. No.A/9058/66.

·········"········

FURTHER TO ADMINISTRATIVE INSTRUCTIONS ISSUED
UNDER THIS OFFICE A/9033/49 of 13-6-18.

1.   The Battalion Training Staffs of the 2/7th West Yorks and
2/7th West Riding Regiments will be prepared to leave IV Corps
area on 15th instant and take with them all their belongings.

2.   No Transport personnel or Transport will accompany them.
The following deletions will therefore be made from Table and
Addendum accompanying this office A/8742/66 of 6-6-18.

                                                Remarks.

(i) Personnel.
     ✱ Grooms   2.   ✱ To be cross-posted
     ✱ Drivers (1st line)   2   within Brigade or
       Driver A.S.C.   sent to Base.
        (Train Transport)   1

(ii) Horses.
       Riding.   7   )
       Draught.   3   )   Remain with other
       Heavy Draught.   )   Transport of 2/7th W.Yorks
        (Train Transport)   2.   )   and 2/7th W.Riding.
)   Separate instructions
(iii) Vehicles.   )   being issued.
       Bicycles.   3   )
       Cart, Offs.Mess.   1   )
       Cart, Water.   1   )
       Wagon, G.S. for   )
        Baggage & supplies. 1.   )

                                              C.J.Saunders
                                                        Major,
14/6/1918.   D.A.A.G., 62nd (West Riding) Division.

DISTRIBUTION.
    185 Inf.Bde.   6 copies. (3 for Adv.Hqrs. & 3 for Rear Hqrs.)
    186 Inf.Bde.   6 copies   "   "   "   "   "   "   "
    62 Div.Train. 1 copy.
    "G".   1 copy.

SECRET.   Copy No........
                                                                  62nd Div.A/9434/49.

ADMINISTRATIVE INSTRUCTIONS IN CONNECTION WITH
62nd (W.R) DIVISION ORDER NO.123
of 22.6.18.

1. The following will hand over in present and take over in new Area (where applicable) by mutual arrangement with Officer Commanding similar detail in 37th Division.
   Relief to be complete by 6 a.m. June 26th 1918.

   A.P.M. and Traffic Control.
   O.C. S.A.A. Section.
   Baths Officer (taking over baths at PAS and HENU)
   Divisional Gas Officer.

2. The following will be relieved by 37th Division by 6 a.m. on 26th June 1918:-
   (a) Water Point Wardens in Divisional Area.
   (b) Burial Party at BIENVILLERS.
   (c) Town Major & Staff, SOUASTRE.
   (d) Town Major & Staff, FONQUEVILLERS.

   On relief detail in (a) will take over Water Points in new Area under arrangements to be made by Divisional Water Officer.
   (b), (c) and (d) will rejoin their units.

3. The following will not move :-

   Headquarters and 527 & 528 Coys Divisional Train.
   D.A.D.O.S.
   Salvage Coy.
   Mobile Veterinary Section.

4. RESERVE RATIONS.
   Rations in FONQUEVILLERS (2016 tins P.M. 2000 lbs Biscuit) will be handed over to incoming unit of 37th Division by 9th D.L.I. and a receipt obtained.

5. TENTS.
   All tents, trench shelters and tarpaulins other than Mobilisation equipment will be handed over to relieving units of 37th Division and a receipt obtained.

                                            J Langton
23.6.18.
                                                            Major,
                                       D.A.Q.M.G. 62nd (W.R) Division.

DISTRIBUTION.

Copy No.1	"G".	Copy No.12.	62nd (W.R) Divl.Train.
2-4	"Q"	13.	9th D.L.I.
5.	62nd (W.R) Div.Arty.	14.	D.G.O.
6.	185th Inf.Bde.	15.	D.G.R.O.
7.	186th Inf.Bde.	16.	Baths Officer.
8.	187th Inf.Bde.	17.	Divl.Water Officer.
9.	D.A.D.V.S.	18.	T.M. SOUASTRE.
10.	A.P.M.	19.	T.M. FONQUEVILLERS.
11.	D.A.D.O.S.	20.	O.C. Salvage Coy.
		21.	O.C. S.A.A. Section.
		22.	37th Division.
		23.	IV Corps "Q".

24. G.R.E.   25. Signal Co.   26. A.D.M.S.
27. M.G.Bn.   28. Div.Reception Camp.   29 Camp Commandant.

62nd Div. A/9729/24.

INFLUENZA

1. The following measures will be carried out forthwith to check the spread of the present influenza epidemic.

   The constant personal supervision of every officer and N.C.O. is required to ensure that they are observed.

   The main principles to be followed are the avoidance of crowding and the most thorough airing of billets and tents.

2. Until further orders no Entertainments or Church Services will be held other than in the open air.

3. **TENTED CAMPS.**
   Strict orders to be issued that all tents to be kept brailed up, and during fine weather no man to be in his tent during the day.
   All kits, etc., to be cleared out of tents in day time.

4. **BILLETS.**
   (a) No man to be in his billet during day except in the case of wet weather.
   (b) Arrangements to be made that all meals are consumed in the open.
   (c) All old straw to be cleared out of billets forthwith.
   (d) The most thorough measures possible taken to air all billets during the day.
   (e) Billets with windows to have these always kept open (so far as air raid precautions allow).

5. In billets and tents where cases have occurred, the billet or tent will be thoroughly aired and cleaned and the usual medical precautions taken against infection. All kits and blankets (if any) being removed.

   Occupants of infected billets etc., who have not developed the complaint should be kept isolated under Unit's arrangements.

6. **DIVISIONAL RECEPTION CAMP.**
   Drafts arriving will be accommodated in separate lines and not join their units for a period of 4 days after arrival and then only after medical examination. These drafts will be kept under constant medical supervision during the 4 days mentioned above, so that cases can be immediately detected.

7. **OFFICERS' QUARTERS.**
   All precautions outlined above refer also to Officers' billets and tents where applicable.

                                HAROLD. F. LEA   Lieut Colonel.
29.6.1918.   A.A. & Q.M.G. 62nd (West Riding) Division.

DISTRIBUTION.

185th Infantry Brigade.	5	62nd Bn M.G.Corps	1
186th Infantry Brigade	5	9th Bn. D.L.I.	1
187th Infantry Brigade	5	Signal Co.	1
62nd Divisional Artillery	4	Camp Commandant	1
C.R.E.	4	General Staff	1
A.D.M.S.	4	Sen.Chaplain C of E	1
62nd Divl. Train	5	Sen.Chaplain Non C Of E	1
A.P.M.	1	Entertainment Officer	1
		Claims Officer	1

APPENDIX E

CASUALTIES DURING JUNE 1918.

OFFICERS.

1.6.18.	2/Lieut.	HOUGHTON.	W.G.	5th K.O.Y.L.I.	Wounded.
2.6.18.	"	CHAMPION.	A.S.	2/4th K.O.Y.L.I.	do.
4.6.18.	Capt.	HAIGH.	A.R.	5th West Rid. Rgt.	do.
5.6.18.	2/Lieut.	MANN.	G.	62nd Bn M.G.C.	do.
5.6.18.	"	JOSLIN.	G.A.	312th Bde R.F.A.	do.
5.6.18.	Lieut.	BANTON.	J.H.	8th West Yorks Rgt.	do.
7.6.18.	"	WILKINSON.	T.W.M.	8th West Yorks Rgt.	W.at duty.
9.6.18.	2/Lieut.	DODD.	G.H.	West Yks Rgt.attd 5th West Rid.Rgt.	Wounded.
15.6.18.	Lieut.	HORNE.	L.J.	2/4th K.O.Y.L.I.	Killed.
11.6.18.	2/Lieut.	KNOWLES.	J.E.	2/7th West Yorks R.	Wounded.
21.6.18.	Lieut.	COOPER.	D.E.	Signal Coy.	Wounded.
23.6.18.	2/Lieut.	DONELLY.	W.	5th K.O.Y.L.I.	Wounded.
23.6.18.	2/Lieut.	BOTTOMLEY.	F.	5th K.O.Y.L.I.	Wounded.

Other Ranks.

Killed	....	54.
Wounded	....	353.
Missing.	....	12.

APPENDIX F

REWARDS GRANTED DURING JUNE 1918.

Victoria Cross.   1.   203590 Pte T. Young
                                9th Bn DLI (see attached)
D.S.O.   1.
M.C.   3.
Bar to Military Medal.   1.
Military Medal.   12.

REINFORCEMENTS RECEIVED DURING JUNE 1918.

	Offrs.	O.R.
8th West Yorkshire Regiment.	-	41
2/5th West Yorkshire Regiment.	-	58
2/7th West Yorkshire Regiment	-	20
1/5th Devonshire Regiment.	-	9
5th West Riding Regiment	-	61
2/4th West Riding Regiment.	-	122
2/7th West Riding Regiment	-	9
2/4th Hampshire Regiment	-	115
5th K.O.Y.L.I.	1	208
2/4th K.O.Y.L.I.	2	118
2/4th York & Lancaster Regiment	-	111
62nd (W.R) Divisional Artillery	-	40
62nd (W.R) Divisional Engineers	-	84
62nd (W.R) Divisional Signal Company	-	7
62nd (W.R) Divisional Train.	-	10
62nd (W.R) Divisional R.A.M.C.	4	49
62nd Bn. Machine Gun Corps	5	65
9th Bn. Durham Light Infantry (Pioneers)	-	60
	12	1187

S P E C I A L   O R D E R

by

Major General W.P.Braithwaite, C.B.,

Commanding 62nd (West Riding) Division.

2nd June 1918.

The Divisional Commander has the honour to announce that His Majesty The King has conferred the VICTORIA CROSS on No.203590 Private THOMAS YOUNG, 9th Battalion Durham Light Infantry (Pioneers).

" For conspicuous gallant conduct in face of the enemy near - - - - from 25th March to 31st March 1918.

This stretcher bearer during the whole course of the operations showed a most magnificent example of courage and devotion to duty. On nine different occasions he went out in front of our line in broad daylight under heavy rifle, machine gun and shell fire which was directed on him, and brought back wounded to safety, those too badly wounded to be moved before dressing he dressed under this harassing fire, and carried them unaided to our lines and safety, he rescued and saved nine lives in this manner.

His untiring energy, his disregard to personal danger in the performance of his duties, and the great skill he showed in dealing with casualties, are beyond all praise. For five days he worked unceasingly evacuating wounded from the seemingly most impossible places."

Harold Lea.

Lieut.Colonel,

A.A.& Q.M.G., 62nd (West Riding) Division.

62nd Division

A. & Q.

62nd DIVISION

J U L Y, 1 9 1 8.

CONFIDENTIAL.

WAR DIARY

OF

HEADQUARTERS, 62ND (WEST RIDING) DIVISION 'A'.

1st JULY 1918. to 31st JULY 1918.

VOLUME XIX.

Army Form C. 2118.

HEADQUARTERS (ADMINISTRATIVE) WAR DIARY or INTELLIGENCE SUMMARY.
(West Riding) Division.

JULY 1918
p. 1.

Place	Date	Hour	Summary of Events and Information	Remarks and references to Appendices
PAS.	1		Weather Fine — D.A.Q.M.G. proceeded on leave. Major W.O. WRIGHT D.S.O. Staff Captain 186 Inf Bde attached to Divisional HQ's Foot as D.A.Q.M.G.	A.Q.
PAS	2		Weather Fine: Much warmer —	A.Q.
PAS	3		Weather Fine	
PAS	4		ditto	
PAS	5		ditto	
PAS	6		ditto	
PAS	7		ditto — Conference at Div. HQ's. A.E.S.O.1, A.A.&Q.M.G., and Staff Captains Infantry Brigades re Action in Event of Battle Position and Entrenchment at	A.Q.
PAS	8		ditto Administrative Instructions issued as result of above — Balance of Men above 920 in 8th and 2/5 W.Yorks, namely 124 in 8th and 72 in 2/5 W.Ypo sent to join 9th KOYLI in 21st Division. Bde above 920 in Tour of 2/4 D.of W's sent to Reserve — M2 210 o5 Staff/Other Officers above 40 in 8th and 2/5 W.Ypo, 5th and 2/4 D/W's posted to other Bn's in Division to bring latter up to 40 Officers per Bn.	A.Q. Appendix A A.Q. A.Q.
PAS	9		186 Inf Bde Sports in Afternoon	A.Q.

HEADQUARTERS WAR DIARY
(ADMINISTRATIVE)
INTELLIGENCE SUMMARY
(West Riding) Division

Army Form C. 2118.

JULY 1918
p.2.

Place	Date	Hour	Summary of Events and Information	Remarks and references to Appendices
PAS	9		Weather fine in morning, some much needed rain in afternoon, fine evening, rain in night.	
PAS	10		Estimate of accommodation for Camp Adm^r required to replace Tents forwarded to Corps	Appendix B
do	11		G.O.C. and A.A. & Q.M.G. visited XXII Corps in morning. Div^l H.Q.s Sports in afternoon. Intimation Rec^d that A.O.T.N.E. was changed to DOULLENS for entraining Station. 187 Bde forwarded to Corps.	Appendix C
do			Fresh Entrainment Instructions issued X. Capt H.S. INGEYRE D.S.O. Yorks Regt.	Appendix C
do	12		Appt. Bde Major 185 Inf Bde (pending confirmation) vice Capt H. RUTHVEN M.C. who went to Hospital owing to Broken Collar Bone sustained in Horse accident.	GRO
do			185 Inf Bde Sports in afternoon. Maj. Genl BRAITHWAITE returned from leave.	GRO
do	13		Brig.-Genl. Vis^l. HOWARD assumed Command 185 Inf Bde.	GRO
do			Orders received for Division to move by Strategical Train from Rwd Army to XIIInd Corps area concerning Entrainment from Ph'L'E huts -	
do			All M.T. to go by Rail. Administrative Instructions issued.	GRO
do	14		Entrainment commenced from DOULLENS N (187 Bde) DOULLENS S (185 Bde) MONDICOURT	
			186 Bde Dvl. Troops split amongst Bde Points - Artillery from all 3 Stations. First Train left DOULLENS N. 16.42 - Same at 3 hour intervals at each Station	GRO

Army Form C. 2118.

HEADQUARTERS WAR DIARY or INTELLIGENCE SUMMARY
(ADMINISTRATIVE)
(West Riding) Division.

JULY 1918 page 3

Place	Date	Hour	Summary of Events and Information	Remarks and references to Appendices
IN the TRAIN	15th		Entrainment continued. Divl. HQs Entrained MONCHOURT 6.12 am — Division proceeded to CHAMPAGNE. 1st Train (containing 187 Bde HQs) arrived destination — SOMMESOUS — about 7 p.m. Orders received that on Detrainment Divisional Personnel of Infantry Bns were to be moved in Lorries to CITRONS Region, Wheel transport, Field Coys, Field Ambulances, Train Coys et moved by Road. Staging 1 Night en Route. All orders given by French. Detrainment continued at following 3 Stations SOMMESOUS, MAILLY le CAMP and ARCIS Sur AUBE - Troops entrained on CITRONS Road - and moved forward to following Destinations 185 Bde JUVIGNY Area. 186 Bde FAVRIÈRES Area. 187 Bde AULNAY Area. Field Coys to NONTROSES, Field Ambces to AULNAY M.G. Bn to VRAUX.	
ARCIS	16th		Detrainment continued. Divl. HQs arrived MAILLY about 3 pm and moved to VRAUX. About 5 pm information received that Divisional Area was moved to TOURS Area. Divl. Arty Transmerced to Detrain about 9pm and moved by March Route, staging 1 Night in New Area namely POCANCY, ST. MARD and ROUFFY BN.	
TOURS SUR MARNE	17th		Divl. HQs moved to TOURS Sur MARNE - Bdes to following Areas - 185 Inf Bde TOURS - 186 Inf Bde ATHIS - 187 Inf Bde BISSEUIL - M.G.s CHAMPIGNEUL	

Army Form C. 2118.

WAR DIARY or INTELLIGENCE SUMMARY.

(Erase heading not required.)

HEADQUARTERS (ADMINISTRATIVE) (West Riding) Division.

JULY 1918 p 4

Place	Date	Hour	Summary of Events and Information	Remarks and references to Appendices
TOURS	17th		(continued) R.E.'s continued — Field Ambces with Bdes. — Detachment continued smoothly — Situation generally very changeable — Embussing continued until Feeds Bus Park finished — there were then 6 detached Companies awaiting Busing, 3 at MAILLY and 3 at SERMIERS — Bus owing to System L'Evéque Only 3 R.E. Coys travelled on each Bn Train. Remaining Coy arriving some 4 hours later. Detrainment complete about 8pm on 17th.	
~~TOURS~~ TOURS	18th		Concentration of Division completed by evening — Field Coys arrived last — 1 Tent Subsection of Field Ambulance sent to VERTUS to open up British Hospital there — Preliminary Orders rec'd to take over a Divisional Area in the II Italian Corps — 187 Bde moved up to SERMIERS to support positions. Order for Relief of Italian Corps Cancelled. Divn moved to Billeting Area (6) NOON — 185 Inf Bde ST IMOGES, 186 Inf Bde GERMAINE, 187 Inf Bde relieved at SERMIERS — M.G. Bn and R.E's at LA NEUVILLE Previous to ST IMOGES. Div'l H.Q's at GERMAINE — Rear Echelon under	
TOURS	19th		DDMS [other?] TOURS — 3 of the 6 detached Coys sent to join Units	

Army Form C. 2118.

WAR DIARY
or
(ADMINISTRATIVE) INTELLIGENCE SUMMARY.

HEADQUARTERS
(West Riding) DIVISION.

JULY 1918 p.5

Place	Date	Hour	Summary of Events and Information	Remarks and references to Appendices
ST. IMOCKS	20th		Weather fine. 185 and 187 Inf Bdes attacked 8am 62 Division attacking on right 51st Div on left, 186 Inf Bde in Support. 187 Inf. Div. Regt, 185 Bde on left, 186 Inf Bde advanced and captured BOURN?, 185 Bde held up at MAREUIL. Estimated Casualties — 5th Devons 10 Officers and 150 o Ranks — 8th W.Yks 15 and 200, 2/5th W.Yks 15 and 200 — 2/4 W.Ridings 2 and 125, 5th KOYLIs 2 and 50, 2/4 Yorks & Lancs 2 and 50. Noticeable feature of move to Assembly Positions was the complete stalk? of? of the Roads and difficulties of Traffic Control with troops of French Italian & British Divisions on same Roads.	
do	21st		Weather Fine. Division attacked Chen de COURT TREON at 10.30am with 2/4 D.L.I and Coy of 5th KOYLI also 2/4 York and Lancs. Attack not successful. Small advance made. Cyclist Patrols Battalion placed at disposal of Division and detailed to 186 Inf Bde. — 73rd Prisoners fr. 20th 21st July 3 officers 530 O Rs	
			Total Estimated Casualties from beginning of Place
			185 Inf Bde 5th Devons 10 Offrs 200 ORs 186 Inf Bde 5th W.Ridings 7 and 200 187 Inf Bde 5th KOYLI
			8th W.Yks 10 — 270 — 2/4 do 11 — 385 2/4 KOYLI 9 and 200
			2/5 do 12 — 320 — 2/4 Hants 10 — 250 2/4 York & Lancs 150
			M.G.C. 25 ORs

Army Form C. 2118.

WAR DIARY
or
INTELLIGENCE SUMMARY. JULY 1918 p. 6

HEADQUARTERS (ADMINISTRATIVE) (West Riding) Division.

(Erase heading not required.)

Place	Date	Hour	Summary of Events and Information	Remarks and references to Appendices
ST IMOGES	22nd		Weather Fine. 186th Inf Bde attacked and Captured BOIS DE PETIT CHAMPS with 5th Bn D of W's Regt. 200 Prisoners 30 M.G.'s reported taken — Total Prisoners taken since 20th July, 7 Officers 253 O.R's 60 M.G.'s — Total Est. Casualties since Commencement of Phase — 9th D.L.Infantry 7 Officers and 240 O.Ranks, 185th Inf Bde 5th Devons 9 Officers and 302 O.Ranks 2/5 W.Yks 12 and 400, 1/8 W.Yks 2/4 Y and 200 Otherwise no change from 21st Inst	
ST IMOGES	23rd		Weather Fine. 185 and 186 Inf Bdes attacked and Captured MONTAGEX and COURTON and Consolidated on line forward of those villages — All Objectives for Day Taken — Total Prisoners since 20th Inst. 7 Officers 428 O.R's — Divl. HQ's moved in evening to HAUTVILLERS where HQ's settled in same buildings with 51st Divmn Forward Signal Office and APM Remp. left at ST IMOGES — Further Total Estimated Casualties — 5th W.Riding 13 Officers and 400 men — 9th D.L.I. 7 and 240, M.G.B. 1 and 56.	

Army Form C. 2118.

WAR DIARY or INTELLIGENCE SUMMARY.

HEADQUARTERS (ADMINISTRATIVE) (West Riding) DIVISION.

JULY 1918 PT

(Erase heading not required.)

Place	Date	Hour	Summary of Events and Information	Remarks and references to Appendices
HAUTVILLERS	24th		Weather Fine. 187 Inf. Bde withdrawn for Reorganisation to NOGENT. Advice received of approx. 1600 Reinfts on the way — Arrangements made to receive them at TOURS s/MARNE where Reception Camp is established — PM	
do	25th		Weather Fine. A Quiet Day. Approx. 1700 Reinfts arrive for various Units as advised — During Night Waggon Lines of 185 Inf Bde Bombed. Several Horse & man Casualties. Heavy bombing JEPERNAY in evening — Total Estimated Casualties since commencement of Operations	

187 Inf Bde

3rd Devons	10 Offrs 331 ors	5th W. Ridings	13 and 400
8th 1st Yks	13 — 344 —	do	11 and 385
2/5 do	14 — 401 —	2/4 do	10 and 250

187 Inf Bde

		Div. Troops
5th Koyli	9 and 300	9th D.L.I 7 and 320
2/4 do	9 and 250	62nd B" N.G. 1 and 85
2/4 Hants	10 and 250	2/4 Yorks L 9 and 250

Artillery, RE and other Units Casualties were light.

HEADQUARTERS WAR DIARY or INTELLIGENCE SUMMARY

Army Form C. 2118.

(West Riding) Division.

July 1918. p. 8.

Place	Date	Hour	Summary of Events and Information	Remarks and references to Appendices
HAUTVILLERS	26th		Weather fine in morning with Rain in Evening - A Quiet day.	
do	27th		Much Rain during day. Dinan attacked at 7 a.m. in conjunction with 51st Division. Leave Allotment via HAVRE of 2 Officers & 48 men for day received. In consequence of Morning's Advance and Evidence that Germans were retreating Advd Divl HQrs moved to NANTEUIL at 6 pm, sharing place with G Office 51st Divl HQs and 177 Infantry Brigade, remainder of HQs remaining at HAUTVILLERS - 51st Divl HQs moved similarly - Corps Cavalry Regt placed at disposal of Division.	4
do	28th		No Rain but dull - 155 Infantry Brigade attacked and captured Mont de BLIGNY in morning. 63 Prisoners taken. Further Leave Allotment of 16 per day received for Devons 5 Tomts.	4
			Further Estimated Casualties during day brought totals to following:-	
			165 Inf Bde 15 Officers 14 Oth 220 ORanks 189 Inf Bde 5 NCO Y.K.L. Offs 300 ORanks BR Workers 15 450 13 375 /5 4 12 400 9/L 9/L 19 379	

Army Form C. 2118.

HEADQUARTERS WAR DIARY / INTELLIGENCE SUMMARY
(ADMINISTRATIVE)

(West Riding) Division.

JULY 1918   p. 9.

Place	Date	Hour	Summary of Events and Information	Remarks and references to Appendices
HAUTVILLERS	29th		Warning Order received for Div: We withdrawn preparably to entrainment of another area, on night 30/31st. Artillery to entrain 12 mn. 31st at rate of 6 trains per diem at CHÂLONS s/MARNE & COOLUS. Infantry & commence entraining 12 mn. 2nd August at rate of 18 trains per diem at CORBON — COOLUS — VITRY LA VILLE. Weather fine. Total Casualties since 20th inst. 10 officers 538 O.Rs. 91 M.G's. 8 75 mm guns recaptured. 1 Searchlight	
do	30		Weather fine. Order of March Post of Brigade Group before Command St French Army D.I.V. MAGENTA. G. Offices & MAGUIS returned to HAUTVILLERS from NANTEUIL.	

Army Form C. 2118.

WAR DIARY or INTELLIGENCE SUMMARY

HEADQUARTERS (ADMINISTRATIVE) ___ (West Riding) Division.

JULY 1918. page 10.

Place	Date	Hour	Summary of Events and Information	Remarks and references to Appendices
HAUTVILLERS	31st		Weather fine.	
			Order of the Day by General BERTHELOT and Special Order by Lt-General Sir A.J. Godley KCB, KCMG Commdg XXII Corps dated 31.7.18 received. (See Appendix).	
			Special Order of the day issued by G.O.C. 62nd Division (see Appendix) D	See Appendix
			Casualties, reinforcements & rewards for month of July 1918.	E
	31.7.18		Divisional H.Q.s moved to BISSEUIL	

[signature] Lieut.Col.
aa aa amg for Major General
Commanding 62nd (W.R.) Division

E Casualties during July.
F Rewards granted during July
G Reinforcements received during July.
H Operations in RHEIMS Area July 20th to 31st -
Administrative Notes - Supply arrangements letter to Expeditionary Force Canteens

S E C R E T.   62nd Div. A/10048/49.

ADMINISTRATIVE INSTRUCTIONS IN THE EVENT OF ORDERS BEING RECEIVED TO TAKE UP 'BATTLE POSITIONS'

Further to this office A/9121/49 dated 15/6/18 and A/9130/49 dated 18/6/18, the latter to 62nd Div. Arty only.

With reference to PROVISIONAL DEFENCE SCHEME, LEFT RESERVE DIVISION, IV CORPS, so far as an attack on the Corps Front is concerned.

1. AMMUNITION.
   Liaison Bombardiers will report to present Infantry Brigade Headquarters, namely:-

   185th Infantry Brigade.   AUTHIEULE.
   186th   -do-   HENU.
   187th   -do-   COUIN.

2. BAGGAGE.
   H.D. horses of baggage wagons have already reported to units.
   Baggage for which transport is not available will be dumped under guard under Brigade arrangements and moved back as opportunity offers to the point on the SARTON - ORVILLE Road where the baggage wagons will have already moved as ordered by para.2 of A/9121/49.

3. NUCLEUS PERSONNEL.
   Nucleus and all other personnel not required in action will move by march route to Divisional Reception Camp, ORVILLE, taking one day's plus the unexpended portion of the current day's rations with them.
   O.C. Divisional Reception Camp will arrange to accommodate and ration such personnel thenceforward until they are ordered to rejoin their units, and will forward a daily state to Divisional Headquarters showing numbers of O.Rs by Units, and Officers by name.

                                    C.J.Saunders Major
                                    for Lieut. Colonel.
                                    A.A. & Q.M.G. 62nd (West Riding) Division.

8/7/18.

Distribution:-
   To all recipients of A/9121/49 and A/9130/49.

IV Corps 'Q'.

Return in accordance with Q/GG/40 dated 6.7.18, para.1.

ACCOMMODATION REQUIRED IN LEFT RESERVE (G.H.Q. RESERVE) DIVISION AREA, IV CORPS.

The figures given below are based on the distribution of troops on July 9th 1918, on the assumption that they will be the same during the coming Winter.

Personnel now in weather-proof billets are only taken into account for Recreation Rooms, and in some cases, Mess and Dining Huts.

TABLE 'A'.

		NUMBERS	TO BE	ACCOMMODATED.	
CLASS OF ACCOMMODATION	OFFICERS	OTHER RANKS	NURSES	Q.M.A.A.C.	REMARKS.
Sleeping	276	6793	-	-	33 Huts.
Officers' Messes	199	-	-	-	47 Huts.
Dining Rooms	-	7747	-	-	13 Huts.
Recreation Rooms	-	9941	-	-	{ 2 Large Huts { 15 Small Huts.
To supplement existing Field Ambulance } Hospital Accommodation. }	10	290	-	-	

For details by Areas and Units see below, Table 'B'.

TABLE 'B'.

AREA AND UNIT.	HOW NOW SITUATED.	CLASS OF ACCOMMODATION AND NUMBERS TO BE ACCOMMODATED.										
		SLEEPING			OFFICERS' MESSES.			DINING ROOMS.			RECREATION ROOMS.		FIELD AMBULANCE TO SUPPLEMENT EXISTING HOSPITAL ACCOMMODATION.
		No. of Offrs	No. of O.Rs	No. of Separ- ateHuts	No. of Offrs.	No. of Huts.	No. of O.Rs.	No. of O.Rs.	No. of Separ- ateHuts	No. of O.Rs.	No. of Separ- ateHuts	No. of Patients	No. of Separate Huts.

AREA AND UNIT.	HOW NOW SITUATED.	Sleep Offrs	Sleep O.Rs	Sleep SepHuts	Mess Offrs	Mess Huts	Mess O.Rs	Dining O.Rs	Dining SepHuts	Rec O.Rs	Rec SepHuts	Patients	Sep Huts
COUIN BRIGADE GROUP													
Brigade H'Qrs	In tents at COUIN.	-	50	-	-	-	50	-	1	-	-	-	-
'A' Battalion.	ditto	30	800	-	30	5	800	800	5	800	1	-	-
'B' Battalion.	ditto	30	800	-	30	5	800	800	5	800	1	-	-
'C' Battalion.	ditto	30	800	-	30	5	800	800	5	800	1	-	-
M.G. Company.	Temporarily now in Trenches. Normally at COUIN.	10	200	-	10	1	200	200	1	-	-	-	-
Field Coy R.E.	Tents at SOUASTRE.	7	211	-	7	1	211	211	1	-	-	-	-
Field Ambulance.	AUTHIE MILL I.15.b.2.7.	10	231	-	-	-	-	-	-	231% 150@	1	90.O.Rs	6 small
HENU-THIEVRES BRIGADE GROUP.													
'A' Battalion.	In Tents D.14.a.	30	800	-	30	5	800	800	5	800	2	-	-
'B' Battalion.	Billets HENU.	-	-	-	-	-	-	-	-	800	1	-	-
'C' Battalion.	Billets THIEVRES.	-	-	-	-	-	-	-	-	800	1	-	-
Field Coy R.E.	Tents and Billets HURTEBISE FARM.	6	-	-	-	-	-	-	-	-	-	-	-

Unit	Location							
Field Ambulance	Tents & Billets HENU.	8						120 O.Rs 8 small
AUTHIEULE-AMPLIER-TERRAMESNIL BDE GROUP.								
Brigade H'Qrs.	Tents AUTHIEULE.		75					
'A' Battalion.	SUMMER CAMP, AMPLIER.	20	800	20	3	800	5	800	1
'B' Battalion.	Tents and Billets TERRAMESNIL.	29						800	1
'C' Battalion.	Tents and Billets AUTHIEULE.							800	1
Field Coy. R.E.	Tents & Billets MARIEUX.	8							
Field Ambulance.	Tents & Billets TERRAMESNIL.	5	80			250	1	250	
Train Coy A.S.C.	Tents AUTHIEULE.	4	100	4	1	100	1		10 Off. 80 O.R. 2 large 1 small
DIVNL. ARTILLERY.									
1 Brigade R.F.A.	Tents & Billets ORVILLE.	2	180			650	4	650	1
1 Brigade R.F.A.	Tents & Billets SARTON.	6	250			790	4	790	1
D.A.C.	Tents & Billets AMPLIER.	10	570	16	2	570	4	570	1
1 Company A.S.C.	Tents ORVILLE.	5	155	5	1	155			
PAS AREA.									
Divisional H.Q. & Signal Company.	PAS CHATEAU SUMMER HUTS.		200			400	2		
D.A.D.O.S. and SAlvage Company.	Tents, FAMECHON Rd.	2	100						

Qrs and 2 Coys Divisional Train	Tents, FAMECHON Road.	2	100	-	-	-	-	-	-
..rs and 2 Coys ..visional Train	Tents, FAMECHON Road.	12	221	12	221	2	-	-	-
..ob. Vet. Section.	Tents, MONDICOURT Road.	1	20	-	-	-	-	-	-
Pioneer Battalion (1 Coy) Probably only temporarily detached.	Tents, GOUIN	5	150	5	150	1	-	-	-
		276	6793	199	7747	47	9941	13	10 Off. 290 O.R. / 2 large 15 small

% personnel.   @ patients.

[signed]
Brigadier General.
Commanding 62nd (West Riding) Division.

9th July 1918.

SECRET.   62nd Div.A/10241/49.

ADMINISTRATIVE INSTRUCTIONS WITH REGARD TO DIVISION
ORDER G.428 OF 13.7.18.
                                                                              Copy No. 24.

1. **BILLETS AND CAMPS.**

   All billets will be settled before departure.
   Camps will be left standing after handing over to Area Commandants.
   Receipts for all tents, tarpaulins and shelters will be taken and forwarded to Divisional Headquarters.
   Billeting parties will be detailed to take over billets at destination: these will travel by the first train from each station.
   R.A. will make their own arrangements.

2. **DIVISIONAL RECEPTION CAMP.**

   All men at Brigade and Divisional Classes will rejoin units at their respective entraining stations under orders of O.C. Reception Camp.

3. **LEAVE.**

   All Staff Officers and Officers Commanding Units, will be recalled from leave forthwith.
   No Officers will proceed on leave after 13th July. Other Ranks may go up to and including 15th July.

4. A.P.M. will arrange for 1 N.C.O. and 3 men to report to the R.T.O. at each entraining station half an hour before entrainment commences.

5. **STATES.**

   Duplicate states will be made out showing strength of units, number of horses and axles and the train on which they are to travel. These will be handed to the Staff Officer detailed by Divisional Headquarters, half an hour before the troops arrive.

6. The following Officers are detailed to superintend :-

DOULLENS NORTH	Captain W.S.Caulfeild
DOULLENS SOUTH	Lieut. E.C.Gore
MONDICOURT	Captain R.Candlish.

   These officers will leave by the last train from their respective stations.
   They will report progress of entrainment to Armies concerned, showing by units the departures from noon to noon and a final telegram reporting completion of the entrainment.

7. **RATIONS.**

   Rations for consumption on 14th will be carried on the man.
   "   "   "   " *15th will be delivered by Divisional Train early on 14th and will be carried in cookers etc.,
   "   "   "   " 16th will be in supply wagons.
   "   "   "   " 17th will be in M.T.Column.
   "   "   "   " *18th will be drawn by Divisional Train & from Field Supply, DOULLENS and 19th carried on Railway Train.
                                                                              Depot

   * Divisional Train will deliver early on 14th as usual.
   The Divisional Train will refill on 14th and Supply wagons will at once join units travelling full with rations for consumption on 15th.

                                                                              P.T.O.

- 2 -

x These rations will be dumped by Divisional Train at entraining stations to be loaded by units as they entrain.
An Officer will be detailed to ensure these train rations being loaded on each train, and a sufficient party detailed to load them: this Officer will report completion to entraining Officer on duty at entraining station.

8. All Area and Corps employment will be recalled forthwith.

9. SURPLUS KIT.

Lorries, number of which will be notified separately, are being put at Brigade and separate Units' disposal to move surplus kit either to WAVANS or to entraining stations as may be desired.
In the latter case, it will be loaded on the train, under Brigade and Units arrangements, and taken to new area.
No dumps will be left in present area.

10. Time tables of trains will be forwarded as soon as received.

Harold Lea

13.7.18.

Lieut.Colonel,
A.A. & Q.M.G. 62nd (West Riding) Division.

DISTRIBUTION.

Copy No. 1.	A.D.C. for G.O.C.	Copy No.10.	A.D.M.S.62nd (W.R) Divn.
2-5	General Staff.	11.	D.A.D.V.S.62nd (W.R) Div.
3.	185th Infantry Brigade.	12.	A.P.M.62nd (W.R) Divn.
4.	186th Infantry Brigade.	13.	62nd Bn.M.G.C.
5.	187th Infantry Brigade.	14.	9th D.L.I.
6.	62nd (W.R) Divl.Arty.	15.	62nd (W.R) Div.Rec.Camp.
7.	C.R.E.62nd (W.R) Divn.	16.	Camp Comdt.62nd (W.R) Div.
8.	62nd (W.R) Divl.Sig.Coy.	17.	4th Corps "Q".
9.	62nd (W.R) Divl.Train.	18.	22nd Corps "Q".
		19.	Capt.R.Candlish.
		20.	Lieut.E.C.Gore.
		21-22	File.

SPECIAL ORDER OF THE DAY
by
Major General W.P.BRAITHWAITE, C.B.
Commanding 62nd (West Riding) Division.

31st July 1918.

The operations which commenced on the 20th July, were brought to a successful termination at midnight on the 30th July.

During the whole of this period the 62nd (West Riding) Division has had continuous fighting, manoeuvring, and marching in new and, hitherto, unknown country of a character entirely different from anything in which it has operated before during this campaign. Especially have the densely wooded slopes of the BOIS DE REIMS been a difficulty for troops unaccustomed to Wood Fighting.

But neither the difficulty of the country, nor the determined and bitter resistance of the enemy, have militated against the victorious operations of the Division.

The Division made a great name for itself at the Battle of CAMBRAI. It enhanced that reputation at BUCQUOY where it withstood the attacks of some of the best of the German troops up to that time flushed with success. It has, in this great battle, set the seal on its already established reputation as a fighting force of the first quality.

During the period it has been fighting with its comrades of the French Army and side by side with the 51st (Highland) Division, the 62nd (West Riding) Division has utterly defeated the 123rd German Division, which had to be withdrawn on the 22nd instant, and the 50th German Division (an assault Division of the first rank) shared a similar fate a few days later.

The fortitude, steadfastness and valour of all ranks has been beyond praise.

MARFAUX, CUITRON, BOUILLY, the clearing of the BOIS DU PETIT CHAMP, attest your gallantry, while ESPILLY, NAPPES, the advance up the ANDRE VALLEY and the capture of BLIGNY and the MONTAGNE DE BLIGNY, are evidence of your sustained valour.

To every Officer, Warrant Officer, Non-commissioned Officer and Private Soldier I tender my grateful thanks and express my unstinted admiration of their victorious efforts. They have gloriously upheld the highest traditions of the British Army.

It is with intense pride that, once again after a great victory, I have the honour to sign myself as Commander of the 62nd (West Riding) Division.

Walter Braithwaite
Major General

SPECIAL ORDER

By

Lieutenant-General Sir A.J. GODLEY, K.C.B., K.C.M.G.,

Commanding XXII Corps.

The following Order of the Day by General Bortholot commanding Fifth (French) Army, together with the Corps Commander's reply to it, are published for the information of all ranks.

The Corps Commander wishes this Order to be distributed as widely as possible, and to be read out on Parade, and takes this opportunity of expressing to the Commanders, Staffs and all Ranks of the 51st (Highland) and the 62nd (West Riding) Divisions, and all the Corps Troops, his thanks for the loyal assistance that he has had from them during the recent arduous operations.

He takes this opportunity of again expressing his admiration of the conspicuous valour and endurance of the troops and trusts that it may be his good fortune to have them again under his command in any future operations.

(Sgd) A.M. DE LA VOYE.

D.A & Q.M.G.

Headquarters,
31.7.1918.

Vme Armée
Etat-Major
3me Bureau

No. 1863/3

Q.G., le 30 Juillet 1918.

ORDRE GENERAL No. 63.

Au moment où le XXII C.A. Britannique est appelé à quitter la Vme Armée, le Général Commandant l'Armée lui exprime toute la reconnaissance et toute l'admiration qu'ont mérité les hauts faits qu'il vient d'accomplir.

A peine débarqué, tenant à honneur de participer à la contre offensive victorieuse qui venait d'arrêter la furieuse ruée de l'ennemi sur la MARNE et commençait à le rejeter en désordre vers le Nord, précipitant ses mouvements réduisant à l'extrême la durée de ses reconnaissances, le XXII C.A. s'est jeté avec ardeur dans la mêlée.

Poussant sans répit ses efforts, harcelant, talonnant l'ennemi il a, pendant 10 jours successifs d'apres combats, fait sienne cette vallée de l'ARDRE largement arrosée de son sang.

Grâce au courage héroïque et à la ténacité proverbiale des fils de la GRANDE-BRETAGNE, les efforts continus et répétés de ce brave Corps d'Armée n'ont pas été vains.

21 Officiers, plus de 1300 soldats prisonniers, 140 mitrailleuses 40 canons enlevés à l'ennemi, dont 4 divisions ont été successivement malmenées et refoulées,
la haute vallée de l'ARDRE reconquise avec les hauteurs qui la dominent au Nord et au Sud,
tel est le bilan de la participation Britannique à l'effort de la Vme Armée.

ECOSSAIS de la MONTAGNE, sous le Commandement du Général CARTER-CAMPBELL, Commandant la 51me Division,
Enfants du Yorkshire, sous le Commandement du Général BRAITHWAITE, Commandant la 62me Division,
Cavaliers NEO-ZELANDAIS et AUSTRALIENS,
Vous tous, Officiers et soldats du 22me C.A., si brillamment commandés par le Général Sir A. GODLEY, vous venez d'ajouter une page glorieuse à votre histoire.

MARFAUX, CHAUMUZY, MONTAGNE de BLIGNY, ces noms prestigieux pourront être écrits en lettres d'or dans les annales de vos régiments.

Vos amis Français se souviendront avec émotion de votre brillante bravoure et de parfaite camaraderie de combat.

LE GENERAL COMMANDANT LA Vme ARMEE,

'BERTHELOT'

Headquarters,
XXII Corps, 30th July 1918.

My dear General,

I have received your most kind letter of farewell and Order of the Day addressed to me and the XXII Corps, and both on my own behalf and on behalf of all the officers, non-commissioned officers and men of the Corps I thank you most deeply.

That we have been fortunate enough to participate under your Command in this, the Second Battle of the Marne, will ever be a source of great pride to us all, and we count ourselves lucky to have been so closely associated with you and our gallant French comrades of your Army.

It is with deep regret that we leave your Command, where we have been very happy and where we hope we have made many friends.

Your Order will be highly valued by us all. I am having copies made which will be circulated to all Regiments before they leave and will be read to the troops, so that all will know that their efforts have been appreciated and will be aware of the high praise you have been good enough to bestow.

I would like to take this opportunity of asking you to convey to your Staff our great appreciation of all the help they have given us. No trouble has been too great for them to take on our behalf and everything possible has been done for us.

In the name of the XXII Corps I wish the Fifth Army and its Commander continued success and prosperity, and we all hope that the best of good fortune may attend you till the final victory is assured.

Yours sincerely,

(Sd.) ALEX. J. GODLEY.

TRANSLATION

Vme Armée

Etat-Major
3me Bureau

No. 1863/3

Q.G., July 30th, 1918.

ORDER OF THE DAY No. 63.

Now that the XXII British Corps has received orders to leave the Fifth (French) Army, the Army Commander expresses to all the thanks and admiration which the great deeds, that it has just accomplished, deserve.

The very day of its arrival, feeling in honour bound to take part in the victorious counter-attack which had just stopped the enemy's furious onslaught on the Marne, and had begun to hurl him back in disorder to the North, the XXII Corps, by forced marches and with minimum opportunity for reconnaissance, threw itself with ardour into the battle.

By constant efforts, by harrying and by driving back the enemy for ten successive days, it has made itself master of the Valley of the ARDRE, which it has so freely watered with its blood.

Thanks to the heroic courage and proverbial tenacity of the British, the continued efforts of this brave Army Corps have not been in vain.

21 Officers and 1300 Other Ranks taken prisoners, 140 Machine Guns and 40 Guns captured from an enemy, four of whose Divisions have been successively broken and repulsed; the Upper Valley of the ARDRE, with its surrounding heights to the North and South, reconquered; such is the record of the British share in the operations of the Fifth Army.

Highlanders under the orders of General Carter-Campbell, commanding the 51st Division; Yorkshire lads under the orders of General Braithwaite, commanding the 62nd Division; Australian and New Zealand Mounted Troops; all officers and men of the XXII Army Corps, so ably commanded by General Sir A. Godley, you have added a glorious page to your history.

MARFAUX, CHAUMUZY, MONTAGNE de BLIGNY --- all those famous names will be written in letters of gold in the annals of your regiments.

Your French comrades will always remember with emotion your splendid gallantry and your perfect fellowship in the fight.

' BERTHELOT '

le General Commandant,
la Vme Armée.

NAMES OF OFFICERS.

Unit.	Rank.	Initials.	Name.	Nature of Casualty.	Date.
5th Devon Regiment.	Captain.	A.G.W.	CHURCH.	Killed.	20.7.18.
	T/2/Lieut.	J.	SMITH, King's Liverpool Regt.	Killed.	20.7.18.
	Captain.	V.R.	WINNICOTT.	Wounded.	20.7.18.
	2/Lieutenant.	G.D.	HALL.	Wounded.	20.7.18.
	2/Lieutenant.	H.M.	PATTERSON.	Wounded.	20.7.18.
	2/Lieutenant.	F.M.	STRINGFELLOW, Lanc. Fus.	Wounded.	20.7.18.
	2/Lieutenant.	H.J.	MITCHELL, M.C.	Wounded.	20.7.18.
	2/Lieutenant.	J.G.	THOMAS.	Wounded.	20.7.18.
	2/Lieutenant.	R.J.	PATON.	Wounded.	20.7.18.
	Major. (T/Lt-Col)	H.V.	BASTOW, Alexandra P. of W. Yks Rgt.	Wounded at duty.	20.7.18.
	2/Lieutenant.	R.W.	COLEMAN, R.Warwick Rgt.	Wounded.	22.7.18.
	2/Lieutenant.	R.	HAY.	Killed.	28.7.18.
	Lieutenant.	J.E.	SKELTON.	Wounded.	28.7.18.
	2/Lieutenant.	F.S.	HUISH.	Killed.	27.7.18.
	2/Lieutenant.	J.S.	LORAM.	Wounded.	27.7.18.
8th West Yorks Regiment.	2/Lieutenant.	T.R.	WILLIAMS.	Killed.	20.7.18.
	T/2/Lieutenant.	S.H.	BRAY.	Killed.	20.7.18.
	2/Lieutenant.	W.H.	DAWSON.	Killed.	20.7.18.
	Lieutenant.	T.W.M.	WILKINSON.	Killed.	20.7.18.
	Captain.	G.G.	KINDER, M.C.	Killed.	20.7.18.
	2/Lieutenant.	E.H.	SHUTTLEWORTH.	Killed.	20.7.18.
	Lieut.A/Captain.	J.E.	APPLEYARD.	Killed.	20.7.18.
	T/2/Lieutenant.	P.B.	WESLEY.	Wounded.	20.7.18.
	Lieutenant.	J.H.	BANTON.	Wounded.	20.7.18.
	2/Lieutenant.	W.	OLIVER.	Wounded.	20.7.18.
	2/Lieutenant.	H.	HORTON.	Wounded.	20.7.18.
	2/Lieutenant.	W.	METCALFE.	Wounded.	23.7.18.
	2/Lieutenant.	F.	ABE.	Killed.	23.7.18.
	Captain.	N.	MULLER. (Not in July A.L.but appears in Col.1034b)	Killed.	28.7.18.
	Lieutenant.	P.H.	BATTISHILL, M.C.	Wounded.	28.7.18.
	Lieutenant.	A.F.	JAMES.	Wounded.	28.7.18.
	2/Lieutenant.	R.	PEARSON, Yorkshire Regt.	Wounded & Missing.	28.7.18.

8th West Yorks Regiment. (Continued).	2/Lieutenant.	F.O.	LAMB. Yorkshire Regt.	Missing.	28.7.18.
2/5th West Yorks Regiment.	2/Lieutenant.	W.A.	CLIFFE. Yorkshire Regt.	Wounded.	28.7.18.
	2/Lieutenant.	P.	FIRTH.	Wounded & Miss:	29.7.18.
	Lieut.(A/Captain)	K.W.	GRIGSON. M.C. The Devon Regt.	Killed.	20.7.18.
	2/Lieutenant.	G.A.	De VILLE.	Killed.	20.7.18.
	Lieut.(A/Captain)	R.F.	WHITE.	Wounded.	20.7.18.
	Lieutenant.	A.	DICKES.	Wounded.	20.7.18.
	Lieutenant.	E.R.	WAUGH.	Wounded.	20.7.18.
	2/Lieutenant.	F.G.	WESTON.	Wounded.	20.7.18.
	2/Lieutenant.	P.	DE LACY.	Wounded.	20.7.18.
	2/Lieutenant.	L.T.	SAWNEY. M.C.	Wounded.	20.7.18.
	2/Lieutenant.	R.	DONKERSLEY. M.C.	Missing Bel'd Killed.	20.7.18.
	2/Lieutenant.	E.H.	BARDSLEY.	Wounded.	20.7.18.
	2/Lieutenant.	J.H.	SIMPSON.	Wounded.	20.7.18.
	2/Lieutenant.	R.B.	WALKER.	Wounded.	20.7.18.
	2/Lieutenant.	W.B.	SCHINDLER.	Missing.	20.7.18.
	Lieutenant.	B.M.	RILEY.	Wounded.	22.7.18.
	2/Lieutenant.	E.M.	KERMODE. D.S.O.,M.C., D.C.M	Died of wds.	26.7.18.
	2/Lieutenant.	W.T.	COLE. 4th Bn Yorkshire Regt.	Killed.	29.7.18.
	2/Lieutenant.	W.	JENNINGS. Yorkshire Regt.	Missing.	29.7.18.
5th West Riding Regiment.	Lieutenant.	F.H.	WAITE.	Wounded.	20.7.18.
	Captain.	F.A.	SYKES.	Wounded.	20.7.18.
	2/Lieutenant.	D.A.S.	HAIGH.	Wounded.	20.7.18.
	2/Lieutenant.	R.J.	MACHIN.(Shown in index to July A.L.Wounded at duty. 21.7.18. as Col.1208b but does not appear in body)		
	Lieutenant.	E.	TANNER. M.C.	Wounded.	20.7.18.
	2/Lieutenant.	J.C.D.	MOORE.	Died of wds.	20.7.18.
	2/Lieutenant.	F.R.W.L.	THORPE.	Wounded (Gas)	24.7.18.
	2/Lieutenant.	H.	GREENWOOD. West Yorks.	Wounded.	22.7.18.
	2/Lieutenant.	P.R.	BARNES. West Yorks.	Wounded.	22.7.18.
	2/Lieutenant.	L.F.	WALKER. West Yorks.	Wounded.	22.7.18.
	Lieutenant.A/Capt.	C.V.	BERNAYS. M.C.	Wounded.	22.7.18.
	2/Lieutenant.	E.R.	STOREY.	Missing.	22.7.18.
	Lieut.(A/Capt)	J.B.	COCKHILL. M.C.	Wounded at duty.	22.7.18.
2/4th West Riding Regiment.	2/Lieutenant.	J.I.	CHRISTMAS.Alex.O. of W.Yks Regt.	Wounded.	20.7.18.
	Captain.	A.B.	KEILLAR.	Wounded.	20.7.18.
	Captain.	H.E.	HINCHCLIFFE.	Wounded.	20.7.18.
	Lieutenant.	G.McG.	FLETCHER.	Wounded.	20.7.18.
	Lieutenant.	H.H.	PEET.	Wounded.	20.7.18.
	Lieutenant.	P.G.	CONACHER.	Wounded.	20.7.18.

2/4th West Riding Regiment. (Contd)	2/Lieutenant.	W.F.	MOORE.	Wounded.	20.7.18.
	2/Lieutenant.	H.O.	SYKES.	Wounded.	20.7.18.
	Lieutenant.	W.H.	MASSIE.	Wounded.	20.7.18.
	2/Lieutenant.	J.	MAUDE. D.C.M., West Yks Regt.	Missing.	20.7.18.
	2/Lieutenant.	H.R.	STENT. R.A.F.	Missing	20.7.18.
	Captain.	W.	SMITHSON.	Wounded at duty.	22.7.18.
	2/Lieutenant.	F.K.	MARSDEN.(Shown in index Wounded. to July A.L.as "F.K."but in Col.1209d as "F.R")		29.7.18.
2/4th Hampshire Regiment.	2/Lieutenant.	H.L.	WILLSHER.	Wounded.	20.7.18.
	Major.	G.M.J.	MOLYNEUX. D.S.O.	Wounded.	20.7.18.
	2/Lieutenant.	N.E.	SMITH. Lanc.Fusiliers.	Killed.	20.7.18.
	Lieutenant.	A.	SCOTT. Middlesex Rgt.	Wounded.	20.7.18.
	2/Lieutenant.	R.O.	CLAPCOTT.	Wounded.	20.7.18.
	2/Lieutenant.	H.L.	THURGOOD. W.Riding Rgt.	Wounded.	20.7.18.
	2/Lieutenant.	S.W.O.	DIXON.	Wounded.	20.7.18.
	2/Lieutenant.	F.C.	HOLBROOK. Gloucester R.	Wounded at duty.	21.7.18.
	2/Lieutenant.	T.R.	JOHNSON.	Wounded.	26.7.18.
	Lieutenant (A/Cpt)	W.H.	LEDGARD.	Wounded at duty.	22.7.18.
	Lieutenant.	C.F.	WILSON.	(Wounded (Died of Wds.	22.7.18. 27.7.18.
	Lieut.(A/Capt)	W.H.	LEDGARD.	Wounded.	25.7.18.
186 Trench Mortar Battery.	Lieutenant.	M.E.	BORNEMANN. W.Riding R.	Wounded.	20.7.18.
	Lieutenant.	M.	HOWARTH. W.Riding R.	Wounded.	22.7.18.
5th K.O.Y.L.I.	T/Lieut (A/Capt)	W.H.	SHORT.	Killed.	20.7.18.
	T/2/Lieutenant.	C.H.	CROFTS. K.O.R.L.	Killed.	20.7.18.
	Lieutenant.	A.	BURNELL.	Killed.	20.7.18.
	T/2/Lieutenant.	W.G.	PRETSELL. M.C.	Killed.	21.7.18.
	2/Lieutenant.	A.	MARR. West Yorks Rgt.	Wounded.	20.7.18.
	2/Lieutenant.	F.R.	CORSON. West Yorks Rgt.	Wounded.	20.7.18.
	2/Lieutenant.	J.	WAGSTAFFE. West Yks Rgt.	Wounded.	20.7.18.
	2/Lieutenant.	G.R.	MASKELL. West Riding Rgt.	Wounded.	20.7.18.
	Lieutenant.	J.	INGLE.	Wounded.	22.7.18.
2/4th K.O.Y.L.I.	T/2/Lieutenant.	R.N.	MILBURN.	Killed.	20.7.18.
	Lieutenant (A/Cpt)	J.H.	WELLINGTON. M.C. East Yorks Regt.	Wounded.	20.7.18.
	Lieutenant.	A.	WOODGER. East Yorks R.	Wounded.	20.7.18.
	2/Lieutenant.	P.G.	RUSSELL.	Wounded.	20.7.18.

4.

Unit	Rank	Name	Casualty	Date
2/4th K.O.Y.L.I. (contd).	T/2/Lieutenant.	F. COCKER. M.C.	Wounded.	20.7.18.
	T/2/Lieutenant.	J. BLACKSTOCK.	Wounded.	20.7.18.
	T/2/Lieutenant.	R.M. MACBETH.	Wounded.	20.7.18.
	T/2/Lieutenant.	C.V. SMITH.	Wounded.	20.7.18.
	2/Lieutenant.	J.W. BALDOCK.	Wounded.	20.7.18.
	2/Lieutenant.	E. NICHOLSON. West Yorks Regt.	Wounded.	23.7.18.
	2/Lieutenant.	C.E. INCHLIFFE. M.M.	Wounded & M.	20.7.18.
	2/Lieutenant.	J. McCORMICK.	Killed.	28.7.18.
	2/Lieutenant.	C. HIRST.	Wounded.	27.7.18.
	2/Lieutenant.	T.C. HUNTER. West Yorks Regt.	Wounded.	27.7.18.
2/4th York & Lanc.	Captain.	C.G. KIRK. New Armies.	Killed.	20.7.18.
	T/2/Lieutenant.	J.ROBSON. (Not in A.L.)	Killed.	20.7.18.
	Captain.	J. ELLSE.	Wounded.	20.7.18.
	2/Lieutenant.	H.V. WARD.	Wounded.	20.7.18.
	T/2/Lieutenant.	G. LONGDEN.	Wounded.	21.7.18.
	2/Lieutenant.	E.A. THACKERAY. West Yorks Regt.	Wounded.	20.7.18.
	T/2/Lieutenant.	F. PROUDFOOT.	Wounded.	20.7.18.
9th Bn D.L.I.(Pioneers)	Lieutenant.	H.V. STRACHAN.	Wounded.	21.7.18.
	Lieutenant.	H.V. CHISHOLM.	Wounded.	21.7.18.
	Lieutenant.(A/Cpt).	T. HARKER. M.C.	Wounded.	21.7.18.
	2/Lieutenant.	J. DAWSON.	Wounded.	21.7.18.
	Lieutenant.	T.B. RENTON.	Wounded.	21.7.18.
	2/Lieutenant.	A. GIBSON.	Wounded.	21.7.18.
	Lieutenant.	W.J. TESSEYMAN.	Wounded.	21.7.18.
	2/Lieutenant.	B. SANDERSON.	Wounded.	23.7.18.
	Captain.	J.A.C.SCOTT. M.C., R.A.M.C. Attd 9th Bn D.L.I.	Wounded.	28.7.18.
62nd Bn Machine Gun Corps.	Lieutenant.	B.C. ORME. 5th K.O.Y.L.I.	Wounded.	20.7.18.
	2/Lieutenant.	H.H. STIRLING. M.G.C.	Wounded.	20.7.18.
	2/Lieutenant.	E.T. WEBSTER. M.G.C.	Wounded.	20.7.18.
	2/Lieutenant.	W. MORGAN.	Wounded.	23.7.18.
	Lieutenant (A/Maj)	F. LISMORE. M.C.	Wounded.	28.7.18.
	2/Lieutenant.	G.W. WARDLE.	Wounded.	28.7.18.
	2/Lieutenant.	A.L. PENTELOW.	Wounded.	28.7.18.
	2/Lieutenant.	A.F.L. WEBSTER.	Wounded. (Gas)	30.7.18.
310th Brigade R.F.A.	Lieutenant.	P.K.B. REYNOLDS.	Wounded.	20.7.18.
	2/Lieutenant.	H.E. STEPHENS.	Wounded.	22.7.18.
X	2/Lieutenant.	J.S. GREEN.	Wounded. (GAS)	19.4.18.

312th Brigade R.F.A.	2/Lieutenant.	J.N.	WHITWORTH.	Wounded.	20.7.18.
	2/Lieutenant.	W.	BURT.	Wounded.	20.7.18.
	2/Lieutenant.	V.A.a.H.	DIAPER.	Wounded.	22.7.18.
2/2nd W.R.Field Ambulance.	Capt (A/Major)	G.	STEELL. R.A.M.C.	Wounded.	24.7.18.

X   This officer's name has been included as the casualty was reported through XXII Corps.

CONFIDENTIAL.

62nd (WEST RIDING) DIVISION.

RETURN OF CASUALTIES FOR MONTH OF JULY 1918.

UNIT.	Officers.				Other Ranks.				REMARKS.
	Killed.	Wounded.	Missing.	Sick.	Killed.	Wounded.	Missing.	Sick.	
310th F.A.Brigade.	-	3	-	-	2	21	-	24	
312th F.A.Brigade.	-	3	-	-	9	26	-	12	
Divl Ammunition Column.	-	-	-	-	-	3	-	13	
X.62 T.M.B.	-	-	-	-	-	-	-	1	
Royal Engineers.	-	-	-	1	1	11	-	34	
8th West Yorks.	9	8	3	-	79	367	19	71	
2/5th West Yorks.	4	10	3	-	51	286	100	44	
1/5th Devons.	4	11	-	1	44	293	32	58	
5th West Riding.	1	11	1	-	46	276	26	78	
2/4th West Riding.	-	11	2	1	44	265	47	54	
2/4th Hants.	2	10	-	2	44	180	47	139	
5th K.O.Y.L.I.	4	5	-	-	57	283	14	60	
2/4th K.O.Y.L.I.	2	11	1	29	29	313	61	45	
2/4th Y & L.	2	5	1	1	56	357	40	35	
9th Bn Durham L.I. (Pnrs).	-	9	-	-	43	236	19	29	
62 Bn M.G.Corps.	-	8	-	-	12	126	1	-	
2/1st W.R.Field Amb.	-	-	-	-	-	1	-	3	
2/2nd W.R.Field Amb.	-	1	-	-	3	10	-	14	
2/3rd W.R.Field Amb.	-	-	-	-	2	9	-	7	
186 T.M.B.	-	2	-	-	-	-	-	5	
187 T.M.B.	-	-	-	-	-	-	-	4	
Army Service Corps.	-	-	-	-	-	-	-	13	
Total.	28	108	10	6	521	3063	406	741	

62nd (WEST RIDING) DIVISION.

HONOURS AND REWARDS GRANTED DURING THE MONTH OF JULY 1918.

MILITARY CROSS

T/2nd Lieut J.E.TILLOTSON D.S.O.   2/7th West Yorkshire Regt.
Lieut H.SMITH   C/312th Brigade R.F.A.

2nd BAR TO MILITARY MEDAL.

241315 Sergt E.RAYWOOD M.M. and Bar   5th Bn K.O.Y.L.I.

BAR TO MILITARY MEDAL.

241908 L/Corpl. H.CORBETT M.M.   2/4th York & Lancaster Regt.

MILITARY MEDAL.

786598	Corpl. E.FIRTH	X/62nd Medium T.M.Battery.
70957	Sergt. W.STEVENSON	312th Brigade R.F.A.
117895	Bomdr. J.R.ROBERTS	312th Brigade R.F.A.
781506	Corpl. E.BURTON D.C.M.	Y/62nd T.M.B.
202196	Corpl. W.HARRIS	5th Bn K.O.Y.L.I.

REINFORCEMENTS RECEIVED DURING JULY 1918.

	Offrs.	O.R.
8th West Yorkshire Regiment	12	219
2/5th West Yorkshire Regiment.	7	267
1/5th Devonshire Regiment.	2	208
5th West Riding Regiment	6	177
2/4th West Riding Regiment	9	70
2/4th Hampshire Regiment.	-	351
5th K.O.Y.L.I.	4	231
2/4th K.O.Y.L.I.	9	123
2/4th York and Lancaster Regiment.	-	106
Royal Artillery	-	54
Royal Engineers	1	45
Divisional Signal Company	-	17
Divisional Train	-	11
R.A.M.C.	2	20
62nd Bn. Machine Gun Corps	9	98
9th Durham Light Infantry	6	217
252 Divisional Employment Company	1	8

H

ADMINISTRATIVE NOTES ON OPERATIONS IN JULY 1918 IN
RHEIMS AREA INCLUDING MOVE BY STRATEGICAL TRAINS
FROM PAS AREA.
=====================

1. **STRATEGICAL TRAINS.**

    MONDICOURT.

    As an entraining station, only two flats can be dealt with at once, and train has to be shunted continuously both for loading and unloading vehicles. An extension of ramp would be of great benefit.

    Information regarding "halte repas" is vague and untrustworthy. This seems to be a point that might very easily be remedied, and it is worth while doing. Watering of horses would be easier, and if troops are to go almost immediately into a fight, it is essential that they should be fit; the uncertainty of a stop for getting to latrines was a marked drawback on a journey of over 30 hours, inducing discomfort to officers and men.

    Every Division packs its trains differently, and Mounted Units trains return for Infantry, consequently when trains are used for one Division, and rushed back for another, men have often to occupy trucks that have had horses in them, for 30 hours and are fouled with manure and urine, and have had no cleaning done to them.

2. **TRAVELLING IN FRENCH BUSSES.**

    French busses only hold 16 men. The French appear to count "one bayonet one seat in a bus", and as detrainment took place in some cases 50 kilometres from concentration area, the march was very long. This affected units like R.A.M.C., Machine Gun Companies, T.M.Batteries (both Medium and Light) and all parties for Baths, Salvage etc. As these latter are mainly composed of "B" men, it made marching particularly difficult, more especially as they are units that have no transport.

    When arranging with the French for bussing it is well to get from the C.R.A.(French Officer of Bureau Automibile) some elastic authority for where the busses are to run.

    When detraining at ARCIS-sur-AUBE, MAILLY, and SOUS SOMME exact destinations were laid down on the supposition that the Division was to be in reserve of 4th French Army behind CHALONS- during the detrainment this was varied to being in reserve to 5th French Army in EPERNAY area. French Staff Officers were sent to stop busses, and French Town Majors instructed that the British Troops would not be accommodated in the villages originally indicated. But fresh orders as to where busses were to go and what villages were to be occupied were not issued, the result was that bus convoys were halted and French Officers in charge were unable to continue the transport of troops till they had new orders from their superiors. The personal presence of the Divisional Commander going round by car was alone able to unravel the difficulty.

    When embussing to return an arrangement was made with the French to place lorries and busses at our disposal for a certain time and detailed orders were issued <u>by the Division.</u>

    The French were most anxious to assist, but their system is different to ours, and in their own case is very rigid.

3. ACCOMMODATION IN FRENCH AREA.

Billets in French Villages.

It appears to be the custom to allocate villages, but there is no very apparent means of finding out what available accommodation there is in a village. The French Town Major has full information when you got there, but as a Brigade may be located in several villages all at a considerable distance from the detraining station and from each other it is a difficult task for a Staff Captain to make the necessary personal reconnaissance.

Billeting in French Areas emphasises a long felt want for Staff Captains to be provided with motor bicycles. In addition to billeting in the houses there appear to be in all French Areas a considerable number of Military huts, but it is not till you get on the spot that you find these out.

During the actual operations there was no accommodation and troops bivouaced in the woods. The bivouacing of the French Troops was very noticeable; a small wood might very possibly contain 1000 French Troops, but not one was to be seen; if their transport was with them it was most carefully drawn up along the hedge of the wood and well camouflaged by branches of trees. The importance of this on a front "where very active operations were going on " was soon realised as the German Air Service was very active, and their night bombing was continual. After the experience in such an area it seems essential that formal wagon lines should be abandoned and every effort made to hide both animals and vehicles. Had wagon lines similar to our former Divisional Artillery lines near COUIN been used, it seems doubtful if the Divisional Artillery would have had any horses left at all; this applies in proportion to all regimental wagon lines.

4. SUPPLIES.

A general report on supplies is attached and marked "A". The following points seem to require attention :-

Rum. Every assistance was given by 22nd Corps to get up rum for the troops, but it is thought that a reserve supply should always be sent with troops who are detached from the British Areas. This operation started in brilliant summer weather, but this weather broke and many days and nights of the operations were soaking wet. The operations during which the troops were bivouaced, including the period of coming out of the line up to re-entraining, was from the 19th July to the 3rd August; throughout this time the troops were without shelter and for 10 days they were fighting hard. Had a reserve of rum been sent up automatically for the detached Corps there is little doubt that in the very trying conditions existing the Corps Commander would have sanctioned further issues of rum, which would have been of inestimable value to the troops.

E.F.Canteen. Copies of a letter written by the Division and of the report made by the Commander of the 22nd Corps to G.H.Q. South, are attached, and marked "B" and "C". These speak for themselves, and it is hoped that when Divisions are detached from British Areas the E.F.C. may be notified in good time and directed to start sending up supplies to the new area at once; it is suggested that the best method of doing this is to add trucks of E.F.C. Supplies to the Pack train.

3.

During this operation the things that the troops missed most were the ordinary E.F.C. supplies such as cigarettes and tobacco.

5. AMMUNITION.

The supply of ammunition went without a single hitch throughout the operations and this is largely attributed to the fact that the ammunition section of the M.T. Company was placed entirely at the disposal of the Division during the operations.

On two occasions ammunition at the rate of 600 rounds per 18 pounder and 500 rounds per 4.5" was ordered to be placed at the guns; this was successfully done within 24 hours.

The system of liaison bombardiers from the S.A.A. Section D.A.C., with the Infantry Brigades worked well and at no time was there any shortage of ammunition reported.

Trench Ammunition. T.M.C. should be included on the first ammunition train. It only came up when specially demanded.

6. ORDNANCE SUPPLIES.

In view of the uncertainty of the operations the whole of the stores were not concentrated in one dump.

Rear and advanced dumps were formed, the latter only holding an amount of stores which could be moved by lorry at half an hours notice. To lessen the strain on first line transport, stores were delivered to units and indents collected.

The Corps Dump formed at TROYES, containing in addition to guns and Field Artillery stores such things as horse shoes, clothing, oil, wheels etc., was rather far back being at one time nearly 70 miles from the Divisional forward stores.

Further no stores could be drawn from this dump without obtaining the sanction of G.H.Q., South, through Corps. This entailed some little delay and, while it is recognised that important stores must be controlled by higher authority, it is suggested that D.A.Ds.O.S. of Divisions could well be entrusted with the necessary authority to draw such stores as horse shoes, oil, clothing, etc.

As the Division went into the area fully equipped this did not effect them adversely in any way.

With regard to the Base, telegrams for stores were acted upon in the usual prompt and efficient manner.

7. SURPLUS BAGGAGE AND STORES.

Neither the length of our stay, nor our rôle in the French Zone could be foreseen. All our laundry stores and a large proportion of units' baggage surplus to Load Tables was taken down in the trains.

No Motor Transport could be obtained from the French for this; it was therefore dumped at the various detraining stations and finally concentrated by our own lorries at the most central of them.

Clean clothing was brought forward to the troops when required, and as opportunity offered, and proved a great boon.

4.

As our return entraining stations were within lorry distance of our dumps, it was possible to move the latter by lorry in time to entrain them with us. Had distance and time not permitted, the problem of recovering stores would have been very difficult.

If engaged in similar operations again, baggage should conform strictly to Load Tables. Plus 2 or 3 lorry loads of clean clothing for immediate requirements, the French apparently do not give their own units lorries for moving stores, and are not prepared for demands of this nature.

TRANSPORT.

Owing to the M.T.Company being originally placed at the disposal of the Division there was no difficulty regarding transport for ammunition and supplies, but after 4 days the M.T.Company was taken over by Corps, only the gun ammunition and S.A.A. lorries being left at the disposal of the Division.

During this latter period there was no abnormal demand, so the loss of the Company was not much felt, but it is considered as a matter of principle that, except in exceptional circumstances, during active operations, the M.T. Company should be entirely at the disposal of the Division to which it belongs.

9. PRISONERS OF WAR.

Owing to lack of previous knowledge of the country and the operations of the Division altering from one part of the front to another, the collection and escort down of prisoners of war was not at first very efficient.

It does not, however, seem thoroughly understood in Brigades that the immediate sending down of prisoners for examination by the General Staff is of the utmost importance; there seems to be an inclination for them to be kept at Brigade Headquarters, and elsewhere for interrogation through Interpreters; this is a wrong principle and prisoners should be sent down at the earliest possible opportunity. The information to be gained from prisoners frequently affects the next days operations and should therefore be at the disposal of the Divisional Commander as soon as possible after they have been captured; this information may often be of such a nature as to modify the plans for the next days fighting and may very possibly modify they in such a way as to be of immense assistance to the fighting troops.

More particularly should effort be made to send down officer or N.C.O prisoners without waiting to make up a batch.

10. BURIAL PARTY.

A burial party of 30 men was detailed but did not prove enough. In order to carry out burials on a battlefield satisfactorarily, to avoid stray burials all over the place, and to ensure identification of bodies, it is necessary to work systematically from one flank to the other.

5.

In this operation it was no easy matter to find the dead in the thick woods and standing corn; more particularly were these difficulties felt when the burying party got anywhere near the firing line and had to work by night. Burials were started from the right of the battlefield and unfortunately the most exposed and noticeable bodies were those on the NANTEUIL - MARFAUX - CHAUMUZY Road which was practically the left of the Divisional battlefield and therefore was only reached towards the end of the operation.

The total number of dead buried was British 418; Germans 7; French 1; and the number of unidentified bodies was 38.

It still appears to be the common practice in Battalions to take off the identity disc from the dead bodies; this may help Battalions in their returns, but entirely defeats the work of the Divisional Burials Officer and should be stopped; if there is time to cut off the identity disc there is equally time to make a note of who the man is, and what his number is ; and by working in this way the risk of whoever cuts off the identity disc becoming a casualty and the disc being lost, is avoided.

11. DRESS.

Before moving up into action, Greatcoats and Haversacks were dumped in billets in the Reserve Area (about 15 miles in rear of assembly positions). It would have been an impossible task for the men to have undertaken the march from the Reserve Area to assembly positions if they had carried full marching order.

When fighting, packs were carried containing Iron Rations, Small kit etc., and Waterproof Sheet Capes - even this load was found too heavy.

After the operations the Greatcoats were collected by lorry from where they had been dumped, and carried to the bivouac area where the Division was concentrated prior to the return train journey - fortunately the distance involved was not very long and time permitted, otherwise their collection would have been a serious difficulty.

The need for the lightening of the Infantry Soldiers' Kit was more than ever apparent during these operations.

12. OPERATING WITH FRENCH TROOPS.

Very little difficulty was experienced while working with the French. On occasions when certain supplies did not come up it was found possible to buy in bulk from the French and they always were ready to assist. The actual relation between British and French Troops was at all times cordial and no difficulties at all were experienced. The chief difficulty of different languages was generally readily overcome, but it was observed that there were far fewer French Officers with any working knowledge of English than British Officers with a working knowledge of French, and French was the language generally used.

13. SALVAGE.

It was found possible to deal with returned stores, salvage, and ammunition empties on the following lines.

Units, assisted by the Salvage Company, collected salvage etc. This was sent to the refilling points by supply wagons and sent to D.A.D.O.S. Dump by the empty returning supply lorries. It was there sorted and sent to the R.O.O.

Main Dressing Station in ST. IMOGES was cleared direct by empty returning supply lorries.

Empty ammunition boxes and cases were sent back to Ammunition Railhead by the ammunition lorries.

The chief items collected in 10 days were :-

Ammunition Boxes	4500	Ammunition Cases	10000
Guns, Lewis	18	Guns, Lewis, parts	5
Magazines, L.G.	194	Rifles S.M.L.E.	800
S.A.A.Boxes full	110	Shells, live, 18 pdr.	245
Cases, cartridge, 4.5"How.	510	Boxes, 4.5"How, empty	178
Boxes, 18 pdr, empty	100	Shells,Stokes,Boxes,full	118
Grenades,boxes,full	122	Grenades,boxes,empty	58
Greatcoats	75	Equipment, sacks	42
Valises, bundles	30	Haversacks, bundles	76
Helmets, steel	700	Bayonets & Scabbards, sacks	31
Limbers, G.S.	2		

"A".

NOTES ON SUPPLY ARRANGEMENTS.

The following observations on the supply arrangements for the period in question are appended, viz :-
On receipt of entraining orders and details,
 (a) Station.
 (b) No. of Train.
 (c) Units and strengths for each train.*

* As each train consisted of Units in a more or less composite form, and A.B.55's for these composite entraining strengths were not available, estimates were made of attached men and animals and adjustments on normal strengths made in accordance with details given in the entraining table. This was found to be satisfactory and practicable, and as units arrived for entraining, the Train rations were delivered. The Mechanical Transport entrained at No. 4 Station but a direct issue was made in this case by S.O., 62nd Div. M.T.Company.

Train rations were drawn and delivered in accordance with strengths shewn on A.F.W.3317, and the Supply Details of 185th, 186th and 187th Infantry Brigades detailed to take charge of the issue at the 3 Stations involved. The Supply Personnel of Divisional Troops were allocated to the 3 Stations to assist in the issue.

The following table will indicate (subject to conditions stated in foot note) the ration position of the Division up to arrival in area of detrainment, entrainment having started on 14.7.18.

CONSUMPTION DATE.	REMARKS.
July 14th 1918.	In possession of Unit.
July 15th 1918.	Carried on Man and Animal.
July 16th 1918.	Train Ration.
July 17th 1918.	Train Ration.
July 18th 1918.	On Supply Wagons.
July 19th 1918.	On M.T.Lorries.

To meet above position for the requirements of Entraining days, the Supply Wagons were filled twice on the 14th. 1st. delivery was for consumption 15th. 2nd. delivery moved by Unit.

(N.B) In cases however of Units entraining on the 14th. inst, and in the early hours of the 15th. inst, the train ration was of course consumed on the 15th and 16th and rations issued normally for the 15th. consumption, were therefore carried in 1st Line Transport and consumed on the 17th.

Similar arrangements were made for the return journey.

Immediately on arrival in New Area the supply wagons which accompanied Units on the train journey, dumped rations in units lines, and were subsequently called in by Officers Commanding Divl. Train Companies, and the following procedure was adopted throughout the operations. Supplies were loaded at Railhead and dumped immediately. Divisional Train supply wagons on return from Units refilled immediately from dump and remained full overnight - the mobility of the Divisional Supply Service being thus transferred from the M.T.Company to the Divisional Train thereby releasing the supply lorries for other duties.

SUPPLIES.

In operations of the kind under review, experience has taught the extreme importance of adequate supplies being available in the immediate vicinity of Railhead.

In the present instance this state of scarcity was not met, until the operations had been effective some time and even then, the situation was not sufficiently eased to completely guard against such contingencies as the non-arrival of hay and oat trucks etc, and to obviate long journeys to collect supplies for completion. In the case of hay we were able to obtain our first demand from the French but afterwards the supply of French baled hay was exhausted, and their subsequent supply was all loose hay obtained direct from the land.

The French Transport is peculiarly adapted for transporting loose hay, but we had to proceed to a station some miles distance to collect, as it would have been useless to have attempted to use a lorry or a Mark 10 G.S.Wagon for the carriage of anything like the hay requirements of the Division.

Frozen Meat.

The Division was based on HAVRE, but the first arrivals of frozen meat were entirely bad chiefly owing to the unsuitable type of truck used for the journey of 3 or 4 days, and also to the excessive heat. 30% Fresh meat could be satisfactorily dealt with.

Fuel.

It was found that the Units located in Forest Country did not require fuel-wood, and for future operations in wooded areas this can be eliminated from the section. With regard to coal, 25 tons weekly was ordered by the Division and this quantity could be dealt with. It was pointed out at the time that units in the Forward Areas were in a favourable position to meet fuel requirements from local resources.

Solidified Alcohol.

Although only a small proportion of the fuel ration was utilized, it is considered that the weekly allowance of solidified Alcohol viz 10500 ozs. was hardly sufficient for special operations of this nature, and the weekly allotment should be increased to 15000 ozs.

Bread.

During the whole period covering the operations, the bread arrived in a very unsatisfactory state being for the most part pitted with mould, although not actually condemnable. I am unable to give a reason as to the cause of the mould other than the packing of old bread. The establishment of the Advanced Field Bakery would have obviated this position, but up to the time of completion of operations, this was not in a position to commence baking. Full fresh bread ration could be dealt with and is desirable.

Rum.

A reserve of Rum should be available with Divisional M.T.Coy. (vide para 4)

Supply Personnel - Move of.

Owing to the long distance between Refilling Points when the Division was on the move, considerable difficulty was experienced in obtaining transport for the lower category Supply Clerks and loaders. On one occasion, a refill had to be commenced with only 3 men, as the remainder were unable to do the journey in sufficient time for the commencement.

XXII Corps "A"   62nd Div. No. A/10382/23

    With reference to the supply of Canteen goods from E.F.C. now being arranged, it is suggested that the Committee of the E.F.C. be approached with a view of rendering such supply more elastic and prompt.

    The present method is hedged round with demands for guarantees and specimens of signatures etc.

    It is considered that once the railway communication is known to be assured, an official telegram from the Headquarters of a Division to the E.F.C. is a sufficient guarantee, and the goods should be delivered forthwith. The point of demanding a "personal" guarantee is particularly foreign to the usual practice of the service.

    The E.F.C. is not a trading concern, but an Army institution for the benefit of the troops, and the benefit of the troops demands prompt action unfettered by formalities.

    The E.F.C. is practically a semi official annexe to the Supply Service, and should progress pari passu with that service; if the E.F.C. could liaison with the Supply Service and be ready to function as soon, it would be of great benefit to the troops.

    This is more especially the case when a Division or Corps is isolated from the main areas occupied by the British Armies.

    It is hoped that the Corps Commander may see his way to represent this very strongly and to urge that the present formalities insisted on be abolished at an early date, so that the men may obtain the benefits they have a right to expect - and now lack - from the E.F.C.

25/7/1918.
                    (Sgd) W.P. BRAITHWAITE, Major-General.
                    Commanding 62nd (West Riding) Division.

C O P Y.   "C"   62nd Div. No. A/41/23.
G.H.Q. (South).   No. Q. 101/1/4.

It has been represented by one of the Divisions under my command, and I quite agree, that the arrangements made by the E.F.C. for the supply of canteen stores to troops operating in French Areas leave much to be desired.

The troops under my command entrained in British area on the 14th July, and trucks of canteen stores are only now arriving, and that only as the results of efforts made by you and my own staff.

I was obliged to agree to supply a guarantee for 50,000 francs, and my Divisional Commanders have had to do the same, before stores were despatched, a formality which, considering that the E.F.C. is presumably an institution for the benefit of the troops and not a trading concern, appears to be quite unnecessary and which seems to suggest that the E.F.C. are more concerned with the risk of financial loss than with the needs of the fighting man.

I suggest that the rules governing the running of the E.F.C. might be made more elastic for British troops detached and operating in French areas.

It should be a simple matter to load and attach trucks to the first pack trains arriving in French areas and to thereby supply some of the soldiers' immediate needs with, so far as I can see, practically no risk of financial loss

After the first few days the supplies could then be adjusted to the units requirements.

The E.F.C. is, I believe, managed by business men, and I think you will agree that no pushful business man working for his own profit would allow such a ready market as 2 Divisions and some thousands of Corps troops represent to go unsupplied for the space of 7 or 8 days. As the E.F.C. hold a monopoly, they should, I consider, more than ever realise their obligations to the troops.

(Sgd) A.J.GODLEY,
Lieut-General,
Headquarters,   Commanding XXII Corps.
27/7/1918.

CONFIDENTIAL.

WAR DIARY.

OF

HEADQUARTERS, 62ND (WEST RIDING) DIVISION 'A'.

1st AUGUST 1918.   to   31st AUGUST 1918.

VOLUME XX.

Army Form C. 2118.

WAR DIARY
or
INTELLIGENCE SUMMARY.
(Erase heading not required.)

August 1918.

Place	Date	Hour	Summary of Events and Information	Remarks and references to Appendices
BISSEUIL.	1st		2nd Artillery completed entrainment for SOMME Area. Infantry Brigades move to Area as follows:- 185. I.B. to CHATEAU SARRAN (MARNE) and bivouacs in woods in neighbourhood. 186. I.B. to OIRY and Woods in neighbourhood 187. I.B. to Bivouacs in woods S. of R. MARNE near BISSEUIL. 16th I.B. marched past General BERTHELOT en route. See order of the day by General Berthelot Commanding 5th French Army and Order by G.O.C XXII Corps Weather fine + hot. Orders received for entrainment to Somme area.	Appendix A " "
do	2nd		62nd M.G. Batt: and 9th D.L.I. (Pioneers) from ST IMOGES to woods S. of MARNE near BISSEUIL and bivouacked. Weather fine in morning, heavy rain in afternoon.	

Army Form C. 2118.

WAR DIARY
or
INTELLIGENCE SUMMARY.
(Erase heading not required.)

August 1918.
Page 2.

Place	Date	Hour	Summary of Events and Information	Remarks and references to Appendices
BISSEUIL	3rd		Entrainment commenced. See orders attached. Weather wet. Detrainment of 62nd Div. Artillery completed in Tincques Area — 1 Bde. Hanover to BVS, 1 Bde to COUIN and BVS to ST LEGER	Schedule BM BM
"	4th		Divisional HQ entrained at EPERNAY & CANDAS (regulating station). Entrainment of troops still in progress. Weather dull & showery.	Schedule BM
PAS	5th		HQ Division opened at PAS CHATEAU having detrained at MONDICOURT about 5 pm. Detrainment of Division Completed. Weather dull & much rain.	Schedule BM

WAR DIARY
INTELLIGENCE SUMMARY

August 1918. (Page 3)

Army Form C. 2118.

Place	Date	Hour	Summary of Events and Information	Remarks and references to Appendices
PAS.	6th		Division resting in PAS Area. H.Q. PAS CHATEAU. 185 T.B. HQ at AUTHIEUX VAUCHELLE. 186. H.Q. at AUTHIE ST LEGER. 187. HQ at HENU. 9th D.L.I. (Pioneers) ST LEGER. N.& 8th Btns de WARNIMONT. Weather fine. 2 Coys + G.H.Q reserve.	Appendix B
PAS.	7th		Orders received re posting 2/5th London 1-62nd Divison vice 2/5th W. Yorks l.to disbanded. Reinforcements as follows:- 2/4 Bn W.Yorks Regt. 10 Officers 261. O.R. — 5th Bn W. 9 Officers 293 O.R — 2/4th York & Lancasters 7 Officers + 164 O.R. — 9th SLI. 4 Officers + 130 O.R. — 2/4th KOYLI. 3 Officers 200 O.R. — 5th KOYLI. 224 O.R. — 8th W. YORKS 3 Officers 147 O.R.	
PAS.	8th		XXII Corps call of names recommended for honours as under:- Legion of Honour 7 — Medaille Militaire 2 — Croix de guerre 100 — of several operations in Marne district.	

WAR DIARY
or
INTELLIGENCE SUMMARY

August 1918. Page 4

Place	Date	Hour	Summary of Events and Information	Remarks and references to Appendices
P.A.S.	9th		1 Corp. - GHQ reserve. Weather fine. Refitting Division continues - 7/20th London arrived from L. of C. (Nieuport Area), detrained at DOULLENS 4pm and marched to Billets at THIEVRES	GM
P.A.S.	10th		Reinforcements. 5th Devons 3 Officers & 100 O.R. - 5th R/W. 1 Officer - 2/4 Hants 86 O.R. - M.G. 13th 19. O.R. - 2/26th London 1 Officer a 13 O.R.	GM
P.A.S.	11th		Reinforcements 2/26th London 1 Officer - 152 O.R.	GM
P.A.S.	12th		Reinforcements. 2/4 D of Ws 8. O.R. - 5th R/W. 8 O.R. - 8 W. Yorks 1 Officer 39 O.R. - 2/5th W.Y. 12 O.R. - 1/5 KOYLI. 4 O.R. - 2/4 KOYLI. 21 O.R. - 9 S.W. 3 O.R. - 2/4 HLI 4 O.R.	GM

WAR DIARY
or
INTELLIGENCE SUMMARY.
(Erase heading not required.)

Army Form C. 2118.

August 1918.
Page 5.

Place	Date	Hour	Summary of Events and Information	Remarks and references to Appendices
PAS.	12th (Cont.)		M.G.13: 3 Officers + 60 O.R.	
	(10th att. in addition on 10th/12th)		Recommendations for french Honours despatched to XXII Corps as required by them	
			Letter received on 8th Inst.	
	13th		Weather Fine	
	14th		Weather Fine	
PAS.	15th		Recommendations for Immediate Honours and Awards in connection with MARNE Battle forwarded to XXII Corps	
PAS.	15th		Divl. HQ moved to AUTHIE to make room for HQrs 63rd (R.N.) Division who for their H.Q. & batt- moved to HQrs at PAS.	BO

Army Form C. 2118.

WAR DIARY
or
INTELLIGENCE SUMMARY.
(Erase heading not required.)

August 1918. Page 6.

Place	Date	Hour	Summary of Events and Information	Remarks and references to Appendices
AUTHIE	16th		Reinforcements. 24 NCOs & 44 O.R. - M.G. Bn. 2 NCOs 31 O.R. - Officers as under to be transferred forthwith from 8th W. Yorkshire Regt. to 9th W. Yorks. 3 — 10th D.Y. 3 — 15th W.Y. 5. Weather hot & fine	BM0
AUTHIE	17th		Weather hot & fine	BM0
do	18th		Weather fine. 1st: I.B. ordered to clear troops out of VAUCHELLE. Bde HQ and 3 Cos to Bus. 2/s: London moved to LOUVENCOURT, one Co to Bus. Field Ambulance to LOUVENCOURT.	BM0

Army Form C. 2118.

August 19ᵗʰ 1918.
Page 2.

WAR DIARY
or
INTELLIGENCE SUMMARY.
(Erase heading not required.)

Instructions regarding War Diaries and Intelligence Summaries are contained in F. S. Regs., Part II. and the Staff Manual respectively. Title pages will be prepared in manuscript.

Place	Date	Hour	Summary of Events and Information	Remarks and references to Appendices
GRENAS	19ᵗʰ		Weather dull & drizzly.	
			Division moves SAULTY area. Div. HQ. GRENAS. (Château).	
			185ᵗʰ Inf Bde POMMERA area. — 166ᵗʰ in SOMBRIN area. — 187ᵗʰ Sus Sᵗ LEGER area.	
			M.G. 15ᵗʰ & 9ᵗʰ D.L.I. to LA BEZIQUE Camp.	
			Division in Reserve to VI Corps — Move of Troops took place on night 19/20 Aug. GWJ	
BAVINCOURT	20ᵗʰ		Weather dull, drizzly.	
			Division moves to areas as follows:— All moves taking place on night 20/21 August	
			Div HQ, C.R.A, C.R.E, A.D.M.S. & Div Train to BAVINCOURT.	
			185ᵗʰ I.B. to GAUDIEMPRÉ — Sᵗ AMAND & LA CAUCHIE.	
			187ᵗʰ I.B. " BAVINCOURT & SAULTY.	
			Other units no change.	BWJ
BAVINCOURT	21ˢᵗ		Weather misty early turning bright & warm.	
			Orders received to move back to IV Corps area on night 21/22 August.	

Army Form C. 2118.

August 1918.
Page 2.

WAR DIARY
or
INTELLIGENCE SUMMARY.
(Erase heading not required.)

Place	Date	Hour	Summary of Events and Information	Remarks and references to Appendices
DOULLENS.	21st	10pm	Divl HQ. opens at DOULLENS 10pm and came under III Corps. 185th I.B at VAUCHELLE - 186th at PAS - 187 at AUTHIE S LEGER. BPD	
DOULLENS.	22nd		Orders received Divl HQ move to PAS. stone they found. Weather bright & very hot.	
PAS.			Divl HQ moves PAS. 4pm. Units of Division no more. Division now in GHQ Reserve. Probability of some days stay in this Area. Bar to Military Medal and Military Medal awarded to GOC XVII Corps for operation July 1918.	
PAS.	23rd		Weather fine + W: Orders rec'd to move to III Corps Area on night 24/25 August. More duty, carried out and Brigades located as under by midnight - 185 Inf/Bde camp - STAPMAND - 186 Inf/Bn camp SAULTY 187 Inf/Bde camp LA BEVIQUE and LA CAUCHIE - MGBn GAUDIEMARC - Pioneers GUINCOURT and HUMBERCOURT Divl HQ's share rear 2nd Division HQs at BEZIQUE. Surplus Infantry to 900 for Bn moved to Reception Camp ORVILLE where Total of about 700 for Division thus collected	

Army Form C. 2118.

WAR DIARY
or
INTELLIGENCE SUMMARY.
(Erase heading not required.)

AUGUST 1918 p. 9

Place	Date	Hour	Summary of Events and Information	Remarks and references to Appendices
LA BEZIQUE	24		Weather cooler and Dull – Orders received that Third Army was to Advance and Enemy to be given no respite – Division ordered to relieve 3rd Division EAST of Railway and near BONIFICORT – More carried out covering 7am. 186 and 187 Inf Bdes moved by Bus and then to MONCHY and thence by March Route 187 Inf Bde throw over on left of 3rd Division front and took over whole on Right 186 get the line in Gavrelle Valley – Division bivouacked in Gavrelle Valley – Advanced HQs consisting of GOC, GSO1, Rear HQs to BIEN VILLERS – During Night 24/25 186 and 187 Inf Bdes took over Line from 3rd Division, 186 Bde on Right and 187 Inf Bde on Left - 185 Inf Bde in Reserve in Gavrelle Valley	GM
BIEN VILLERS and QUESNOY	25		Weather fine 6h16'. 186 and 187 Inf Bdes attacked in keeping 186 Inf Bde through SAMIGNIES, and 187 Inf Bde through MORY, both directed finally on VRAUX – VRAUCOURT – Both Bdes gained Objective but suffered moving to exposed flanks. Heavy Counter Attack on 187 Inf Bde and Prussels repulsed with Bayonet and Heavy losses inflicted on Enemy	GM

WAR DIARY
or
INTELLIGENCE SUMMARY.

Army Form C. 2118.

August 1918. p.10.

Place	Date	Hour	Summary of Events and Information	Remarks and references to Appendices
	25th		Who are reported to have had 70 killed by the fork Francs alone. Prisoners of War Captured 1 Officer 40 O.R's Estimated Casualties 5th W.Riding Regt 2 Officers 100 O.R.s	GM
BRANCOURT and GUESNOY	26th		Weather continued dull and showery — Roads very bad — Attacks of 18th and 187th Brigades continued. Former attacking Old Thine Army Line towards BEVRGNATRE and latter through MORY. Enemy caught by L.G. Fire retiring in the open and heavy losses inflicted, notably by 187 Bde. Prisoners of War Captured 1 Officer 52 O.R.s Estimated Casualties 5th K.O.Y.L.I. 2 Officers 150 O.R.s 2/4th KOYLI — do 250 do 2/4th Yorks L — do 350 do Since 25th inst.	GM

Army Form C. 2118.

WAR DIARY
or
INTELLIGENCE SUMMARY.

(Erase heading not required.)

August 1918. p. 11.

Place	Date	Hour	Summary of Events and Information	Remarks and references to Appendices
BIHUCOURT and QUESNOY P'T	27		Weather fine and cool. Operations 187 Inf Bde in conjunction with Guards attacked along Spur running N of VRAUCOURT. Heavy Counter attack forced Troops back to Original line. Bn. had reached Sugar Factory. Commander in Chief wired Bde. HQrs during afternoon and Congratulated Division. Prisoners of War Captured 8 Officers 150 o.r's, including B'n Commander & Staff. 5th W. Ridings 4 Officers and 150 o.r's, 2/4 W. Ridings Estimated Casualties from 25th inst. 2 Officers and 60 o.R's.	BJH
BIHUCOURT & QUESNOY P'T	28		Weather Dull in Morning. Fine later. Major General W.P. BRAITHWAITE C.B. appointed to Command a Corps. Left to take over Temporary Command of XIII ~ Corps. Major General Sir R.D. WHIGHAM K.C.B. from 59th Division, assumes Command of 62nd (West Riding) Division from 28th Inst. Operations: 187 Inf Bde relieved in left sector by 185 Inf Bde during night 27/28th. Attack was pushed forward towards Sugar Factory — No change on 186 Inf Bde front — 185 Bde advanced Position. Supply Railhead moved to BUSMÉTAUMONT. Reinft Ditto to SAPINY. Prisoners taken Capture 5 o.R's. Estimated Casualties from 25th inst. 5th W. Ridings 5 Officers 200 o.r's 2/4 Hants 2 Offrs 90 o.r's 5th KoyR 6 do 250 do 2/4 Noyk 10 do 400 do	BJH

T2134. Wt. W708-776. 50C000. 4/15. Sir J. C. & S.

Army Form C. 2118.

WAR DIARY
or
INTELLIGENCE SUMMARY.
(Erase heading not required.)

August 1918 p.12.

Place	Date	Hour	Summary of Events and Information	Remarks and references to Appendices
BIENVILLERS and GUESNY PK	29th		Weather Showery and Dull. Roads in forward area breaking up. Operations: Attack pushed forward - 185 Inf Bde clearing BANNS and VRAMCOURT Trenches. 186 Inf/Bde captured Horse Lines on BEUGNATRE - FAVREUIL Rd. Divl Reception Camp moved from OVILLE to BIENVILLERS - Rejht Railhead changed to SAULTY. Prisoners of War Captured total approx 150. Estimated Casualties for 28th inst. 2/Lt Nuartz 30 O.R.s Honours Awards received from XVII Corps. 1 Bar to DSO - 4 DSO's; 2 2nd Bars to MC, 9 Bars to MC, 57 MC's attached. 2 D.C.M.S. 1 Bar to MM - 4 MM's	see DROC attached
BIENVILLERS and FAVREUIL	30th		Weather Dull. Operations. Operations: 185 and 186 Inf/Bdes attacked VAUX-VRAMCOURT and gained footing therein. Advd Divl HQs moved to FAVREUIL 7pm. Park Train did not arrive in Divisore so Rations failed for Various Reserve Supply Dumps in Area. Lorries did not finish Dumping till 6 am on Morning 30/31st. Prisoners of War Captured 3 Officers 290 O.R's Estimated Casualties. None Reported.	

WAR DIARY or INTELLIGENCE SUMMARY

Army Form C. 2118.

August 31st 1918
p. 13.

Place	Date	Hour	Summary of Events and Information	Remarks and references to Appendices
RAINVILLERS and COURCELLES	31st		Weather Showery in Morning. Fine later.	

Operations. Enemy Counterattacked and drove our Troops out of VAUX - 186 Inf. Bde.
Formed Defensive Flank: Bdes ordered to consolidate on present line.
Rear Div. HQ's move for BIENVILLERS to COURCELLES in Morning - Supply Railhead
moved to BOYELLES

Prisoners further Captured 7 Officers 139 ORs

Estimated Casualties to close of Phase ie. 31st Aug / 1st Sept:-
156/INF Bde
155 INF Bde. 5th Devons 3 Officers 60 ORs | 5th N. Fus 9 Offrs 270 ORs | 5th Argyll 4 Offrs 153 ORs
8th W. Yorks nil | 2/4 do 4 Offrs 266 do | 2/4 Argyll 10 do 192 do
9/2th Seaforths 7 Officers 180 ORs | 3/4 Hants 3 Offrs 165 do | 2/4 Yand 2.8 ok. 214 do.

The 187 Inf Bde Casualties in seeking showing considerable decrease on those of first reported

War Material Reported Captured since 25 Inst
8 Field Guns
147 Machine Guns
15 Trench Mortars
10 Anti-Tank Rifles

And a considerable amount of Ammunition and Equipment, Rifles &c not yet counted.

Army Form C. 2118.

WAR DIARY
or
INTELLIGENCE SUMMARY.
(Erase heading not required.)

Instructions regarding War Diaries and Intelligence Summaries are contained in F. S. Regs., Part II. and the Staff Manual respectively. Title pages will be prepared in manuscript.

Place	Date	Hour	Summary of Events and Information	Remarks and references to Appendices
			Appendix D = Casualties during August.	
			" E = Honours and Awards during August.	
			" F = Reinforcements during August.	
			Lancelot Kiggell ~ Major General Comdg 62nd (W.R.) Division	

App. A

SPECIAL ORDER
BY
Lieutenant-General Sir A.J. GODLEY, K.C.B., K.C.M.G.,
Commanding XXII CORPS.

The Corps Commander has been desired by the General-Officer-Commanding Fifth (French) Army to express his great satisfaction at the appearance and bearing of the troops which he reviewed this morning. The Corps Commander wishes to add his appreciation of the excellent turn-out, good march discipline and smartness of the representative detachments of the Corps Mounted Troops, 51st (Highland) Division and 62nd (West Riding) Division, and to thank them for the evident pains which they had taken, though only just out of the Battle, to so worthily uphold the credit of the British Army before the French Generals and Staffs.

Alu De la Voye

Headquarters.
1.8.18.

D. A. & Q. M. G.
XXII CORPS.

SECRET.

62nd Div. No. A/273/67.

185th Infantry Brigade.
186th Infantry Brigade.
187th Infantry Brigade.
D.A.D.O.S. 62nd (W.R.) Divn.
General Staff.

App. B.

Copy of G.H.Q. letter O.B./2218 of 5/8/18 is forwarded for information :-

"Third Army.   O.B./2218.

      Owing to the shortage of reinforcements the 2/5th West Yorks. Regt. will be absorbed by the 8th West Yorks Regt. under orders to be issued by the A.G.
2.   Surplus equipment and transport will be disposed of under the orders of the Q.M.G.
3.   The 2/20th London Regt. is posted to the 185th Infantry Brigade in place of the 2/5th West Yorks Regt.
4.   The 2/20th London Regt. will be transferred from the L of C. Area to the Third Army in accordance with G.H.Q. telegram No. O.B. 2218 issued to-day.

                     (sd) G.P.DAWNAY, M.G.
G.H.Q.   for Lieutenant-General.
5/8/18.   C.G.S.   "

      The orders from A.G. have not been received, but these are practically as follows:-

      8th West Yorks. Regt. will be made up to 900 other ranks from men of the 2/5th West Yorks. Regt.

      The balance of men from the 2/5th West Yorks. Regt, will be distributed among Yorkshire Battalions of the 62nd Division to bring them up to 900 strong - no men of the 2/5th West Yorks. Regt. will leave the Division or go to the Base.

      Further instructions regarding the arrival of the 2/20th London Regt. and the disposal of equipment and transport of 2/5th West Yorks. Regt. will be issued later.

                    (sd) HAROLD.F.LEA.   Lieut-Colonel.
7th August 1918.   A.A.&.Q.M.G., 62nd (West Riding) Division.

App. C

DIVISIONAL ROUTINE ORDERS
by Major-Gen. Sir. R.D.Whigham, K.C.B., D.S.O,
Comdg. 62nd (West Riding) Division.

August 31st. 1918.

ADMINISTRATIVE STAFF.

No.1483. HONOURS AND AWARDS.

The Divisional Commander has the honour to announce that the Field-Marshal Commanding-in-Chief has awarded, under authority granted by His Majesty the King, the undermentioned decorations for gallantry in Operations on the MARNE from the 20th to 29th July 1918.

BAR TO THE DISTINGUISHED SERVICE ORDER.

Maj.(A/Lt.Col) L.W.P.HART, D.S.O.	Lincoln Rgt attd York and Lancs Rgt.

THE DISTINGUISHED SERVICE ORDER.

Lt.(A/Capt) J.B.COCKHILL, MC.	West Riding Regt,
Capt.(A/Lt.Col) N.A.ENGLAND.	W,Rid,Rgt. attd West Yorks Rgt.
Maj.A/Lt.Col) E.V.BASTOW.	Yorks Rgt. attd Devon Regt.
Maj.(A/Lt.Col) C.A.CHAYTOR.	K.O.Y.L.I.

SECOND BAR TO THE MILITARY CROSS.

Capt. P.BENTLEY, MC.	K.O.Y.L.I.
Capt. J.A.O.SCOTT, MC.	R.A.M.C. attd Durham L.I.

BAR TO THE MILITARY CROSS.

Lt. H.TREACHER, MC.	R,Suss.Rgt attd Devon Regt.
Capt. R.SMITH, MC	York & Lancs Regt.
Lt. (A/Capt) S.C.MAXWELL, MC	York & Lancs Regt.
Lt. H.JOHNSON, MC	Durham Light Infantry.
2/Lt. G.A.ELLIS. MC	B/312th Brigade R.F.A.
Lt.(A/Maj) F.LISMORE. MC	M.G.Bn.London Rgt attd M.G.Bn
Capt.(A/Maj) L.A.POLLAK. MC	M.G.Bn.
Capt. A.F.WILSON, MC	R.A.M.C. attd York & Lancs Rgt.
Lt. J.R.STANSER MC.	York & Lancs Rgt. attd Sig Co.

THE MILITARY CROSS.

Lt. T.ROBBINS.	Lancs Fus. attd H.Q. 62nd Divn.
Capt. J.WINDEATT	Devon Regiment.
2/Lt. J.H.EDGAR.	Liverpool Rgt attd Devon Regt.
2/Lt. C.W.STEER.	Devon Regt.
2/Lt. J.C.MITCHELL.	do
2/Lt. R.W.COLEMAN.	Warwick Rgt attd Devon Regt.
2/Lt. A.BULLOCH.	West Yorks Regt.
2/Lt. A.NAYLOR.	do
Lt. H.J.GRAVES.	Yorks Rgt attd West Yorks Rgt.
Capt. T.P.REAY.	West Yorks Regt.
2/Lt. I.R.S.HARRISON.	do
Lt. H.R.BURROWS.	do
Lt. J.C.AIREY.	Royal Scots. attd West Yorks Rgt.
2/Lt. A.J.GWYNN.	West Yorks Regt.
2/Lt. W.J.McKINTOCK.	do
Lt. B.M.RILEY.	do
Lt. E.H.BARDSLEY.	do
Capt. W.SMITHSON.	West Rid. Rgt attd 186 Bde H.Q.

over

THE MILITARY CROSS (contd.)

2/Lt. F. CHAPMAN.	West Riding Regt.
2/Lt. P.R. BARNES.	West Yorks attd West Riding Rgt.
2/Lt. R.J. MAUHIN.	West Riding Regt.
2/Lt. L.V. WALKER.	West Yorks attd West Riding Rgt.
Lt.(A/Capt) J. STOCKS.	West Riding Regt.
2/Lt. B. STOTT.	do
2/Lt. A.C. POTTER.	do
2/Lt. F.K. MARSDEN.	do
2/Lt. H.A. WALKER.	do
Lt.(A/Capt) W.H. LEDGARD.	Hants. Regt.
Lt.(A/Capt) H.C.B. COTTAM.	do
2/Lt. E.P. FENN.	do
2/Lt. S.D. GREENHALGH.	Lancs Fus. attd Hants Regt.
2/Lt. F.C. HOLBROOK.	Glouc. Rgt attd Hants Regt.
Capt. T.A.M. OLIPHANT.	K.O.Y.L.I.
2/Lt. P. MOORE.	West Yorks attd K.O.Y.L.I.
2/Lt. E. CALLEAR.	do
2/Lt. G.C. GRAY.	do
2/Lt. C. HIRST.	K.O.Y.L.I.
Capt. J. MILSE.	York & Lancs Regt.
Capt(A/Maj) J.E.D. STICKNEY.	do
2/Lt. J.A. LONGMIRE.	W. Riding Rgt attd York & Lancs Rgt.
2/Lt. E.A. THACKERY.	West Yorks Rgt attd York & Lancs Rgt.
Lt. W.E. MEIKLE.	Durham Light Infantry.
2/Lt. I. DODDS.	do
Lt.(A/Capt) C.H.R. GEE.	do
2/Lt. P.N. MASON.	M.G. Bn.
2/Lt. H.E.A. MADGE.	M.G. Bn.
Lt. E.S. LLOYD.	Sig. Secn. 312th Bde R.F.A.
Capt. P.W. HURD.	R.A.M.C. attd K.O.Y.L.I.
Capt. J.M. PRINGLE.	R.A.M.C. attd West Yorks Regt.
Capt.(A/Maj) G. STIELL.	R.A.M.C. attd 2/2nd W.R. Fld Amb.
Capt. J.W. FREW.	R.A.M.C. attd 2/3rd W.R. Fld Amb.
Capt. W.J.L. BICKEY.	R.A.M.C. attd West Riding Regt.
Revd. P.F. HINDE.	A.C.D. attd York & Lancs Rgt.
200455 C.S.M. W.H. HOYLE.	West Riding Regt.
5441 C.S.M. F.W. WATSON, DCM.	K.O.Y.L.I.

THE DISTINGUISHED CONDUCT MEDAL.

204679 Sergt. E.T. HEPPER.	Devon Regiment.
240835 Pte. S. RICE.	do
306963 Sergt. J.T. HORNER.	West Yorks Regt.
201802 Pte. J. SMITH, MM	do
203773 Pte. H. STEDMAN.	do
253027 Sergt. R.W. CAMPBELL.	do
240598 CSM. C.E. WATERHOUSE.	West Riding Regt.
12275 CSM. K. HANSBY.	do
235044 Sergt. D. MADEN.	do
200800 Pte.(A/L.Cpl) W. FOULDS, MM	do
19908 CSM. J.H. MANN.	do
41137 Pte. A. BROOMHEAD.	K.O.Y.L.I.
242411 Sergt. J. IOWSLEY.	do
200797 Sergt. J. WALSH.	do
241168 Pte. W. DALE.	York & Lancs Regt.
325306 Sergt. W. WILSON.	Durham Light Infantry.
325637 Cpl. E. GILL, MM	do
325465 L/Cpl. J. MASTERS.	do
42323 Sergt. W. HAZELL.	M.G. Bn.
20100 Cpl.(A/Sgt) J. SHEPHERD.	do
9632 Bo/Cpl. C.P. REED.	do
482140 Sergt. H. ELLIS, MM	Div. Signal Coy.
401178 Cpl.(A/Sgt) E. HIRST, MM	2/1st W.R. Fld. Ambce.
403136 L/Sgt. J.H. BARBER.	2/2nd W.R. Fld Ambce.

BAR TO THE MILITARY MEDAL.

~~No. Pte.~~ C. REID. ~~14~~   Durham Light ~~Infantry.~~

tTHE MILITARY MEDAL.

20928 Pvte. H. SMITH,   West Yorks Regt.
201109 Sergt. H.T. CHURCHER.   Hants Regt.
201432 L/Cpl. G.A. WINPENNY.   K.O.Y.L.I.
201471 Corpl. J. BAKER.   do

(Authority G.H.Q. MS/H/10539 dated 26th August 1918)

Also the MILITARY CROSS to the undermentioned:-

1st Lieut. W.H. HOUSE.   M.O.R.C., U.S.A. attd 62nd D.A.C.
1st Lieut. G.S. OSINCUP.   do   attd West Rid. Regt,

(Authority MS/AM/63 dated 26th August 1918)

No. 1494. FAIR WEATHER TRACKS.

Fair weather horse transport tracks are now open as follows:-

WEST to EAST. A.16.c.3.3. to A.16.d.2.1. level crossing.
EAST to WEST. Ditto but North of road.
            Reference ERVILLERS Special Sheet.

No. 1495. WATER&

The following Watering Points have now been finished and come into operation:-

DOUCHY. 3 standards for water carts, 420' horse troughs.
        1 petrol can filler.
BOIRY ST RICTRUDE. 2 standards for water carts.
                   1 petrol can filler & 300' double troughs.
MOYENNEVILLE. 2 standards for water carts, 240' troughs for
              watering in course of erection.
The following Pumping Plants have now been removed to forward areas:-
        SAULTY NORTH.
        GROS TISON FARM.
The water points supplied have been closed down - they are as follows:-
    SAULTY NORTH. Horse troughs and water cart filling point
                  at V.1.b.3.5.
    GROS TISON FARM. Horse trough GROS TISON FARM.
                     Horse dip, water troughs and water cart
                     filling point at C.1.b.3.0.

ERVILLERS. Water Points now working:- 480' troughing B.14.a.7.5.
                                      100'   do   B.14.c.5.5.
    do   Water cart filling point
                                                B.14.d.4.0.

No. 1496. LEAVE TRAIN SERVICE.

TO BOULOGNE.   Dept. BEAUMETZ 8.08.
                                          SAULTY   8.40.
                                          WARLINCOURT 8.52.
                                          MONDICOURT 9.10.
                                          DOULLENS
                                              (Nord) 10.12.
                                    Arr. BOULOGNE 17.52.

LEAVE TRAIN SERVICE (contd.)

To PARIS.
    By returning Supply Train   Depart SAULTY   12.40
                                                   DOULLENS
                                                   (Exchange) 19.30.
                                                   ABBEVILLE   21.10.
    By Personnel Train   Arr. ROUEN   2.07.
            Thence by passenger train to PARIS.

    Personnel will leave Railhead 2 days before arrival at ROUEN.

No.1497. HORSE WATERING.

    Sufficient men to provide pumping parties will always accompany horse watering parties.

                                        HAROLD F. LEA, Lieut-Colonel.
                                              A.A. & Q.M.G.

NOTICE&

MOBILE VETERINARY SECTION.

    2/1st (W.R.) Mobile Veterinary Section is now located at F.10.c.5.9 (DOUCHY-AYETTE Road) with Advanced Veterinary Aid Post in COURCELLES.

APPENDIX D

CASUALTIES DURING AUGUST 1918.

OFFICERS.

23/8/18.	Lieut.	MASSY-BERESFORD		310th Bde. R.F.A.	Killed.
24/8/18.	T/2/Lt.	CRANSTON.	J.B.	8th West Yorks.	Wounded (Gas).
25/8/18.	2/Lieut.	MOORE.	P.	West Yorks Regt. attd. 5th K.O.Y.L.I.	Wounded.
25/8/18.	2/Lieut.	BUTTERFIELD.	H.E.	5th K.O.Y.L.I.	Wounded.
25/8/18.	2/Lieut.	PORTER.	J.T.	2/4th K.O.Y.L.I.	Killed.
25/8/18.	2/Lieut.	HALL.	G.	2/4th K.O.Y.L.I.	Wounded.
25/8/18.	2/Lieut.	MAYLOR.	A.	2/4th K.O.Y.L.I.	Wounded.
25/8/18.	2/Lieut.	WIGGINS.	S.	5th K.O.Y.L.I. attd. 2/4th K.O.Y.L.I.	Wounded.
25/8/18.	2/Lieut.	FOX.	R.T.	2/4th K.O.Y.L.I.	Killed.
25/8/18.	2/Lieut.	LONGMIRE.	J.A.	West Riding Regt attd. 2/4th York & Lancs.	Wounded.
25/8/18.	2/Lieut.	WINFIELD.	W.M.	Lancs. Fus. attd. 2/4th York & Lancs.	Wounded.
25/8/18.	2/Lieut.	PARTINGTON.	H.	Lancs. Fus. attd. 2/4th York & Lancs.	D. of Wounds
25/8/18.	2/Lieut.	LOWE.	W.	2/4th York & Lancs.	Wounded.
25/8/18.	2/Lieut.	DRAPER.	J.R.	2/4th York & Lancs.	Wounded.
25/8/18.	Lieut. (A/Capt.)	WILKINS.	L.A.	2/4th York & Lancs.	Killed.
25/8/18.	Lieut.	NORMAN.	A.	2/4th York & Lancs.	Wounded.
25/8/18.	2/Lieut.	SEDDONS.	H.	Lancs. Fus. attd. 2/4th York & Lancs.	Wounded & Missing.
25/8/18.	2/Lieut.	WALKER.	W.	6th Lancs. Fus. attd. 5th West Riding Regt.	Died of Wounds.
25/8/18.	2/Lieut.	MELLALIEU.		Lancs. Fus. attd. 5th West Riding R.	Wounded.
25/8/18.	2/Lieut.	CHAPMAN.	F.	8th West Riding R. attd. 5th West Riding R.	Wounded.
25/8/18.	2/Lieut.	MACHIN.	R.J.	2nd West Riding R. attd. 5th West Riding R.	Wounded.
25/8/18.	2/Lieut.	FLATOW.	E.W.	2/4th West Rid. R.	Wounded.
25/8/18.	Lieut.	HOLLARD.	H.L.	A.S.C. attd. 2/4th K.O.Y.L.I.	Wounded.
26/8/18.	2/Lieut.	RICHMOND.	C.B.	2nd Lancs. Fus. attd. 2/4th Hants. Regt.	Wounded at Duty.
26/8/18.	Capt.	BENNETT.	J.F.	9th Bn. Hants. attd. 2/4th Hants. Regt.	Killed.
26/8/18.	2/Lieut.	PENDERGAST.	F.G.	7th Lancs. Fus. attd. 2/4th West Rid. R.	Wounded.
27/8/18.	T/2/Lt.	CALLEAR.	E.	West Yorks. attd. 5th K.O.Y.L.I.	Wounded.
27/8/18.	T/2/Lt.	TEE.	R.F.	5th K.O.Y.L.I.	Wounded.
27/8/18.	Lieut. (A/Capt.)	SKIRROW.	G.	West Yorks. attd. 2/4th K.O.Y.L.I.	Killed.
27/8/18.	Capt.	BEAUMONT.	G.	5th West Riding R.	Wounded at Duty.
27/8/18.	2/Lieut.	RODGER. (M.C.)	J.L.	2/4th K.O.Y.L.I.	Wounded.
27/8/18.	2/Lieut.	COOPER.	G.	2/4th K.O.Y.L.I.	Wounded.
27/8/18.	2/Lieut.	SWABY.	S.T.	West Yorks. attd. 2/4th K.O.Y.L.I.	Wounded.
27/8/18.	2/Lieut.	JOHNSTON.	R.B.	2/4th K.O.Y.L.I.	Wounded (Gas)
28/8/18.	2/Lieut.	HOLBROOK.	F.C.	Glouc. Regt. attd. 2/4th Hants. Regt.	Wounded.
29/8/18.	T/2/Lt.	GUMM.	P.F.	Glouc. Regt. attd. 1/5th Devon Regt.	Wounded.
29/8/18.	T/2/Lt.	BOARDMAN.	J.T.	Lancs. Fus. attd. 5th West Rid. R.	Wounded.
29/8/18.	2/Lieut.	DRABBLE.	H.	4th West Rid. R. attd. 5th West Rid. R.	Wound

Date	Rank	Name	Initials	Regiment	Status
29/8/18.	2/Lieut.	CLAY.	G.F.	2nd West Yorks. attd. 5th West Rid. Regt.	Wounded at Duty.
29/8/18.	2/Lieut.	SAUNDERS.	A.G.	5th Devon Regt.	Wounded.
30/8/18.	T/2/Lt.	WALLWORK.	F.	5th Devon Regt.	Wounded.
30/8/18.	Lieut. (A/Capt.)	JONES.	R.G.	2/20th London R.	Killed.
30/8/18.	Capt.	REYNOLDS.(M.C.)	A.	2/20th London Regt.	Wounded.
30/8/18.	2/Lieut.	BRIGHT.	W.L.	2/20th London Regt.	Wounded.
30/8/18.	2/Lieut.	SMOUT.	P.L.	7th London Regt. attd. 2/20th London Regt.	Wounded.
30/8/18.	2/Lieut.	DYBALL.	A.F.	2/20th London Regt.	Wounded.
30/8/18.	2/Lieut.	MORRISON.	R.	Lancs. Fus. attd. 5th Devon Regt.	Killed.
30/8/18.	T/2/Lt.	DUNN.	H.B.	5th Devon Regt.	Killed.
30/8/18.	T/2/Lt.	LOOK.	J.L.	Glouc. Regt. attd. 5th Devon Regt.	Wounded.
30/8/18.	2/Lieut.	READ.	F.E.	2/20th London Regt.	Wounded.
30/8/18.	Lieut.	COPELAND.	J.	2/4th West Riding R.	Wounded.
30/8/18.	2/Lieut.	ADKINSON.	C.E.	7th Lancs. Fus. attd. 2/4th West Rid. R.	Wounded.
30/8/18.	T/2/Lt.	WARD.	J.E.	2nd West Rid. R. attd. 2/4th West Rid. R.	Wounded.
30/8/18.	Lieut. (A/Capt.)	WATKINSON.	E.G.	5th West Rid. Regt.	Wounded at Duty.
31/8/18.	2/Lieut.	BARNES.	F.	2/20th London Regt.	Wounded.
31/8/18.	Lieut. (A/Major)	WHITEAWAY.	E.G.L.	5th Devon Regt.	Wounded at Duty.
31/8/18.	T/Capt.	PICKFORD.	A.F.I.	62nd Div. Train. (525 Coy A.S.C.)	Injured.
31/8/18.	Capt.	GELDARD.(MC)	N.	2/4th West Riding R.	Wounded.
31/8/18.	2/Lieut.	GRANT.	R.L.	2/4th West Riding R.	Wounded.

OTHER RANKS.

Killed..............213.
Wounded............1231.
Missing.............111.

APPENDIX E

REWARDS GRANTED DURING AUGUST 1918.

Bar to D.S.O.	1.
D.S.O.	4.
2nd Bar to M.C.	2.
Bar to M.C.	9.
M.C.	62.
D.C.M.	24.
Bar to M.M.	22.
M.M.	333.

REINFORCEMENTS RECEIVED DURING AUGUST 1918.

APPE

	Offcrs.	O.R.
8th West Yorkshire Regiment.	9	275
2/5th West Yorkshire Regiment.		116
1/5th Devonshire Regiment.	22	464
2/20th London Regt.	3	198
5th West Riding Regiment.	20	452
2/4th West Riding Regiment.	14	421
2/4th Hampshire Regiment.	7	267
5th K.O.Y.L.I.	5	463
2/4th K.O.Y.L.I.	12	611
2/4th York & Lancaster Regiment.	18	479
Royal Artillery.	1	89
Royal Engineers.	2	75
Divisional Signal Company.	-	-
Divisional Train.	-	26
R.A.M.C.	2	56
62nd Bn Machine Gun Corps.	8	166
9th Bn Durham Light Infantry.	15	205
252 Divisional Employment Company.	-	2

Army Form C. 2118.

WAR DIARY
or
INTELLIGENCE SUMMARY.   September 1918   p 3
(Erase heading not required.)

Place	Date	Hour	Summary of Events and Information	Remarks and references to Appendices
COURCELLES and TRIANGLE WOOD	6th		Weather Fine and Warm	
	7th		Weather Dull with Occasional Showers	
do	8th		Weather Dull. High Wind. G.O.C. presented Medal Ribbons on Parade to 185th Inf Bde	
do	9th		Orders received for 62nd Division to move forward this spring evening. On completion of move units will be situated as follows:— 185th Inf Bde. Gp.H.Q. Neighbourhood FREMICOURT. 186th " S.W. corner HAVRINCOURT WOOD 187th " VELU WOOD 9th Bn D.L.I. S.W. corner HAVRINCOURT WOOD Field Companies R.E. will concentrate at VAULX WOOD Divisional H.Qrs. will move to I.17.a.5.9 on morning of 10th Sept. Moves performed 24 hours Orders for move of Field Ambulances Action of Divisions on either flank of 62nd Division	

WAR DIARY or INTELLIGENCE SUMMARY

Army Form C. 2118.

September 1918

Place	Date	Hour	Summary of Events and Information	Remarks and references to Appendices
COURCELLES and TRIANGLE COPSE	Sept. 9		Administrative Instructions reference 62nd Divisional Order No 141 of 8/9/18	APPENDIX A A/45/49
	10		G.O.C. commanding 62nd Division issued an appeal to all ranks for a big effort to be made to capture the high ground on which stands the village of HAVRINCOURT. Attack orders. Barrage, Brigade Group, as contained in D.O. 141 carried out. Weather – dull, high wind, occasional heavy rain. Tracks too heavy for traffic.	
			Weather – dull, wind fresh, occasional heavy rain. Routes to be used on night 11th/12th September.	
COURCELLES and Southern and Western BELGIAN HORTHIES	11		Field Coys. moved to a point E of BERTINCOURT and during evening 2 their assembly positions in S.W. corner of HAVRINCOURT WOOD. Zero hour 5.25 A.M. 12th Sept.	
	12		Weather – dull, dry wind, occasional heavy rain. Prisoners to-day : 9 Officers, 550 O.R. Total since 24th Aug: 58 Officers, 1968 O.R. Corps Commander sends his hearty congratulations to all ranks of the 62nd Division for his highly successful operation of this date. The capture of HAVRINCOURT under circumstances of considerable greater difficulty than on the first occasion that the 62nd Division carried it out is a fine feat of arms of which the Division may well be proud.	

T2134. Wt. W708–776. 50000. 4/15. Sir J.C. & S.

Army Form C. 2118.

WAR DIARY
or
INTELLIGENCE SUMMARY.

September 1918 p. 5.

(Erase heading not required.)

Place	Date	Hour	Summary of Events and Information	Remarks and references to Appendices
COURCELLES and Southern and Western BEUGNY & MORCHIES	12		Sum. General Sir H.P. Braithwaite K.C.B. arrives. Bell Aine 62.	
			Total estimated casualties from 1st Sept.	
			5th Bn. Duke of Wellingtons Regt. 2 Officers and 104 O.R.	
			2/4th " 3 " 120 O.R.	
			2/4th Bn. Hampshire Regt. 6 " 200 O.R.	
			5th Bn. Kings own Yorkshire L.I. 6 " 233 O.R.	
			2/4th " 5 " 239 O.R.	
			2/4th Bn. York & Lancaster Regt. 10 " 234 O.R.	
			9th Bn. Durham Lgt. Inf. (Pioneers) 8 " 143 O.R. — Division Heavily counterattacked but without success	App.
	13		Weather — fine, fresh wind, cold.	App.
			Prisoners:	
			Total estimated casualties since 1st September 42 Officers 1393 O.R's.	
	14		Weather — fine, fresh wind, mild	App.
			Warning orders for Division to be relieved, less Artillery, on night 15/16 Septr.	
			Division in last 24 hours 7 Officers 211 o Ranks	
			Special congratulatory order by Div. Comdr.	App. B

Army Form C. 2118.

WAR DIARY
or
INTELLIGENCE SUMMARY.

(Erase heading not required.)

September 1918 p.6.

Place	Date	Hour	Summary of Events and Information	Remarks and references to Appendices
Courcelles and Sunken Rd	15th		187 Inf. Bde moved to S. of HERMIES. Situation nothing to record. Estimated Material Captured 12" to 14" not included. 4 Field Guns, 12 Trench Mortars, 46 Machine Guns. Actual Casualties incurred during Operations Attached administrative accounts in connection with 6th Oct and 13th Sept/18.	Attached Appendix D
Triangle Copse	16th		Command of Right Sector VI Corps front passed to G.O.C. 3rd Division 3.10 a.m. On Relief Division distributed as under. 185 Inf.Bde to HERMIES, 186 Inf.Bde to BEUGNY, 187 Inf Bde to BEHAGNIES, 9th D.L.I to VAULX - All Troops in Dug-outs and Shelters. Divl H.Qrs to TRIANGLE Copse.	GM GM
do	17th		186 Inf.Bde Group moved to COURCELLES Area, 155 Inf.Bde Group to West of VAULX	GM
do	17th to 21st		During these days - Divisional baths Reorganised, incorporated Reinforcements and did certain Amount of Training	GM
do	22nd		General Plan of Operations for Capture of MARCOING issued	GM

Army Form C. 2118.

WAR DIARY
or
INTELLIGENCE SUMMARY.
(Erase heading not required.)

September 1918.
Page 6.

Place	Date	Hour	Summary of Events and Information	Remarks and references to Appendices
TRIANGLE COPSE	23rd	—	Major J. Smyth D.S.O. R.A.O. handed over appointment of S.M.O. to Captain D.S. Boyefield "The Lincolnshire Regt", on being appointed S.A.D.M.S. 7 Corps.	
"	24th	—	Orders received for Division to move forward to front. Weather fine. Administrative instructions after 62 Divy Order G.481/58 g 22/9/18 amendment to above Administrative Instructions.	Appendix E.F.
"	25.	—	Below now formed as follows:- 185 Inf. Group from VAUX to BEUGNY — 187 from BARASTRE - SAPIGNIES to FREMICOURT — 186 from GOMIECOURT to VAUX troops bivouacked in + around villages. Divl HQ remained TRIANGLE COPSE. Amendment to Administrative Instructions issued on 24/9/18 refer 62 Divn G.481/59>>19/18 left	Appendix G.
"	26.	—	Divl HQ Landers left TRIANGLE COPSE to go to Advanced HQ. G office remained.	

Army Form C. 2118.

WAR DIARY
or
INTELLIGENCE SUMMARY.
(Erase heading not required.)

September 1918. Page 7.

Place	Date	Hour	Summary of Events and Information	Remarks and references to Appendices
HERMIES & BEAUMETZ	26"		at HERMIES, "Q" in Catacombs at BEAUMETZ and "A" bivouaced with Rear H.Q. at TRIANGLE COPSE. Offr. Such Police moved to following positions:- 18 St trenches S.E. of HERMIES — 186" L/BEAUMETZ — 187 trenches near HERMIES.	W
	27"	Zero hour 5.20 am	3rd Division passed through 3rd Division to Capture RUMILLY. Railheads Supplies VELU — Ammunition HERMIES Sch. Heap. S.A.A. Section moved from near ERVILLERS to RUYAULCOURT. Two G.S. wagons per Rle were attached from 13th A.A.H.T.Co. One Supply Tank attached to each Infantry Bde. Prisoners of War cage established near YORKSHIRE BANK. HERMIES.	W

WAR DIARY
or
INTELLIGENCE SUMMARY.

(Erase heading not required.)

Army Form C. 2118.

September 1918. Page 8.

Place	Date	Hour	Summary of Events and Information	Remarks and references to Appendices
HERMIES & BEAUMETZ.	28th		Weather fine.	
HAVRINCOURT & HERMIES.	29th		"G" Office opened at HAVRINCOURT at 10 a.m. "O" Office moved to HERMIES & Hd. Qtrs. vacated by "G". Special congratulatory order by Divl. Comdr.	Appendix H

WAR DIARY
or
INTELLIGENCE SUMMARY.

Army Form C. 2118.

September 1918. Page 9.

Place	Date	Hour	Summary of Events and Information	Remarks and references to Appendices
HAVRINCOURT & BEAUCAMP HERRIES	30"		Weather fine. Casualties during operations commencing 27th to end of month. Killed 20 Officers & 248 O.Ranks. — Wounded 44 Officers & 1135 Other Ranks — missing 3 Officers & 262 Other Ranks. Guns captured 38, M.G. captured 219, + large quantities of small arms, ammunition etc.	Appendix L

Army Form C. 2118.

WAR DIARY
or
INTELLIGENCE SUMMARY.
(Erase heading not required.)

Appendix J = Casualties during September.
     "   K = Reinforcements joined during September.
     "   L = Reinforcements.

Feetatfark Kolen
Anderson Major General
Commanding 62nd (2R.) Division.

SECRET. 62nd Div. A/45/49.
Copy No..........

ADMINISTRATIVE INSTRUCTIONS REFERENCE 62ND (WEST RIDING) DIVISION ORDER NO.141 OF 8.9.18.

1. **S.A.A.**

    S.A.A. Section will be at I.34.c. central.

2. **PRISONERS OF WAR CAGE** will be at Cross Roads in J.32.d.8.6.

    STRAGGLERS' POSTS will be at J.20.c.9.3, J.13.a.6.8.

3. **WATER.**

    (i) **Water Points.**

SAPIGNIES	Good supply.
FAVREUIL	Limited supply.
BEUGNATRE	Not working satisfactorily.
FREMICOURT	Good supply.
BEUGNY	" "
I.29.b.	Limited supply. Water supplied by Motor lorries.
VELU Station	A good supply anticipated and now partially working.
CANAL P.91b.9.9.	Working order.
" P.4.c.2.8.	Good supply hand pumps.
" J.36.a.6.1	Working order.
HERMIES J.30.a.4.4.	2 troughs filled by lift and force pump from pond.
I.26.central	2, 9000 gallon tanks filled by compresser plant.

    (ii) **Water Cart Filling Points.**

SAPIGNIES H.8.d.7.4.	Good supply.
FAVREUIL	Limited supply.
FREMICOURT	Good supply.
I.29.b.	Limited supply, water supplied by motor lorries.
VELU Station	Working order.

4. **CANAL DU NORD.**

    Bathing and washing is forbidden.

5. **BILLETS & HORSE STANDINGS.**

    No men will be billeted in houses, barns or billets marked "RAUDE".

    On no account will horses or mules be put in horse lines, or standings or houses marked "PFERDE, KRANKE, LAZARETT, LAZ, or RAUDE."

6. **MOBILE VETERINARY SECTION.**

    Mobile Veterinary Section will be established at FREMICOURT by 10 a.m. 11th instant, and will report what locality has been selected for advanced station.

7. Nuclei will be sent to Reception Camp at BIENVILLERS.

8. **MEDICAL.**

   A.D.M.S. will issue orders with regard to evacuation.
   Additional bearers will be supplied as follows :-

   From 185th Inf.Bde. to report to 2/1st Fld.Amb. 20 men.
   "   186th   "   "   "   " " 2/2nd "   20 "
   "   187th   "   "   "   " " 2/3rd "   20 "

   These men will be taken from bands.

9. **LIGHT RAILWAYS.**

   It is reported that the Light Railway on the East side of the Canal from P.4.b.0.9 to K.31.a.0.2 is in working order.
   There are four large trucks at P.4.b.0.9 which have been easily drawn by one mule.

10. **CANAL DU NORD CROSSINGS.**

    The canal can be crossed at the following points :-

    (a) On Foot   P.4.b.0.9.   J.34.a.9.7.   J.36.a.5.0.   J.36.b.9.3.

    (b) Wagons L.G.S.   P.4.b.0.9.

11. **GAS.**

    Supplies of spare respirators will be sent forward to Brigade Gas Officers.
    Chloride of lime can be drawn on demand from coal dump on BRVILLERS - HAMLINCOURT road.
    The Divisional Gas Officer will be at the Advanced Dressing Station.

9.9.18.

Lieut.Colonel,
A.A. & Q.M.G. 62nd (West Riding) Division.

DISTRIBUTION.

Copy No. 1.	A.D.C. for G.O.C.	Copy No. 11.	A.D.M.S.
" 2.	"G"	12.	62nd (W.R) Div.Sig.Co.
3-4	"A" & "Q".	13.	62nd Bn.M.G.C.
5.	185th Infantry Brigade.	14.	9th D.L.I.
6.	186th Infantry Brigade.	15.	A.P.M.
7.	187th Infantry Brigade.	16.	Divl.Gas Officer.
8.	62nd (W.R) Divl.Arty.	17.	D.A.D.V.S.
9.	C.R.E.	18.	Mob.Vet.Section.
10.	62nd (W.R) Divl.Train.	19.	Baths Officer.
		20.	Water Officer.
		21-22	War Diary.
		23.	D.A.D.O.S.

App. B.

SPECIAL ORDER OF THE DAY
BY
Major General Sir R.D. Whigham, K.C.B. D.S.O.
Commanding 62nd (West Riding) Division.

September 14th 1918.

The following congratulatory letters from the General Officer Commanding Third Army, and the General Officer Commanding Sixth Corps, on the recent operations are published for the information of all ranks :-

Extract from a personal letter received by the Divisional Commander from the General Officer Commanding Third Army.

" I set the 62nd Division a very hard task yesterday, but the importance of it was so great that I determined to try it.

The Division has done it, and done it splendidly, and so I write to let you know how proud I am of their achievement."

From the General Officer Commanding Sixth Corps. 12/9/18.

" Corps Commander sends his hearty congratulations to all ranks of the 62nd Division for their highly successful operation of this date. The capture of HAVRINCOURT under circumstances of considerably greater difficulty than on the first occasion that the 62nd carried it out was a fine feat of arms of which the Division may well be proud."

Lieut.Colonel,
A.A. & Q.M.G. 62nd (West Riding) Division.

SECRET.
Copy No....21....
62nd Div. A/55/49.

Correction to para. 2 of ADMINISTRATIVE
INSTRUCTIONS dated 9.9.18.
----

1. <u>PRISONERS OF WAR CAGE</u> will be at VELU I.30.d.9.6.

[signature]

10.9.18.
                          Lieut.Colonel,
    A.A. & Q.M.G. 62nd (West Riding) Division.
<u>DISTRIBUTION.</u>
All recipients of 62nd Division A/45/49.

App. C

CASUALTIES FROM 12.9.18 to 18.9.18.

	K.		W.		M.		W.at duty.		
	Offs.	O.R.	Offs.	O.R.	Offs.	O.R.	Offs.	O.R.	
5th Devon Regt.	1	26	5	89	-	5	-	-	
8th West Yorks Regt.	-	3	-	12	-	-	-	2	
2/20 London Regt.	3	18	1	97	-	19	-	-	
5th West Riding Regt.	1	26	2	59x	-	-	-	2	x 5 gas.
2/4th West Riding Regt.	-	19	3	196	-	-	2	-	
2/4th Hants Regt.	1	34	7x	136	-	58	-	-	x 1 W.& M.
186 T.M.B.	-	-	-	3	-	-	-	-	
5th K.O.Y.L.I.	1	17	3	147	-	79	-	-	
2/4th "	-	16	4	74	-	23	-	-	
2/4th Y & L.	-	10	6	99	-	24	-	-	
9th D.L.I.	1	18	1	81	-	18	2	1	
62 Bn M.G.C.	-	8	1	37x	-	2	-	2	x 1 gas.
310th Bde. R.F.A.	-	-	-	13	-	-	-	2	
312th Bde. R.F.A.	-	3	1	7	-	-	1	-	
62nd D.A.C.	-	1	-	4	-	-	-	-	
2/2nd W.R.Fld Amb.	-	-	-	4	-	-	-	-	
2/1st W.R.Fld Amb.	-	-	-	1x	-	-	-	-	x 1 gas.
2/3rd W.R.Fld Amb.	-	-	-	7x	-	-	-	-	x 4 gas.
461st Field Coy.	-	-	-	1	-	-	-	-	
62 Div. Signal Coy.	-	-	-	1	-	-	-	-	
A.C. Dept.	-	-	-	-	-	-	1	-	
	8	199	34	1068	-	228	6	9	11 gas 1 Off W.& M.

SECRET.   62nd Divn. A/63/49.

Copy No. ......

ADMINISTRATIVE INSTRUCTIONS WITH REFERENCE TO 62ND (WEST RIDING) DIVISION ORDER NO.143 DATED 15/9/18.

1. S.A.A. Section will move to south of MORY, and report exact location by wire.

2. All Infantry attached to Field Ambulances will move with Field Ambulances and return to their units on 17th instant.

3. Mobile Veterinary Section will move to the vicinity of GOMIECOURT, reporting exact location by wire.

4. Baths and clean clothing store will be located at SAPIGNIES.

5. The wholesale canteen will be at COURCELLES.

6. DADOS. will be at COURCELLES.

7. SALVAGE. All salvage will be handed into nearest Corps Salvage Dumps; the exact locations have been previously published in D.R.Os.
   Returned stores will be sent to D.A.D.O.S. as usual.

8. Train Companies will move under orders of O.C. Train.

15.9.18.

Lieut.Colonel,
A.A. & Q.M.G. 62nd (West Riding) Division.

DISTRIBUTION.

Copy No. 1. - A.D.C. for G.O.C.	Copy No.13. 62nd Bn. M.G.C.
2 - "G"	14. 9th D.L.I.
3-4 - "A" & "Q".	15. D.A.P.M.
5. - 185th Infantry Brigade.	16. Divl. Gas Officer.
6. - 186th Infantry Brigade.	17. D.A.D.V.S.
7. - 187th Infantry Brigade.	18. Mob. Vet. Section.
8. - 62nd (W.R) Divl. Arty.	19. Baths Officer.
9. - C.R.E.	20. Water Officer.
10. - 62nd (W.R) Divl. Train.	21-22. War Diary.
11. - A.D.M.S.	23. D.A.D.O.S.
12. - 62nd (W.R) Divl. Sig. Coy.	24. "A" Rear.
	25. Salvage Officer.
	26. 6th Corps "Q".
	27. S.A.A. Section.

S E C R E T.   62nd Divn. A/3137/49.

Copy No..........

APP. E.

ADMINISTRATIVE INSTRUCTIONS
with reference to 62nd Division G.481/S of 22.9.18.

1. **RAILHEADS.**

   Supplies: all Divisions VELU, probably on Zero day.
   Heavy Ammunition: FREMICOURT.
   Light Ammunition: HERMIES Slag heap at P.4.a.

2. **ROADS.**

   The XVII Corps will have running rights on the BAPAUME - CAMBRAI Road, and the roads running into it from the North, i.e., from VAULX VRAUCOURT and LAGNICOURT.
   The VI Corps will have running rights over the FREMICOURT - VELU - BERTINCOURT - RUYAULCOURT - HAVRINCOURT Wood - HAVRINCOURT Village Road, and over the BERTINCOURT - HERMIES Road. Roads are available for this Corps as under for supplies and ammunition:-

   (a) For the Right Division : VELU - BERTINCOURT - RUYAULCOURT - HAVRINCOURT Wood - to HAVRINCOURT Village.

   (b) For the Left Division : VELU - BEAUMETZ - DOIGNIES - HERMIES - ramp into Canal at K.31.a. thence out of the Canal at K.32.a or K.15.a.

   The Canal bed will be available for double lorry traffic from the ramp in K.31.a. to the lock in K.15.a.
   Should the ramp at K.31.a. become impassable then the Left Division must send lorries via route (a), but this should not be done except in case of necessity.
   The Left Division will probably, if the weather is dry, be able to get horse transport from DOIGNIES to DEMICOURT and thence on to the Crossing in K.15.a.

3. **LIGHT RAILWAY.**

   The light railway can now operate as far as K.32.a. and will be extended through HAVRINCOURT to RIBECOURT and onwards.
   At present this railway is only to be used for ammunition and R.E. stores, and is not available for supplies.

4. **WATER.**

   Water points are as under:-

I.5.d.9.4.	Water carts, lorries and horse watering.
J.15.b.4.2.	-ditto-
J.35.c.1.5.	Water carts and lorries.
J.36.a.3.4.	Horse watering only.
J.36.c.4.9.	-ditto-
K.15.a.3.2.	Advd. storage, drinking water only (projected)
K.27.a.6.2.	-ditto-
K.31.a.2.2.	Water carts and lorries, drinking water only (projected).
L.7.c.5.7.	Borehole (projected).
L.25.d.8.9.	Well (projected).

-2-

4. WATER (contd.)

The points marked "projected" are expected to be established by the evening of Z day.
When the forward Division is relieved it will hand over two water lorries per Brigade to this Division.

5. POLICE.

The IV Corps will police its own roads, but the 3rd Division will police the sleeper road in HAVRINCOURT Wood. Columns of vehicles are not to exceed 6 in each column whilst on the sleeper road, and at least 50 yards interval is to be maintained between columns.

Tanks are not allowed to use the sleeper road and are also forbidden to use the ramp at K.31.a.

The 3rd Division will detail specially selected men for Traffic Control at the ramp at K.31.a. and the culvert at K.32.a.3.8.

The 3rd Division is responsible for Traffic Control in HERMIES and HAVRINCOURT and the Guards Division for Traffic Control in BEAUMETZ LES CAMBRAI, DOIGNES and DEMICOURT. The Guards Division will police water points erected by the VI Corps North of the line running through J.21, 22, 23 Eastwards, and the 3rd Division water points South of this line.

6. PRISONERS OF WAR.

The VI Corps Cage will be at J.20.a.3.2. BEAUMETZ.
The Divisional Cage will be at BOGGART HOLE K.33.b.2.6.
As soon as possible the A.P.M. will arrange a forward collecting post, which will be notified to all concerned.

7. S.A.A.

The S.A.A. Section will close at present location at 9 a.m. on Y d-ay, and be ready for issue of ammunition at P.10.d (RUYAULCOURT) at 2 p.m. on Y day.

The S.A.A. Section will close at P.10.d. at 7 a.m. on Z day and open at K.21.d.7.5. (HAVRINCOURT) at 1 p.m. on Z day.

8. SUPPLIES.

The delivery of supplies will be normal.
Refilling will be on the BERTINCOURT - RUYAULCOURT Road.

9. SUPLUS STORES.

All surplus stores, blankets, greatcoats, packs etc., will be stored in the areas at present occupied. Each Infantry Brigade and each unit of Divisional Troops will arrange its store.

A guard will be left in charge of store, and the N.C.O. in command will be furnished with written instructions that should any Division or Formation order him to move, he will ask that the question be referred to Headquarters 62nd Division.

It is not expected that these stores will be brought forward again till the advance ceases.

10. TENTS AND SHELTERS.

All tents and shelters remain on charge of Formations and Units not occupying them.

Any further supply of canvas is very doubtful and it should be carried forward with units' wagon lines.

-3-

10. TENTS AND SHELTERS (contd.)

To assist in this, 2 G.S. wagons are allotted to each Infantry Brigade, and 1 to the 62nd Bn M.G.C. These wagons will be ordered to report on Y morning to Headquarters of Formations and Units concerned.

11. SUPPLY TANKS.

One supply tank is allotted to each Infantry Brigade. All arrangements will be made direct with O.C. 2nd Tanks Supply Company, location A.30.central.
These tanks are not to be pushed forward until the evening before Zero.

12. WAGON LINES.

Infantry Brigades, etc., will keep Divisional Headquarters 'Q' acquainted with the location of their wagon lines.

13. REINFORCEMENTS.

No reinforcements will join units after the 23rd September.
Formations and Units will notify O.C. 62nd Divisional Reception Camp as early as possible of the numbers and date of arrival of nuclei and surplus personnel sent to Reception Camp. They will also arrange that a sufficient supply of cooking utensils is sent with each party.

14. BILLETS AND HORSE STANDINGS.

No men will be billeted in houses, barns or billets marked "RAUDE".
On no account will horses or mules be put in horse lines or sta-ndings or houses marked "PFERDE, KRANKE, LAZERYT, LAZ, or RAUDE". No buildings will be occupied by animals without authority from a Veterinary Officer.

15. MEDICAL.

A.D.M.S. will issue orders with regard to evacuation.
Additional bearers will be supplied from bands as under, and will report to their respective Field Ambulances at 10 a.m. on Y day:-

185th Inf. Brigade 30 to 2/1st W.R. Field Ambulance.
186th Inf. Brigade.30 to 2/2nd W.R. Field Ambulance.
187th Inf. Brigade 30 to 2/3rd W.R. Field Ambulance.

16. MOBILE VETERINARY SECTION.

The Mobile Veterinary Section will be established at P.13.a. by 5 p.m. on Y day.
An Advanced Aid Post will be at J.36.a. at 6 a.m. on Z day.

Harold Lea
Lieut.Colonel.
24th September 1918.   A.A. & Q.M.G. 62nd (West Riding) Division.

-4-

DISTRIBUTION.

1. A.D.C. FOR G.O.C.
2. 'G'.
3-4. 'A' & 'Q'.
5. 185th Infantry Brigade.
6. 186th Infantry Brigade.
7. 187th Infantry Brigade.
8. 62nd (W.R.) Divisional Artillery.
9. C.R.E.
10. 62nd (W.R.) Divisional Train.
11. A.D.M.S.
12. 62nd (W.R.) Divisional Signal Company.
13. 62nd Bn. M.G.C.
14. 9th D.L.I.
15. D.A.P.M.
17. D.A.D.O.S.
18. D.A.D.V.S.
19. Mobile Veterinary Section.
20. Salvage Officer.
21. 62nd Divisional Reception Camp.
22. S.A.A. Section.
23. Water Officer.
24. VI Corps 'Q'.

SECRET.

62nd Divn. A/2164/49.

Copy No.......

ADDITION AND AMENDMENTS TO
ADMINISTRATIVE INSTRUCTIONS - 62ND DIV A/2137/49.
DATED 24.9.18.

app F.

ADDITION.

Insert after para.16:-

17. GAS.

The Divisional Gas Officer will be at A.D.S. at RUYAULCOURT. Supplies of bicarbonate of soda, chloride of lime, cloth union and spare respirators may be drawn from him there.

AMENDMENTS.

(1) 6. PRISONERS OF WAR.

For "BOGGART HOLE K.33.b.2.6" read "near YORKSHIRE DUMP.K.32.b.2.7.".

(ii) 8. SUPPLIES.

For "BERTINCOURT - RUYAULCOURT Road" read "road running through P.4.a. and c".

Harold Lea
Lieut.Colonel,
24th September 1918.   A.A. & Q.M.G., 62nd (West Riding) Divn.

DISTRIBUTION.

To all recipients of A/2137/49 dated 24.9.18,
plus 62nd Divisional Gas Officer.

App. G.

SECRET.   62nd Divn. A/2138/42.

                                    Copy No.......

AMENDMENT TO ADMINISTRATIVE INSTRUCTIONS
62nd Divn. A/2137/42 dated 24.9.18.

With reference to para. 2 (b) of above,

"For the Left Division". No lorries will be allowed, until further orders, to run from HERMIES down the ramp into the Canal, except those working for the C.E. of the Corps. These lorries will be provided with a special pass signed by the C.E. or his Staff Officer.

All other lorries, whether carrying ammunition or supplies, will, until further orders, use BERTINCOURT - RUYAULCOURT P.18.c. - HAVRINCOURT WOOD Sleeper Road - K.32.b. - HERMIES route.

The 3rd Division is responsible for seeing that no lorries whatever, except those mentioned for the C.E., proceed from HERMIES towards the Ramp.

The Right Division will not use the HERMIES - Ramp Road for wheeled transport until the Left Division report to Corps that the Canal is passable for transport East of DEMICOURT. VI Corps will then issue further traffic instructions.

                                    [signature]
                                         Lieut.Colonel.
25.9.18.   A.A. & Q.M.G. 62nd (West Riding) Division.

DISTRIBUTION.

To all recipients of A/2137/42 dated 24.9.18.

APP. H.

62ND (WEST RIDING) DIVISION.

SPECIAL ORDER OF THE DAY
by
Major-General Sir R.D. WHIGHAM, K.C.B., D.S.O.

29th September 1918.

The Major General Commanding has great pleasure in publishing for the information of all ranks of the Division the contents of a letter, which he has received from the Corps Commander, concerning the action of two companies of the 8th Battalion West Yorkshire Regiment on the 27th instant.

The incident referred to is explained in the following copy of a telegram despatched to VI Corps Headquarters on the morning of the 28th instant :-

"A.G.126. 28.
It has now been ascertained that acting on the principle of pressing an advantage wherever gained two companies 8th West Yorks reached N.W. outskirts of MARCOING yesterday morning about noon AAA Owing however to 187th Brigade on right being unable to get forward from RIBECOURT on account of M.G. fire from HIGHLAND Ridge and strong opposition in HINDENBURG Support Line in L.27 and to the left flank of West Yorks Coys. being exposed to M.G. fire from PREMY CHAPEL and NINE wood, these Coys. suffered severe casualties losing Capt. STEAD and Capt. HIRST wounded AAA Other casualties in these two Coys. not yet ascertained AAA The unfortunate obscurity as to situation in PREMY CHAPEL prevented this area from being dealt with by our Artillery from 12 noon to 2 p.m. till after 6 p.m. AAA The Commanders of these two Coys. seem to have shown great dash and initiative.

62nd Divn."

The following is a copy of the Corps Commander's letter :-

"G.O.C. 62nd Division.

Please convey to the survivors of the two Coys. 8th West Yorkshire Regiment my high appreciation and admiration of their initiative, dash, and gallantry in pushing up to the outskirts of MARCOING yesterday in spite of all obstacles. It is by resolution and bravery such as they displayed, that great victories have been won in the past history of the British Army.

I heartily congratulate the whole Battalion yourself, and your splendid Division of the inspiriting incident in front of MARCOING.

(sd) A. HALDANE, Lieut. Genl.
Commanding VI Corps.

28.9.1918.

29th September 1918.
(sd) Harold F. Lea, Lieut. Colonel,
A.A. & Q.M.G. 62nd (West Riding) Division.

App. I

CASUALTIES FROM 27-9-18 - 1-10-18.

	Killed.		Wounded.		Missing.	
	Off.	O.Rs.	Off.	O.Rs.	Off.	O.Rs.
1/5th Devon Regt.	3	77	8	158	-	12
8th West Yorks.	5	32	7	177	5	131
2/20th London Rgt.	2	25	2	72	-	9
5th West Riding Rgt.	1	1	1	7	1	-
5th West Riding Rgt.	2	14	3	103	-	2
2/4th West Riding Rgt.	2	23	2	190	-	32
2/4th ████ Rgt.	1	19	2	96	-	5
5th K.O.Y.L.I.	2	7	2	56	-	14
2/4th K.O.Y.L.I.	1	24	2	155	-	22
2/4th York & Lanc.	1	17	7	111	-	27
62nd Bn MGC	-	5	4	48	-	4
9th D.L.I.	-	1	-	2	-	-
Royal Engineers	2	2e	1e	11	-	- e at duty
Signal Coy.	-	-	-	7	-	-
R.A.M.C.	-	-	1	2	-	-
Royal Artillery.	-	1	-	7	-	-
62ND DIVISION.	20	248	42	1166	5	262

APPENDIX. J.

CASUALTIES DURING SEPTEMBER 1918

OFFICERS.

1/9/18	2/Lieut.	BRYSON.	W.M.	East Yorks. Yeo. attd. 8th West Yorks	Killed.
1/9/18	T/2/Lt.	CLIDERO.	H.	Yorks Regt. attd. 8th West Yorks.	Killed.
1/9/18	T/Lieut.	McCULLOCH.	A.G.	Yorks. Regt. attd. 8th West Yorks.	Wounded.
1/9/18	T/2/Lt.	GLENNIE	J.	Yorks Regt..attd. 8th West Yorks.	Wounded.
1/9/18	2/Lieut.	WRIGHT.	H.R.	8th West Yorks.	Wounded.
2/9/18	Lt. (A/Capt)	BURROWS.	H.R.	8th West Yorks.	Wounded.
2/9/18	Capt.	COOPER.	S.R.	8th West Yorks	W. at Duty.
2/9/18	T/2/Lt.	CRABTREE, MC	R.M.	8th West Yorks.	W. at Duty.
2/9/18	Lt.(A/Capt)	MORIER.	C.E.	5th W.Riding Regt.	Wounded.
2/9/18	Capt.	VASEY.	F.T.	9th Bn. Durham L.I.	Wounded.
2/9/18	Lt.	PLUMMER. MC	H.C.B.	9th Bn. Durham L.I.	W. at Duty.
2/9/18	Lieut.	JOHNSON.	J.F.	9th Bn. Durham L.I.	Wounded.
2/9/18	Lt.(A/Capt)	RICKABY.	J.D.	9th Bn. Durham L.I.	W. at Duty.
2/9/18	2/Lieut.	BOYD.	F.J.	62nd Bn. M.G.Corps.	W. at Duty.
2/9/18	T/2/Lt.	BILLING.	J.	East Yorks. attd. 5th K.O.Y.L.I.	Killed.
2/9/18	T/2/Lt.	NEILSON.	W.C.	East Yorks. attd. 5th K.O.Y.L.I.	Killed.
2/9/18.	T/2/Lt.	BOTTOMLEY.	F.	K.O.Y.L.I. attd. 5th K.O.Y.L.I.	Killed.
2/9/18.	Lt.(A/Capt)	LYNN.DSO.,MC.	A.C.	5th K.O.Y.L.I.	Wounded.
2/9/18.	T/Lieut.	HOUGHTON.	R.A.	K.O.Y.L.I. attd. 5th K.O.Y.L.I.	wounded.
2/9/18.	T/2/Lt.	BOWDEN.	J.S.	K.O.Y.L.I. attd. 5th K.O.Y.L.I.	Wounded.
2/9/18.	T/2/Lt.	HOWELLS.	C.P.	Yorks. Regt. attd. 5th K.O.Y.L.I.	Wounded.
2/9/18.	T/2/Lt.	MARTIN.	A.E.	K.O.Y.L.I. attd. 2/4th K.O.Y.L.I.	Killed.
2/9/18.	2/Lt.(A/Capt)	TOWNEND.	R.	2/4th K.O.Y.L.I.	Wounded.
2/9/18.	Lieut.	SUTHERLAND.	J.F.	A.S.C. attd. 2/4th K.O.Y.L.I.	Wounded.
2/9/18.	2/Lieut.	FISHER.	J.H.	West Yorks. attd. 2/4th K.O.Y.L.I.	Wounded.
2/9/18.	2/Lieut.	POLLARD.	G.E.W.	2/4th K.O.Y.L.I.	Wounded.
2/9/18.	Capt.	RODGERS.	J.	2/4th York & Lancs.	Killed.
2/9/18.	T/2/Lt.	HALLMARK.	P.H.	York & Lancs. attd. 2/4th York & Lancs.	Killed.
2/9/18.	2/Lieut.	SIMPKIN.	A.L.	2/4th York & Lancs.	Wounded.
2/9/18.	2/Lieut.	MAY.	W.B.	2/4th York & Lancs.	Wounded.
2/9/18.	2/Lieut.	BRYDEN.	G.A.	Lancs. Fus. attd. 2/4th York & Lancs.	Wounded.
2/9/18.	2/Lieut.	JOHNSON.	J.D.	Lancs. Fus. attd. 2/4th York & Lancs.	Wounded
2/9/18.	T/2/Lt.	OWEN.	L.	York & Lancs. attd. 2/4th York & Lancs.	Wounded.
2/9/18.	T/2/Lt.	JOHNSON.	L.W.	K.O.R.L. attd. 2/4th K.O.Y.L.I.	Wounded.
1/9/18.	2/Lieut.	STUART.	F.R.	312th Bde. R.F.A.	Wounded.
1/9/18.	2/Lieut.	GREEN.	W.J.	312th Bde. R.F.A.	Wounded.
7/9/18.	2/Lieut.	STEER.	K.R.	2/4th York & Lancs.	Injured (Acc.)
12/9/18.	A/Capt.	NOON.	A.C.	5th Devon Regt.	Wounded.
12/9/18.	A/Capt.	STOCKS.	J.	2/4th West Riding Regt.	Wounded.
12/9/18.	2/Lieut.	DUNNETT. MC	J.H.	2/4th West Riding Regt.	Wounded.
12/9/18.	2/Lieut.	POTTER.	A.C.	2/4th West Riding Regt.	Wounded.
12/9/18.	Capt.	LUPTON. MC	B.C.	2/4th West Riding Regt.	W. at Duty.
12/9/18.	2/Lieut.	STOTT.	W.	2/4th West Riding Regt.	W. at Duty.
12/9/18.	2/Lieut.	HEWITT.	J.B.C.	312th Bde. R.F.A.	W. at Duty.
12/9/18.	2/Lieut.	BENTHAM.	H.	5th West Riding Regt.	Wounded.
12/9/18.	2/Lieut.	BRYANT.	H.	2/4th Hants. Regt.	Killed.
12/9/18.	2/Lieut.	WEEKS.	H.S.	2/4th Hants. Regt.	Wounded.

12/9/18.	2/Lieut.	GADSBY.	C.A.	6th West Riding R. attd. 2/4th Hants R.	Wounded.
12/9/18.	2/Lieut.	WILSON.	W.J.	2/4th Hants. Regt.	Wounded.
12/9/18.	2/Lieut.	ISAACS.	F.C.	2/4th Hants. Regt.	Wounded.
12/9/18.	2/Lieut.	UFFINGTON. Viscount.	G.O.B.	2/4th Hants. Regt.	Wounded.
12/9/18.	Lieut.	FRENCH.	E.S.	5th K.O.Y.L.I.	Killed.
12/9/18.	2/Lieut.	KILNER.	A.	2/4th K.O.Y.L.I.	Wounded.
12/9/18.	2/Lieut.	FISHER.	T.D.	Lancs. Fus. attd. 2/4th York & Lancs.	Wounded.
12/9/18.	2/Lieut.	CAIRD.	C.F.	2/4th York & Lancs.	Wounded.
12/9/18.	2/Lieut.	FORREST.	W.R.	9th Bn. Durham L.I.	Killed.
12/9/18.	2/Lieut.	ABERDEEN. DCM	S.	9th Bn. Durham L.I.	Wounded.
13/9/18.	2/Lieut.	PORRITT.	J.	5th West Riding Regt.	Wounded.
13/9/18.	2/Lieut.	ROSSINGTON.	A.	6th West Riding Regt. attd. 5th W.Rid.Regt.	Killed.
13/9/18.	Capt.	BULLEY.	C.P.	2/4th Hants. Regt.	Wounded.
13/9/18.	2/Lieut.	BRADBURY.	J.C.L.	2/4th York & Lancs.	Wounded.
13/9/18.	T/2/Lt.	KNOX.	J.P.	2/4th York & Lancs.	Wounded.
11/9/18.	Lieut.	GIRVAN.	A.	62nd Bn. M.G.Corps.	Wounded.
25/9/18.	Lieut.	NICHOLSON.	K.B.	312th Bde. R.F.A.	W. at Duty.
12/9/18.	T/2/Lieut.	CLARKE.	F.J.F.	5th K.O.Y.L.I.	Wounded.
12/9/18.	2/Lieut.	FERNIE.	J.S.	5th K.O.Y.L.I.	Wounded.
12/9/18.	2/Lieut.	PRATT.	E.B.	2/4th Hants.Regt.	Wounded.
12/9/18.	2/Lieut.	MORTON.	E.	5th K.O.Y.L.I.	Wounded.
12/9/18.	2/Lieut.	PITMAN.	A.T.	2/4th K.O.Y.L.I.	Wounded.
12/9/18.	2/Lieut.	WILKINSON.	F.	2/4th K.O.Y.L.I.	Wounded.
13/9/18.	2/Lieut.	BATY.	J.W.	2/4th K.O.Y.L.I.	Wounded.
12/9/18.	2/Lieut.	SAGAR.	F.	2/4th York & Lancs.	Wounded.
12/9/18.	T/2/Lt.	HART.	E.M.	5th Devon Regt.	Wounded.
13/9/18.	T/2/Lt.	GREGORY.	J.J.	2/4th York & Lancs.	Wounded.
13/9/18.	Lieut.	RIDLEY.	T.	9th Bn. Durham L.I.	W. at Duty.
14/9/18.	2/Lieut.	HERDMAN. MM	W.	9th Bn. Durham L.I.	Wounded.
13/9/18.	T/Lieut.	BEDFORD. MC	R.	9th Devon Regt. attd 5th Devon Regt.	Wounded.
13/9/18.	T/Lieut.	BUTCHER.	P.G.	8th Bn. attd. 5th Devon Regt.	Wounded.
14/9/18.	2/Lieut.	HALL.	G.D.	5th Devon Regt.	Wounded.
14/9/18.	T/2/Lt.	STOCK.	A.E.	5th Devon Regt.	Wounded.
14/9/18.	T/2/Lt.	SUTTON	D.C.W.	R.W.Kent Regt. attd. 2/20th London Regt.	Killed.
14/9/18.	T/2/Lt.	ELLEN.	H.J.	2/20th London Regt.	Killed.
14/9/18.	2/Lieut.	HIRST. MM	J.	2/20th London Regt.	Killed.
14/9/18.	2/Lieut.	HOLTON.	G.J.P.	1st C.of Lon. Yeo.attd. 2/20th London Regt.	Wounded.
15/9/18.	T/Chap.tothe forces 4th class C. of E. WRIGHT. M.C.		A.B.	Army Chaplains Dept.	W. at Duty.
27/9/18	Lt.(A/Capt) STEAD.		C.B.	8th West Yorks.	Wounded.
27/9/18.	Lt.(A/Capt) HIRST.		G.M.	8th West Yorks.	Wounded.
27/9/18.	2/Lieut.	SHENTON.	H.E.	8th West Yorks.	Wounded.
27/9/18.	2/Lieut.	TURNER.	F.J.	West Yorks. attd. 8th West Yorks.	Killed.
27/9/18.	2/Lieut.	GRAVES.	H.J.	13th West Yorks attd. 8th West Yorks.	Wounded.
27/9/18.	2/Lieut.	ODDY.	A.E.	West Yorks attd. 8th West Yorks.	Killed.
27/9/18.	2/Lieut.	AXE.	F.	East Yorks. attd. 8th West Yorks.	Missing.
27/9/18.	2/Lieut.	W.J.WHITTALL.		5th West Yorks. attd. 8th West Yorks.	Missing.
27/9/18.	2/Lieut.	TINGLE.	R.L.A.	5th West Yorks. attd. 8th West Yorks.	Missing.
27/9/18.	2/Lieut.	CROFT.	C.E.	West Yorks. attd. 8th West Yorks.	Missing.
27/9/18.	2/Lieut.	PALMER.	A.E.	West Yorks. attd. 8th West Yorks.	Killed.
27/9/18.	Lieut.	EALES.	C.W.	1/5th Devon Regt.	Killed.
27/9/18.	2/Lieut.	EVANS.	J.E.	1/5th Devon Regt.	Killed.
27/9/18.	2/Lieut.	O'NEILL.	J.A.	1/5th Devon Regt.	Wounded.
27/9/18.	2/Lieut.	KNIGHT.	A.E.	1/5th Devon Regt.	Wounded.
27/9/18.	2/Lieut.	BARGETSON.	S.M.	1/5th Devon Regt.	Wounded.
27/9/18.	2/Lieut.	LOWE.	T.N.R.	1/5th Devon Regt.	Wounded.
27/9/18.	2/Lieut.	HOSKINS.	W.A.V.	1/5th Devon Regt.	Wounded.

Date	Rank	Name	Initials	Unit	Status
27/9/18.	2/Lieut.	JACKSON.	F.	2/20th London Regt.	Killed.
27/9/18.	Lieut.	SLAUGHTER.	V.	2/20th London Regt.	Killed.
27/9/18.	2/Lieut.	HERBERT.	S.	2/20th London Regt.	Wounded.
30/9/18.	2/Lieut.	COTTIS.	W.J.	2/20th London Regt.	Wounded.
27/9/18.	2/Lieut.	SPENCE.	G.F.	West Yorks. attd. 5th K.O.Y.L.I.	Wounded.
27/9/18.	2/Lieut.	STOTT.	W.C.H.	5th K.O.Y.L.I.	Killed.
27/9/18.	2/Lt.(A/Capt)	HIRST. MC	C.	2/4th K.O.Y.L.I.	wounded.
27/9/18.	2/Lieut.	ECKERSLEY. MM	J.	2/4th York & Lancs.	Wounded.
27/9/18.	2/Lieut.	SMITH.	H.C.F.	2/4th York & Lancs.	Wounded.
27/9/18.	Lt.(A/Capt)	OXLEY-BOYLE.	R.F.C.	62nd Bn. M.G.Corps.	Wounded.
28/9/18.	2/Lieut.	MATTHEWS.	A.C.	3rd Hants. attd. 2/4th Hants. Regt.	wounded.
28/9/18.	2/Lieut.	POWRIE.	W.	2/4th York & Lancs.	Killed.
28/9/18.	Lieut.(T/Maj.)	LUNDGREN.	C.W.	2/4th York & Lancs.	W. at Duty.
28/9/18.	2/Lieut.	MURRELL-TALBOT	E.R.	5th York & Lancs.attd. 2/4th York & Lancs.	W. at Duty.
28/9/18.	A/Capt.	PENNINGTON MC	B.C.	2/4th York & Lancs.	Wounded.
28/9/18.	2/Lieut.	HILL.	G.M.	2/4th York & Lancs.	Wounded.
29/9/18.	2/Lieut.	YOUNG.	R.A.	2/4th York & Lancs.	Wounded.
28/9/18.	2/Lieut.	CHARLESWORTH.	G.V.	5th West Riding Regt.	Killed.
28/9/18.	2/Lieut.	BARNETT.	G.M.	6th West Rid. R. attd. 5th West Riding Regt.	Killed.
28/9/18.	2/Lieut.	BRIGGS.	S.E.	7th West Rid. R. attd. 5th West Riding Regt.	Wounded.
28/9/18.	2/Lieut.	MORTON. MC	T.E.	West Yorks Regt.attd. 5th West Riding Regt.	Wounded.
28/9/18.	Capt.	LOCKWOOD.	C.H.	7th West Rid. R. attd. 5th West Riding Regt.	Wounded.
28/9/18.	Lieut.	WILSON.	E.	West Yorks. attd. 185th L.T.M.B.	Wounded.
28/9/18.	2/Lieut.	PILBROW.	S.E.	62nd M.G.Bn.	Injured. (Acc)
29/9/18.	Capt.	FREW.	J.W.	2/3rd Fld. Ambce.	Wounded.
29/9/18.	Capt.	HILL.	G.M.	2/4th West Riding Regt.	wounded.
29/9/18.	2/Lieut.	CROOKSON.	A.E.	West Rid. Regt. attd. 2/4th West Riding Regt.	wounded.
29/9/18.	2/Lieut.	DODSWORTH.	R.D.	62nd Bn. M.G.Corps.	wounded.
29/9/18.	2/Lieut.	BARRACLOUGH.	G.W.	2/4th W.Riding Regt.	Killed.
29/9/18	2/Lieut.	WOOD.	A.	5th K.O.Y.L.I.	Killed.
29/9/18.	Lieut.	WILSON.	C.H.	5th K.O.Y.L.I.	D. of Wounds.
30/9/18.	Capt.	SIMPKIN	A.W.	13th Yorks Regt. attd. 8th West Yorks.	Killed.
30/9/18.	2/Lieut.	PERCIVAL.	J.L.	8th West Yorks.	Killed.
30/9/18.	2/Lieut.	FERGUSON.	F.	West Yorks. attd. 8th West Yorks.	Wounded.
30/9/18.	2/Lieut.	HALL.	F.	East Yorks. attd. 8th West Yorks.	wounded.
30/9/18.	2/Lieut.	GRAM.	J.E.	4th Yorks. attd. 2/4th West Rid. Regt.	Killed.
30/9/18.	2/Lieut.	BILTON.	B.W.	62nd Bn. M.G.Corps.	wounded.
30/9/18.	Lt. Col.	ENGLAND.	N.A.	8th West Yorks.	W. at Duty.
30/9/18.	Lieut.	WILLIS.	F.	9th Devons. attd. 1/5th Devon Regt.	Killed.
30/9/18.	A/Capt.	EDGAR. MC	J.H.	1/5th Devon Regt.	Wounded.
30/9/18.	2/Lieut.	STANLEY.	J.H.	1/5th Devon Regt.	Wounded.
30/9/18.	2/Lieut.	OSBORNE.	T.L.	1/5th Devon Regt.	Wounded.
30/9/18.	Capt.	COTTAM. M.C.	H.C.B.	2/4th Hants.Regt.	Killed.
30/9/18.	2/Lieut.	TURNER.	T.	2/4th Hants. Regt.	Wounded.
30/9/18.	2/Lieut.	HOWELLS.	C.P.	Yorks Regt. attd. 5th K.O.Y.L.I.	Killed.
30/9/18.	A/Capt.	SPENCER.	G.E.	2/4th K.O.Y.L.I.	Wounded.
30/9/18.	Major.	FROGGATT. MC	W.	461st Fld. Coy.	W. at Duty.

OTHER RANKS.

Killed   551
Wounded   2760
Missing   623

APPENDIX K.

REWARDS GRANTED DURING SEPTEMBER 1918.

    2nd Bar to M.M.   1

    Bar to M.M.   10

    M.M.   184.

62nd (West Riding) Division.

REINFORCEMENTS RECEIVED DURING SEPTEMBER 1918.

App. L.

	Offrs.	O.R.
8th West Yorkshire Regiment.	7	195
1/5th Devonshire Regiment.	12	108
2/20th London Regiment	-	12
5th West Riding Regiment	7	342
2/4th West Riding Regiment	1	427
2/4th Hampshire Regiment	16	326
5th K.O.Y.L.I.	5	386
2/4th K.O.Y.L.I.	9	378
2/4th York & Lancaster Regiment	14	424
Royal Artillery	-	84
Royal Engineers	2	42
Divisional Train	1	7
Royal Army Medical Corps	-	4
Machine Gun Battalion	5	137
9th Durham Light Infantry (Pioneers)	4	96
	83	2968

DIVISIONAL ROUTINE ORDERS.
by Major General Sir R.D.Whigham, K.C.B, D.S.O.
Commanding 62nd (West Riding) Division.

21st September 1918.

ADMINISTRATIVE STAFF.

No.1532. HONOURS & AWARDS.

The Divisional Commander has the honour to announce that the Commander of the VI Corps, under authority delegated to him, has awarded decorations as under :-
(Authority VI Corps H.R.155.)

BAR TO MILITARY MEDAL.

31067	Sgt.	S.Chapman, M.M.	Army Brigade R.F.A.
94005	Gnr.	C.English, M.M.	do
26073	"	E.Wendrop, M.M.	R.F.A. attd. T.M.Bty.
240115	Sgt.	E.J.Crispin, M.M.	Devon Regiment.
240244	Pte.	C.W.White, M.M.	do
208050	Sgt.	E.Spivey, M.M.	West Riding Regt.
241658	Pte.(L/Cpl)	E.W.Shearsmith M.M.	West Riding Regiment.
9154	Pte.	T.Blyth M.M.	do
266273	Pte.	B.Cockerill, M.M.	do
242641	Pte.(L/Cpl)	J.Bell M.M.	K.O.Y.L.I.

MILITARY MEDAL.

75560	Gnr.	J.Beattie	Army Brigade R.F.A.
47575	Sgt.	E.J.Nix	do
21797	Gnr.(L/Bdr)	J.B.Cowie	do
50320	BSM.	K.Bartlett	do
71668	Sgt.	F.Bowers	do
66325	Gnr.	J.Whiteside	do
58845	Gnr.	A.Siggers	do
70202	Bdr.	A.Moore.	do
67550	Pte. (A/Cpl)	W.H.Matthews.	Devon Regiment.
240173	Pte. (A/L/Cpl)	E.J.Willis	do
240586	Sgt.	W.Q.Lethbridge	do
240770	Pte.	F.Bearne	do
263057	Pte.	R.Pallett	KOYLI attd. do
202150	Cpl.	J.Essery	do do
241145	Pte.	W.Grate	Devon Regiment.
240713	Pte.	R.C.Southern	do
210434	Pte.	A.Blight	do
33772	Pte.(A/L/Cpl)	J.J.Lang	do
43397	Rfn.	W.Bird	West Yorks Regiment.
305958	Sgt.	J.Hipps	do
305111	Rfn.	D.C.Pratt	do
42889	Rfn.	A.Stockdale	do
306774	Rfn.	L.Greenwood	do
8055	Rfn.	F.Cooper	do
305208	Rfn. (L/Cpl)	J.Markinson	do
236016	Rfn. (L/Cpl)	H.R.Shepherd	do
201544	Rfn.	G.Lumbley	do
211444	Pte.	J.H.Willoughby	W.Yorks attd T.M.Bty.
650662	Sgt.	F.Powell	London Regiment.
650905	CSM.	J.B.Selkeld	do
650629	Sgt.	F.W.Cook	do
633050	Pte.	A.Barron	do
650149	Pte.	A.Smith	do
631687	Pte. (A/L/Cpl)	G.Giddings.	do
650925	Pte. (A/Cpl)	C.Robinson	do
36604	Pte.	G.Earl	do
653040	Pte.	A.Westall	do
650313	Pte. (L/Cpl)	G.F.Crawley	do
650643	pte.	D.Woolfe.	do

235653	Pte.	T.Ward	West Riding Regiment.
34488	Pte.	C.Koy	do
240883	Pte.	R.Jennings	do
306037	Pte.	H.Shaw	do
14367	Cpl.	G.Roberts	do
241222	Pte. (L/Cpl)	C.Rhodes	do
235629	Pte. (L/Cpl)	I.Levy.	do
203121	Pte.	S.Mackroll.	do
268800	Pte.	W.Barker	do
240139	CSM.	W.Hulse	do
34531	Pte.	H.Walker	do
242651	Pte.	E.Walton	do
34759	Pte.	W.McClintock	do
241691	Pte.	L.H.Cook	do
306313	Pte.	H.W.Stead	do
322103	Pte.	J.A.Dodd	do
263171	Pte. (A/L/Cpl)	G.Mitchell	do
205531	Pte.	R.Hegarty	do
263035	Sgt.	F.Clayton	do
303764	Sgt.	E.Redfearn	do
22372	Pte.	A.Bailey	do
235711	Pte.	H.Robinson	do attd. T.M.B.
200877	Sgt.	E.H.Hoyle	West Riding Regiment.
201614	Pte.	V.Barber	do
200315	Cpl.	H.Hixon	Hampshire Regiment.
42296	Pte. (L/Cpl)	V.Ford	do
202475	Pte.	G.H.Cawte	do
201152	Sgt. (A/CQMS)	A.E.Barney	do
356839	Pte.	F.Morson	do
201339	Pte.	S.Brandon	do
200757	Pte.	J.Ellis	do
202461	Pte.	F.W.Clarke	do
201652	Pte.	C.J.Banning	do
200343	CSM.	J.H.Tilson	do
201825	Pte.	P.West	do
202815	Pte.	F.Tappendon	do
202428	Pte.	A.G.Street.	do
8470	Pte.	W.Purdue	do
303850	Sgt.	G.Redman	do
33560	Pte.	F.Tonkin	do
25199	"	A.E.Kibby	do
241656	Sgt.	B.Kirkham	K.O.Y.L.I.
240668	Pte.	H.Stocks	do
241189	Pte.	G.Buck	do
241146	Sgt.	P.Fox	do
55081	Pte.	J.Errington	do
35875	Pte.	W.Dungworth	do
63215	Pte.	J.W.Shaw	do
242287	Pte. (L/Cpl)	A.Reynolds	do
45520	Pte.	J.Turner	do
36812	CQMS	E.S.Woods	do
200111	Pte.	E.Johnson	do
40620	Pte. (L/Cpl)	J.W.James	do
39442	Cpl.	H.Carr	do
11787	Sgt.	J.W.Parker	do
37455	Pte.	G.W.Jackson	do
263188	Pte.	W.Hum	do
63455	Pte.	W.Potts	do
263113	Pte. (L/Cpl)	R.Mitchell	do
201154	Cpl.	H.Hampson	do
41329	Pte. (L/Cpl)	J.C.Kay	do
52885	Pte.	J.Prosser	do
201197	Pte.	T.Heaps.	do
201817	Pte.	H.Ward	do
202215	Pte.	F.Wadsworth	do
202313	Pte.	A.Williamson	do
235832	Pte.	W.Haigh	do

2984 Sgt. G.Blakemore	York & Lancs Regiment.
200949 Sgt. P.S.Askham	do
200824 Sgt. G.Wyman	do
20491 Pte. F.Adamson	do
263175 Pte. B.T.Flatt	do
200476 Pte. S.Bradshaw	dp
57651 Pte. F.White	do
263042 Pte. W.H.Ledger	K.O.Y.L.I. attd. T.M.B.
64401 Cpl. T.Condon	Machine Gun Battalion.
26630 Cpl. A.Hindle	do
67761 Pte. (L/Cpl) B.Gibson	do
137277 Pte. G.H.R.Whybrow	do
63949 Pte. (L/Cpl) W.T.Thorne	do
60242 Pte. J.Johnson	do
126041 Pte. F.White	do
87182 Pte. (L/Cpl) W.J.Wilson	do
32796 Pte. J.C.Russell	do
105266 Pte. W.France	do
11266 Pte. J.Wilson	do
87841 Pte. H.Muhleck	do
7084 Pte. (L/Cpl) H.Haigh	do
119135 Pte. (L/Cpl) C.Kelly.	do
403330 Pte. C.V.Wright R.A.M.C.	West Riding Field Ambulance.
403642 Pte. R.Cockerham do	do
32370 Pte. T.B.Norris	Devon Regiment.
8798 Sgt. G.Bettridge	Hampshire Regiment.

No.1533. <u>SALVAGE DUMPS.</u>

<u>Corps Salvage Ammunition Dump</u> at A.10.d.9.5, has been transferred to VICTORY SALVAGE AMMUNITION DUMP, A.28.d.9.4. (Sheet 57c).

<u>Corps Main Dump BOYELLES</u> has now been closed and for the time being MORY dump (B.23.a.3.5.) will be used as the main dump.

HAROLD. F. LEA   Lieut Colonel,
A. A. & Q. M. G.

<u>N O T I C E S.</u>

The Wholesale Canteen is now established at BEHAGNIES.

Reference to Notice in D.R.O. of September 10th, the day by which this weeks allotment must be cleared will be noon Tuesday September 24th 1918.

LOST. Between BEHAGNIES and TRIANGLE COPSE, a small red flag bearing a 'Pelican'. Information to Camp Commandant, 62nd Div H.Q.

DIVISIONAL ROUTINE ORDERS.
by Major General Sir R.D. Whigham, K.C.B., D.S.O.
Commanding 62nd (West Riding) Division.

23rd September 1918.

ADMINISTRATIVE STAFF.

No. 1534. HONOURS AND AWARDS

The Divisional Commander has the honour to announce that (i) the Commander of the V Corps, under authority delegated to him, has awarded decorations as under :-
(Authority R.A. 38th Div. Q.5850/20.)

MILITARY MEDAL.

50531	Sergeant	EGGETT. G.H.	D/310th Bde. R.F.A.
960755	Sergeant	DARLING. G.	B/310th Bde. R.F.A.
786188	Sergeant	WAKEFIELD. E.	D/312th Bde. R.F.A.
178962	Gunner.	GETHING. H.	D/312th Bde. R.F.A.
686749	Bombdr.	BLAKELEY. J.	D/310th Bde. R.F.A.
686809	Corpl.	MITCHELL. J.	D/310th Bde. R.F.A.
940004	B.S.M.	BROWN. J.D.	D/312th Bde. R.F.A.

(ii) The Commander of the VI Corps under authority delegated to him has awarded decorations as under :-
(Authority VI Corps H.R.155 of 21/9/18)

BAR TO MILITARY MEDAL.

16176   Cpl. CLARKE. W. (MM)   93rd Army Bde. R.F.A.

MILITARY MEDAL.

32104   Sgt. SIDLEY. W.   93rd Army Bde. R.F.A.

No. 1535. NOMINAL ROLL OF OFFICERS AND OTHER RANKS OF JEWISH FAITH.

H.Q's formations and separate units will forward to this office not later than 27th instant, nominal rolls of officers and other ranks of the Jewish Faith, serving under their command.

HAROLD.F.LEA, Lieut-Colonel.
A.A.&.Q.M.G.

NOTICES.

LOST on night 20/21st between 5 p.m. and 6 p.m. from vicinity of Horse Lines H.2.c.7.5. Chestnut Gelding, Rider, 15.2. star race. brand 186 (faint) off fore, old rope gall near hind. Age 11 years. Information to Headquarters, 186th Infantry Brigade.

DIVISIONAL ROUTINE ORDERS.
by Major General Sir. R.D.Whigham, K.C.B., D.S.O.
Commanding 62nd (West Riding) Division.

28th September 1918.

ADMINISTRATIVE STAFF.

No. 1539. HONOURS AND AWARDS.

The Divisional Commander has the honour to announce that the Commander of the VI Corps has, under authority delegated to him, awarded decorations as under :-

SECOND BAR to MILITARY MEDAL.

325479	Pte.(A/L/Cpl.) G.Landreth, M.M.		Durham L.I.

BAR to MILITARY MEDAL.

325217	Pte.	J.Waitt,	M.M.	Durham L.I.
240893	CSM.	J.C.Davis,	M.M.	York & Lancs.

MILITARY MEDAL.

268251	Spr.	J.G.Arch.	Div. Signal Coy.
482271	"	(A/L/Cpl) A.E.Lake	do
405302	Pte.	H.Shaw	W.Riding Fld. Amb.
65038	"	F.J.Tipping	do
M/22855	"	J.Burdon A.S.C.,M.T. attd.	do
401489	"	A.Williamson	do
401173	Cpl.	(A/Sgt) G.J.Micklethwaite	do
M2/102446	Pte.	W.Coleshill A.S.C.,M.T. attd.	do
201310	"	(A/L/Cpl) J.G.Moore	Durham L.I.
325617	"	(A/L/Cpl) T.Waters	do
76439	"	(A/L/Cpl) A.E.Jones	do
325386	"	(A/L/Cpl) R.Farrow	do
325833	"	(A/L/Cpl) T.W.Robson	do
325832	"	(A/L/Cpl) J.Hudson	do
325851	Cpl.	A.Jones	do
325932	Pte.	A.Fortune	do
325082	Sgt.	F.Noble	do
326790	Cpl.	H.S.Clay	do
325915	Pte.	J.H.Williamson	do
77892	"	G.Skilbeck	do
350981	"	C.Wood	do
325642	"	H.Tebb	do
31720	"	F.Wright	do
86196	Sgt.	C.H.Johnson, D.C.M.	Army Brigade,R.F.A.
43641	Gnr.	C.H.Hunter	do
640558	"	A.S.Malcolm	do
479989	Spr.	H.Wilson	Div.Sig.Coy. attd. Divl.Arty.
306197	CSM.	W.Wheeler	West Yorks. Regt.
305213	Sgt.	H.Swarbrick	do
42393	Cpl.	C.Pamment	do
15/1744	"	W.G.West	do
201025	"	R.Earl	do
27605	Rfn.	A.Clunie	do
58868	"	J.H.Hakey	do
205506	"	R.E.Harrison	do
306818	Sgt.	J.Stanhope	do
306413	"	W.Lockridge	do
325143	Rfn.	F.Collier	do

P.T.O.

-2-

241361	Pte.	P.Toplis	K.O.Y.L.I.
25080	"	E.Norfolk	do
240194	Cpl.	L.Calvert	do
63218	Pte.	E.Smith	do
34064	"	W.H.Rendle	do
18805	Sgt.	H.Drage	do
42828	Pte.	J.Phillips	K.O.Y.L.I.
57603	Cpl.	S.Thompson	York & Lancs.
263185	Pte.	T.W.Kirton	do
255	"	H.Dickinson	do
201550	Sgt.	A.Hodgson	do
39445	Pte. (A/L/Cpl)	W.Winterbottom	do
202774	"	J.Jubb	do
58081	"	G.Dickins	do
57365	"	E.J.Todd	do

(Authority VI Corps H.R.155 of 23/9/18.)

also that the Military Medal has been awarded the undermentioned :-

No. 90085   Gunner W.HEAD   Bde. R.F.A.

HAROLD.F.LEA. Lieut-Colonel.
A.A.&.Q.M.G.

Appendix A

Location Reports

for

month

of

September 1918.

SECRET. LOCATION FORECAST.

62ND (WEST RIDING) DIVISION.

No.	Unit.	Position at 8 a.m. 2nd Septr.
5	8th W.Yorks Regt.	I.7.central
12	186th T.M.Bty.	A.30.c.1.8.
13	187th.Inf:Bde.H.Q.	B.27.central
	'C' Coy.Div.M.G.Bn.	B.27.central
28	Div.Train H.Q.	A.20.a.3.5.
	Adv.Vety.Aid Post	GOMIECOURT
34.	1st Gun Carrying Co.Tanks	A.2.a.8.4.
35	12 Tank Battn 'D' Coy.	B.8.c.5.5.
	REMAINDER : UNCHANGED.	

J.C. Airey Lt
for Lieut.Colonel,
General Staff, 62nd.(West Riding) Division.

1.9.18.

SECRET. **LOCATION FORECAST.**

62ND (WEST RIDING) DIVISION.

No.	Unit.	Position at 12 noon 4th Sept.
1.	Divl. Hd. Qrs.	A.24.c. (Triangle Copse)
	Rear H.Q.	A.16.c.4.3.
2.	Div. Arty. H.Q.	B.13.c.3.2.
	Right Group H.Q.	H.3.central
	Left do.	B.27.c.9.6.
3.	185th. Inf: Bde. H.Q.	SAPIGNIES H.8.b.2.2.
4.	1/5th Devon Rgt.	B.28.a.6.8.
5.	8th W. Yorks Rgt.	I.7.central
6.	2/20th London Rgt.	B.28.a.5.8.
7.	185th T.M. Bty.	B.19.a.4.7.
8.	186th. Inf: Bde. H.Q.	H.2.c.7.4.
9.	5th D. of W. Rgt.	A.22.b.3.5.
10.	2/4th. do.	A.28.c.9.4.
11.	2/4th Hants Rgt.	A.22.b.3.5.
12.	186th. T.M. Bty.	A.16.b.8.4.
13.	187th. Inf: Bde. H.Q.	BEH WOOD B.25.central.
14.	5th K.O.Y.L.I.	B.25.c.7.9. (BIHU WOOD)
15.	2/4th. do.	G.6.b.9.7.
16.	2/4th. Y. & L. Rgt.	B.19.b.4.4.
17.	187th. T.M. Bty.	A.24.c.
18.	9th Bn. D.L.I. Pioneers.	A.29.a.central.
19	62nd. Bn. M.G.C. H.Q.)	
	A Coy	
	B Coy	A.15.a.3.7.
	C Coy	
	D Coy)	
20.	C.R.E.	A.23.d.5.4.
21.	457th Fd. Coy. R.E.	A.29.d.6.7.
22.	460th. do.	H.1.d.8.5.
23.	461st. do.	A.29.b.5.5.
24.	A.D.M.S.	A.16.c.4.3.
25.	1/1st W.R. Fd. Amb.	BEHAGNIES H.1.b.8.2.
26.	2/2nd. do.	GOMIECOURT CHATEAU F.11.a.2.9.
27.	2/3rd. do.	COURCELLES A.14.b.7.2.
28.	Div. Train H.Q.	A.20.a.3.5.
29.	525th Coy. A.S.C.	do
30.	526th. do.	F.4.a.9.1.
31.	527th. do.	F.3.d.6.6.
32.	528th. do.	F.4.a.9.1.
33.	Div. Reception Camp.	BIENVILLERS.

F. Robbins Lieut
for Lieut. Colonel,
4.9./.1918. General Staff, 62nd. (West Riding) Division.

S E C R E T.   LOCATION FORECAST.
62ND. (WEST RIDING) DIVISION.

War Diary.

No.	Unit.	Position at 8 am 5th Septr.
2.	Div.Arty. H.Q.	A.24.c. (TRIANGLE COPSE)
4.	1/5th Devon Regt.	H.2.a.1.3.
5.	8th W.Yorks Regt.	G.12.d.2.6.
6.	2/20th London Regt.	H.1.b.8.9.
7.	185th.T.M.Bty.	H.6.b.2.2.
30.	526th Coy.A.S.C.)	
31.	527th. do.)	ERVILLERS - HAMELINCOURT Road.
32.	528th. do.)	

REMAINDER-UNCHANGED.

4.9.18.

Lieut.Colonel,
General Staff, 62nd.(West Riding) Division.

SECRET. LOCATION FORECAST.

62ND (WEST RIDING) DIVISION.

No.	Unit.	Position at 12 noon 8th Sept.
18	9th Bn.D.L.I. Pioneers.	I.2.c.3.7.
21	457th Fd.Coy.R.E.	C.27.b.4.7.
22	460th do	I.9.d.6.8.

REMAINDER - UNCHANGED.

(sd) J.C.Airey, Lieut.

for Lieut.Colonel,
General Staff, 62nd.(West Riding) Division.

7.9.18.

SECRET. **LOCATION FORECAST.**
62ND (WEST RIDING) DIVISION.

No:	Unit.	Position at 12 noon, 11th September.
1.	Divnl. Hd.Qrs.	I.17.a.5.9.
	Battle Hd.Qrs.	J.34.c.7.0.
	Rear Hd.Qrs.	COURCELLES (A.16.c.4.3.)
2.	Div.Arty. H.Qrs.	I.17.a.5.9.
	Right Group H.Q.	R.E. Dump, VAULX.
	Left do.	I.21.central.
	No.3 Group	VELU.
3.	185th.Inf:Bde.H.Qrs.	FREMICOURT I.25.b.3.8.
4.	1/5th Devon Rgt.)	
5.	8th W.Yorks Rgt.)	
6.	2/20th London Rgt)	Huts in I.26. and I.27.
7.	185 T.M.Bty.)	
8.	186th Inf:Bde.H.Qrs.	J.36.d.9.5.
9.	5th D.of Ws.Rgt.)	
10.	2/4th. do.)	S.W. corner
11.	2/4th Hants Rgt.)	HAVRINCOURT WOOD.
12.	186 T.M.Bty.)	
13.	9th D.L.I.Pioneers)	
14.	187th.Inf:Bde.H.Qrs.)	
15.	5th K.O.Y.L.I.)	
16.	2/4th. do.)	VELU WOOD - J.31.
17.	2/4th Y.& L.Rgt.)	
18.	187 T.M.Bty.)	
19.	62 Bn.M.G.C. H.Qrs.	I.17.a.5.9.
20.	C.R.E.	I.4.central.
21.	457 Fd.Coy.R.E.	C.27.b.4.7.
22.	460 do	I.9.d.6.8.
23.	461 do	I.3.a.2.6.
24.	A.D.M.S.	COURCELLES (A.16.c.4.3.)
25.	2/1st W.R.Fd.Amb.	BEHAGNIES (H.1.b.8.2.)
26.	2/2nd. do.	O.4.d.9.9.
27.	2/3rd. do.	VELU.
28.	Div.Train H.Qrs.	A.20.a.3.5.
29.	525 Coy.A.S.C.	H.24.d.central.
30.	526th. do.)	
31.	527th. do.)	HAPLINCOURT.
32.	528th. do.)	
33.	Div.Reception Camp.	BIENVILLERS.
34.	Mob.Vet.Section.	FREMICOURT.
35.	S.A.A.Section.	I.34.c.central.
36.	P.O.W. Cage.	VELU, I.30.d.9.6.
37.	Stragglers' Posts.	J.20.c.9.3. and J.13.a.8.8.
38.	M.D.S.	O.4.d.9.9.
39.	37th Div.H.Qrs.	I.36.d.9.1.
40.	IIIth Inf:Bde.H.Q.(37 Div)	P.11.b.1.1.
41.	2nd Div.H.Qrs.	C.26.a.6.7.
42.	5th Inf:Bde.H.Qrs.(2 Div)	J.20.d.0.4.

10th Septr. 1918.

J.C. Airey Lt.
for Lieut.Colonel,
General Staff, 62nd.(West Riding) Division.

SECRET.

LOCATION FORECAST.
62ND. (WEST RIDING) DIVISION.

No.	Unit.	Position at 12 noon 18th Sept.
1.	Divnl.Hd.Qrs.	TRIANGLE COPSE (A.24.c.6.0.)
	Rear Hd.Qrs.	COURCELLES (A.16.c.4.3.)
2.	Divnl.Arty.H.Q.	TRIANGLE COPSE (A.24.c.6.0.)
3.	185th Inf.Bde.H.Q.	B.27.central.
4.	1/5th Devon Rgt.	H.11.d.6.9.
5.	8th W.Yorks Rgt.	B.28.d.6.1.
6.	2/20th London Rgt.	H.3.a.
7.	185th T.M.Bty.	H.4.a.1.2.
8.	186th Inf.Bde.H.Q.	H.2.c.7.5.
9.	5th D.of Ws.Rgt.	A.29.c.5.5.
10.	2/4th do	A.29.a.6.6.
11.	2/4th Hants Rgt.	A.28.c.9.1.
12.	186th T.M.Bty.	A.28.b.9.5.
13.	9th D.L.I.(Pioneers)	I.2.c.3.7.
14.	187th Inf.Bde.H.Q.	SAPIGNIES.
15.	5th K.O.Y.L.I.)	SAPIGNIES.
16.	2/4th do)	BEHAGNIES.
17.	2/4th Y & L Rgt)	Area.
18.	187th T.M.Bty)	
19.	62nd Bn. M.G.C.H.Q.	H.2.a.5.5.
20.	C.R.E.	I.4.central.
21.	457th Field Co.R.E.	I.36.b.8.6.
22.	460th do	I.36.a.central.
23.	461st do	I.36.b.
24.	A.D.M.S.	TRIANGLE COPSE (A.24.c.6.0.)
25.	2/1st W.R.Fld.Amb.	BEHAGNIES (H.1.b.8.2.)
26.	2/2nd do	A.14.b.6.4.
27.	2/3rd do	H.2.a.5.5.
28.	Div.Train H.Q.	A.20.a.3.5.
29.	525th Coy.A.S.C.	H.24.d.central.
30.	526th do)	
31.	527th do)	ERVILLERS - Hamelincourt Road.
32.	528th do)	
33.	Div.Reception Camp.	BIENVILLERS.
34.	A.D.V.S.	TRIANGLE COPSE (A.24.c.6.0.)
35.	12th Squadron R.A.F.	B.30.a.

J.C. Airey Lt.
for Lieut-Colonel,
Gomora; Staff 62nd (West Riding) Division.

17.9.1918.

S E C R E T.

LOCATION LIST.
62nd (WEST RIDING) DIVISION.

N° 1

No.	Unit.	Position 12 noon 24th Sept.	Moving 25 Sept.
1.	Divnl.Hd.Qrs.	TRIANGLE COPSE (A.24.c.6.0.)	
2.	Divnl.Arty.H.Q.	Triangle copse (A.24.c.6.0.)	
3.	185 Inf:Bde.H.Q.	B.27.central	BEUGNY Area.
4.	1/5 Devon Rgt.	H.11.d.6.9.	do.
5.	8th W.Yorks Rgt.	C.25.a.3.1.	do.
6.	2/20 London Rgt.	H.3.a.	do.
7.	185th T.M.Bty.	H.4.a.1.2.	do.
8.	186 Inf:Bde.H.Q.	H.2.c.7.5.	VAULX Area.
9.	5th D.of Ws.Rgt.	A.29.c.5.5.	do.
10.	2/4th do.	A.29.a.6.6.	do.
11.	2/4th Hants Rgt.	A.28.c.9.1.	do.
12.	186th T.M.Bty.	A.28.b.9.5.	do.
13.	9th D.L.I. (Pioneers)	I.2.c.3.7.	
14.	187 Inf:Bde H.Q.	SAPIGNIES.	FREMICOURT Area
15.	5th K.O.Y.L.I.)	SAPIGNIES.	do.
16.	2/4th do.)	Behagnies	do.
17.	2/4th Y & L Rgt)	Area.	do.
18.	187th T.M.Bty.)		do.
19.	62nd Bn. M.G.C.H.Q.	H.2.a.5.5.	Old Huts L.7.
20.	C.R.E.	A.29.b.8.2.	
21.	457th Field Co.R.E.	I.28.d.8.2.	
22.	460th do.	I.36.a.central.	
23.	461st do.	I.35.b.9.9.	
24.	A.D.M.S.	TRIANGLE COPSE (A.24.c.6.0.)	
25.	2/1st W.R.Fld.Amb.	BEHAGNIES (H1.b.8.2.)	
26.	2/2nd do.	A.14.b.8.4.	
27.	2/3rd do.	H.2.a.5.5.	
28.	Div.Train H.Q.	A.20.a.3.5.	
29.	525th Coy.A.S.C.	H.24.d.central.	
30.	526th do.)		
31.	527th do.)	ERVILLERS - HAMELINCOURT Rd.	
32.	528th do.)		
33.	Div.Reception Camp.	BIENVILLERS.	
34.	A.D.V.S.	TRIANGLE COPSE (A.24.c.6.0.)	
35.	12th Squadron R.A.F.	B.30.a.	

24.9.18.

J.C. Airey Lt
for Lieut-Colonel,
General Staff 62nd (West Riding) Division.

S E C R E T.   LOCATION LIST   No. 2.

62ND (W.R.) DIVISION.

No:	Unit.	Position 12 noon 26th. Sept.
3.	185 Inf: Bde. H.Q.	I.29.b.1.5
4.	1/5th Devon Rgt.	I.27.b.9.9.
5.	8th W. Yorks Rgt.	I.26.b. and 27.a.
6.	2/20 London Rgt.	I.29.b.1.9.
7.	185th T.M. Bty.	I.29.b.1.9.
9.	5th D. of Ws. Rgt.	H.3.a.
10.	2/4th do.	C.25.a.3.1.
11.	2/4th Hants. Rgt.	H.11.d.6.9.
12.	186th T.M. Bty.	H.4.a.1.2.
14.	187 Inf: Bde. H.Q.	H.30.a. central.
15.	5th K.O.Y.L.I.)	
16.	2/4th do.)	FREMICOURT
17.	2/4th Y & L Rgt.)	AREA.
18.	187th T.M. Bty.)	
19.	62nd Bn. M.G.C. H.Q.	H.2.d.5.5.
26.	2/2nd W.R. Fld. Amb.	BEAUMETZ AREA.
27.	2/3rd do.	BEUGNY.

REMAINDER UNCHANGED.

J. F. Taylor, 2nd. Lt.
for
Lieut-Colonel,
25 : 9 : 18.   General Staff, 62nd (West Riding) Division.

CONFIDENTIAL.

WAR DIARY

OF

HEADQUARTERS, 62ND (WEST RIDING) DIVISION "A".

1st OCTOBER 1918 TO 31st OCTOBER 1918.

VOLUME XXII.

WAR DIARY or INTELLIGENCE SUMMARY

Army Form C. 2118.

OCTOBER 1918.

Place	Date	Hour	Summary of Events and Information	Remarks and references to Appendices
HERMIES and HAVRINCOURT	1st		Relief of 62nd by 3rd Division proceeded with. Divisional HQ & 'G' at HERMIES. 'A&Q' and AA & QMG remained at HAVRINCOURT. 195 Nyssa to BOGGARTS HOLE (LISON LODGE LANE) 196 Nyssa to Angola on HERMIES Havrincourt Road. 157 Hyflda Triangle Wood near FLESQUIERES. — 9/ DLI Havrincourt — M.G.G.H FLESQUIERES —	GW
do	2nd		Weather Fine —	GW
do	3rd		Weather Fine. 'A' Office moved from Triangle Copse nr GOUZEAUCOURT to HERMIES. Baths at HAVRINCOURT convent — Water Difficulty	GW

WAR DIARY
INTELLIGENCE SUMMARY

October 1918 p. 2

Army Form C. 2118.

Place	Date	Hour	Summary of Events and Information	Remarks and references to Appendices
HERMIES	4th		Weather fine & cold — Whole of Divisional H.Q's concentrated at HERMIES — Divisional Reception Camp concentrated at BERTINCOURT to-day — having stayed previous night at GOMIECOURT —	G.W.
do	5th		Weather dull — G.O.C. presented Medal Ribbons & Parcel to 184th Inf. Bde — Time changed to winter time at midnight 5/6th	
do	6th		Weather dull. G.O.C. presented Medal Ribbons on Parade to 184 Rif Bde — and inspected N.C.O's Class at Reception Camp. Warning Order that Division would probably move forward on 8th Inst.	G.W.
do	7th		Weather dull. Rain in evening — Preparations made to take over sector HQs from 3rd Division at FLESQUIERES on 8th Inst.	G.W.
do	8th		Weather dull — VI Corps attacked 0530 hours — 3 Brigades moved forward to area between HAVRINCOURT and MARCOING in evening, covering 1820 — Coming into Support of Guards Division — Remainder of Division did not move	G.W.

Army Form C. 2118.

WAR DIARY
or
INTELLIGENCE SUMMARY.
(Erase heading not required.)

October 1918. p. 3.

Place	Date	Hour	Summary of Events and Information	Remarks and references to Appendices
FLESQUIÈRES	9th		Weather Fine. Divisional HQ's moved to FLESQUIÈRES 1000 hours – During afternoon Divisional Comdr. issued orders to Area Comdrs. – 185 Bde of DLI 2 Field Coys to MASNIÈRES 186 Bde 62 8th M.Gun Coys to RUMILLY 187 Bde 1 Field Coy to Area East of Canal d'Escaut Lot W/T other 2 Brigades. Some Congestion on Roads owing to IV Corps using same Roads – VI Corps Annual Relieves issued	M Difficulties
MASNIÈRES	10th		Weather Fine. Moves as under. Divl. HQs to MASNIÈRES 185 Bde no change 186 Bde to SERANVILLERS taking over from 3rd Guards Bde. 187 Bde to RUMILLY taking over from 126 Inf Bde Roads remarkably good and Billets quite habitable in all Villages – Water supply presented no difficulties	GN

Army Form C. 2118.

WAR DIARY
or
INTELLIGENCE SUMMARY.
(Erase heading not required.)

October 1916 F. 4

Place	Date	Hour	Summary of Events and Information	Remarks and references to Appendices
P'tit Chantenal ESTOURNEL	11th		Weather Dull. Some Rain. — Roads very slippery. — Good Country. Tanks unpassable. Div. HQrs to P'tit Chantenal, ESTOURNEL. Moves — 185 Inf Bde to CATTENIERES, also M.G.Bn & 1 Coy. 186 Inf Bde, 16y N.L.R" to LANNIERES. 187 Inf Bde to ESTOURNEL, ISONEL, ROSTRENNOUAT. 9th DLI from Coy to WAMBAIX	
do	12th		Very good Billets. Scarcely at all damaged — 271 ORs Reinforcements arrived for 1/30 Londons Rgt.	A
do	13th		Weather continues dull and damp. No moves. Weather as before. Moves as follows — 185 Inf Bde and 168" Lew/Coy to BEVIEERS. 186 Inf Bde and 1 Coy M.G.Bn to BOUSSIERES, with Bde HQs and 1 Bn remaining at CATTENIERES. 189 Inf Bde, 9th M" DLI DAC, Train HQs to CATTENIERES	A A A
do	14th		Weather Fine and Bright — Roads drying up rapidly — No moves —	A
do	15th		Weather Dull. Some Drizzle during Morning — Special Order published re men of Division when Captured, had revealed Information to the Enemy. Supply Railhead opened CAMBON-ANNIEN. — Train distribution till 8 pm.	A Appendix B

Army Form C. 2118.

WAR DIARY
or
INTELLIGENCE SUMMARY.
(Erase heading not required.)

October 1915 P. 5.

Place	Date	Hour	Summary of Events and Information	Remarks and references to Appendices
ESTOURMEL	16		Weather dull. Conference at HQ 5185 Inf/Bde in morning. Approx 250 OR Reinfts arrived by March Route (2 days) from STANNERS and joined 185 and 186 Inf/Bdes.	BM
do	17th		Weather Dull. Division took over Left Sector Corps Front. Relieving portion of Guards Division who continued to hold Northern Sector. Brigades etc disposed as follows. 186 Inf/Bde + 74 Yorkshire Holding the Line. HQs and 2ohs QUIEVY. 185 Inf/Bde Reserve NEUVILLES. 187 Inf/Bde Reserve CATTENIERES M.G.Coy to QUIEVY. Supply Train unloaded FREMICOURT owing to Railway Breakdown – Some trouble due to lack of lorries finally overcome.	BM
BEVILLERS	18th		Weather Misty then Fine. Divn HQs moved to BEVILLERS in morning – Administrative Instructions to coincide with proposed attack SOLESMES issued	BM Appendix C.
do	19th		Weather dull. 20 Infantry and 1 Cavalry Divisions sent to Interviewing Committee at CAMBRAI – 185 Inf/Bde moved to QUIEVY. This accommodation in BEVILLERS being taken over by 187 Inf/Bde – Again 1 of 3rd Division moved into CATTENIERES. Orders issued for Reception Camp Moves to IGNIEZ on 21st inst and to stop August 24/25 Cat at MARCOING – Corps provide 5 lorries for move	BM

T.J134. Wt. W708-776. 50C000. 4/15. Sir J.C. & B.

Army Form C. 2118.

WAR DIARY
or
INTELLIGENCE SUMMARY.
(Erase heading not required.)

October 1918 p.6

Place	Date	Hour	Summary of Events and Information	Remarks and references to Appendices
BEVILLERS	20th		Weather Wet. All Day. Third Army attacked – 6nd Division's objective SOLESMES and ST PYTHON. Zero 0200 hours – 186 R.M.L.I. leading – 185 Support – forcing though them 8/th Village had been captured to further objective – 189. R/F Acte in Reserve at QUIEVY. All Objectives taken by Midday – Certain number of Civilians found in ST PYTHON and brought to BEVILLERS where accommodated for —	
			Estimated Casualties at 6pm. 8th W.Yorks 1 and 60. 9th Durhams 50 ors. 5th D.L.I's 40 ors. 2/4 Dyke's 1 and 25. 9/th Hants 1 and 47. 2/h York's 1 and 40. Prisoners yet Captured – Rough Back. Cap. 9 Officers NSO ORanks	
	21st		New Material reported Captured. 3 Field Guns Several M.G. Guns. Weather dull but drying up. A Quiet Day. Divisions Consolidating on Objectives gained – About 3,500 Civilians found in SOLESMES System. Majority wished to remain – Total Pyrs though Cage up to 1700 hours since commencement of Operations 100 Officers 504 ors. Further estimated Casualties being 8th W. Yorks up to 2 and 70 Londons up to 100 ors	

Army Form C. 2118.

WAR DIARY
or
INTELLIGENCE SUMMARY.
(Erase heading not required.)

October 1918 p. 7

Place	Date	Hour	Summary of Events and Information	Remarks and references to Appendices
BEVILLERS	22nd		Weather Dull. 3rd Division passed through 62nd Division during evening to make further advance. — Brigades withdrawn to support Bullecourt as under — 185 Inf Bde — to QUIEVY — 186 Inf Bde to BEVILLERS — 9th York & Lancs rejoined 187 Inf Bde at CATTENIÈRES — D.L.I remained at QUIEVY — MGOA concentrated at BEVILLERS and 3 Field Cos at QUIEVY. Estimated Casualties not accurate since 14/15 October to — Devons 1 and 10, W Yorks 2 and 120, Londons 120 — 5th KRR 40 — 2/4 do 1 and 40 — Hants 1 and 50 — Yorks and Lancs 1 and 60. Prisoners Officer Captured since 29th October _____ 11 Officers 519 o.Ranks.	Attack Cancelled Appx A
do	23rd		Weather Fine and Warm. VI Corps attacked with 2nd and 3rd Divisions 0400hrs — Attack Successful — 62 Ambce Reception Camp Established at 16NH4 near ESTOURMEL. Total Prisoners Captured since 20th but now reported as 12 officers 657 o.Ranks —	GM
do	24th		Weather Dull and fairly warm. — 200 German Prisoners employed on clearing BEVILLERS. Divisional Candidates for November = 12 in number — dispatched to VI Corps School DAPONE. Proceeded on leave. Capt K.P. Leonard 9/4 Duke of Wellingtons acting — 187 Inf Bde moved to QUIEVY taking over billets recently by 7th Inf Bde. 9th & 10th D.L.I moved to SOLESMES to work on Roads forward of there.	GM

Army Form C. 2118.

WAR DIARY
or
INTELLIGENCE SUMMARY.
(Erase heading not required.)

October 1918 p. 8

Place	Date	Hour	Summary of Events and Information	Remarks and references to Appendices
BEUVILLERS	25		Weather fine until late afternoon then light drizzle. - 2 Odo R.F.A. return to DIVISION for Rest and Refit. At present accommodated at VERTAIN will probably move back shortly. - D.T.C. to return when no longer required by 3rd Divn. GM	
do	26th		Weather fine and warm. - 315F and 312E Bdes moved to Billets at QUIEVY. GM	
do	27		Weather Fine - Sunday - Watering of Artillery Horses at QUIEVY a difficulty - 3 more Water Tank Lorries obtained from Corps - Enemy gun at QUIEVY - Comparative Statement Casualties, Prisoners, Stores Captured and Materiel Captured Since 23/8/18 APPENDIX "E" GM	E
do	28th		Weather fine and warm. Soldiers reconnoitred with a view to establishing Div. HQs here as well as Bde HQs on 31st Inst. Dark Car proceeded to FONTAINE MRAN for Bdays Tank Course - Brig Genl T.W. Vick. Harrison CBS CMC arrived to assume cmd of the 2dn. GM	
do	29th		Weather Fine and warm. Soldiers reconnoitred with a view to 188 Inf Bde - 157 Bde HQs and LAs moving there on 31st in addition to Divisional HQs. Bgdo HQs not completed for about a week. GM	

Army Form C. 2118.

WAR DIARY
or
INTELLIGENCE SUMMARY.
(Erase heading not required.)

October 1918 p. 9.

Instructions regarding War Diaries and Intelligence Summaries are contained in F.S. Regs., Part II. and the Staff Manual respectively. Title pages will be prepared in manuscript.

Place	Date	Hour	Summary of Events and Information	Remarks and references to Appendices
BEVILLERS	30		Weather Fine – 3rd Division HQ s to be established in QUIEVY necessitated move of 7% Field Ambulance to another part of Village. Asst Asst DAC & 186 Infantry reached from Leave. Asst Dir. Car from Corps in PONTAMELBON on Capoden.	JN
SOLESMES	31		Weather Fine Return. Div HQ s moved to Billets in SOLESMES vacated by 3rd Div. HQ's in evening – Brigade's moved as under. 186 Inf.Bde to SCLEMPIS 187 Inf.Bde. HQ's to SOLESMES, 2/4 York Lancs to BEVILLERS remaining 2 B/ns. to ROMERIES – MGB". to QUIEVY. 90. Remainder of Division. No Change – During latter part of October the supply train returning to Corpoden and German Mines exploding on the Railway – So many Coal the Peak Rain did not cease till the day after it was done, and then whole days at the Railhead. As this would probably seriously hamper possible future Operation arrangements made to Dump a reserve of Rations at ROMERIES.	

Army Form C. 2118

WAR DIARY
or
INTELLIGENCE SUMMARY
(Erase heading not required.)

Appendix F = Casualties during October.
  "   G = Rewards during October.
  "   H = Reinforcements.

[signature]
Major General
Commanding 2nd (R) Division

app. A

VI Corps A/2096/13.

62nd Division.

BURIAL OF DEAD DURING AN ADVANCE.

1. VI Corps A/2096/12 dated 16/8/18 is cancelled.

2. **GENERAL SCHEME.**

The instructions contained in A.G.3212/0 of 22/7/18 will be generally followed.

The areas for which Divisions are responsible will be notified by Corps 'A' from time to time. Generally speaking, Divisions will be given an area corresponding, as near as practicable, to the area over which they have fought. When two Divisions relieve each other alternately, the same area will be given to each Division, and the Divisional Burial Parties will work jointly in that area.

3. **STAFF.**

Each Divisional Burial Party will consist of @ 2 officers (including D.B.O.) 1 Sergeant, 3 Corporals and 50 men, of which the present Divisional Burial Staff will form the trained nucleus.

From the Labour personnel allotted to C.B.O., men will be allotted to each Division, and will come under the orders of D.B.O. This party will be additional to Divisional party
(@ A Chaplain may be appointed to assist D.B.O. as a Second Burial Officer)

4. **WORKING OF DIVISIONAL AREAS.**

Only in the case of units in the line - and then only in the case of necessity - will units bury dead during an advance. Bodies should be collected by units at suitable collecting stations, the locations of which should be notified by the unit through Brigade Headquarters to the D.B.O. These collecting stations should be chosen at existing cemeteries if possible, or at spots suitable for cemeteries. D.B.Os will then arrange for burial, either at the collecting station, if suitable, or at a cemetery elsewhere. If for any reason bodies must be buried before the Divisional parties reach reach the area (i) a wire should be sent to the D.B.O. or C.B.O. who will arrange for burial before the general clearance, or (ii) bodies should be buried in an existing cemetery.

D.B.Os will arrange to search thoroughly each portion of the area allotted to them before another portion is commenced, and will keep a map record of the area searched. D.B.Os who discover isolated dead of the Division with whom they share responsibility for the area allotted to them will notify the D.B.O. of that Division who will arrange burial.

Any bodies of men of Corps Troops units or of Divisions not working in the area concerned will be buried by the D.B.O. who finds the bodies.

5. **CEMETERIES.**

Existing Cemeteries will be used as much as possible. The positions of these have been communicated to D.B.Os concerned.

Where no cemetery is available, suitable positions will be chosen by D.B.Os. The minimum number of cemeteries necessary for the adequate completion of the work will be used. D.B.Os will place 1 N.C.O. in charge of each cemetery until burials are finished therein.

6. **CHAPLAINS.**

All Chaplains should co-operate with D.B.O. as much as possible.

Divisions will nominate one Chaplain (C/E), 1 Chaplain (Non C/E), and if possible, 1 Chaplain (R/C) per day. These Chaplains on duty will keep in close touch with D.B.O., and will take all services required. It will not be possible always for services to be held before graves are filled in, but they can be held sometime the same day.

7. **MARKING OF GRAVES.**

When available, G.R.U. crosses (with copper plates attached) will be used as far forward as possible, the smaller crosses being used where necessary. Crosses etc., will be distributed to convenient centres by C.B.O.

In forward sectors, the numbered discs will be used. D.B.Os are responsible for the distribution of discs. All numbering of graves will be from left to right, when facing the head of the graves.

D.B.Os and Chaplains who come across old graves which appear not to have been registered will forward all available particulars to the C.B.O.

P.T.O.

(2.)

and will mark the cross over the grave with the letter 'N' (to signify 'notified').

8. REGISTRATION.
Corporal in charge of cemetery will keep a record of all burials in A.B. 152 (in duplicate) as follows:-

---

CEMETRY_____ Date_____ 1918.

No. of Grave.	Regtl. No.	Rank.	Initials.	Name.	Regt.	Religion.	Identification.

(Signed)_____ C.F.(C/E.)   (Signed)_____ C.F.(Non.C/E.)
                        Chaplain.   Chaplain.

One page will be used for each row of (10 names). Chaplains will sign at foot of page (as shown) giving their denomination. It will then be understood that each Chaplain named has held a service for the men of the same denomination who are shewn on that page.

One copy of this Cemetery return will be handed to D.B.O. The remaining copy will be kept in book for reference. When books are finished, they will be forwarded by D.B.O. to Division "A".

From these Cemetery returns, D.B.O. will make up daily the return as shewn in A.G's letter, and will forward same to C.B.O. Copies of forms will be supplied to all D.B.Os.

9. EFFECTS AND SALVAGE.
Effects and Salvage will be dealt with as laid down in A.G's letter. Detailed instructions will be sent to D.B.Os.

6/10/18.   (sd) W. de H. Haig, Major,
                              D.A.A.G. 6th Corps.

Copy to D.A.C.G. D.A.P.C. D.D.M.S. C.B.O.

app. B.

C O N F I D E N T I A L.　　　　　　　　62nd Div. A/2874/1.

G.O.C. 185th Infantry Brigade.
"   186th Infantry Brigade.
"   187th Infantry Brigade.
G.O.C.R.A.
C.R.E.
A.D.M.S.
O.C. 62nd Divisional Train.
O.C. 9th Bn Durham Light Infantry.
O.C. 62nd Bn. Machine Gun Corps.
O.C. 62nd Divisional Signal Company.

　　　　The attached translations of a German document found in CAMBRAI are forwarded for your information and are to be read to all ranks of the units under your command.

　　　　It is to be explained to them that the individuals who have given such precise information to the enemy, concerning not only the dispositions for the battle of HAVRINCOURT but also the still more important strategical dispositions of the British Army in East and West and the provision of reserves at home, have jeopardised the lives of their comrades and endangered the successful conduct of the war.

　　　　That these men should thus have disgraced themselves as soldiers of so splendid a Division as I have the honour to command is incomprehensible to me, all the more so in view of the very precise information and instructions on the subject issued so recently from General Headquarters.   I refer to G.R.O.4791 of 17.8.18 and S.S.730 issued w-ith it.

　　　　This G.R.O. and the memorandum are in future to be read to all ranks <u>at least once a week</u>, and I hold Battalion, Battery Company and Platoon Commanders personally responsible that every individual in their respective commands clearly understands that every prisoner taken by the enemy owes it to his country that when examined by his captors <u>he gives no more than his name.</u>

　　　　The names of all individuals of the 2/4th Hants Regt and 5th K.O.Y.L.I. who were reported missing on 13th September last will be carefully recorded.

　　　　　　　　　　　　　　　　　　　　R. Whigham

　　　　　　　　　　　　　　　　　　　　　　Major General.
14th October 1918.　　　　Commanding 62nd (West Riding) Division.

N.B.　A sufficient number of copies of this memorandum for issue down to Companies is forwarded.   These are not to be taken into the front line but are to be collected at Brigade Headquarters before units go into action.

Intelligence Officer, G.H.Q.
Attached to the 17th Army.   H.Q. 15.9.18.

Statements of :-
12 prisoners of B.C. & D.Coys. 2/IV/Hants R. 186th Inf. Brigade.
23 prisoners of A.B.C. & D.Coys. 1 & 2/V/Yorks.L.I. 187th I.Brigade,
62nd Division, captured on the 13th Sept. at 10.00 hrs on the
railway line East of HAVRINCOURT during German counter-attack.

Composition is given as follows :-

186th Brigade.	187th Brigade.
2/IV/W.Rid.R.	2/IV/Yorks L.I.
1 & 2/V/W.Rid.R.	1 & 2/V/Yorks L.I.
2/IV/Hants R.	2/IV/York & Lanc.R.

Historical. After the fighting near MONCHY the 186th Inf. Brigade went into bivouacs West of GOMIECOURT about the 1st Sept. and the 187th Inf. Brigade South of ERVILLERS about the 3rd. Nothing is known of the location of the 185th Inf. Brigade.

Whilst in rest attack exercises were practised by the whole Brigade.

At 16.00 hrs on the 10th Sept. 186th and 187th Brigades left their bivouacs and proceeded via BAPAUME, 186th Brigade to quarters in HAPLINCOURT WOOD and the 187th Brigade to the large wood by VELU.

On Wednesday, the 11th, the Brigades moved forward at dusk to take up their assembly positions South-West of HAVRINCOURT which were reached between 12 and 1 o'clock on the night of the 11th/12th Sept.

Relief. The prisoners know that they relieved troops with Yellow horse-shoes on their coat-sleeves (37th Division).

Prisoners of the 2/IV/Hants R. were told before the attack that after reaching their objective they were to be immediately relieved; by whom this relief was to take place is not known. In general these fellows attached little value to the promise of relief as such promises are usually not fulfilled.

Troops on Flanks. The 186th Brigade was South and the 187th Brigade was on the North along the N. and N.E. edges of HAVRINCOURT Village. Some of the prisoners believed that on the right of them N.Z.troops were to make a simultaneous attack. The presence of the 2nd Division is confirmed.

Other Troops. Some prisoners of a draft which had joined the 2/IV/Hants R. on the 8th Sept. saw in their train men of the York & Lancs. and W.Riding Regts of their Division; also Highland Light Infantry, Seaforth Highlanders and Americans. The Units of these latter troops could not be ascertained.

One of the prisoners belonged until the end of August to the 2/IV/Hants Reserve Battalion in BELFAST - strength of this unit 900 to 1000 men. In the same place there were about 50 of a Northumberland Regt. Troops of a Wiltshire Reserve Battalion are stationed in DUBLIN.

Dispositions. Of the 187th Brigade, the V/Y.L.I. occupied the railway embankment from North of the village to South of the Cemetery, in touch with the 2/IV/York.L.I. on the left, the 2/IV/York & Lanc. R. in support.

Of the 186th Brigade, the 2/IV/Hants R. occupied the railway at the East Edge of HAVRINCOURT and the 2/IV/W.R.R. East of Chateau Park, the V/W.R.R. in support. Nothing could be ascertained of the situation of the positions of the 185th Brigade.

Company Strengths. Before the attack on the 12th, Company strengths are said to be as follows :-

-2-

  2/IV/Hants Regt. 3 - 4 Officers,   120 O.R.
  1 & 2/V/York L.I. 3 Officers,   110 O.R.

  Prisoners of the 1 & 2/V/Yorks L.I. said that about 8-10 O.R. were left at transport lines as nucleus.
  People of the 2/IV/Hants R. state the ration strength to be about 150 per Company.

<u>Intentions of the Enemy.</u> Prisoners knew nothing about the further offensive intentions of the enemy.

<u>The attack on the 12th.</u> This took place after a short intensive artillery preparation. During the attack the artillery creeping barrage moved forward in accordance with an exact and carefully thought out plan and the attacking troops had to follow closely. The attack began 12th Sept. at 0600 hrs in a South Westerly direction towards the Village of HAVRINCOURT. After gaining the Village the attack was continued in an Easterly direction. This change of front, also the heavy German artillery fire, caused great disorder. The different Companies were mixed up and the Commanders could no longer control their men. Owing to the weak German resistance in the village they were able to press forward as far as the Eastern edge of HAVRINCOURT where the Germans defended themselves most energetically and the objective (the trench some 300 metres East of the Village) could not be gained. Contradictory statements are given as to the manner in which the units were formed up for this attack. Of the 2/IV/Hants R. A.B.C. Companies attacked one after the other, each Company having a special objective; B. Company which had to take the German trench East of the Village could not do so. The 2/IV/W.R.R. after reaching the village had to proceed through the Chateau Park as far as the Eastern edge of the latter where they had to dig themselves in. The V/Yorks. L.I. attacked with C.Company in the first wave, A and B. Companies passing through them at the second wave with D.Company following in support. After taking the village the North and North-East edge was occupied.

<u>GENERAL DETAILS.</u>

<u>Personal.</u> All the men come from the labouring classes, ages from 19 to 41 years. They all announced that they were glad that the war was now over so far as they were concerned.

<u>Method of Capture.</u> They were cut off and captured by the German counter-attack from the Church Yard which lies N.E. of the village.

<u>Losses.</u> Estimated for the attack on the 12th as being very slight, owing to the very weak German defence. Prisoners of the 2/IV/Hants R. and the V/Yorks. L.I. saw some of their own people caught by English artillery fire, they are unable to state any definite figure. During the German counter-attack on the 13th. the losses are said to have been considerably higher. Some of the older prisoners estimate the total losses during the fighting on the 12th and the 13th at about 50%. The losses in the attacks at the end of August by MONCHY were said to have been moderate.

<u>Reinforcements.</u> The 2/IV/ Hants R. suffered the heaviest losses in the fighting on the MARNE and received about the middle of August a draft of 350 men of which C Company received 150, B Company 18 and the remainder going to A and D Companies. The V/Yorks L.I. received a draft on the 9th September strength 120 men, who were distributed evenly throughout the companies. This draft of 1000 strong left ETAPLES on the 9th September at 0715 hours (length of train) about 20 coaches). Prisoners did not remember exactly what places they passed on route,

but the journey from ABBEVILLE was over a newly laid double track as far as DOULLENS and from there on single line as far as SAULTY, 15 Kms N.E. of DOULLENS, arriving at 1830 hrs, thence by march route to Battalion bivouacs in the vicinity of ERVILLERS.

The combed out workers from war industries were sent to the front as reinforcements as soon as they were trained. Those who were not yet trained went to Reserve Battalions in ENGLAND. One of the prisoners was called up in April, 1918 and trained in SOUTH SHIELDS. After 4½ months training he was transferred to his present Battalion at the end of August.

In SOUTH SHIELDS there is the 3rd Durham Training Reserve Battalion, strength of 8 Companies each of 500 men, in all about 4,000 men strong.

The effect of German Arms. The nightly air raids upon camps and bivouacs are very demoralising to the troops although losses have very rarely been occasioned thereby.

State of Health. Is stated to be excellent.

Approach Route. Troops marched from HAPLINCOURT and VELU WOODS via BERTINCOURT, RUYAULCOURT and thence in a N.E.direction in the vicinity of the Spoil Heap S.W. (?) to HAVRINCOURT where the assembly positions were taken up.

Artillery Positions. During the march into assembly positions prisoners observed a great concentration of artillery. Batteries were strongly massed at the spoil heap S.E. (sic) of HAVRINCOURT.

Organisation. In April 1916, the 75th English Division was transferred from INDIA to EGYPT and still remains there.

In May, 1918, the 2/IV/Somerset Light Infantry of the 232nd Brigade, 2/IV/Hants Regt. 233rd Brigade, 2/V/Devon Regt, 234th Brigade, were withdrawn and transported to ROUEN via ALEXANDRIA and MARSEILLES. The 2/IV/Hants Regt. was attached to the 62nd Division but it is not known to which Divisions the Somerset and Devon Battalions were sent.

The 2/IV/Hants Regt. has 9 Lewis Guns per Company, 1 of which is detailed for A.A. defence at Company H.Q.

The V/Yorks. L.I. has 8 Lewis Guns per Company.

Commanders.
    2/IV/Hants Regt.
        B Company   Lieut. WEEKS.
        C -do-   Lieut. ISAACS.
        D -do-   Capt. BULLEY.

    V/Yorks. L.I. Battalion Commander Lieut.Col. PETER.
        B. Company   Lieut. FRENCH.
        C. -do-   Capt. OLIPHANT.
        D. -do-   Lieut. WILSON.

Transportation Details. The transportation of the three Battalions of the 75th Division from ALEXANDRIA to MARSEILLES took place in the Steamer 'EMPRESS of INDIA'. They travelled in a convoy of 7 steamers protected by 10 destroyers; 'U' Boats were not sighted.

Battalion Signs. 2/IV/Hants Regt. On both sleeves a Yellow oblong; on the back below the collar, 2 upright yellow and black bands.
        1 & 2/V/Yorks. L.I. A blue diamond on both sleeves.
        2/IV/Yorks L.I.   red   -ditto-
        2/IV/York & Lancs. Regt. yellow -ditto-

Furlough. Is open.

Political. Nothing is known of a new General Election. Should this take place the Prime Minister, Lloyd George, will probably obtain a majority.

Morale. In the Army and at home very war weary, one hopes for a speedy peace though they are certain of a further winter of war and heavy fighting in the next year.

Economical. One of the prisoners is a collier from Durham. In April exempted people, and men fit for garrison duty were combed out in the Northumberland and Durham districts. The number of these is said to be 50,000, nearly all of which were called up as fit for active service. Prisoner states that colliers in other areas were similarly called up and the scarcity of coal owing to the lack of labour will be very considerable during the coming winter. 10 cwt of coal was formerly delivered to the colliers for every days work; since March owing to the coal shortage this arrangement could not be maintained and the colliers received as compensation 5/6d every 14 days. This sum does not amount to the value of the coal as the colliers sold the supplies delivered to them for 15/-d a ton. The prisoner knew that munition workers at the ages of 18 to 30 were called up at the same time as the colliers and their places were filled by women. Owing to these measures the output of munitions has been rendered very difficult and a further calling up of these workers for military service is not likely to be continued.

(sd) REINCKE,
Lt. and Intelligence Officer.

app. C.

SECRET.   62nd Div. A/3048/49.

                                                Copy No........

ADMINISTRATIVE INSTRUCTIONS
to accompany 62nd (West Riding) Division Order No.154.

1. **S.A.A.**

   The S.A.A. Section is located at C.23.c.
   Corps Dump for light ammunition H.29.b.

2. **PRISONERS OF WAR.**

   VI Corps Cage is at I.3.c.3.8. The Divisional Cage will open at C.29.a.2.8 on 19th instant at 6 .1800.
   A forward collecting post will be established at D.13.c.9.5 at 1800. 19th instant.
   Stragglers' Post at D.14.c.5.2.
   Collecting Station at D.13.c.9.5.

3. **SUPPLIES.**

   Supplies will be normal.

4. **BLANKETS AND PACKS.**

   Blankets and packs will be dumped under guard at the last place Battalions are stationed at before going into action.

5. **WAGON LINES.**

   Infantry Brigade, etc., will keep Divisional Headquarters 'Q' acquainted with location of wagon lines.

6. **MEDICAL.**

   A.D.M.S. will issue orders with regard to evacuation.
   Additional bearers will be supplied from regimental bands as usual - 30 men to each affiliated Field Ambulance.

7. **MOBILE VETERINARY SECTION.**

   The Mobile Veterinary Section is established at FRESNOY FARM C.27.c.0.5.
   An Advanced Veterinary Aid Post will be at QUIEVY C.24.b.8.6.

8. **BURIALS.**

   The D.B.O. will be at A.D.S. QUIEVY, D.14.c.0.1. where there will always be a representative to give any necessary information. All bodies should be sent to A.D.S. for burial.

                                       Harold S. Lea
                                            Lieut.Colonel.
18.10.1918.   A.A. & Q.M.G. 62nd (West Riding) Division.

DISTRIBUTION.

1. A.D.C. for G.O.C.
2. 'G'.
3-4. 'A' & 'Q'.
5. 185th Infantry Brigade.
6. 186th Infantry Brigade.
7. 187th Infantry Brigade.
8. 62nd (W.R.) Divisional Artillery.
9. C.R.E.
10. 62nd (W.R) Divisional Train.
11. A.D.M.S.
12. 62nd (W.R) Divisional Signal Coy.
13. 62nd Bn. Machine Gun Corps.
14. 9th Bn. Durham Light Infantry.
15. D.A.P.M.
16. D.A.D.O.S.
17. D.A.D.V.S.
18. Mobile Veterinary Section.
19. Div. Burials Officers.
20. Div. Gas Officer.
21. Div. Salvage Officer.
22. S.A.A. SEction.
23. VI Corps 'Q'.

SECRET.   62nd Div. A/3120/49

Copy No......

AMENDMENT TO
ADMINISTRATIVE INSTRUCTIONS TO ACCOMPANY
62ND (WEST RIDING) DIVISION ORDER NO.154.
- - - - - - - - - - - - - - - -

Cancel para.2 and substitute:-

2. PRISONERS OF WAR AND STRAGGLERS.

(a) 62nd Divisional P.O.W. Cage is at QUIEVY D.13.c.9.5.
from 1800 hours, 19th inst.
VI Corps Cage will be at I.3.c.2.8. near BEAUVOIS on
CAMBRAI le CATEAU Road.

(b) Stragglers Post will be at D.19.a.8.8. QUIEVY.
Collecting station at D.13.c.9.5.   do

[signature]

19.10.1918.   Lieut Colonel.
              A.A.&.Q.M.G. 62nd (West Riding) Division.

To all recipients of 62nd Division A/3048/49 of 18.10.18.

app D

CASUALTIES FROM 20/10/18 to 24/10/18.

	Killed		Wounded		Missing		
	Off.	O.Rs.	Off.	O.Rs.	Off.	O.Rs.	
1/5th Devon Regt.	-	-	1	8x	-	-	x 1 Injured.
8th West Yorks.	-	-	3	79	-	17	
2/20th London Regt.	-	-	-	76	-	4	
185th T.M.Battery	-	-	-	10✻	-	-	✻ 2 at duty
5th West Riding Regt.	-	-	-	33x	-	2	x 1 Injured
2/4th West Riding Regt.	-	-	1	59	-	-	
2/4th Hants. Regt.	-	-	1	16	-	1	
186th T.M.Battery.	-	-	-	1	-	-	
5th K.O.Y.L.I.	-	-	-	1x	-	-	x 1 Injured.
2/4th K.O.Y.L.I.	-	-	-	-	-	-	
2/4th York & Lancs.	-	-	1	38	-	12	
9th Bn. Durham L.I.	-	-	2	2	-	-	
62nd Bn. M.G.Corps.	-	7	1	34	-	2	
310th Bde. R.F.A.	-	-	-	2x	-	-	x 1 Injured
312th Bde. R.F.A.	-	-	-	8	-	-	
62nd D.A.C.	-	-	-	1x	-	-	x 1 Injured.
457th Field Coy.	-	-	-	3	-	-	
460th Field Coy.	-	-	-	1	-	-	
461st Field Coy.	-	-	-	3	-	-	
62nd Divl. Signal Coy.	-	-	-	16%	-	-	% 15 Gas.
2/1st W.R.Fld. Ambce.	-	-	-	5	-	-	
2/2nd W.R.Fld. Ambce.	-	-	-	1✻	-	-	✻at duty.
62nd Divl. Train.	-	-	-	1x	-	-	x Injured.
TOTAL DIVISION.	-	7	10	398	-	38	

appx H.

62nd (West Riding) Division.

REINFORCEMENTS RECEIVED DURING OCTOBER

	Officers.	O.Ranks.
185th Infantry Brigade H.Q.	–	1
8th West Yorks Regiment	11	488
1/5th Devonshire Regiment.	15	288
2/20th London Regiment	3	77
5th West Riding Regiment	11	248
2/4th West Riding Regiment	16	326
2/4th Hampshire Regiment	9	184
5th Bn K.O.Y.L.I.	12	336
2/4th Bn K.O.Y.L.I.	10	135
2/4th York & Lancs Regiment	3	247
62nd Bn Machine Gun Corps	4	126
9th Bn Durham Light Infantry	4	48
Royal Engineers	1	57
Divisional Train	–	5
Royal Army Medical Corps	4	34
252 Employment Company	–	24
Divisional Ammunition Column.	–	7
	103	2631.

STATEMENT OF CASUALTIES INCURRED SINCE AUGUST 25th to DATE.

PERIOD.	K. Offs.	K. O.R.	W. Offs.	W. O.R.	M. Offs.	M. O.R.
August 25th and following days.	18	294	70	1639	1	323
September 12th ditto.	8	199	40	1077	–	228
September 27th ditto.	21	248	42	1135	4	262
October 20th ditto.	–	64	10	398	–	38
TOTAL.	47	805	162	4249	5	851

Total Casualties since 25/8/18
Officers.	Other Ranks.
214	5905

PRISONERS CAPTURED.

	Through Divl. Cage. Offs.	Through Divl. Cage. O.R.	Through Field Amb.	TOTAL PRISONERS.
August 25th and following days.	32	1078	151	1261
September 12th ditto.	19	886	66	971
September 27th ditto.	24	1300	195	1519
October 20th ditto.	12	657	30	699
TOTAL.	87	3921	442	4450

Total Prisoners since 25/8/18
Officers.	Other Ranks.
87	4363

APPENDIX F.

CASUALTIES DURING OCTOBER 1918.

OFFICERS.

1.10.18.	2/Lieut.	STEPHENS.	C.T.	62 Bn M.G.Corps.	Wounded.
3.10.18.	Lt.& Q.M.	GADSBY.	C.G.	2/4th Bn K.O.Y.L.I.	Wounded.
4.10.18.	Lieut.	MURRAY.	G.A.	62 Div.Sig.Coy.	Killed.
8.10.18.	Lieut.	ALEXANDER.	A.C.	9th Bn D.L.I.	Wounded.
18.10.18.	2/Lt.	BRIGGS.	T.	6th Lanc.Fuslrs.atd. 5th W.Rid.Rgt.	Killed.
20.10.18.	2/Lt.	READING.	S.J.	2/4th West Riding.	Wounded.
20.10.18.	2/Lt.	MATTHEW.	A.C.	3rd Bn. 2/4th Hants.	Wounded.
20.10.18.	2/Lt.	MCMILLAN. M.C.	J.	62 Bn M.G.C. (Cameronians Scottish Rifles)	Wounded.
20.10.18.	2/Lt.	DUGDALE.	T.C.	2/4th York & Lanc.	Wounded.
20.10.18.	Lt (A/Cpt)	PYMAN.M.C.	J.	Yks Rgt. attd 8th West Yorks.	Wounded.
20.10.18.	2/Lieut.	SHARPE.	C.	8th West Yorks.	Wounded.
20.10.18.	2/Lieut.	COWLING.	F.W.	9th D.L.I.	Wounded.
21.10.18.	2/Lieut (T/Lt)	SKARDON.	H.J.	5th Devon Rgt.	Wounded.
22.10.18.	T/Lieut.	CLARKSON.M.C.	A.	8th West Yorks.	Wounded.
22.10.18.	2/Lieut.	CRANE.	H.J.	9th D.L.I.	Wounded.
23.10.18.	Lt-Col.	ENGLAND.	N.A.,D.S.O.	8th West Yorks.	W.at duty.

OTHER RANKS.

Killed.	67.
Wounded.	451.
Missing.	22.

app.G.

HONOURS AND REWARDS.
OCTOBER 1918.

D.S.O.	7.
Third Bar to M.C.	1.
Bar to M.C.	18.
M.C.	74.
D.C.M.	43.
2nd Bar to M.M.	1.
Bar to M.M.	38.
M.M.	273.

Original

Vol 23

CONFIDENTIAL.

WAR DIARY

of

62ND (WEST RIDING) DIVISION, 'A' BRANCH.

-o-o-o-o-o-o-o-o-

From
1st November 1918.
to
30th November 1918.

VOLUME XXII.

Army Form C. 2118.

HEADQUARTERS WAR DIARY
INTELLIGENCE SUMMARY. NOVEMBER 1918 (P.1)
(ADMINISTRATIVE)
(West Riding) Division.

Place	Date	Hour	Summary of Events and Information	Remarks and references to Appendices
SOLESMES	1		Intimation received that Advance would shortly be resumed - ESCARMAIN reconnoitred for Div. H.Q. Push train late again.	VI Corps SG 882
			Mobile column of 10 lorries placed at disposal of 62 Div. Arty from Zero onwards.	Q206 Q210
			Additional 3 lorries allotted by Corps for purpose of distributing rations to French civilians in SOLESMES (3800) and ROMERIES (640).	
SOLESMES	2		13,500 iron Rations and 27,500 lbs Oats drawn by train & taken to ESCARMAIN to be kept as emergency supply, following moves took place for relief of 2nd Div. by 62nd Division.	
			Unit — from — to	Bde. H.Q. R20 8.1.6
			187 Bde. POMERIES LINE	ESCARMAIN
			186 Bde. SOLESMES ESCARMAIN	POMERIES (2 Bns)
			185 Bde. QUIEVY POMERIES (2 Bns) SOLESMES (1 Bn)	SOLESMES
			62nd Bn M.G.C. QUIEVY ROMERIES	Under orders 185 Bde.

WAR DIARY

INTELLIGENCE SUMMARY.

HEADQUARTERS (West Riding) Division

Army Form C. 2118.

P.2

NOVEMBER, 1918

Place	Date	Hour	Summary of Events and Information	Remarks and references to Appendices
SOLESMES	3	1600	One Supply Tank allotted each of 186 & 187 Inf. Bde, to be handed over to 185 Inf. Bde, when latter pass through. Divl. H.Q. closed SOLESMES and opened ESCARMAIN same hour, Infantry Brigades moved forward to assembly positions	P.O./89 G.258
ESCARMAIN	4	1200	Divl H.Q. closed ESCARMAIN and opened RUESNES; morning attack very successful. Prisoners: (1) through Corps Cage to 1800 hours. 7 off 6130 o.r. (2) " N.Z. Divn Cage " " 2 " 142 " (3) " Fld. Ambces. " " 3 " 65 " Total 12 off. 8200 o.r. Estimated casualties 23 off. 5150. o.r.	G/63
RUESNES	5	1200	185 Inf. Bde. continued advance from line E. of FRASNOY. Divl. H.Q. closed RUESNES and opened FRASNOY same hour. Casualties in attack slight. Prisoners - 1 off 430 o.r.	
do	6		Advance resumed, and line carried forward to BAVAI Road. Light casualties. Prisoners - 8. {Total captures from ZERO 4th to 1800 hours 6th - 13 off 8710 o.r.} {Estimated casualties same period 32 off 7950 o.r.}	

Army Form C. 2118.

WAR DIARY
INTELLIGENCE SUMMARY. NOVEMBER, 1918. P.3.

HEADQUARTERS
(West Riding Division)

Place	Date	Hour	Summary of Events and Information	Remarks and references to Appendices
FRASNOY	7		Attack resumed from BAVAI–AVESNES Road towards MAUBEUGE by 186 Inf. Bde. with two Bns. 185 Bde. attached. Third day of rain & mist. Roads in bad condition. Hard ration drawn at CAMBRAI ANNEXE and issued to troops; train did not arrive at all on 6th, owing to mine explosions at MARCOING. Supply problem becoming acute, owing to distance of units from railhead & delay in moving latter up to SOLESMES. Two extra lorries allotted for purpose of bringing food to french civilians – number of latter greatly increased by capture of BAVISIAUX, LE TRECHON, OBIES, MECQUIGNIES and other villages on 6th.	Q 612
		1000	G.O.C. and "G" moved to new H.Q. at BAVISIAUX.	

Army Form C. 2118.

WAR DIARY
INTELLIGENCE SUMMARY. NOVEMBER 1918.

HEADQUARTERS ADMINISTRATIVE (West Riding) Division.

T.P.4

Place	Date	Hour	Summary of Events and Information	Remarks and references to Appendices
FRASNOY	7		P.O.W. through Cage - 11. Estimated casualties Zero 4th to 1800 7/11/18 -32 off, 8,570 O.R. Three extra lorries allotted by Corps for bringing forward	Q 663
"	8	0930	"A" and "Q" moved to BAVISIAUX. Morning attack carried line to Railway W. of MAUBEUGE. New railhead opened SOLESMES for supply to leave-trains. Total estimated casualties to 1800, 8/11/18 - 34 off - 8570 O.R.	
BAVISIAUX	9	1200	"Q" moved to NEUF MESNIL. MAUBEUGE, SOUS LE BOIS and LOUVROIL occupied during morning. "A" + "Q" moved from BAVISIAUX to LE TRECHON.	
LE TRECHON	10	1000	"A" + "Q" closed LE TRECHON and opened NEUF MESNIL. Whole Division concentrated in and near SOUS LE BOIS. No advance attempted.	
NEUF MESNIL	11	1000	Sid H.Q. closed NEUF MESNIL and opened SOUS LE BOIS same hour.	
		1200	G.O.C. addressed representative gathering of officers of Division in THEATRE, SOUS LE BOIS.	

Army Form C. 2118.

WAR DIARY
or
INTELLIGENCE SUMMARY.
(Erase heading not required.)

HEADQUARTERS
ADMINISTRATIVE
(West Riding Division)

NOVEMBER 1918

P.5

Place	Date	Hour	Summary of Events and Information	Remarks and references to Appendices
			ARMISTICE	
NEUF MESNIL	11	0230	Wire received from Corps that GERMANY had accepted terms of armistice.	
			Hostilities ceased from 1100 hours onwards.	
SOUS LE BOIS.			Pack Late again - due to great delay of Column on roads, breaking down & ditching of lorries, and extreme strain imposed on drivers. Supplies still 24 hours behind i.e. - rations for consumption on 11th arrived some morning.	
			Large dump of coal and supply of loose hay (variously computed at 300-1500 tons) found and drawn from Sup. units of Division, saving this affected In Pack & supply Column	
			Supply Dump at ESCARMAIN of one day's rations (except Hay) for whole Corps moved to BAVAI.	
			From 11th 38 lorries put at disposal of Division for supply & other purposes. Reckoning number of lorries	

WAR DIARY

Army Form C. 2118

HEADQUARTERS (ADMINISTRATIVE) (West Riding) Division.

INTELLIGENCE SUMMARY — NOVEMBER 1918

Place	Date	Hour	Summary of Events and Information	Remarks and references to Appendices
SOUS LE BOIS	11th		Broken down, this number represented no increase in transport available. Ten G.S. wagons allotted to each of 185 & 186 Inf. Bdes. for moving up dumps, and to D.A.D.O.S. for bringing up Div. Baths. Party of 1100 officers + men from Reception Camp moved by march route from IGNIEL DIT LES FRISETTES to SOLESMES. Permanent Reception Camp + staff remained at ST TYTHON.	
		2200	Word received that 62nd Divn. as part of first Corps would be attached to Fourth Army for march of occupation into Germany.	G544 A/G.834 G598
do	12th		Baths opened at Sous Le Bois and supplies of clean clothing brought up from SOLESMES. Reception Camp moved from AMFROIPRET to SOUS LE BOIS. Party from Reception Camp moved from SOLESMES to AMFROIPRET.	
do	13th		D.A.D.O.S. and Canteen stores brought up — naval lorries supplemented by 8 supply lorries saved from train. Reception Camp marched from AMFROIPRET to SOUS LE BOIS and rejoined their units. Notes for advance & forward of moves for first stage of march to Germany received from Corps. Preliminary instructions issued by "G".	

WAR DIARY

INTELLIGENCE SUMMARY

Army Form C. 2118

P. 7

HEADQUARTERS (ADMINISTRATIVE)
(West Riding) Division.

NOVEMBER - 1918

Place	Date	Hour	Summary of Events and Information	Remarks and references to Appendices
SOUS LE BOIS	15th		Orders issued for advance of 62nd Div: — march table and billeting orders attached. Great difficulties in getting up stores from SOLESMES, owing to lorries promised by Corps not being supplied. Orders issued for personnel unfilled to march, not to go to Reception Camp but be accommodated in Billets in SOUS LE BOIS. Capt. G. Beaumont, 2/4th Bn. Duke of Wellington Regt. to be in charge. Approximate numbers 9 officers 700 O.R. Cable Section attached to 62nd Div. Signal Coy from 15th. 132nd A.T. Coy. R.E. attached 62nd Div. from 15th. 1 sect. 194th Tunnelling Coy. R.E. attached 62nd Div. assisting in bringing up stores owing to further shortage of transport.	D.O. 162 A/4316/49 C 723
do	16th		Owing to breakdown of pontoon bridge, SOUS LE BOIS, march table altered. All moves postponed for 24 hours, with exception of move of Serial No 6 [Advanced Guard]	G 737. G 751 D.O. 162

Army Form C. 2118.

P.8

WAR DIARY
or
~~INTELLIGENCE SUMMARY~~
(Erase heading not required.)

HEADQUARTERS
ADMINISTRATIVE
(West Riding Division)

November 1918

Instructions regarding War Diaries and Intelligence Summaries are contained in F.S. Regs., Part II. and the Staff Manual respectively. Title pages will be prepared in manuscript.

Place	Date	Hour	Summary of Events and Information	Remarks and references to Appendices
SOUS LE BOIS	Nov: 16th		2 Troops Australian Light Horse } Attached 185th Bde. Group from 16th	G 723
	17th		1 Coy & A Cyclist Battn. }	
			Advance resumed by Advanced No.6 Group only. Very frosty – roads hard & in good condition.	
	18th		Hard frost during night. Some snow during day. Thaw commenced during afternoon. Divisional Headquarters closed & reopened at the Château, Ham SUR HEURE same hour.	
			185th Brigade Group moved to area MONTIGNIES ST CHRISTOPHE – BOUSIGNIES – BERSILLIES L'ABBAYE	G 783
			14th Bde. RHA (less B.A.C.) moved to above area.	
			186th Brigade Group moved to area COUSOLRE and COLLERET	D.O.162 and G 797
			187th " " " " CERFONTAINE and OSTERGNIES with one Battn.
HAM SUR HEURE		10.00	FERRIERE LA GRANDE	
			Divl. Artillery Group moved to area ROUSIES – LOUVROIL and FERRIERE LA GRANDE	
			D.A.D.O.S., Canteen Officer, & E.S.Os. Officer with their respective Staffs established at HAM SUR HEURE	

Army Form C. 2118.

WAR DIARY
of
HEADQUARTERS
ADMINISTRATIVE
(West Riding) Division
INTELLIGENCE SUMMARY
November 1918

P9

Place	Date	Hour	Summary of Events and Information	Remarks and references to Appendices
HAM SUR HEURE	Novr 19		Thaw continued during day, foggy towards evening Moves as under carried out:- Advanced Guard, 185 Bgde Group remained in area NALINNES - HAM SUR HEURE 185 Bgde Group to area GOZEE & THUIN 186 " " " THUIN (exclusive) - RAGNIES - BIERCEE - LEERS ET FOSTEAU 187 " " " MONTIGNIES ST CHRISTOPHE - BOUSIGNIES - BERSILLIES L'ABBAYE. 62nd Divl Artillery Group b area SOLRE SUR SAMBRE - HANTES WIHERIES - FONTAINE VALMONT. Arrangements for disposal of Released Prisoners of War issued	D.O.182 G.797 A/4475/44
	20		Weather mild, foggy until morning & evening Moves as under carried out:- Advanced Guard, 185 Bgde Group b area } GERPINNES - TONCRET - ACOZ - VILLERS POTERIE 185 Bgde Group b area 186 " " " TANCIENNE - NALINNES 187 " " " HAM SUR HEURE - MARBAIX - GOZEE - BIESMES. 62nd Divl Artillery Group b area THY-LE-CHATEAU - BERZEE - COUR-SUR-HEURE	D.O.183

Army Form C. 2118.

WAR DIARY
INTELLIGENCE SUMMARY.
(Erase heading not required.)

(West Riding Division)

November 1918

P10

Instructions regarding War Diaries and Intelligence Summaries are contained in F.S. Regs., Part II. and the Staff Manual respectively. Title pages will be prepared in manuscript.

Place	Date	Hour	Summary of Events and Information	Remarks and references to Appendices
HAM SUR HEURE	Nov. 21	1430	Weather: fairly early morning, milder during day. Roads very heavy. Divisional Headquarters closed & reopened same hour LOVERVAL.	
LOVERVAL			Warning order: Division will continue advance to MEUSE 24th and 25th prox.	G.912 G.933
	22		Frosty & very cold, stationary. R.E. HQrs & 3 Field Companies & 9th Bn. D.L.I. moved to METTET	
	23		Frosty, roads hard & in good condition. Pack horse late, good difficulties experienced in feeding troops. Information received that Division will shortly be transferred to IX Corps.	G.974
	24		Heavy white frost early morning. Resuming advance during day. Moves as under carried out:— 185 Inf. Bde. Group to area ST GERARD — DENEE — GRAUX and area FURNAUX — BIESMEREE — METTET. 186 " " DEVANT LES BOIS — BIESME — GOUGNIES 187 " " ACOZ — VILLERS POTERIE — JONCRET — NALINNES 62nd D.A. GERPINNES — FROMIEE — HANZINNE — SOHZEE — TARCIENNES. Advanced T.M.H. Collecting Station — BIESME. Supply situation acute: supplies for consumption 25th arrived R.P.s about 11 P.M.	D.O. 164

WAR DIARY

HEADQUARTERS (ADMINISTRATIVE) (West Riding) Division

November 1918

Army Form C. 2118.

Place	Date	Hour	Summary of Events and Information	Remarks and references to Appendices
LOYERVAL	Nov 25	1000	Weather mild. Some rain during day. Roads becoming very heavy. Divisional Headquarters closed & reopened BIOUL same hour. Moves as under carried out:- 185 Bde. Group to area YVOIR – EVREHAILLES – HOUX – ANHEE – HAUT LE WASTIA – WARNANT – ANNE VOIE ROUILLON. 186 " " BIOUL – ST GERARD – DENEE. 187 " " PONTAURY – GRAUX – METTET. 62nd D.A. " " FURNAUX – MAREDRET – ERNETON SUR BIERT – BIESMEREE. Released P. of W. Collecting station. – Buses based on Main Road to East N.W. of DENEE. Supply situation again acute. Two days supplies – replaceable in kind – requisitioned in CHARLEROI.	D.O. 164
BIOUL	26		Weather mild. Roads still heavy. Moves as under carried out:- 185 Bde. Group to area CINEY – SOVET – SPONTIN – BRAIBANT. 186 " " DORINNE – PURNODE – EVREHAILLES. 187 " " ANHEE – HAUT LE WASTIA – WARNANT. 62nd D.A. " " MARTEAU – FAY – SOSOYE – MAREDRET. Released P. of W. Collecting Station. – DORINNE.	D.O. 165

Army Form C. 2118.

WAR DIARY
INTELLIGENCE SUMMARY.
(Erase heading not required.)

November 1918

HEADQUARTERS (ADMINISTRATIVE) (West Riding) Division.

Instructions regarding War Diaries and Intelligence Summaries are contained in F. S. Regs., Part II. and the Staff Manual respectively. Title pages will be prepared in manuscript.

P/2

Place	Date	Hour	Summary of Events and Information	Remarks and references to Appendices
BIOUL	Nov. 27	1200	Weather mild, a good deal of rain during the morning clearing about towards afternoon. Some fog. Divisional Headquarters closed and reopened LEIGNON same hour. Moves as under carried out:—	D.O. 165
LEIGNON			185 Bde Group to area CHAUDE LA FONTAINE LIBION — HAID — XHIPPE — LEIGNON — CHAPOIS.	
			186 " " SURFONTAINE — BARSENALLE — CORBION — REUX — CONTOUX — CONNEUX — FAYS	
			187 " " CROIX — JET — ACHENE — LIROUX — TAVIET — SORINNE — ONTHAINE	
			62nd D.A. THYNES — GEMMECHENNE — LAYERS — LISOGNE — ROMEREE.	
			Returned R.of W. Collecting Station. — LEIGNON	
	28		Weather foggy early, much rain later in the day. Roads very heavy. Railhead changed to DINANT. Rations for consumption 29th due to arrive 23.00 hrs.	G. 35
	29		Weather mild, becoming foggy towards evening. Field Coy R.E. from XHIPPE and 9th Bn. D.L.I. [Pioneers] moved to HAVERSIN. To-day's Rations did not arrive until much after midday.	
	30		Weather mild, some fog. Inspection of Divl. Signal Company by G.O.C.	

WAR DIARY
or
INTELLIGENCE SUMMARY.

Army Form C. 2118.

Place	Date	Hour	Summary of Events and Information	Remarks and references to Appendices
			Appendix A = Reinforcements received during November	
			" B = Honours Rewards " "	
			" C = Casualties incurred " "	
			Lawley Jean [?] Lieutenant and Major General Commanding 62nd (West Riding) Division	
	30th November 1918.			

Appendix 'A'

REINFORCEMENTS RECEIVED DURING MONTH OF NOVEMBER 1918.

	Officers.	Other Ranks.
8th West Yorkshire Regiment	7	83
1/5th Devonshire Regiment	4	49
2/20th London Regiment	2	109
5th West Riding Regiment	6	146
2/4th West Riding Regiment	10	232
2/4th Hampshire Regiment	7	81
5th K.O.Y.L.I.	3	179
2/4th K.O.Y.L.I.	7	118
2/4th York & Lancaster Regiment	-	146
9th Durham Light Infantry (Pnrs.)	3	44
62nd Bn. Machine Gun Corps	8	79
Royal Artillery	-	22
Royal Engineers	2	33
Royal Army Medical Corps	3	8
Divisional Signal Company	-	5

Appendix B

HONOURS AND REWARDS RECEIVED DURING NOVEMBER, 1918.

Victoria Cross	1
Distinguished Service Order	1
Military Crosses & Bars	30
Distinguished Conduct Medals	13
Military Medals and Bars	198.

Appendix C

CASUALTIES DURING NOVEMBER 1918.

Rank	Name	Unit	Status
2nd Lieut.	C.P.Mollison,	62nd Bn.M.G.C.	Wounded at duty
" "	W.J.Phillips,	do.	Wounded
Lieut.	F.D.Roberts,	186th L.T.M.B.	do
2nd Lieut.	W.Campbell,	2/4th K.O.Y.L.I.	Killed
T/Lt.A/Capt.	C.B.Dixon,	2/4th York & Lancs.	wounded
2nd Lieut.	C.Revitt,	do	do
Captain	H.Brown,	5th K.O.Y.L.I.	do
Lieut.	C.Evers	do	do
Lieut.	S.C.Bywater,	do	do
2nd Lieut.	T.R.Allott,	do	do
A/Major	E.M.Body,	40th Bde.R.F.A. attd.	killed
Lieut.	J.A.Brown,	312th Brigade R.F.A.	wounded
2nd Lieut.	W.R.Ashplant,	1/5th Devons Regt.	do
2nd Lieut.	G.B.Yonge,	do	do
Lieut.	E.Clapham,	5th West Riding Regt.	do
2nd Lieut.	W.Saunders,M.C. M.M.	do	do
2nd Lieut.	E.Ellis,	do	do
2nd Lieut.	J.A.Ward,	do	do
2nd Lieut.	L.Martin,	do	do
2nd Lieut.	J.H.Vanstone,	do	do
Lieut.	W.C.R.Rowland,	2/4th West Riding Regt.	killed
2nd Lieut.	H.R.Harper,	do	do
Lieut.	S.L.Roch-Austin,	do	Died of Wds.
Lieut.	R.H.Porter,	Devon Yeo.att. do	wounded
2nd Lieut.	H.M.Slack,	2/4th West Riding Regt.	do
2nd Lieut. A/Capt.	W.Brierley,	2/4th Hants Regt.	do
2nd Lieut.	C.A.Geer,	do	do
2nd Lieut.	A.L.King,	do	Injured.
2nd Lieut.	H.S.Phillips.	5th K.O.Y.L.I.	wounded
2nd Lieut.	W.H.Bosworthick,	5th Devon Regt.	killed
2/Lt.A/Capt.	P.D.Rooke,	2/4th K.O.Y.L.I.	wounded
2nd Lieut.	F.Cotterill,	2/4th K.O.Y.L.I.	do
Lieut.	W.P.Holt,M.C.	310th Brigade R.F.A.	do
Lieut.	K.A.Latter,	do	do
2nd Lieut.	G.Carruthers,	5th West Riding Regt.	do
Lieut.	H.C.H.Broadwood,	do	Wounded at duty.
2nd Lieut.	F.N.Chapman,	2/4th West Riding Regt.	Wounded.

Other Ranks.

Killed	123
Wounded	702
Missing.	61

Vol 24

CONFIDENTIAL.

WAR DIARY

of

62ND (WEST RIDING) DIVISION, "A" BRANCH.

From

1st December 1918

To

31st December 1918.

VOLUME XXIII.

Army Form C. 2118.

HEADQUARTERS (ADMINISTRATIVE)
December, 1917
(West Riding) DIVISION.

WAR DIARY
INTELLIGENCE SUMMARY.
(Erase heading not required.)

Instructions regarding War Diaries and Intelligence Summaries are contained in F. S. Regs., Part II. and the Staff Manual respectively. Title pages will be prepared in manuscript.

Place	Date	Hour	Summary of Events and Information	Remarks and references to Appendices
LEIGNON	DEC 1		White frost, cold during day. Roads slippery.	
	2		Railhead moved to CINEY. Regns of 13th & 21st Army Auxiliary Horse Transport Companies reported. Regns of 16th & 18th " " " " arrived from VI Corps & IX Corps	
		11.00	Foggy early morning becoming milder during the day. G.O.C. presented Medal ribbons to recipients of rewards 185th Inf. Brigade. Forage for consumption 3rd inst. drawn from DINANT late in the evening	
	3	11.00	Dull, some rain during day. Roads heavy. G.O.C. presented Medal ribbons to recipients of rewards 186th Inf. Brigade.	
	4		Heavy, some rain.	
	5	11.00	Fine, clear. G.O.C. presented Medal ribbons to recipients of rewards 187th Inf. Brigade	

WAR DIARY or INTELLIGENCE SUMMARY

Army Form C-2118.

(West Riding) Divisional Administrative HQ

December 1918 p. 2

Place	Date	Hour	Summary of Events and Information	Remarks and references to Appendices
LIGNON	6th		Divisional Orders issued for move to night G/10 December Inclusive — General Advance of Division to commence on 6th Inst. but 155 and 156 Inf Bdes to move forward short distance on 6th Inst to shorten subsequent marches — Accordingly 155 Bde Group moved to Area PESSOUX, BAMPHOX - CONDROZ and FANON. 9/156 Inf Bde moved to LEIGNON	
do	7th		A & O/106. Reconnoitred ELSENBORN Camp. Weather Fine. Moves ordered in D.O.166 to 8th Inst cancelled owing to failure of Division not moving.	
do	8th		Weather Fine. Guards Division notified us no move on 9th. More 9/62nd Division therefore postponed further 24 hours. So no move on 9th.	
do	9th		Weather Wet in morning. Fine later. Orders issued for Division to recommence march on 10th Inst.	
do	10th		Weather Dull. Division marched to areas laid down in D.O.66 — Billets just adequate. D.O.167 for 12th and 13th received.	
do	11th		Weather Dull. Rain after Noon. March continued — Dec 6 HQrs moved to Chateau MANOIR LUSSUS — Rathead to BOMAL (very bad) Rest Camp for Convalescents 13th Bat cleared by Noon — So Supply position satisfactory so far as to regards of March.	

WAR DIARY or INTELLIGENCE SUMMARY

Army Form C. 2118.

December 1918 p 3

Place	Date	Hour	Summary of Events and Information	Remarks and references to Appendices
AYWAILE	12ᵗʰ		Weather very perfect day. Reconnaissance made of area just EAST of Frontier — Butsdorf — Information received that Army would not advance on EISENBORN area as originally planned but would move to BHIE Division to take 16 March. Head of Column reaching CHEVRON Area — Orders received that MINERS would finally be demobilised — Workers remained. Weather wet till afternoon. Division continued March. Head of Column reaching GRAND TRIBURE.	Appendix B
do	13ᵗʰ		Wet Weather. Raid between WEBBO MONT and TROIS PONTS very bad	9ᵗʰ
VIELSALM	14ᵗʰ		Weather Wet. Divisional HQ's moved to VIELSALM — Crossing VIELSALM-5 completed and whole Division accommodated in SALM Valley — Billets fair, food good.	9ᵗʰ
do	15ᵗʰ		Weather Dull. Very little Rain — No moves except 250 Cdn Regt who crossed Frontier at 12 Noon — Formal Entry into Germany made by Divisional Commander and Staff.	9ᵗʰ
do	16ᵗʰ		Weather dull — Some Rain — March continued — 185 and 186 Inf Bns completely over Frontier — 155 Bde in BORN, AMEL, HEPPENBACH Area — 186 Bde in STAVELOT — Signals in RECHT and POTEAU — 189 Inf Bde Hqs STAVELOT —	9ᵗʰ
do	17ᵗʰ		Weather wet — DAAG and GSO3 proceeded to Corps HQ's SCHLEIDEN to reconnoitre final Area with a view to allotting Group Areas — Return that they should remain until 20ᵗʰ inst. Divisional HQ's hoped to MALMEDY — March of Division continued — Whole of Division now in Germany —	9ᵗʰ

WAR DIARY
or
INTELLIGENCE SUMMARY

December 1918
p 4

Place	Date	Hour	Summary of Events and Information	Remarks and references to Appendices
MENDEN	18th		Weather Wet – Division halted – German population quiet and amenable. Instructions re distribution of Confidential Reports GRO 582 issued	
do	19th		Weather Wet – No Moves. Instructions re Peace Gazette 1919 issued	
do	20th		Weather Wet no Moves	
do	21st		G.O.C. Brigade proceeds on Leave – Major Sir R Dougherty assumes Command. Weather fine – March continued over EIFEL Mountains and RHINE crossed. Forest Very heavy and trying. Coy Marches to Billets – 185 Inf/Bde Group to areas HOLLENTHAL-VOENBRETH and BULLINGEN-HONNINGEN. 186 Inf/Bde Group MIEL-MODERSCHEID-HEPPENBACH. 187 Inf/Bde Group NONTIDIE area – RA Group RESCHEIDT Area	

Army Form C. 2118.

WAR DIARY
or
INTELLIGENCE SUMMARY.
(Erase heading not required.)

December 1918 p 5.

Place	Date	Hour	Summary of Events and Information	Remarks and references to Appendices
SCHEIDEN	22nd		Weather Fine – Div. HQs moved to KREUZHAUS SCHEIDEN – March of Division continued 185 Group had reaching 515716, 187 Group billeted at KUSKIRCHEN Barracks. SCHEIDEN – 500 Officers 2000 men arrived from Reception Camps and	
do	23rd		Weather Fine – March Continued into Final Area – Heads of Groups as follows – 185 SCHEIDEN – 186 BLUMENTHAM – 187 WOLLERSHEIM RA SCHEIDEN – Administrative information re Wehrkreis issued	Appendix C
do	24		Weather Fine – March continued 185 and 187 Groups reached Final Area	
do	25		Weather Fine – CHRISTMAS Day – Dinners served in Final Areas – Map attached HQs Groups as follows – 185 Bell Group FICKS, 186 Group MECHERNICH 187 Group VLATTEN, RA Group GEMÜND – Composition of Groups altered for Final Areas arranged that (a) Each Field Coy went to 185 to its affiliated Bripad (b) 9th D.A.I. to 185 Tr/Mor Group – MGD" to 186 Tr/Mor Group (c) 1st FA HA Bde and BAC to RA Group	Appendix D

WAR DIARY or INTELLIGENCE SUMMARY

December 1918

Place	Date	Hour	Summary of Events and Information	Remarks and references to Appendices
SCHINNEN	26		Weather fine – Snow later –	(W)
	27		Instructions recd to send approx 500 Coalminers to Concentration Camps at DUREN and COLOGNE on 30th Inst.	(W)
	28		Demobilization wires arriving all day – CAPT CAVENDISH O.C. 262 Employment Coy appointed Senior Demobilization Officer –	(W)
	29		Demobilization – Areas and Rates altered ↑ two hours occasionally – Instructions recd to send 250 Coalminers to Concentration Camps on 31st Inst –	(W)
	30th		Demobilization and Area Concentration – Scheme received from GHQ to make Divisional Areas coincide with Corps Areas – various difficulties foreseen –	(W)
	31st		Weather fine – G.O.C. and A.A.&Q.M.G. proceeded Corps HQs to Conference re Areas – Demobilization continues –	(W)

WAR DIARY
or
INTELLIGENCE SUMMARY.

(Erase heading not required.)

Army Form C. 2118.

HEADQUARTERS (ADMINISTRATIVE)
(West Riding Div...)

Place	Date	Hour	Summary of Events and Information	Remarks and references to Appendices
Appendix A			Honours & Rewards during December.	

31st Decr 1915.

Maunders Mayn
Brig General.
Commanding 62nd West (Riding) Division

app. A.

62nd (West Riding) DIVISION.

HONOURS AND REWARDS GRANTED DURING DECEMBER 1918:-

VICTORIA CROSS.

205353 Cpl.(A/Sgt) J.DAYKINS, 2/4th York & Lancaster Regt.

34506 Pte Henry TANDY, D.C.M., M.M., 5th Duke of Wellington's Regiment.

BAR TO MILITARY MEDAL.

34578	Sgt (A/C.S.M.) J.J.S.ELLIOTT,M.M.	2/4th West Riding Rgt.
34507	Pte W.H.CRABTREE M.M.	ditto.
201025	Cpl R.EARL.M.M.	8th West Yorks Regt.
306764	Sgt E.REDFEARN.M.M.	2/4th West Riding Rgt.

MILITARY MEDAL.

482297	2nd Cpl E.KNOWLES.	No.2 Sect.Div.Signal Coy.
73649	Gnr M.F.CHAMPION.	310th Brigade R.F.A.
55597	Cpl F.RODDY.	2/4th York & Lancaster Regt.
201544	Pte (A.L/Cpl) P.MATTHEWS	2/4th West Riding Regt.
34720	Pte J.CARDON.	ditto.
265479	C.S.M., E.PEACOCK.	ditto.
22367	Pte W.TRANTER.	ditto.
24135	Pte J.RODGERS.	ditto.
34860	Pte M.McGARVEY.	ditto.
40086	Pte J.L.T.REAY.	ditto.
201000	Sgt H.HEY.	ditto.
240774	Cpl (A/Sgt) F.J.SPARKES.	1/5th Devon Regt.
781817	Sgt H.W.T.BUTCHER.	312th Brigade R.F.A.
786046	Sgt W.LUPTON.	ditto.
78372	Gnr E.J.AUSTIN.	ditto.
5341	B.S.M. G.TURNER.	ditto.
403117	Cpl G.F.THOMAS.	2/2nd W.R.Field Amb.
46188	Sgt H.DRIVER.	62nd Bn Machine Gun Corps.
P.5965	Pte (A/L.Cpl) J.W.DENT.	M.M.P.attd 62nd Divl H.Q.
623583	Pte A.SMALE.	252 Emply Coy attd 62 Div. Traffic Control.
241941	Pte (L/Cpl) A.WHITEHEAD.	W.Yorks attd 62nd Div. Traffic Control.
240070	Sgt L.W.WOOLCOTT.	1/5th Devon Regt.
240755	Pte (L/Cpl) E.COLLMAN.	ditto.
240526	Pte J.LEACH.	ditto.
67383	Pte H.SALTER.	ditto.
32322	Pte F.J.L.DUNFORD.	ditto.
240396	Pte (L/Cpl) F.M.DOLLEN.	ditto.
51273	Pte F.TAYLOR.	ditto.
240823	Pte (A.L/Cpl) G.WOTTON.	ditto.
37059	Cpl (A/Sgt) B.T.SULLIVAN.	ditto.
52146	Rfn W.WARDELL.	8th West Yorkshire Regt.
52119	Rfn F.REDDING.	ditto.
305314	Sgt H.THREADGOULD.	ditto.
236316	Rfn F.CARTER.	ditto.
29366	Rfn F.HOLDSWORTH.	ditto.
652750	Sgt A.LEWIS.	2/20th London Regt.
200735	Sgt E.GREENWOOD.	2/4th West Riding Regt.
201355	C.S.M., E.C.CORNEY.	2/4th Hampshire Regt.
201206	Pte (L/Cpl) E.E.HIGGINS.	ditto.
201193	Cpl F.L.ARNOLD.	ditto.
201824	Pte H.J.MOODY.	ditto.
357322	Pte (L/Cpl) F.STEVENS.	ditto.
200464	Pte F.BUSHBY.	ditto.
202749	Pte F.W.COOPER.	ditto.
200966	Sgt C.PAINTING.	ditto.

MILITARY MEDAL (contd)

```
202496    Pte (L/Cpl) J.KEARLEY.          2/4th Hampshire Regt.
 20570    Pte A.B.ACKERMAN.                   ditto.
200897    Pte A.J.PIPER.                      ditto.
201459    Pte E.STONE.                        ditto.
201830    Pte (L/Cpl) T.ADAMS.                ditto.
205099    Pte I.SPENCER.                      ditto.
200183    Sgt F.LANDSDOWNE.                   ditto.
200763    Pte W.MEAGER.                       ditto.
 11417    Pte (L.Cpl) C.CAVELL.               ditto.
 40672    Pte G.W.R.CUTHBERT.                 ditto.
 11227    Pte S.BUSHELL.                      ditto.
 43613    Pte G.H.PHILLIPS.                   ditto.
 38737    Pte G.J.NORTHIN.                 2/4th K.O.Y.L.I.
 35987    Cpl F.BARMBY. K.O.Y.L.I. attd. 187th T.M.Battery.
T4/251921 Sgt E.A.O.MARTIN.              62nd Divisional Train.
T4/260554 Dvr A.MACKELLER.                   ditto.
T/364956  Dvr A.S.JORDAN.                    ditto.
T4/253750 Cpl T.CARTER.                      ditto.
T4/250935  "  H.SIMPSON.                     ditto.
T4/253666 Dvr W.LOCKWOOD.                    ditto.
201844    Cpl T.E.IBBOTSON.              2/4 York & Lanc.Regt.attd
                                              187th T.M.Battery.
```

app B

62nd Div. No. A/5390/72.

To _____

For information and necessary action.

1.   The Return required by paras. 6 and 7 will reach this office at the earliest possible moment and will be rendered to Divisional Headquarters by the following:-

H.Q's. R.A. for 62nd Divl. Artillery, with separate return for 14th A.H.A. Brigade and B.A.C.
185th, 186th and 187th Infantry Brigades, each for their Brigade Headquarters, 3 Battalions, and T.M.Bty.
C.R.E. for 3 Field Coys.
9th Bn. Durham L.I.
62nd Bn. M.G. Corps.
A.D.M.S. for 3 Field Ambulances with separate return for 33rd Sanitary Section.
O.C., Train for all Train Coys.
Camp Commandant for all men belonging or attached to Divl. Headquarters who are not administered by O.C., 252 Divl. Employment Coy, who will report for the remainder.
62nd Divl. Signal Coy. for whole Coy. including Infantry Brigade and Artillery Sections.
62nd Divl. M.T. Coy.
O.C., 62nd Divl. Reception Camp for <u>all</u> men at the Reception Camp on the day this order is received. Any men concerned being sent to join Units after that date will take a slip with them stating whether or no they have been included in Reception Camp figures. Reception Camp will wire Consolidated Return as para. 7, and will also forward statement by D.R.L.S. showing, by Units, how Return is made up.

<u>Note for all formations.</u>
            Separate Return in each case where men of 16th or 18th A.A.H. Coys. are concerned.

2.   In view of the urgency of the matter, the return will be rendered by wire wherever possible, and will not be delayed pending the receipt of further forms or instructions. If the location of the dispersal station is in doubt, it should be taken as that in which the railway station nearest to place of employment is situated.

                                                C.K. Saunders
                                                Major.
13th December 1918.   D.A.A.G., 62nd (West Riding) Division.

Copies are forwarded for distribution to Battalions, Field Coys. and similar formations.

Subject:- Release of Coalminers.　　　　　　　　　　　URGENT.

IX Corps No. 8182/3.A.

62nd Division.

1.　　The release will commence shortly of all men, registered in their A.B. 64 as Industrial Group No. 3 (Coalminers), excluding Shale Workers).

2.　　The release will be regulated by allotment of numbers for each of the 5 Dispersal Stations mentioned in para. 10 of Demobilization Circular Memo. No. 1.

3.　　This allotment will be issued by G.H.Q., through formations, in due course.

4.　　The following amendment should be made to para. 10 of Demobilisation Circular Memo. No. 1 :-

"Areas VIa and VIb will now be affiliated to SHORNCLIFFE, instead of RIPON."

5.　　Full instructions, together with necessary Army Forms for despatch of Coalminers, will be issued shortly.

6.　　Units and Formations will report BY WIRE to the next superior formation, the number of coalminers, registered as above, whom they have for dispersal at each dispersal Station (as laid down in para. 10 of Demobilisation Circular Memo. No.1., amended as above).

7.　　Each formation, in forwarding the return, will consolidate the returns received by them, so that the wire in each case will read:-

```
DUDDINGSTON - (Number)
OSWESTRY    - ( -do- )
RIPON       - ( -do- )
CHISLEDON   - ( -do- )
SHORNCLIFFE - ( -do- )
```

8.　　The matter will be treated as very urgent.

9.　　No coalminers who are regular soldiers with Colour Service to complete will be sent home under this scheme.

10.　　Acknowledge.

(sd) J.C. HARDING NEWMAN, Brig-General.
D.A.&Q.M.G., IX Corps.

11/12/1918.

P.T.O.

app C

62nd Div. A/5755/40.

LIST "A".

ADMINISTRATIVE INFORMATION ON AREA ALLOTTED
TO 62nd (WEST RIDING) DIVISION FOR PERMANENT OCCUPATION.

1. CIVIL ADMINISTRATION.

Each village is administered by the 'GEMEINDEVORSTEHER', who has fairly extensive powers within the village.

The inhabitants should be dealt with through him.

A group of villages forms a 'BÜRGERMEISTEREI', under a 'BÜRGERMEISTER'. A large village would form a 'BÜRGERMEISTEREI' in itself.

A group of 'BÜRGERMEISTEREIEN' forms a 'KREIS', under a 'LANDRAT'.

The attached map shows boundaries of above. (issued to Groups & C.R.E.)

2. BILLETS.

The local authorities are bound to furnish all information as to billets and stabling in their area, and are in possession of billeting papers which they serve on inhabitants. They should therefore be made a channel for orders to the population as to billeting.

Their estimates of possible accommodation are, however, based on experience of Peace Time Manoeuvres, and, in consequence do not approach our requirements.

The majority of the Bürgermeisters have been informed that our minimum requirements would be accommodation for troops on the basis of one man for one inhabitant and in certain villages considerably more than this.

3. INFECTIOUS DISEASE.

Isolated cases of Foot and Mouth Disease and Mange are scattered over whole area.

Bürgermeister or Gemeinde Vorsteher should always be asked if any cases are in village before troops enter.

The same applies to disease affecting inhabitants.

Statements as to billets not being available owing to illness should be checked by a medical officer.

4. ROADS.

Lorries should not be sent, without previous reconnaissance, on any road not marked in RED on 1/250,000 map.

Other roads are generally good surface but narrow.

Occasionally they are very bad, even if shown in brown on 1/100,000 map.

Notably: Road along railway from MECHERNICH to SATZULY, barely suitable for H.T.

5. WATER.

Nearly every village has water laid on by pipe line.

Horses should not be watered from any stream contaminated by Lead Mines, these exist at MECHERNICH and neighbourhood, and all streams near by should be tested.

E J Saunders

Lieut-Colonel.

21st December 1918.   A.A.&.Q.M.G., 62nd (West Riding) Division

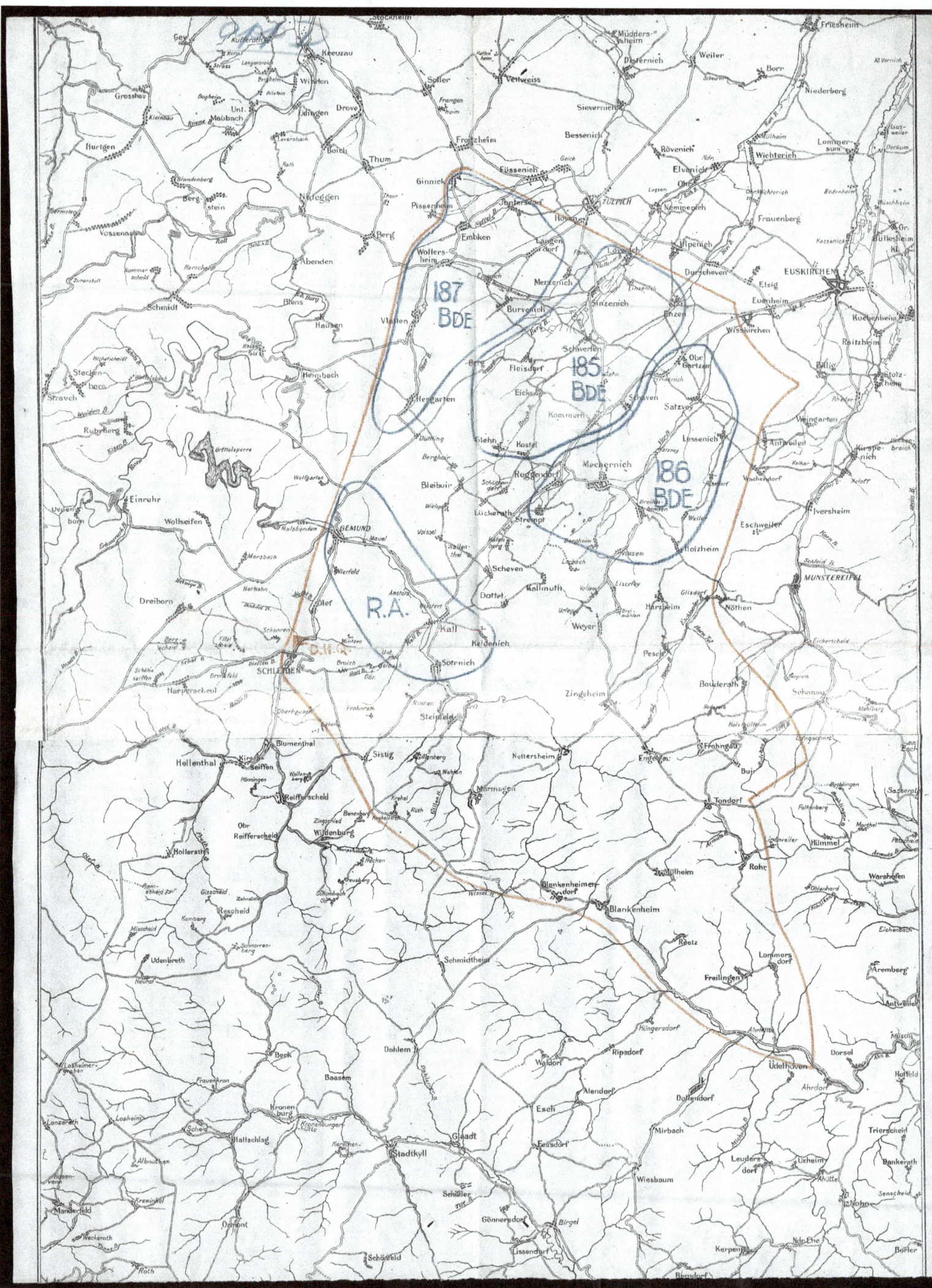

62nd Div.A/6222/72.

IX Corps "A".

DEMOBILISATION.

The Demobilisation situation, as it affects the Division under my Command is broadly as follows :-

Approximately 800 men, mainly Coalminers, have been despatched to Concentration Camps - (31/12/18). and I understand that a further 330 will be called for to depart on every third succeeding day from now onwards.

Since the principle on which these men are selected is

"Demobilisation by individuals in accordance with trade requirements, and not by units in accordance with Military requirements",

the situation from the Military point of view, notably as regards mounted units and specialists, is becoming difficult.

So far, no instructions have been received, as to whether, if at all, reinforcements will be received to balance the withdrawals, and definite information as to the policy which will be followed in this respect would greatly relieve the uncertainty and uneasiness which now prevails.

I do not wish now, to make more than a passing reference to the strain which the frequency of changes and the rapid succession of fresh orders throw on Brigade and Regimental Commanders, and on Divisional, Brigade and Regimental Staffs, whose energies, are already fully taken up with the administration of the occupied enemy Territory.

I do ask, however, that a definite ruling may be given as to how fare the military situation is to be considered in relation to the Demobilisation situation, and whether there is any minimum strength below which units of all arms and services should not be reduced.

31.12.18.   (sd) R.Whigham, Major General,
Commanding 62nd (West Riding) Division.

Demobilisation List.   62nd Div.D/76/A.

  With reference to this office NO.A/5791/72 of 22.12.18, the list given therein of those to whom the privilege of not returning from leave was not granted, applies all through the general scheme of Demobilisation.

  Formations and Units cannot be left without those Officers Warrant Officers and N.C.Os who are essential for Military necessities.

  Not only is it essential for the purpose of maintaining the efficiency of the Formation or Unit, but it is also imperative in order that Demobilisation itself may be properly carried out.

  In every case therefore which appears on the above quoted list, very great care will be taken to ensure that a thoroughly competent and suitable substitute us available before any Officer, Warrant Officer or N.C.O. on that list is allowed to be demobilised.

2.1.19   (sd) Harold F. Lee, Lieut.Colonel,
        A.A. & Q.M.G. 62nd (West Riding) Division.

To all formations and separate Units.   62nd Div.D/101/A.

  Second Army telegram as follows is circulated for information.
  "AD.104. 3rd.

  Army Commander has decided that until a scheme of replacement is arranged Officers and other ranks whose dispersal would seriously affect the efficiency of the unit are not to be sent away even though it results in dispersal allotments not being entirely taken up. Inform all concerned.

  Officers Commanding will, when considering the cases of Officers, Warrant Officers N.C.Os and men for demobilisation, be careful to ensure that all pivotal personnel of all ranks who are essential for Military needs are kept with their units. This more especially applies to specialists, the number of whom will not be allowed to decrease to an extent that is likely to render the unit inefficient. It will also be remembered that there is a limit in mounted branches to the number of men whom it is possible to demobilise, and discrimination must be used so that there is no question as regards efficient men left to look after the animals on charge of units.

4th January 1919.   (sd) Harold F. Lee, Lieut.Colonel,
        A.A. & Q.M.G. 62nd (West Riding) Division.

SECRET.

62ND DIVISION.
ADDENDA TO "STANDING BATTLE ORDERS".

The following note will be added to Standing Battle Orders, page 1 Para 1 (e) grenades.

"A convenient method of carrying 7 grenades instead of 2 is to carry these grenades in an empty S.A.A. bandolier slung over the shoulder.
This method has the advantage of giving the bomb some protection and it is easier to collect them by passing the Bandolier along into reserve dumps as and where required in the captured objectives"

STATEMENT OF CASUALTIES, PRISONERS CAPTURED, AND MATERIAL CAPTURED FROM AUGUST 25th 1918 to NOVEMBER 11th 1918.

CASUALTIES.

PERIOD.	K. O.O.R.	W. O.	W. O.R.	M. O.O.R.	Total Cas. O.O.R.
Aug. 25th & foll. days.	18	294	70	1659	1 323	69	2256
Sept. 12th & foll. days.	0	199	40	1077	- 228	40	1504
Sept. 27th & foll. days.	21	243	42	1135	4 262	67	1645
Oct. 25th & foll. days.	7	64	10	398	- 38	10	500
Nov. 4th & foll. days.	5	117	24	663	- 61	29	861
	52	982	186	4932	5 912	243	6766

PRISONERS CAPTURED.

	Through Divl. Cage O.O.R.	Through Fd. Amb. O.R.	Total Prisoners O.O.R.	BATTLE.
Aug. 25th & foll. days.	1078	151	32 1229	MORY. VAUX. BEHAGNIES.
Sept. 12th & foll. days.	886	66	19 952	HAVRINCOURT.
Sept. 27th & foll. days.	1300	195	24 1495	FLESQUIERES. MARCOING. RIBECOURT. RUMILLY. MASNIERES.
Oct. 25th & foll. days.	657	30	12 687	SOLESMES.
Nov. 4th & foll. days.	808	92	10 900	SOUS LE BOIS. MAUBEUGE.
	4729	534	97 5263	

MATERIAL CAPTURED.

	How. 9.2"	How. 8"	How. 5.9"	How. 4.2"	Gun Naval 6"	Guns H.V. 10 cm.	Guns 77 mm.	Heavy T.Ms.	Light T.Ms.	Machine Guns.	Anti Tank Rifles.	
Aug. 25th & foll. days.	::	::	::	::	1	::	5	4	25	353	27	MORY. VAUX. BEHAGNIES.
Sept. 12th & foll. days.	1	1	1	3	1	::	5	::	13	100	2 X	HAVRINCOURT.
Sept. 27th & foll. days.	::	::	3	2	::	::	61	::	25	320	2	FLESQUIERES. MARCOING. RIBECOURT. RUMILLY. MASNIERES.
Oct. 25th & foll. days.	::	::	::	::	::	::	5	6	1	44	::	SOLESMES.
Nov. 4th & foll. days.	::	2	2	9	::	1	10	::	15	115	1	SOUS LE BOIS. MAUBEUGE.
	1	2	5	14	1	1	85	10	74	932	51	

X Also 16 Guns, calibre not known.

CONFIDENTIAL.

WAR DIARY

OF

62ND (WEST RIDING) DIVISION, "A" BRANCH.

Original

CONFIDENTIAL.

WAR DIARY.

of

62nd (WEST RIDING) DIVISION ADMINISTRATIVE BRANCH.

From 1st January 1919. To 31st January 1919

Original JAN 1919

Army Form C. 2118.

WAR DIARY
or
INTELLIGENCE SUMMARY.
(Erase heading not required.)

Instructions regarding War Diaries and Intelligence Summaries are contained in F. S. Regs., Part II. and the Staff Manual respectively. Title pages will be prepared in manuscript.

HEADQUARTERS (ADMINSTRATIVE)

(West Riding) Division

Place	Date	Hour	Summary of Events and Information	Remarks and references to Appendices
SCAWTON	1st		Weather Fine - Demobilisation and other Administration	
do	2nd		do	
do	3rd		do. Lt Col Newnan C.M.G. 280 Grot Sconol Arty Retured on Demobilisation to weeting of Officers for all Branches of Division	
do	4th		Weather Fine	
do	5th		do	
do	6th		do. G.O.C. and A.A.Q.M.G. proceded on leave - Brig General	
do	7th		ANDERSON GOC Cos G.W. Dick acting assumes Command of Division	
do	8th		Weather Fine. Routine Work	
do	9th		Divisional Agricultural Science Course under D.A.Q.M.G. assembled, OBERHAUSEN	
do	10th		Weary rain Routine Work	
do	11th		Weather Fine Routine Work	
do	12th		do do	

Army Form C. 2118.

original

WAR DIARY
or
INTELLIGENCE SUMMARY.
(Erase heading not required.)

January 1919

HEADQUARTERS (ADMINISTRATIVE)

(West Riding Division)

Instructions regarding War Diaries and Intelligence Summaries are contained in F. S. Regs., Part II. and the Staff Manual respectively. Title pages will be prepared in manuscript.

Place	Date	Hour	Summary of Events and Information	Remarks and references to Appendices
SCHLEIDEN	Jany 13th		9/B Durham Light Infantry ceased Demobilisation temporarily having reached minimum numbers laid down.	
	14th		Heavy snowfall. Routine Work	
	15th		More snow fell. do	
	16th		Weather fine; very cold. Routine Work	
	17th		do do	
	18th to 23rd		Weather fine. Routine Work	
	24th		Weather fine; over 20° frost. Routine Work. 62nd B. M.G.C. & 2/4th B. KOYLI temporarily ceased Demobilisation having reached minimum numbers laid down.	
	25th		More snow fell. Routine Work	
	26th		Weather fine. Routine Work. R.E. Units temporarily ceased Demobilisation having reached minimum numbers laid down.	

Army Form C. 2118.

original

WAR DIARY
or
INTELLIGENCE SUMMARY.

(Erase heading not required.)

January 1919

HEADQUARTERS
(ADMINISTRATIVE)

(West Riding Division)

Place	Date	Hour	Summary of Events and Information	Remarks and references to Appendices
SCHLEIDEN	Jany 26		Major-General Sir R.D. Whigham KCB, DSO, the Divisional Commander, proceeded to G.H.Q.	
			Brigadier General Viscount Hampden, CB, CMG assumed command of the Division	
	27th		Weather fine. Routine Work	
	28th		do. 3/20th Bn London Regt. temporarily ceased Demobilisation having reached minimum numbers laid down.	
	29th		Weather fine. 62nd Divt Artillery ceased Demobilisation having reached minimum numbers laid down	
	30th		G. order received to move of Division either to BONN or COLOGNE should necessity arise.	D.D. 177
	31st		Routine Work Appendix 'A' - Honours Awards received during Jany. B - Reinforcements	

W. Hampden
W.A. April
for Brigadier General
Comdg. 62nd (W.R.) Division

HONOURS AND REWARDS - JANUARY.1919.

Victoria Cross	1
Distinguished Service Order	6
Bar to Military Cross	10
Military Cross	39
Bar to Distinguished Conduct Medal	2
Distinguished Conduct Medal	23
Military Medal	1

Reinforcements Received during January 1919.

	Offrs.	O.R.
8th West Yorkshire Regiment.	2	62
1/5th Devonshire Regiment	2	63
2/20th London Regiment	-	10
5th West Riding Regiment	-	79
2/4th West Riding Regiment	3	101
2/4th Hampshire Regiment	-	53
5th K.O. Yorkshire L.I.	-	72
2/4th K.O. Yorkshire L.I.	-	39
2/4th York & Lancaster Regiment	1	71
9th Durham Light Infantry (Pioneers)	-	47
62nd Bn. Machine Gun Corps	1	160
62nd (W.R) Divisional Artillery	-	43 *
62nd (W.R) Divisional Engineers	2	102
R.A.M.C. 62nd (W.R) Division	-	25
Divisional Signal Company	-	27
Divisional Train	-	16
Divisional Employment Company	-	22

* includes 10 Indians.

Original

WD 26

CONFIDENTIAL.

WAR DIARY.

of

62nd (WEST RIDING) DIVISION ADMINISTRATIVE BRANCH.

From 1st February 1919 To 28th February 1919

Army Form C. 2118.

WAR DIARY *Original*
or
INTELLIGENCE SUMMARY. *February* 1919
(Erase heading not required.)

HEADQUARTERS ADMINISTRATIVE
(West Riding Division)

Instructions regarding War Diaries and Intelligence Summaries are contained in F. S. Regs., Part II. and the Staff Manual respectively. Title pages will be prepared in manuscript.

Place	Date	Hour	Summary of Events and Information	Remarks and references to Appendices
SCHLEIDEN	1		Hard frost continued. Some snow. Routine work. Demobilisation.	
	2		Major C.F. Saunders MC., DAAG, proceeded on leave. Some snow fell. Keen frost. Routine work	
	3		Bright frosty day. Routine Work	
	4		2/Lt. P. Nesbitt Lance. Rept. ceased demobilisation having reached minimum strength. Cold afternoon. Bright frosty day. Routine Work	
	5		Hard frost during night. Some snow early morning. Routine Work	
	6		Bright frosty day. Routine Work	
	7		Bright frosty day. Routine Work	

Army Form C: 2118.

WAR DIARY
or
INTELLIGENCE SUMMARY.

Original February 1919

(Erase heading not required.)

HEADQUARTERS (ADMINISTRATIVE) (West Riding Division)

Instructions regarding War Diaries and Intelligence Summaries are contained in F. S. Regs., Part II. and the Staff Manual respectively. Title pages will be prepared in manuscript.

Place	Date	Hour	Summary of Events and Information	Remarks and references to Appendices
GHLEIDEN	Feby 8		Bright frosty day. Routine Work. 5 K.B. Devon Regt. ceased Demobilisation having reached minimum strength.	
	9		Frost remained keen. Routine Work	
	10		High Wind & strong sun : snow disappearing though still freezing. Routine Work	
	11		Freezing. Routine Work	
	12		Lieut Col H.F.Lea D.S.O., A.A.& Q.M.G. proceeded on one Month's Special Leave. Frost continued : temperature rather higher. Routine Work.	
	13		Rather warmer; every sign of a thaw. Routine Work	
	14		Colonel F.W. Gosselt C.M.G. D.S.O. proceeded to H.Qrs. 2nd Army to take up Appointment of A.G.S.O.I. Thaw commenced.	

Army Form C. 2118.

WAR DIARY or INTELLIGENCE SUMMARY.

Original February 1919

(Erase heading not required.)

HEADQUARTERS (ADMINISTRATIVE) (West Riding) Division.

Instructions regarding War Diaries and Intelligence Summaries are contained in F. S. Regs., Part II. and the Staff Manual respectively. Title pages will be prepared in manuscript.

Place	Date	Hour	Summary of Events and Information	Remarks and references to Appendices
SCHLEIDEN	Feb 15		Thaw continued. Thaw precautions adopted. 8th B. West Yorks Regt. ceased demobilisation having reached minimum strength laid down.	
	16		Brig. Genl. T.W. The Viscount Hampden, Freiherr v. Dacre pending handover of C.R.A. 62 Div. Brig. Genl. A.T. Anderson CMG RA, CRA 62 Div. assumed command of Division.	
	17		Heavy rain during night, snow practically disappeared. Temperature higher. Apparently necessary for much defrost.	
	18		Mild. a little rain	
	19		Mild.	
	20		Very mild	
	21		1/5th Gordon Highlanders arrived to relieve 2/4th B. Duke of Wellingtons Regt. 186 & 187 Bde. left. They arrived as a complete unit. Less transport animals, which arrived from 2nd B. York & Lancs. Regt.	
	22		Mild weather. Route party heavy & breaking up lastly in places 2/4th B. Duke of Wellington's Regt. proceeded by March Route to 6th Division. 1/6th B. Black Watch arrived. Horses 12th West Yorks Regt. arrived	

Army Form C.2118.

WAR DIARY
or
INTELLIGENCE SUMMARY.

Original February 1919

(Erase heading not required.)

HEADQUARTERS (ADMINISTRATIVE) (West Riding) Division.

Place	Date	Hour	Summary of Events and Information	Remarks and references to Appendices
SCHLEIDEN	23		2/4th Bn. Hampshire Regt. entrained MECHERNICH & proceeded to 29th Division. 4th Bn. Gordon Highlanders arrived MECHERNICH to relieve 2/4th Bn. KOYLI. Horses 1st Cecil Kent Regt. arrived MECHERNICH to be handed to 1/4th Bn. Seaforth Highlanders on arrival	
	24		2/4th Bn. KOYLI marched complete to 6th Division. 1/4th Bn. Gordon Highlanders arrived MECHERNICH to relieve 2/4th Bn. KOYLI.	
	25		9th Bn. Durham Light Infantry entrained MECHERNICH & proceeded to 3rd Division. 5th Bn. KOYLI marched complete to 6th Division. 9th Bn. Seaforth Highlanders arrived MECHERNICH to relieve 9th Bn. D.L.I. Thaw precautions taken off	
	26		Much rain fell during night. Roads very heavy	
	27		Routine work	
	28		1/4th Bn. Seaforth Highlanders arrived MECHERNICH to relieve 5th Bn. KOYLI. Appendix. Honours & Rewards received during February	

W. Mansfield Wynn ? ?
t. Brigadier General
Comdg. 6 Inf Watch Division

HONOURS AND REWARDS - FEBRUARY 1919.

Bar to MILITARY CROSS   1.

CONFIDENTIAL.

WAR DIARY

OF

Highland
(62ND (WEST-RIDING) DIVISION.

ADMINISTRATIVE BRANCH.

1st MARCH 1919 TO 31st MARCH 1919.

VOLUME XXVII.

Original

WAR DIARY or INTELLIGENCE SUMMARY

Army Form C. 2118.

March 1919

Place	Date	Hour	Summary of Events and Information	Remarks and references to Appendices
SCHLEIDEN	1st		Weather showery.	
	2nd		Weather fine. 8th Bn Black Watch (R.H.) arrived MECHERNICH to relieve 2/4 Bn York & Lancaster Regt.	
	3rd		Following duties taken over from 3rd Division:– Second Army Depot. Camp DÜREN. 5 Offrs 122 OR. to MALMEDY to Supply Guard. 3 Offrs 50 OR. to MUNTZIE to Supply Guard 18 OR. to LAN GERMERE for Regt Guard	Do 180
			5 Offrs 220 OR. to HERBESTHAL for Railway. 8th Hvd Yorks 5th Duke of Wellington 107th Inf Bde. 42 OR. to BUIR to guard on Ry. Bridges	
	4th		187th Inf Bde front move to 8th Inf Bde front and in SKG Kl 7th Mich area the occupied – BUIR – GOLZHEIM – FRAUWÜLLESHEIM – BINSFELD – MERZENICH – GIRBELSRATH	DO 181
	5th		Move of 187th Inf Bde front is above.	
	6th		10th A & S Highlanders arrived at ZÜLPICH to relieve 7th Londons	DO 182
	7th		186 Inf Bde front and move to 9th Inf Bde. Area on 15.11.11 2nd March Div is occupied – BODHEIM – NÖRVENICH – HOCHKIRCHEN – KERPEN – BLATZHEIM – NISSERSHEIM – KELZ – BERGERHAUSEN	DO 183
	8th		5 H A & S Highlanders arrived MECHERNICH to relieve 8th Duke of Wellington Regt.	DO 184

Army Form C. 2118.

WAR DIARY
or
INTELLIGENCE SUMMARY.
(Erase heading not required.)

Instructions regarding War Diaries and Intelligence Summaries are contained in F. S. Regs., Part II. and the Staff Manual respectively. Title pages will be prepared in manuscript.

Place	Date	Hour	Summary of Events and Information	Remarks and references to Appendices
SCHLEIDEN	9th		3 Offrs. 122 O.R., Volunteers or returnable, transferred from 5th D/we. of Wellington Regt. to 2/1 K. sure of Wellington Regt.	App
	10th		3 Offrs. 70 O.R., Volunteers or returnable, transferred from 5th D/we. of Wellington Regt. to 2/1 Duke of Wellington Regt.	App
	11th		} Move of 186th Inf. Bde Group into new area completed in accordance with D.O. 183.	
	12th		Division transferred from IX to VI Corps. 6 Offrs. 163 O.R. volunteers or returnable, transferred from 3/4 Londons Regt. to 10th Royal East Kent Regt.	App
	13th		Divl. H.Q. moved from SCHLEIDEN to DÜREN	
DÜREN	14th		185th Inf. Bde Group moved into new area — BLADGACH–MÜDDERSHEIM–DRETENICH–FÜSSENICH–VETTWEISS–JUNTERDORF–HOLGERHEIM–EMBKEN	App 164
	15th		Division becomes HIGHLAND DIVISION.	
	19th		Brig. Gen. J. Campbell, V.C. C.M.T. D.S.O. assumed command of 185th Inf. Bde. Brig. Gen. R.H. Bramble D.S.O. " " 167th " "	
	20th 21st		5 Offrs. 159 O.R. Volunteers or returnable, transferred from 8th West Yorks Regt. to 6th Black Watch Regt. 5th Cameron Highlanders joined the Division.	App

Army Form C. 2118.

WAR DIARY
or
INTELLIGENCE SUMMARY.
(Erase heading not required.)

Instructions regarding War Diaries and Intelligence Summaries are contained in F. S. Regs., Part II. and the Staff Manual respectively. Title pages will be prepared in manuscript.

Place	Date	Hour	Summary of Events and Information	Remarks and references to Appendices
DUREN	22nd		Division Transferred from IX to II Corps	
	24th		Maj. Gen. A.S. Ritchie CMG assumed temporary command of Highland Division	
			51st Gordon Highlanders joined the Division	
	27th		1/5th Devon Regiment transferred to the Southern Division	DD 2
	26th		Field Marshal Sir Douglas Haig visited 4 Corps HQ Division. Said goodbye to 51st Division General and Staff	
	31st		Major General Sir David Campbell, KCB, assumed command of Highland Division	

J. Saunders Major
for Major General
Commanding Highland Division

www.ingramcontent.com/pod-product-compliance
Lightning Source LLC
Chambersburg PA
CBHW080820010526
44111CB00015B/2585